ACTIVITIES 1941–1946

The Collected Writings of John Maynard Keynes

Lord Keynes with Mr Henry Morgenthau at Bretton Woods

(Alfred Eisenstaedt, New York)

THE COLLECTED WRITINGS OF
JOHN MAYNARD KEYNES

VOLUME XXVI

ACTIVITIES 1941–1946
SHAPING THE POST-WAR WORLD
BRETTON WOODS
AND REPARATIONS

EDITED BY
DONALD MOGGRIDGE

MACMILLAN
CAMBRIDGE UNIVERSITY PRESS
FOR THE
ROYAL ECONOMIC SOCIETY

Published for the Royal Economic Society

throughout the world, excluding the U.S.A. and Canada, by

THE MACMILLAN PRESS LTD

London and Basingstoke
Associated companies in Delhi   Dublin   Hong Kong   Johannesburg   Lagos
Melbourne   New York   Singapore   Tokyo

and throughout the U.S.A. and Canada by
THE SYNDICS OF THE CAMBRIDGE UNIVERSITY PRESS
32 East 57th Street, New York, NY 10022, U.S.A.

Printed in Great Britain at the
University Press, Cambridge

British Library Cataloguing in Publication Data

Keynes, John Maynard, *Baron Keynes*
The collected writings of John Maynard Keynes

Vol. 26: Activities 1941–1946, shaping the post-war
world, Bretton Woods and reparations
1. Economics
I. Moggridge, Donald   II. Royal Economic Society
330.15'6   HB171

ISBN 0-333-10737-3
ISBN 0-521-22939-1 (the U.S.A. and Canada only)

This book is sold in the U.K. subject to the standard
conditions of the Net Book Agreement

11/10/80

CONTENTS

General introduction   *page* vii

Editorial note   xiii

1   BRETTON WOODS AND AFTER, APRIL 1944–
        MARCH 1946   1

2   COMMERCIAL POLICY, DECEMBER 1941–
        DECEMBER 1945   239

3   REPARATIONS, SEPTEMBER 1941–   328
        DECEMBER 1945

    Appendix: Selections from the Articles of Agree-
        ment of the International Monetary Fund   402

Acknowledgements   411

List of Documents Reproduced   412

Index   419

GENERAL INTRODUCTION

This new standard edition of *The Collected Writings of John Maynard Keynes* forms the memorial to him of the Royal Economic Society. He devoted a very large share of his busy life to the Society. In 1911, at the age of twenty-eight, he became editor of the *Economic Journal* in succession to Edgeworth: two years later he was made secretary as well. He held these offices without intermittence until almost the end of his life. Edgeworth, it is true, returned to help him with the editorship from 1919 to 1925; Macgregor took Edgeworth's place until 1934, when Austin Robinson succeeded him and continued to assist Keynes down to 1945. But through all these years Keynes himself carried the major responsibility and made the principal decisions about the articles that were to appear in the *Economic Journal*, without any break save for one or two issues when he was seriously ill in 1937. It was only a few months before his death at Easter 1946 that he was elected president and handed over his editorship to Roy Harrod and the secretaryship to Austin Robinson.

In his dual capacity of editor and secretary Keynes played a major part in framing the policies of the Royal Economic Society. It was very largely due to him that some of the major publishing activities of the Society—Sraffa's edition of Ricardo, Stark's edition of the economic writings of Bentham, and Guillebaud's edition of Marshall, as well as a number of earlier publications in the 1930s—were initiated.

When Keynes died in 1946 it was natural that the Royal Economic Society should wish to commemorate him. It was perhaps equally natural that the Society chose to commemorate him by producing an edition of his collected works. Keynes himself had always taken a joy in fine printing, and the Society, with the help of Messrs Macmillan as publishers and the Cambridge University Press as printers, has been anxious to give Keynes's writings a permanent form that is wholly worthy of him.

The present edition will publish as much as is possible of his work in the field of economics. It will not include any private and personal correspondence or publish many letters in the possession of his family. The edition is concerned, that is to say, with Keynes as an economist.

Keynes's writings fall into five broad categories. First there are the books which he wrote and published as books. Second there are collections of articles and pamphlets which he himself made during his lifetime (*Essays in Persuasion* and *Essays in Biography*). Third, there is a very considerable volume of published but uncollected writings—articles written for newspapers, letters to newspapers, articles in journals that have not been included in his two volumes of collections, and various pamphlets. Fourth, there are a few hitherto unpublished writings. Fifth, there is correspondence with economists and concerned with economics or public affairs. It is the intention of this series to publish almost completely the whole of the first four categories listed above. The only exceptions are a few syndicated articles where Keynes wrote almost the same material for publication in different newspapers or in different countries, with minor and unimportant variations. In these cases, this series will publish one only of the variations, choosing the most interesting.

The publication of Keynes's economic correspondence must inevitably be selective. In the day of the typewriter and the filing cabinet and particularly in the case of so active and busy a man, to publish every scrap of paper that he may have dictated about some unimportant or ephemeral matter is impossible. We are aiming to collect and publish as much as possible, however, of the correspondence in which Keynes developed his own ideas in argument with his fellow economists, as well as the more significant correspondence at times when Keynes was in the middle of public affairs.

Apart from his published books, the main sources available to those preparing this series have been two. First, Keynes in his will made Richard Kahn his executor and responsible for his economic papers. They have been placed in the Marshall Library of the University of Cambridge and have been available for this edition. Until 1914 Keynes did not have a secretary and his earliest papers are in the main limited to drafts of important letters that he made in his own handwriting and retained. At that stage most of the correspondence that we possess is represented by what he received rather than by what he wrote. During the war years of 1914–18 and 1940–6 Keynes was serving in the Treasury. With the opening in 1968 of the records under the thirty-year rule, the papers that he wrote then and between the wars have become available. From 1919 onwards, throughout the rest of his life, Keynes had the help of a secretary—for many years Mrs Stephens. Thus for the last twenty-five years of his working life we have in most cases the carbon copies of his own letters as well as the originals of the letters that he received.

There were, of course, occasions during this period on which Keynes wrote himself in his own handwriting. In some of these cases, with the help of his correspondents, we have been able to collect the whole of both sides of some important interchanges and we have been anxious, in justice to both correspondents, to see that both sides of the correspondence are published in full.

The second main source of information has been a group of scrapbooks kept over a very long period of years by Keynes's mother, Florence Keynes, wife of Neville Keynes. From 1919 onwards these scrapbooks contain almost the whole of Maynard Keynes's more ephemeral writing, his letters to newspapers and a great deal of material which enables one to see not only what he wrote but the reaction of others to his writing. Without these very carefully kept scrapbooks the task of any editor or biographer of Keynes would have been immensely more difficult.

The plan of the edition, as at present intended, is this. It will total thirty volumes. Of these the first eight are Keynes's published books from *Indian Currency and Finance*, in 1913, to the *General Theory* in 1936, with the addition of his *Treatise on Probability*. There next follow, as vols. IX and X, *Essays in Persuasion* and *Essays in Biography*, representing Keynes's own collections of articles. *Essays in Persuasion* differs from the original printing in two respects: it contains the full texts of the articles or pamphlets included in it and not (as in the original printing) abbreviated versions of these articles, and it also contains two later pamphlets which are of exactly the same character as those included by Keynes in his original collection. In *Essays in Biography* there have been added a number of biographical studies that Keynes wrote both before and after 1933.

There will follow two volumes, XI–XII, of economic articles and correspondence and a further two volumes, already published, XIII–XIV, covering the development of his thinking as he moved towards the *General Theory*. There are included in these volumes such part of Keynes's economic correspondence as is closely associated with the articles that are printed in them. A supplement to these volumes, XXIX, prints some further material relating to the same issues, which has since been discovered.

The remaining fourteen volumes deal with Keynes's *Activities* during the years from the beginning of his public life in 1905 until his death. In each of the periods into which we divide this material, the volume concerned publishes his more ephemeral writings, all of it hitherto uncollected, his correspondence relating to these activities, and such other material and correspondence as is necessary to the understanding of Keynes's activities. These volumes are edited by Elizabeth Johnson and

Donald Moggridge, and it has been their task to trace and interpret Keynes's activities sufficiently to make the material fully intelligible to a later generation. Elizabeth Johnson has been responsible for vols. XV–XVIII, covering Keynes's earlier years and his activities down to the end of World War I reparations and reconstruction. Donald Moggridge is responsible for all the remaining volumes recording Keynes's other activities from 1922 until his death in 1946.

The present plan of publication is to complete the record of Keynes's activities during World War II with the group of volumes of which this forms one. These volumes will cover his contributions both in the Treasury and at Bretton Woods and elsewhere to the shaping of the post-war world. The volume containing the new material relating to the evolution of the *Treatise* and the *General Theory* has been published separately as volume XXIX. It will then remain to fill the gap between 1922 and 1939, to print certain of his published articles and the correspondence relating to them which have not appeared elsewhere in this edition, and to publish a volume of his social, political and literary writings.

Those responsible for this edition have been: Lord Kahn, both as Lord Keynes's executor and as a long and intimate friend of Lord Keynes, able to help in the interpreting of much that would be otherwise misunderstood; the late Sir Roy Harrod as the author of his biography; Austin Robinson as Keynes's co-editor on the *Economic Journal* and successor as Secretary of the Royal Economic Society. Austin Robinson has acted throughout as Managing Editor; Donald Moggridge is now associated with him as Joint Managing Editor.

In the early stages of the work Elizabeth Johnson was assisted by Jane Thistlethwaite, and by Mrs McDonald, who was originally responsible for the systematic ordering of the files of the Keynes papers. Judith Masterman for many years worked with Mrs Johnson on the papers. More recently Susan Wilsher, Margaret Butler and Leonora Woollam have continued the secretarial work. Barbara Lowe has been responsible for the indexing. Susan Howson undertook much of the important final editorial work on the wartime volumes. Since 1977 Judith Allen has been responsible for seeing the volumes through the press.

EDITORIAL NOTE

This volume is the second of three concerned with Keynes's efforts to shape the post-war world.

The main sources for this volume are Keynes's surviving papers, materials in the Public Record Office and, on occasion, the papers of colleagues and friends. Where the material has come from the Public Record Office, the call numbers for the relevant files appear in the List of Documents Reproduced following page 409.

In this and the other wartime volumes, to aid the reader in keeping track of the various personalities who pass through the pages that follow, we have included brief biographical notes on the first occasion on which they appear. These notes are designed to be cumulative over the whole run of wartime volumes.

In this, as in all the similar volumes, in general all of Keynes's own writings are printed in larger type. Keynes's own footnotes are indicated by asterisks or other symbols, to distinguish them from the editorial footnotes. All introductory matter and all writings by others than Keynes are printed in smaller type. The only exception to this general rule is that occasional short quotations from a letter from Keynes to his parents or to a friend, used in introductory passages to clarify a situation, are treated as introductory matter and are printed in the smaller type.

Most of Keynes's letters included in this and other volumes are reprinted from the carbon copies that remain among his papers. In most cases he has added his initials to the carbon in the familiar fashion in which he signed to all his friends. We have no certain means of knowing whether the top copy, sent to the recipient of the letter, carried a more formal signature.

Chapter 1

BRETTON WOODS AND AFTER, APRIL 1944–MARCH 1946

After publication of the Joint Statement, Keynes had two meetings with M.P.s on the proposals. He reported their results to the Chancellor's Private Secretary on 28 April.

To T. PADMORE, *28 April 1944*

THE MONETARY PROPOSALS

After long discussions with the two groups of M.P.'s I find very little sign of definite opposition. I think there will be a good many questions asked and cautions raised, and certainly an atmosphere of hesitation in some quarters, but very little decided opposition. The upshot would be I should say a clear general view in favour of going ahead in spite of this and that.

At the Conservative group, which included Mr. Hammersley, Sir Alfred Beit, Sir Arnold Gridley, Sir Irving Albery, Sir Archibald Southby, Mr. Spearman, and Mr. Robert Boothby, all ended the evening decidedly in favour, with the exception of Boothby. His arguments produced no impression whatever on his friends and were somewhat a matter of derision towards the end of the evening. I had the impression that Sir Alfred Beit, Sir Arnold Gridley, Sir Archibald Southby and Mr. Spearman were strongly in favour, and Mr. Hammersley and Sir Irving Albery also reasonably happy about it. Beit will, I think, make a speech saying that just as he was opposed to preference concessions, so, on the other hand, he is entirely in favour of a currency move forward along these lines.

When Boothby ventured the remark that there was going to be widespread opposition the others said that they had not come across it, and were not conscious of probable strong opponents, except perhaps Shinwell, Walter Elliott and Boothby.

At the second meeting there were present amongst others, Sir John Wardlaw-Milne, Mr. R. J. G. Boothby, The Rt. Hon. F. W. Pethick-Lawrence, Mr. P. C. Loftus and Lord Hinchinbrook. The doubts raised at this gathering were much more on the lines as to whether we were surrendering our privileges of expansionist policy and the like, and whether we were not submitting to too much international control. But my impression of the final outcome was that there was no sign of opposition and considerable sign of support (apart from Boothby who on this occasion was almost silent and gave signs I thought of being considerably shaken in his opposition). Sir John Wardlaw-Milne seemed decidedly in favour. I think that Mr. Pethick-Lawrence might make a rather colourless speech raising a good many doubts and hesitations, but saying in the end that in spite of all this, he acquiesces without enthusiasm. His attitude may be a little more favourable than that because I have found by experience that on an occasion like this he quite rightly emphasises in talking to one, his doubts rather than any counter-balancing feelings he may have.

I should say that anyone who tries to take the line that this is simply the gold standard over again will not be taken seriously. Nor has anyone pressed the point that the proposed arrangements would interfere with the sterling area. It seemed to me that the Chancellor's reply on this was being accepted as a reliable interpretation. The real ground of hesitation is fear of putting our neck under some sort of yoke, the exact nature of which was not clearly apprehended. It was also generally appreciated that we shall not be particularly well equipped at the end of the war for a free-for-all fight, and that we might easily have more to gain in laying down certain general principles of conduct than we had to lose from this. I found that argument carried a good deal of weight. Indeed, that is only one more illustration of what is the underlying truth, namely that none of these schemes will ever be accepted for their own beautiful eyes or special merits, but because as soon as one faces the probable alternative it is obviously so much worse.

[copy initialled] K

28 April 1944

Before the Parliamentary discussions of the Joint Statement, the British began discussions with the European Allies, taking the opportunity to explain the scheme clause by clause in three meetings on 1, 3 and 8 May. As well as taking part in these discussions, Keynes also met some of the Dominion premiers who were in London for discussions on Article VII, in particular Mr Bruce[1] and General Smuts. He also met his old friend W. S. Robinson,[2] who was advising Mr Curtin.[3]

The House of Commons debate on 10 May brought the following comment to Pethick-Lawrence in reply to a letter expressing sympathy at the critical tone of the proceedings.

To F. W. PETHICK-LAWRENCE, *16 May 1944*

My dear Pethick-Lawrence,

It was very comforting to get your letter. I spent seven hours in the cursed Gallery, lacerated in mind and body, and the only moment of satisfaction came when you rose to speak followed by the Chancellor. I thought both these contributions were first-class. For the rest, apart from another brave speech from Spearman, the whole thing was smeared by this unreasoning wave of isolationism and anti-Americanism which is for no obscure reason passing over us just now. Somewhat superficial perhaps but nevertheless to be reckoned with.

[1] Stanley Melbourne Bruce (1883–1967), 1st Viscount Melbourne; Prime Minister of Australia and Minister for External Affairs, 1923–9; Australian Minister in London, 1932–3; High Commissioner for Australia in London, 1933–45, and Minister for Australia to the Netherlands Government, 1942–5.

[2] W. S. Robinson, Australian financier.

[3] John Curtin (1885–1945), Prime Minister of Australia, 1941–5.

However, I do not feel that any real harm was done. The thing will grind along. We shall produce a further version and when at a later date the House is eventually faced with the alternative of turning their back on all this sort of thing and begin to appreciate what that means, I have not the slightest doubt that they will change their minds.

Sincerely yours,
[copy initialled] K

On 16 May, Viscount Bennett opened a discussion in the House of Lords asking the Government to indicate their assumptions as to post-war policies on other economic matters prior to the debate on the Joint Statement scheduled for 23 May. His suggestion of delaying a decision until more information was available was supported by Lord Strabolgi. At this stage Keynes intervened.

From House of Lords Debates, *16 May 1944*

LORD KEYNES: My Lords, I understand that the proposals of the White Paper are to be debated in your Lordships' House next week, and I do not want to anticipate that debate in any way, but I would like to see whether I can help to answer Lord Bennett's question as to the usefulness of having that debate without more evidence on certain other matters. He is, of course, quite right, as he stated in his preface, that the experts conceived these proposals as part of a wider and more comprehensive scheme of international co-operation to cover other topics. I think it is quite a different thing to say that we can discuss one part of the plan first and to say that our post-war problems can be solved by that means alone without the aid of all the other schemes. For example, the stabilisation policy of the cost of living will be very greatly facilitated if steps could be found to mitigate the fluctuation of international prices of primary commodities. The expansion of our export industries which is so vital to us would be much easier if obstacles to trade can be diminished or done away with altogether. The policy of full

4

employment to which His Majesty's Government are committed would be immensely easier in practice if we could have a concerted policy with other countries, and if we all moved altogether and did not allow what is sometimes called the export of unemployment from one country to another.

It is perfectly true we shall not know how to deal with our post-war problems as a whole until we have a complete plan before us covering all these subjects. That seems to me clear. But it is not so clear that we have, therefore, to postpone everything until we know the complete scheme, which may present great difficulties and for reasons that have been mentioned may have to be delayed for quite an appreciable time yet. To begin with, there is a logical reason for dealing with the monetary proposals first. It is extraordinarily difficult to frame any proposals about tariffs if countries are free to alter the value of their currencies without agreement and at short notice. Tariffs and currency depreciations are in many cases alternatives. Without currency agreements you have no firm ground on which to discuss tariffs. In the same way plans for diminishing the fluctuation of international prices have no domestic meaning to the countries concerned until we have some firm ground in the value of money. Therefore, whilst the other schemes are not essential as prior proposals to the monetary scheme, it may well be argued, I think, that a monetary scheme gives a firm foundation on which the others can be built. It is very difficult while you have monetary chaos to have order of any kind in other directions.

I see no particular reason why the understanding of the monetary scheme would be assisted by further knowledge on the other matters. In fact, if we are less successful than we hope for in other directions, monetary proposals, instead of being less necessary, will be all the more necessary. If there is going to be great difficulty in planning trade owing to tariff obstacles, that makes it all the more important that there should be an agreed orderly procedure for altering exchanges. Therefore I should say that so far from the monetary proposals depending for their success on the rest of the programme, they would be the more necessary if that programme is less successful than we all hope it is going to be. On the other hand, if we have firm ground on this particular issue it will be a great deal easier to reach a satisfactory answer on other questions. It is perhaps an accident that the monetary proposals got started first and are therefore more fully developed; but I am not sure it was not a fortunate accident for the logical reasons I have given. As we cannot talk about everything at once, let us talk about these first.

The next day Keynes briefed Lord Addison[4] who was to open the monetary debate in the Lords.

To LORD ADDISON, *17 May 1944*

Dear Addison,

The great misfortune about the Debate in the House of Commons on the Monetary Proposals was in my judgement the under-current of isolationism and anti-American co-operation which ran through a great many of the speeches. I am sure that you are not at all likely to agree to that, and so I feel it would be very helpful if, in the Debate in the Lords, this note disappears so far as possible.

You ask me to jot down a few suggestions as to the possible line. I do not know if something like the following might be roughly what is in your mind, judging from what you said in conversation:

(1) One naturally welcomes the first concrete attempt at international co-operation in the economic field. Surely it is a considerable thing for the experts of so many nations to have agreed, and one naturally wants to treat the outcome in the most sympathetic spirit possible.

---

[4] Christopher Addison (1869–1951); 1st Baron 1937, 1st Viscount 1945; M.P. (Liberal) for Hoxton Division, Shoreditch, 1910–22; M.P. (Labour) for Swindon, 1929–31, 1934–5; Minister of Health, 1919–21; Minister of Agriculture and Fisheries, 1930–1.

(2) No one is more convinced than the noble Lords on these benches of the vital importance of success in securing international co-operation in the economic field as well as in the political. The fact that we naturally want to examine the proposals closely and to be fully convinced that there are safeguards for all our proper and indeed indispensable national interests, must in no wise be interpreted as being made in any spirit of hostility to the important and most desirable objects in view.

(3) There are certain questions in particular where I, at any rate, would be grateful for further elucidation and enlightenment—and also in some cases of re-assurance. The policy of full employment which we all put in the fore-front of our post-war economic programme, would need for its implementation a volume of exports far beyond what we have reached in recent years. How far do these proposals facilitate this task? How clear is it that we shall be entirely unfettered in our domestic policy? Can we be sure that, whatever may be the level of exchange from time to time, the [one] most appropriate to our internal and external equilibrium will be secured, and that there is no risk whatever of the impediments which are so vivid in our memories, and which were so utterly disastrous in 1931?

But I expect I am running on unnecessarily long. My only object was to suggest the sort of order of things which might help to keep the subsequent debate logical. The actual questions which are bothering you are very possibly not those I have indicated.

You mentioned I think that you would be following very much the same line as Pethick-Lawrence took in the other House. I thought his remarks were extremely helpful. Indeed more positive in their approval than what I have indicated above. So I do hope you will go as far as you can in giving us some sort of blessing. For we need it. We have worked very hard and really believe that the position is far better safeguarded than the superficial critic realises, and that if we allow these negotiations to break down we may quite likely find ourselves forced at a later date into something very much less well safe-guarded than what is now in view.

Sincerely yours,

[copy initialled] K

On 18 May, *The Times* published a letter from Thomas Balogh[5] asking for clarification in plain English as to the relationship between the Joint Statement and planned trading and bilateralism. Keynes replied on the same day.

To the Editor of The Times, *18 May 1944*

Sir,

Since the monetary proposals are concerned only with currency, they involve no commitments about commercial arrangements. But Dr Balogh is, of course, under a strange misapprehension if he believes that they do not even involve commitments about currency. For this would be contrary to the plain meaning and purpose of the plan.

During the transitional period the war-time restrictions can be maintained and adapted, as will be unfortunately inevitable. But after the transitional period, with a saving clause for the abnormal war balances, the members of the fund undertake to maintain inter-convertibility of their currencies. In particular they agree to refrain from bilateral agreements which would have the effect of restricting the availability of foreign-owned funds arising out of current transactions. In other words, we shall all be free, having sold our exports in one country, to spend the proceeds in any other country.

Indeed, this is one of the main objects and merits of the plan. No country has more to gain from it than ourselves. For it is a characteristic of our trade that our important sources of supply

---

[5] Thomas Balogh (b. 1905), Life Peer 1968; economist in the City of London, 1931–9; National Institute of Economic and Social Research, 1938–42; Oxford University Institute of Statistics, 1940–55; Special Lecturer, 1955–60.

are not always our best customers. Moreover, if our permanent policy involves us in having many different kinds of sterling, each subject to different conditions of use, farewell to London as an international centre. Farewell, also, to the sterling area and all that it stands for. Our traditional arrangements were based on the general convertibility of sterling; for who, except in conditions of war and out of a readiness to help us finance it, would bank in London if the funds deposited there were not freely available? To adapt a famous phrase, Schachtian minds ill consort with great Empires. Since we are not (so far as I am aware), except perhaps Dr Balogh, disciples of Dr Schacht, it is greatly to our interest that others should agree to refrain from such disastrous practices.

As to capital movements, whether within or outside the sterling area, members of the Fund agree not to make 'a large or continuing use' of the resources of the Fund to invest abroad. They are free to do what they like out of their own resources. Thus no capital transaction, which would be within our capacity in the absence of the Fund, is put beyond it by the existence of the fund. In any case, some control of overseas capital issues will be required to prevent loans on a scale beyond our capacity.

All this is set forth in the plan in the plain English for which Dr Balogh asks, but which apparently he cannot understand.

Yours, &c.,

KEYNES

Following Lord Addison, Keynes rose to speak in the House of Lords on 23 May.

From House of Lords Debates, *23 May 1944*

LORD KEYNES: My Lords, it is almost exactly a year since the proposals for a Clearing Union were discussed in your Lordships' House. I hope to persuade your Lordships that the year has not been ill-spent. There were, it is true, certain features of elegance, clarity and logic in the Clearing Union plan which have disappeared. And this, by me at least, is to be much regretted. As a result, however, there is no longer any need for a new-fangled international monetary unit. Your Lordships will remember how little any of us liked the names proposed––bancor, unitas, dolphin, bezant, daric and heaven knows what. Some of your Lordships were good enough to join in the search for something better. I recall a story of a country parish in the last century where they were accustomed to give their children Biblical names—Amos, Ezekiel, Obadiah and so forth. Needing a name for a dog, after a long and vain search of the Scriptures they called the dog 'Moreover'. We hit on no such happy solution, with the result that it has been the dog that died. The loss of the dog we need not too much regret, though I still think that it was a more thoroughbred animal that what has now come out from a mixed marriage of ideas. Yet, perhaps, as sometimes occurs, this dog of mixed origin is a sturdier and more serviceable animal and will prove not less loyal and faithful to the purposes for which it has been bred.

I commend the new plan to your Lordships as being, in some important respects (to which I will return later), a considerable improvement on either of its parents. I like this new plan and I believe that it will work to our advantage. Your Lordships will not wish me to enter into too much technical detail. I can best occupy the time available by examining the major benefits this country may hope to gain from the plan; and whether there are adequate safeguards against possible disadvantages. We shall emerge from this war, having won a more solid victory over our enemies, a more enduring friendship from our Allies, and a deeper respect from the world at large, than perhaps at any time in our history. The victory, the friendship, and the respect will have been won, because, in spite of faint-hearted preparations, we have sacrificed every precaution for the future in the interests of immediate strength with a fanatical single-mindedness which has had few parallels. But the full price of this has still to be paid. I wish that this was more generally appreciated in the country than it is. In thus waging the war without counting the ultimate cost we—and we alone of the United Nations—have burdened ourselves with a weight of deferred indebtedness to other countries beneath which we shall stagger. We have already given to the common cause all, and more than all, that we can afford. It follows that we must examine any financial plan to make sure that it will help us to carry our burdens and not add to them. No one is more deeply convinced of this than I am. I make no complaint, therefore, that those to whom the details of the scheme are new and difficult, should scrutinise them with anxious concern.

What, then, are these major advantages that I hope from the plan to the advantage of this country? First, it is clearly recognised and agreed that, during the post-war transitional period of uncertain duration, we are entitled to retain any of those war-time restrictions, and special arrangements with the sterling area and others which are helpful to us, without being open to the charge of acting contrary to any general engagements into which we have entered. Having this assurance, we can make our plans for the most difficult days which will follow the war, knowing where we stand and without risk of giving grounds of offence. This is a great gain—and one of the respects in which the new plan is much superior to either of its predecessors, which did not clearly set forth any similar safeguards.

Second, when this period is over and we are again strong enough to live year by year on our own resources, we can look forward to trading in a world of national currencies which are inter-convertible. For a great commercial nation like ourselves this is indispensable for full prosperity. Sterling itself, in due course, must obviously become, once again, generally convertible. For, without this, London must necessarily lose its international position, and the arrangements in particular of the sterling area would fall to pieces. To suppose that a system of bilateral and barter agreements, with no one who owns sterling knowing just what he can do with it—to suppose that this is the best way of encouraging the Dominions to centre their financial systems on London, seems to me pretty near frenzy. As a technique of little Englandism, adopted as the last resort when all else has failed us, with this small country driven to autarky, keeping itself to itself in a harsh and unfriendly world, it might make more sense. But those who talk this way, in the expectation that the rest of the Commonwealth will throw in their lot on these lines and cut their free commercial relations with the rest of the world, can have very little idea how this Empire has grown or by what means it can be sustained.

So far from an international plan endangering the long tradition, by which most Empire countries, and many other countries, too, have centred their financial systems in London, the plan is, in my judgement, an indispensable means of maintaining this tradition. With our own resources so greatly impaired and encumbered, it is only if sterling is firmly placed in an international setting that the necessary confidence in it can be sustained. Indeed, even during the transitional period, it will be our policy, I hope, steadily to develop the field within which sterling is freely available as rapidly as we can manage. Now if our own goal is, as it surely must be, the general inter-convertibility of sterling with other currencies, it must obviously be to our trading advantage that the same obtains elsewhere, so that we can sell our exports in one country and freely spend the proceeds in any other. It is a great gain to us in particular, that other countries in the world should agree to refrain from those discriminatory exchange practices which we ourselves have never adopted in times of peace but from which in the recent past our traders have suffered greatly at the hands of others. My noble friend Lord Addison has asked whether such an arrangement could be operated in such a way that certain markets might be closed to British exports. I can firmly assure him that none of the monetary proposals will do so provided that if we find ourselves with currencies in a foreign country which we do not choose to spend in that country, we can then freely remit them somewhere else to buy goods in another country. There is no compulsion on us, and if we choose to come to a particular bargain in the country where we have resources, then that is entirely at our discretion.

Third, the wheels of trade are to be oiled by what is, in effect, a great addition to the world's stock of monetary reserves, distributed, moreover, in a reasonable way. The quotas are not so large as under the Clearing Union, and Lord Addison drew attention to that. But they are substantial and can be increased subsequently if the need is shown. The aggregate for the world is put provisionally at £2,500 million. Our own share of this—for ourselves and the Crown Colonies which, I may mention, are treated for all purposes as a part of the British monetary system (in itself a useful acknowledgement)—is £325 million, a sum which may easily double, or more than double, the reserves which we shall otherwise hold at the end of the transitional period. The separate quotas of the rest of the sterling area will make a further large addition to this. Who is so confident of the future that he will wish to throw away so comfortable a supplementary aid in time of trouble? Do the critics think it preferable, if the winds of the trade cycle blow, to diminish our demand for imports by increasing unemployment at home, rather than meet the emergency out of this Fund which will be expressly provided for such temporary purposes?

I emphasize that such is the purpose of the quotas. They are not intended as daily food for us or any other country to live upon during the reconstruction or afterwards. Provision for that belongs to another chapter of international co-operation, upon which we shall embark shortly unless you discourage us unduly about this one. The quotas for drawing on the Fund's resources are an iron ration to tide over temporary emergencies of one kind or another. Perhaps this is the best reply I can make to Lord Addison's doubts whether our quota is large enough. It is obviously not large enough for us to live upon during the reconstruction period. But this is not its purpose. Pending further experience, it is, in my judgement, large enough for the purposes for which it is intended.

There is another advantage to which I would draw your Lordships' special attention. A proper share of responsibility for maintaining equilibrium in the balance of international payments is squarely placed on the creditor countries. This is one of the major improvements in the new plan. The Americans, who are the most likely to be affected by this, have, of their own free will and honest purpose, offered us a far-reaching formula of protection against a recurrence of the main cause of deflation during the inter-war years, namely the draining of reserves out of the rest of the world to pay a country which was obstinately borrowing and exporting on a scale immensely greater than it was lending and importing. Under Clause VI of the plan a country engages itself, in effect, to prevent such a situation from arising again, by promising, should it fail, to release other countries from any obligation to take its exports, or, if taken, to pay for them. I cannot imagine that this sanction would ever be allowed to come into effect. If by no other means, than by lending, the creditor country will always have to find a way to square the account on imperative grounds of its own self-interest. For it will no longer be entitled to square the account by squeezing gold out of the rest of us. Here we have a voluntary undertaking, genuinely offered in the spirit both of a good neighbour and, I should add, of enlightened self-interest, not to allow a repetition of a chain of events which between the wars did more than any other single factor to destroy the world's economic balance and to prepare a seed-bed for foul growths. This is a tremendous extension of international co-operation to good ends. I pray your Lordships to pay heed to its importance.

Fifth, the plan sets up an international institution with substantial rights and duties to preserve orderly arrangements in matters such as exchange rates which are two-ended and affect both parties alike, which can also serve as a place of regular discussion between responsible authorities to find ways to escape those many unforeseeable dangers which the future holds. The noble Lord, Lord Addison, asks how the Fund is to be managed. Admittedly this is not yet worked out in the necessary detail and it was right that he should stress the point. But three points which may help him, are fairly clear. This is an organisation between governments, in which central banks only appear as the instrument and agent of their government. The voting power of the British Commonwealth and that of the United States are expected to be approximately equal. The management will be in three tiers—a body of expert, whole time officials who will be responsible for the routine; a small board of management which will make all decisions of policy subject to any over-riding instructions from the Assembly, an Assembly of all the member governments meeting less often and retaining a supervisory, but not an executive, control. That is perhaps even a little better than appears.

Here are five advantages of major importance. The proposals go far beyond what, even a short time ago, anyone could have conceived of as a possible basis of general international agreement. What alternative is open to us which gives comparable aid, or better, more hopeful opportunities for the future? I have considerable confidence that something very like this plan will be in fact adopted, if only on account of the plain demerits of the alternative of rejection. You can talk against this plan, so long as it is a matter of talking—saying in the same breath that it goes too far and that it does not go far enough, that it is too rigid to be safe and that it is too loose to be worth anything. But it would require great fool-hardiness to reject it, much more fool-hardiness than is to be found in this wise, intuitive country.

Therefore, for these manifold and substantial benefits I commend the monetary proposals to your Lordships. Nevertheless, before you will give them your confidence, you will wish to consider whether, in return, we are surrendering anything

15

which is vital for the ordering of our domestic affairs in the manner we intend for the future. My Lords, the experience of the years before the war has led most of us, though some of us late in the day, to certain firm conclusions. Three, in particular, are highly relevant to this discussion. We are determined that, in future, the external value of sterling shall conform to its internal value as set by our own domestic policies, and not the other way round. Secondly, we intend to retain control of our domestic rate of interest, so that we can keep it as low as suits our own purposes, without interference from the ebb and flow of international capital movements or flights of hot money. Thirdly, whilst we intend to prevent inflation at home, we will not accept deflation at the dictate of influences from outside. In other words, we abjure the instruments of Bank rate and credit contraction operating through the increase of unemployment as a means of forcing our domestic economy into line with external factors.

Have those responsible for the monetary proposals been sufficiently careful to preserve these principles from the possibility of interference? I hope your Lordships will trust me not to have turned my back on all I have fought for. To establish those three principles which I have just stated has been my main task for the last twenty years. Sometimes almost alone, in popular articles in the Press, in pamphlets, in dozens of letters to *The Times*, in text books, in enormous and obscure treatises I have spent my strength to persuade my countrymen and the world at large to change their traditional doctrines and, by taking better thought, to remove the curse of unemployment. Was it not I, when many of to-day's iconoclasts were still worshippers of the Calf, who wrote that 'Gold is a barbarous relic'? Am I so faithless, so forgetful, so senile that, at the very moment of the triumph of these ideas when, with gathering momentum. Governments, parliaments, banks, the Press, the public, and even economists, have at last accepted the new doctrines, I go

16

off to help forge new chains to hold us fast in the old dungeon? I trust, my Lords, that you will not believe it.

Let me take first the less prominent of the two issues which arise in this connexion. Namely, our power to control the domestic rate of interest so as to secure cheap money. Not merely as a feature of the transition, but as a permanent arrangement, the plan accords to every member government the explicit right to control all capital movements. What used to be a heresy is now endorsed as orthodox. In my own judgement, countries which avail themselves of this right may find it necessary to scrutinise all transactions, as to prevent evasion of capital regulations. Provided that the innocent, current trans-actions are let through, there is nothing in the plan to prevent this. In fact, it is encouraged. It follows that our right to control the domestic capital market is secured on firmer foundations than ever before, and is formally accepted as a proper part of agreed international arrangements.

The question, however, which has recently been given chief prominence is whether we are in any sense returning to the disabilities of the former gold standard, relief from which we have rightly learnt to prize so highly. If I have any authority to pronounce on what is and what is not the essence and meaning of a gold standard, I should say that this plan is the exact opposite of it. The plan in its relation to gold is, indeed, very close to proposals which I advocated in vain as the right alternative, when I was bitterly opposing this country's return to gold. The gold standard, as I understand it, means a system under which the external value of a national currency is rigidly tied to a fixed quantity of gold which can only honourably be broken under *force majeure*; and it involves a financial policy which compels the internal value of the domestic currency to conform to this external value as fixed in terms of gold. On the other hand, the use of gold merely as a convenient common denominator by means of which the relative values of national

17

currencies—these being free to change—are expressed from time to time, is obviously quite another matter.

My noble friend Lord Addison asks who fixes the value of gold. If he means, as I assume he does, the sterling value of gold, it is we ourselves who fix it initially in consultation with the Fund; and this value is subject to change at any time on our initiative, changes in excess of 10 per cent. requiring the approval of the Fund, which must not withhold approval if our domestic equilibrium requires it. There must be *some* price for gold; and so long as gold is used as a monetary reserve it is most advisable that the current rates of exchange and the relative values of gold in different currencies should correspond. The only alternative to this would be the complete demonetisation of gold. I am not aware that anyone has proposed that. For it is only common sense as things are to-day to continue to make use of gold and its prestige as a means of settling international accounts. To demonetise gold would obviously be highly objectionable to the British Commonwealth and to Russia as the main producers, and to the United States and the Western Allies as the main holders of it. Surely no one disputes that? On the other hand, in this country we have already de-throned gold as the fixed standard of value. The plan not merely confirms the de-thronement but approves it by expressly providing that it is the duty of the Fund to alter the gold value of any currency if it is shown that this will be serviceable to equilibrium.

In fact, the plan introduces in this respect an epoch-making innovation in an international instrument, the object of which is to lay down sound and orthodox principles. For instead of maintaining the principle that the internal value of an national currency should conform to a prescribed *de jure* external value, it provides that its external value should be altered if necessary so as to conform to whatever *de facto* internal value results from domestic policies, which themselves shall be immune from criticism by the Fund. Indeed, it is made the duty of the Fund to approve changes which will have this effect. That is why I say that these proposals are the exact opposite of the gold standard. They lay down by international agreement the essence of the new doctrine, far removed from the old orthodoxy. If they do so in terms as inoffensive as possible to the former faith, need we complain?

No, my Lords, in recommending these proposals I do not blot a page already written. I am trying to help write a new page. Public opinion is now converted to a new model, and I believe a much improved model, of domestic policy. That battle is all but won. Yet a not less difficult task still remains, namely, to organize an international setting within which the new domestic policies can occupy a comfortable place. Therefore, it is above all as providing an international framework for the new ideas and the new techniques associated with the policy of full employment that these proposals are not least to be welcomed.

Last week my noble friend Lord Bennett asked what assumptions the experts might be making about other phases of international agreement. I do not believe that the soundness of these foundations depends very much on the details of the superstructure. If the rest of the issues to be discussed are wisely settled, the task of the Monetary Fund will be rendered easier. But if we gain less assistance from other measures than we now hope, an agreed machinery of adjustment on the monetary side will be all the more necessary. I am certain that this is not a case of putting the cart before the horse. I think it most unlikely that fuller knowledge about future commercial policy would in itself make it necessary to alter any clause whatever in the proposals now before your Lordships' House. But if the noble Viscount meant that these proposals need supplementing in other directions, no one could agree with him more than I do. In particular, it is urgent that we should seek agreement about setting up an International Investment Institution to provide funds for reconstruction and afterwards. It is precisely because there is so much to do in the way of international collaboration in the economic field that it would be so disastrous to discourage this first attempt, or to meet it in a carping, suspicious or cynical mood.

The noble Lord, Lord Addison, has called the attention of your Lordships to the striking statement made by Mr Hull in connexion with the National Foreign Trade Week in the United States, and I am very glad that he did so. This statement is important as showing that the policy of the United States Administration on various issues of political and economic preparation forms a connected whole. I am certain that the people of this country are of the same mind as Mr Hull, and I have complete confidence that he on his side will seek to implement the details with disinterestedness and generosity. If the experts of the American and British Treasuries have pursued the monetary discussions with more ardour, with a clearer purpose and, I think, with more success so far than has yet proved possible with other associated matters, need we restrain them? If, however, there is a general feeling, as I think that there is, that discussion on other matters should be expedited, so that we may have a complete picture before us, I hope that your Lordships will enforce this conclusion in no uncertain terms. I myself have never supposed that in the final outcome the monetary proposals should stand by themselves.

It is on this note of emphasising the importance of furthering all genuine efforts directed towards international agreement in the economic field that I should wish to end my contribution to this debate. The proposals which are before your Lordships are the result of the collaboration of many minds and the fruit of the collective wisdom of the experts of many nations. I have spent many days and weeks in the past year in the company of experts of this country, of the Dominions, of our European Allies and of the United States; and, in the light of some past experience I affirm that these discussions have been without exception a model of what such gatherings should be—objective, understanding, without waste of time or expense of temper. I dare to speak for the much abused so-called experts. I even venture sometimes to prefer them, without intending any disrespect, to politicians. The common love of truth, bred of a scientific habit of mind, is the closest of bonds between the representatives of divers nations.

I wish I could draw back the veil of anonymity and give their due to the individuals of the most notable group with which I have ever been associated, covering half the nations of the world, who from prolonged and difficult consultations, each with their own interests to protect, have emerged, as we all of us know and feel in our hearts, a band of brothers. I should like to pay a particular tribute to the representatives of the United States Treasury and the State Department and the Federal Reserve Board in Washington, whose genuine and ready consideration for the difficulties of others, and whose idealistic and unflagging pursuit of a better international order, made possible so great a measure of agreement. I at any rate have come out from a year thus spent greatly encouraged, encouraged beyond all previous hope and expectation, about the possibility of just and honourable and practical economic arrangements between nations.

Do not discourage us. Perhaps we are laying the first brick, though it may be a colourless one, in a great edifice. If indeed it is our purpose to draw back from international co-operation and to pursue an altogether different order of ideas, the sooner that this is made clear the better; but that, I believe, is the policy of only a small minority, and for my part I am convinced that we cannot on those terms remain a great power and the mother of a Commonwealth. If, on the other hand, such is not our purpose, let us clear our minds of excessive doubts and suspicions and go forward cautiously, by all means, but with the intention of reaching agreement.

Later in the debate Lord Balfour of Burleigh raised a matter Keynes had referred to in his letter to *The Times* (above p. 9). The exchange ran as follows.

LORD BALFOUR OF BURLEIGH: *The noble Lord, Lord Addison, referred to the bulk purchase of food. In passing, I would like to refer to a point made by the noble Lord, Lord Nathan, in regard to abnormal war balances, and I would remind him that there is in the scheme a saving clause for abnormal war balances after the transitional period. I think he thought the saving clause was limited to the transitional period. In point of fact in the scheme the saving clause for abnormal war balances does apply even after the transitional period. But the apprehensions which have been aroused are that, for instance, there might be a desire to do a big trade deal between this country, and we will say, New Zealand. I well remember at the time of the slump, when New Zealand was having great difficulty in sending enough of her exports at the reduced prices to pay for her obligations over here, New Zealand said to this country: 'We will give you an undertaking to purchase with the sterling resulting from our butter the whole of the manufactures you chose to sell.' It was very difficult for us to give that undertaking. I do not think we were ever able to. But it is conceivable that New Zealand might want to say to us: 'We will make very large shipments of butter to the United Kingdom, and in return you will send us manufactured goods to the equivalent value.' I have some slight difficulty in reconciling the right to adopt an arrangement of that sort with the very sweeping definition which my noble friend opposite has given us, because it does seem to me that if the sterling proceeds of that big bulk purchase of New Zealand butter are earmarked for United Kingdom sellers of manufactures, that cannot be said to leave New Zealand free to spend the proceeds of her butter money where she likes.*

LORD KEYNES: By her own free will. I said that a country, having sold its exports anywhere, was free to spend the money resulting from those exports anywhere. In the case of both countries it must be of their own free will.

LORD BALFOUR OF BURLEIGH: *Yes, but having of their own*

free will entered into such an agreement, does not it limit the possibility of other nations being similarly free? Lord Keynes' letter to The Times *put it the other way round, but I think I could best illustrate the point by a quotation of what he said to-day. He said: 'We desire to sell in one country and buy in another, therefore it is important to us that others should refrain from discriminatory trade practices.'*

LORD KEYNES: 'Exchange practices' were the words I used.

LORD BELFOUR OF BURLEIGH: *Discriminatory exchange practices. But is it possible to distinguish between my proposal and allocating definitely a block of currency for one particular purpose? The noble Lord said if we buy ourselves with currency and we do not want to sell there, we can spend it elsewhere.*

LORD KEYNES: The distinction is whether it is voluntary. If it is blocked it is not voluntary.

LORD BALFOUR OF BURLEIGH: *I am very much obliged for the explanation, which I think may go some way to relieve the anxiety of those who really do see a danger to our Imperial trade on this particular point.*

Keynes's replies to Balogh and Lord Balfour led to an exchange of notes with D. H. Robertson.

From D. H. ROBERTSON, *22 May 1944*

I have been pondering on your letter to Balogh, in the light of your memorandum.[6]

Great Empires and Schachtian minds, as you say, go ill together. But so, in the (not so) long run, do commercial bilateralism and monetary multilateralism. Suppose we agree with the Danes to take so much per annum of their bacon, provided they take from us so much coal which they could buy cheaper in Poland. Then to the extent of the value of this coal the Danes are *not* 'free', having sold their exports in one country, to spend the proceeds in any other country'. Whether the Danish sterling is or is not paid into some sort of Special Account before being disbursed for coal is a mere matter of

[6] *JMK*, vol. XXIV, pp. 33–65.

mechanism. In fact a trade agreement of this kind (which was the usual model of our agreements made in the 30s) is *more* restrictive than our present Payments Agreements, for it stipulates that Danish sterling must be spent on *British coal* (or agricultural machinery, or whatever it may be), and not merely on *something British*.

So the Baloghs and the Boothbys are right, from their point of view, in seeing the cloven hoof in the Monetary Plan. For they quite frankly do not regard commercial multilateralism as being either possible or desirable for this country, even at the end of a transitional period conceived of as being of the order of five years in length. And so far as I can make out (though it is very difficult to make out), this view has now prevailed, at the official level, in the Treasury.

It may of course be that those of us who still think otherwise,—that it is both our duty and our interest to work towards a truly multilateral system, and that the goal is not unattainable—are the victims of wishful thinking, nostalgia and all the other now fashionable terms of abuse. Certainly I would not minimise the danger of the bilateral drugs which we and others must use during early years becoming a habit; and one of my fears now is that we may use them to a greater extent than is necessary, and so render our emergence to health more difficult, out of excessive *amour propre* in respect of the terms on which we will accept American help.

But anyway this distinction by *time*, embodied in the concept of the 'transitional period', is not obviously fallacious. What makes me apprehensive about your own position, is that I think you are in danger of digging in on a distinction by *content*—a distinction between the monetary and the commercial—which has only a superficial validity, and may prove an intellectual quicksand. If I really held that commercial bilateralism and discrimination were the right policy for this country, I should not, I think, much mind whether they found expression in 'Schachtian' monetary contraptions or not.

I am sending a copy of this to Eady as an attempt to make more explicit something which I said to him on Saturday. D.H.R.

22 May 1944

From D. H. ROBERTSON, *27 May 1944*

MONETARY AND COMMERCIAL BILATERALISM

In your reply to Balfour of Burleigh (Hansard, May 23rd, p. 870 [above, pp. 22–3]) you suggested that the distinction between these turns on the latter being entirely voluntary, while the former contains an element of compulsion.

24

I cannot see any validity in this. Our war-time Payments Agreements (e.g. with Argentina) are just as much the outcome of free negotiation between Governments (or their agents) as our pre-war Trade Agreements (e.g. with Denmark) were. On the other hand, the Agreement being once made, Denmark was just as firmly obligated under the Trade Agreement to spend (part of) her sterling earnings in England as Argentina is under the Payments Agreement.

I am sorry to be so obstinate about this, but I feel that there is still the makings of a first-class misunderstanding here, both at home and with the Americans.

D.H.R.

27 May 1944

To D. H. ROBERTSON *and* SIR WILFRID EADY, *31 May 1944*

MONETARY AND COMMERCIAL BILATERALISM

I remain more (or worse) than unrepentant. The point is that currency multilateralism is quite distinct from commercial multilateralism and that the former does not imply or require the latter. Indeed, currency multilateralism has been in the past the normal state of affairs without in fact being accompanied by commercial multilateralism. The one no more implies the other in the future than it has done in the past. The fact that those people who have a strong sympathy for the one are likely to have a strong sympathy for the other also seems to me to be beside the point. Moreover there is a large and important group, as I discovered in my conversations with Members of Parliament, who are decidedly in favour of currency multilateralism but very dubious about commercial multilateralism.

I turn next to my reply to Lord Balfour of Burleigh. The context of this was whether the obligation to avoid blocking currency and entering into payments agreements prevented one entering into a voluntary bargain for bulk purchases; such bulk purchases being perhaps balanced by another bulk purchase in the opposite direction, though I do not think Lord Balfour was particularly thinking of that. What I told him was that if we acquire New Zealand currency, New Zealand would not be free to block our currency against our will. But if we chose, by a voluntary bargain, to agree to spend that currency on butter, there was nothing in the Monetary Proposals to stop us. Surely that is absolutely clear. I do not see the vestige of an opportunity of misunderstanding with anyone.

That does not mean that if our final decision is against even a moderate version of commercial multilateralism that that will not cause trouble and misunderstanding with the Americans. I am sure it will. I hope Professor Robertson is wrong in believing that the view which is opposed to any version of commercial multilateralism now prevails at the official level in the Treasury. I occupy a middle position and believe that a compromise could be worked out. But if we are going to adopt views of the Baloghian kind then indeed there will be a first-class misunderstanding.

It has been extremely inconvenient to have to discuss the monetary proposals whilst concealing one's opinions about the commercial proposals. That is a consequence of the tergivers-ations of the Cabinet, which we have to submit to but which cannot affect the logical and actual independence of monetary and of commercial multilateralism.

KEYNES

31 May 1944

After the Lords discussion, Keynes wrote to White and Pasvolsky setting out the background.

To H. D. WHITE, *24 May 1944*

My dear White,

The Monetary Proposals came up for debate yesterday in the House of Lords, and I have thought that you might like to get as early as possible, news of the general reaction. I am enclosing a copy of Hansard, and also some pages from today's Press—

—*Times*, *Telegraph* and the *Financial News*. There have also been some very helpful comments elsewhere which possibly Casaday will be sending to you.

From the first publication, the Press, broadly speaking, has been extremely satisfactory. But various underground forces of opposition have been at work and the debate in the House of Commons was about as disappointing as it could be. Until Mr Pethick-Lawrence and the Chancellor of the Exchequer spoke at the end of the debate, the discussion was certainly not one which did credit to the mother of Parliaments.

The trouble is that there is a small group, an insignificant minority, who are bent on far-reaching bilateralism. They have been rather dishonestly raising the bugbear of gold, since the mere suggestion that our proposals can be regarded in the light of a return to gold, is enough to make 99 per cent of the people of this country see red. Taking advantage of this not easily answered misrepresentation together with the rush of imperial sentiment which is going over us just now, they have been able to prevent the serious discussion which one was hoping for, though as I have said, the response of the Press has been exceedingly good.

I do not think that all this need be taken too seriously; it is essentially a superficial and a passing phase. The atmosphere in the House of Lords yesterday was quite free from it, and my sense of the atmosphere afterwards, for what it is worth, is that the tide was turning.

On the other hand, I am afraid it is definitely the case that the commercial proposals will have to be presented in a very different form—I do not think that there need be so much change in the substance—if they are to have a dog's chance of success in either House.

Meanwhile, we are wondering when the invitation is going to come from Mr Morgenthau. For God's sake do not take us to Washington in July, which would surely be a most unfriendly act. We were hoping, you will remember, that the next round would be here. If that is impossible, then at least you must arrange for some pleasant resort in the Rocky Mountains, if you are going to keep your flock in a reasonably good temper.

Yours ever,
[copy initialled] K

To L. PASVOLSKY, *24 May 1944*

My dear Pasvolsky,

You may like to have an early report of yesterday's debate in the House of Lords on the monetary proposals, and I enclose a copy of Hansard. I have also sent White some press cuttings. As was the case when the scheme first came out, the Press has been all that one could wish, fair, objective and sympathetic. But as you will be aware, the proposals had a pretty rough passage in the House of Commons.

The background position is that a very small minority, who are set on extreme bilateralism, have been working extremely hard to create prejudice by taking advantage of imperial sentiment now passing over this country and by misrepresenting the monetary proposals as tantamount to a return to the gold standard. This last suggestion is not very easily dealt with for an ignorant public, and the mere suggestion of it is capable of upsetting almost every single person in this country.

Behind all this, moreover, lies considerable disquiet arising out of rumours about the commercial talks, no authentic version of which has yet been published or has even leaked to any outside circles. This is something on which I should like to have a long heart-to-heart talk with you. A great deal of the sentiment and opposition prevailing in this country at the moment is, in my judgement, superficial and need not be taken too seriously. All the same, a good deal of attention has to be paid to it. It is, I am afraid, absolutely certain that if the commercial proposals were published in this country in their present form, they would meet with overwhelming opposition in both Houses

28

of Parliament, and indeed, throughout the Press. There simply would not be a dog's chance and prejudice would have been aroused which would take a long time to quieten down. To a considerable extent, but not entirely, this is, I fancy, a matter of presentation. The commercial proposals have been drawn up on those lines which are most suitable from the point of view of satisfying American public opinion, and unfortunately in this case, that means lines which are most likely to provoke opposition in this country. You understand that I am writing this quite personally and without consulting anyone else. But I am sure there will have to be a pretty drastic change in presentation and some changes in substance, if we are to make progress.

The great thing is that you should not misinterpret current opinion in this country as being in any respect a reaction against internationalism. It was most striking in the House of Lords yesterday how all the references to the essential necessity of international schemes, if any of us are to live happily hereafter, were warmly applauded and clearly struck the predominant note.

But there is something else which is not to be overlooked. This country is immensely exhausted and has made sacrifices so far as encumbering the future goes, far beyond those of the other United Nations. The big public is just beginning to become acutely aware of our post-war troubles but does not see daylight any more than I do myself. Naturally, therefore, there is great anxiety that we should not be cutting ourselves off from conceivable expedients before we really know what expedients we are likely to need. On the top of that, I think I ought frankly and add, is a somewhat irritated atmosphere, arising out of the naggings about lend-lease, and completely untruthful charges that we are trying to take improper advantages. There also appears to the general public to be a concerted effort to prevent us doing anything at all to improve our export trade prospects after the war, which, whilst it is a luxury to you, is a matter of life and death to us. In matters of this kind, there is in my judgement, a very great defect in the way in which we here handle ourselves. When any particular incident arises, we do not immediately react with any vehemence but take the whole thing most meekly. If we reacted properly, we could get the mischief out of our system and probably get it out of yours, too, and be good friends again. But as we do not, these things get under people's skin, and whilst it is difficult to be at all definite about it, an irritable general atmosphere is present such as did not exist a few months ago. Also, of course, everyone is frightfully wrought up and tense about the coming battle. The ordinary man's life is upset in many new ways. We are so near to the scene of events that we all of us feel almost in the battle. Indeed, a large part of the country is an armed camp and a training area. It is into this atmosphere that reports arrive that, so far as our relations with U.S. are concerned, everything has to be subordinated to a prospective election.

As I have said, all this is not to be taken too seriously, but it is not to be overlooked. I look forward to having a chance of going through it all with you more thoroughly. Yours ever,

[copy initialled) K

In March 1943 Professor Hayek had sent Keynes an article entitled 'A Commodity Reserve Currency'. Keynes accepted it for publication in the issue of the *Economic Journal* for June–September 1943. He also added a short note of his own.

From The Economic Journal, *June–September 1943*

THE OBJECTIVE OF INTERNATIONAL PRICE STABILITY

There are two complaints which it has been usual to lodge against a rigid gold standard as an instrument to secure stable prices. The first is that it does not provide the appropriate quantity of money. This is the familiar, old-fashioned criticism naturally put forward by adherents of the Quantity Theory. The way to meet it is, obviously, to devise a plan for varying appropriately the quantity of gold or its equivalent—for example, the tabular standard of Marshall sixty years ago, the compensated dollar of Irving Fisher forty years ago, or the commodity standard of Professor Hayek expounded in the article printed above.

The peculiar merit of the Clearing Union as a means of remedying a chronic shortage of international money is that it operates through the velocity, rather than through the volume, of circulation. A *volume* of money is only required to satisfy hoarding, to provide reserves against contingencies, and to cover inevitable time lags between buying and spending. If hoarding is discouraged and if reserves against contingencies are provided by facultative overdrafts, a very small amount of actually outstanding credit might be sufficient for clearing between well-organised central banks. The C.U., if it were fully successful, would deal with the quantity of international money by making any significant quantity unnecessary. The system might be improved, of course, by further increasing the discouragements to hoarding.

On another view, however, each national price level is primarily determined by the relation of the national wage level to the national efficiency; or, more generally, by the relation of money costs to efficiency in terms of the national unit of currency. And if price levels are determined by money costs, it follows that whilst an 'appropriate' quantity of money is a *necessary* condition of stable prices, it is not a *sufficient* condition. For prices can only be stabilised by first stabilising the relation of money wages (and other costs) to efficiency.

The second (and more modern) complaint against the gold standard is, therefore, that it attempts to confine the natural tendency of wages to rise beyond the limits set by the volume of money, but can only do so by the weapon of deliberately creating unemployment. This weapon the world, after a good try, has decided to discard. And this complaint may be just as valid against a new standard which aims at providing the quantity of money appropriate to stable prices, as it is against the old gold standard.

In the field of price stabilisation international currency projects have, therefore, as I conceive it, only a limited objective. They do not aim at stable prices as such. For international prices which are stable in terms of unitas or bancor cannot be translated into stable national price-levels except by the old gold standard methods of influencing the level of domestic money costs. And, failing this, there is not much point in an international price level providing stability in terms of an international unit which is not reflected in a corresponding stability of the actual price levels of member countries.

The primary aim of an international currency scheme should be, therefore, to prevent not only those evils which result from a chronic shortage of international money due to the draining of gold into creditor countries but also those which follow from countries failing to maintain stability of domestic efficiency costs and moving out of step with one another in their national wage policies without having at their disposal any means of orderly adjustment. And if orderly adjustment is allowed, that is another way of saying that countries may be allowed by the scheme, which is not the case with the gold standard, to pursue, if they choose, different wage policies and, therefore, different price policies.

Thus the more difficult task of an international currency scheme, which will only be fully solved with the aid of experience, is to deal with the problem of members getting out of step in their domestic wage and credit policies. To meet this it can be provided that countries seriously out of step (whether too fast or too slow) may be asked in the first instance to reconsider their policies. But, if necessary (and it will be necessary, if efficiency wage rates move at materially different rates), exchange rates will have to be altered so as to reconcile a particular national policy to the average pace. If the initial exchange rates are fixed correctly, this is likely to be the only important disequilibrium for which a change in exchange rates is the appropriate remedy.

It follows that an international currency scheme can work to perfection within the field of maintaining exchange stability, and yet prices may move substantially. If wages and prices double everywhere alike, international exchange equilibrium is undisturbed. If efficiency wages in a particular country rise ten per cent more than the norm, then it is that there is trouble which needs attention.

The fundamental reason for thus limiting the objectives of an international currency scheme is the impossibility, or at any rate the undesirability, of imposing stable price-levels from without. The error of the gold-standard lay in submitting national wage-policies to outside dictation. It is wiser to regard stability (or otherwise) of internal prices as a matter of internal policy and politics. Commodity standards which try to impose this from without will break down just as surely as the rigid gold-standard.

Some countries are likely to be more successful than others in preserving stability of internal prices and efficiency wages— and it is the off-setting of that inequality of success which will provide an international organisation with its worst headaches. A communist country is in a position to be very successful. Some people argue that a capitalist country is doomed to failure because it will be found impossible in conditions of full employment to prevent a progressive increase of wages. According to this view severe slumps and recurrent periods of unemployment have been hitherto the only effective means of holding efficiency wages within a reasonably stable range. Whether this is so remains to be seen. The more conscious we are of this problem, the likelier shall we be to surmount it.

KEYNES

Keynes's note brought two comments from Professor Frank Graham of Princeton University, and Benjamin Graham.[7] On receiving these comments, Keynes wrote to the two authors.

To PROFESSOR F. D. GRAHAM, *31 December 1943*

Dear Professor Graham,

Your letter of October 21st with its enclosures only came into my hands in the middle of December, and pressure of official work prevented me from attending to it until the Christmas holidays. Apologies for this delay, which has been unavoidable.

As you point out, your article and that of your namesake only overlap to a certain extent. I am, therefore, replying to them separately. I shall be grateful if you will forward to him the enclosed letter, of which I have added a copy for your own retention.

As for your own article, I should be grateful if you would think it over in the light of what follows.

(1) Your *obiter dictum* about myself and Dr White, I have no right to speak for him. But I have spent many hours in his company discussing these matters and I have never heard him express the opinion you attribute to him, namely that exchange rates should be fixed, subject to the rarest and most difficult exceptions, just as they once used to be, in terms of gold. The chief matter at issue has been quite a different one, namely whether member countries should surrender to an international body the right to decide whether the circumstances are such as to justify a change, or whether they should retain at least some measure of discretion in their own hands. I am hopeful that all this may be cleared up in due course, and meanwhile it would, I think, darken counsel to suggest that there is here an irreconcilable difference of opinion.

At any rate, on this point you and I are, I gather, agreed.

[7] Frank Dunstone Graham (1890–1949); economist, Lecturer-Professor, at Princeton University, 1921–49.
  Benjamin Graham (b. 1897); economist, Lecturer-Professor, Columbia University, 1928–55; U.C.L.A., 1957.

(2) The passage beginning with the last paragraph on your p. 2[8] seems to be fair comment on the assumption (which is possible) that Hayek did not aim, as I thought he did, at *national* currencies stable in terms of a composite commodity. If, on the other hand, he thought of his commodity standard being in exactly the same position as that in which gold would be under the Clearing Union, my objection was misconceived.

In this case the question would arise how far it is worth while to go beyond using buffer stocks to achieve short-term stabilisation of individual commodities (which I ardently advocate) at the cost of the colossal controversy involved in depriving gold production and gold reserves of their present usefulness.

You are clearly right that, if a country is free at any time to alter the value of its currency in terms of the composite commodity, nothing is imposed on it. I was supposing that something more than this was intended.

(3) I do not know on what ground you attribute to me the view stated in the last paragraph of your p. 4. It is not borne out, quite the contrary, by what I have recently written on this matter for official circulation.

(4) The same applies to the last paragraph of your p. 5. I do not know on what your suspicions are founded. It seems to be a confusion with something else. I was speaking of the 'natural', not of the 'desirable', tendency of wages to rise. In my published works I have discussed at great length the balancing pros and cons of the broad issue. In my recent note I was merely concerned with the point that wage policy is a domestic political issue which it is unwise to subject to rigid outside determination. I elaborate this a little further in my letter to Mr Graham. Your comment here goes far beyond anything I have actually said in my note.

(5) The discussion you begin on p. 7 is, in my judgement, the real issue—and a damned, difficult, disobliging one it is. I called

[8] Graham's original note has not survived (Ed.).

35

attention to it without attempting, in that brief note, to carry the discussion very far.

How much otherwise avoidable unemployment do you propose to bring about in order to keep the Trade Unions in order? Do you think it will be politically possible when they understand what you are up to?

My own preliminary view is that other, more reasonable, less punitive means must be found. And it is my strong conviction that such efforts will be hopelessly prejudiced if the trade unions believe that it is an international monetary convention which is at the bottom of all the trouble. I have had the benefit of hearing Mr Bevin on this subject!

However, I welcome your contribution to this discussion, which needs a much franker opening up than it has yet received.

(6) Your p. 8 does not apply equally to an industrial country.

(7) Your p. 9: I should say that this is *not* 'what commodity reserve money would *do*', but what it would *postulate* without the power to do it. That is the other one of my two essential points. (Here you seem to be attributing to Hayek the same more drastic intention that I assumed).

Couldn't you clear up the false issues between us and concentrate more on the essential problem? There seems to me to be an opportunity for an exceedingly interesting and helpful article from you, which I would gladly accept for the *Economic Journal*, centring particularly on what you say from p. 6 onwards of the enclosed.

Yours sincerely,
[copy initialled] K

To BENJAMIN GRAHAM, *31 December 1943*

Dear Mr Graham,

The articles of yourself and Professor Graham make me feel that it was a great mistake for one, who, being occupied on official work, has no leisure except to write briefly on one particular point without the full background of his thought and is not free to publish the more detailed work he has actually been doing on the subject behind the scenes, to write for publication at all. For the result, as your article shows, is to lead to a wild misconception of one's opinions. And nothing is more futile than public controversy about what one has *not* said and does *not* mean.

(1) You say that I 'imply strongly that any mechanism aiming at a stable price level is in itself undesirable'. I said no such thing, and it is the exact opposite of what I believe. After all, I was one of the pioneers (along with yourself) in advocating buffer stocks for this very purpose, and there is no-one in the world who has spent more time than I have in the last two years trying to carry this policy into fruition.

My point was an entirely different one. I was pointing out that a currency stable in terms of a composite commodity, whilst serving certain objects, either did not achieve stable national prices or postulated stable efficiency wages without having the power to impose them. That was my *only* contention in that brief note. I ought to have made it clear that I was thinking primarily of the long term. The avoidance of short-term fluctuations is another matter; though I am not clear about the advantages (in the short term) of stabilising a composite commodity as compared with those of stabilising individual commodities. For the latter is a better means of stabilising the national income of individual raw-material producing countries.

(2) You restate my argument as meaning that 'full employment can be maintained only while money wages are rising faster than efficiency'. Here again I said no such thing, and it is the opposite of what I believe. If money wages rise faster than efficiency, this aggravates the difficulty of maintaining full employment, and, so far from being a condition of full employment, it is one of the main obstacles which a full employment policy has to overcome.

My point was an entirely different one. Some people over here are accustomed to argue that the fear of unemployment and the recurrent experience of it are the only means by which, in past practice, trade unions have been prevented from over-doing their wage-raising pressure. I hope this is not true. I said in my article that, the more aware we were of this risk, the more likely we should be to find a way round other than totalitarianism. But I recognised the reality of the risk.

(3) This leads me to what was intended to be my central point. The task of keeping efficiency wages reasonably stable (I am sure they will creep up steadily in spite of our best efforts) is a political rather than an economic problem. In my country it is quite essential that it should not be handled in obedience to the dictates of an international currency system (which will be identified in labour circles with international bankers). From this point of view, the legal stabilisation of national currencies in terms of a composite commodity would be just as dangerous and objectionable in operation as in terms of gold. That was the point I was concerned to establish. And if my article is to be discussed, that is the only relevant point to raise.

On the use of buffer stocks as a means of stabilising short-term commodity prices you and I are ardent crusaders on the same side, so do not let a falsely conceived controversy arise between us.

Yours very truly,
[copy initialled] K

When he received Professor Graham's article, Keynes published it in the *Economic Journal* for December 1944 under the title 'Keynes vs Hayek on a Commodity Reserve Currency', and added a brief note of his own.

From The Economic Journal, *December 1944*

NOTE BY LORD KEYNES

Prof. Graham's statement of my point of view is a very fair one. But in the note on which he comments I expressed myself much more briefly than the nature of the subject-matter really allowed. So, to diminish the chances of misunderstandings, there are one or two points I should like to re-state and emphasise.

I have no quarrel with a tabular standard as being intrinsically more sensible than gold. My own sympathies have always fallen that way. I hope the world will come to some version of it some time. But the opinion I was expressing was on the level of contemporary practical policy; and on that level I do not feel that this is the next urgent thing or that other measures should be risked or postponed for the sake of it. These are some of my reasons:

1. The immediate task is to discover some orderly, yet elastic method of linking national currencies to an international currency, whatever the type of international currency may be. So long as national currencies change their values out of step with one another, I doubt if this task is made easier by substituting a tabular standard for gold. Indeed the task of getting an *elastic* procedure may be made more difficult, since a tabular standard might make rigidity seem more plausible. Perhaps unjustly, I was suspecting Prof. Hayek of seeking a new way to satisfy a propensity towards a rigid system.

2. In particular, I doubt the political wisdom of appearing, more than is inevitable in any orderly system, to impose an external pressure on national standards and therefore on wage levels. Of course, I do not want to see money wages forever soaring upwards to a level to which real wages cannot follow. It is one of the chief tasks ahead of our statesmanship to find a way to prevent this. But we must solve it in our own domestic way, feeling that we are free men, free to be wise or foolish. The suggestion of *external* pressure will make the difficult psycho-

logical and political problem of making good sense prevail still more difficult.

3. This does not strike me as an opportune moment to attack the vested interests of gold holders and gold producers. Why waste one's breath on what the Governments of the United States, Russia, Western Europe and the British Commonwealth are bound to reject?

4. The right way to approach the tabular standard is to evolve a technique and to accustom men's minds to the idea through international buffer stocks. When we have thoroughly mastered the technique of these, which is sufficiently difficult without the further complications of the tabular standard and the oppositions and prejudices which this must overcome, it will be time enough to think again. On buffer stocks I can enthusiastically join forces with Professor Frank Graham and Mr Benjamin Graham. Though even here I am beginning to feel a slight reserve about whether just this moment, when many materials are scarce, is the right moment to start; they can so easily be turned into producers' ramps, and if they start that way the prospect of a brilliant improvement will have been prejudiced.

All this, I agree, is very low-level talk; for which I apologise. But it was in fact from a low level that I was, in the first instance, addressing Professor Hayek on his dolomite.

KEYNES

With the conclusion of the Parliamentary debates, preparations began for the conference, eventually convened at Bretton Woods, New Hampshire, to which Secretary Morgenthau had invited the representatives of 44 Governments to formulate proposals for an International Monetary Fund 'and possibly a Bank for Reconstruction and Development'. (In addition, he invited a smaller group of nations to a preliminary drafting conference at Atlantic City.) On the proposals, Keynes commented.

To SIR DAVID WALEY, *30 May 1944*

THE MONETARY CONFERENCE

I. *The Scheme of the Conference*

Dr White's conception of all this seems to get 'curiouser and curiouser'. 42 nations, making 43 in all, have been invited for July 1. They are to have no power of commitment or final decision and everything is to be *ad referendum*. Nevertheless it now appears that they are not even to have the semblance of doing any work, since that is to be done before they meet. I had been supposing that after meeting they would appoint two or more Committees, which would then do the work which it is now contemplated to do beforehand, reporting back to a larger body whenever necessary. The American newspapers have indicated that 'the Conference beginning on July 1 may last several weeks'. Unless this is a misprint for several days, it is not easy to see how the main monkey-house is going to occupy itself. It would seem probable that acute alcoholic poisoning would set in before the end.

II. *Date for the meeting of the proposed Drafting Committee*

Dr White proposes a date somewhere about June 10. Place unstated. This is clearly impossible. If the Drafting Committee is not going to be merely an Agenda Committee, but is to do the work, it would seem out of the question that it could meet early enough to have completed its work by July 1. Suppose, for example, it met a week earlier, which would be feasible, that would be rather quick going. There is no indication in Opie's telegram how the Reconstruction Bank is to be treated, i.e. whether it is to be handled by the Drafting Committee or is reserved for some subsequent Committee to be appointed by the main body. If it is agreed that it is not practicable for the Drafting Committee to have really completed its work before July 1, either the Committee should be appointed by the main body as I have previously contemplated, and should begin round about July 1; or alternatively, it might be assembled a week earlier than that and the main body a fortnight later. I hope that the Drafting Committee as well as the main body would meet in New Hampshire.

Twenty-one countries have been invited which clearly have nothing to contribute and will merely encumber the ground, namely, Colombia, Costa Rica, Dominica, Ecuador, Salvador, Guatemala, Haiti, Honduras, Liberia, Nicaragua, Panama, Paraguay, Philippines, Venezuela, Peru, Uruguay, Ethiopia, Iceland, Iran, Iraq, Luxemburg. The most monstrous monkey-house assembled for years. To these might perhaps be added: Egypt, Chile and (in present circumstances) Yugo-Slavia.

III. *Membership of the Drafting Committee*

The U.S. have nominated 10 members of the Drafting Committee, namely: U.S., U.K., Russia, China, Canada, Belgium, Czechoslovakia, the French Committee, Brazil, and Mexico. They express no great enthusiasm for Czechoslovakia, but would like to add Cuba; do not object to the addition of Australia, and would take Holland instead of Belgium but not as well.

If the membership is brought up to twelve by the addition to the original ten of Australia and Cuba, then there remain only seven countries with any serious claim to representation, namely: India, New Zealand, South Africa, Greece, Holland, Norway and Poland. I should select from these Greece and Holland for what they have to contribute. Certainly it would seem quite outrageous and hopelessly unreal to put on to the Committee not only a pack of countries which know nothing of international finance but even Cuba, whilst excluding Holland and her Empire.

Of Dr White's Drafting Committee, Russia, China, Brazil,

Mexico and Cuba, know little or nothing of international finance.

On the whole I think we should firmly resist Cuba; insist very firmly on Holland as well as Belgium; and suggest the substitution of Greece for Czechoslovakia on the ground of the particular contribution which Varvaressos might be able to make. If, however, Varvaressos would be unable to attend then Greece might reasonably be left out.

KEYNES

There then began a series of meetings and discussions in the Treasury on both the Fund and the Bank. On 7 June, after discussions with Sir Wilfrid Eady, Keynes wrote to Sir Richard Hopkins.[9]

To SIR RICHARD HOPKINS, *7 June 1944*

CONFERENCE ON INTERNATIONAL MONETARY FUND

1. Although the invitation made it clear that the Delegates were not to be plenipotentiaries and that the conclusions of the Conference would be referred to the Governments, Remac 414 and 415 indicate the intention of the U.S. Treasury that on the Monetary Fund at least, the Conference shall produce the complete draft of the Convention which would set up the Fund.

The Conference will be pressed for time and although we may be able to have some intimate discussions with the Americans, some of the points we wish to make will have to be made publicly, either at the drafting Committee or in the full

---

[9] On this memorandum D. H. Robertson commented the next day, giving his personal views as a prospective member of the delegation. He was concerned about the prospect of asking the Americans to change the exchange clause, even if the change proposed was sensible. As he did not think 'this combination of the prestige of sovereignty with the stigma of criminality is an attractive or workable one', he pressed for dropping the proposal. He agreed with Keynes on point (*b*). On Keynes's (*c*), he agreed with the arguments against (i), and supported Keynes on (ii). However on (iii) he argued for bringing the Fund into existence before the end of the war and pressed for a five year transition period.

Conference, and presumably with an appeal to voting to decide divergence of view.

Our agreement with the U.S. Treasury is that the Statement of Principles cannot be altered without the joint agreement of themselves and ourselves.

We may therefore have to face a position of some difficulty upon which the general lines of our attitude on important points need to be laid down in advance, for we will not be able to adjourn discussion pending the receipt of further instructions.

2. Three major points are:

(*a*) What is the shape of the Exchange Adjustment Clause?

(*b*) What are we to say to the Americans, and possibly more publicly, about seeing our way through the difficulties of the transition;

(*c*) Do we accept Clause 10 as giving us sufficient freedom within a Convention which we shall have signed, or are we to claim a greater freedom as to time and conditions before we sign?

3. (*a*) *Exchange Adjustment*

In his Memorandum of February 16th, Lord Catto suggested that the Exchange Clauses might be amended so as to include some such wording as the following:

Nothing herein stated shall affect the sovereign right of member-countries to fix and/or amend their exchange rates as they may consider necessary or advisable, but such fixing of rates and/or amendments shall be made in consultation with the Fund: and in the event of action being taken by a member-nation without agreement with the Fund, the latter may, if it considers the action unjustified in the interests of the member-country and/or the proper working of the Fund in the interests of all member-countries, block the subscription of the member-country and suspend the facilities of the Fund so far as such member-country is concerned.

The effect of this would be that countries would not formally abandon their right to alter exchanges, but if they did so, without the agreement of the Fund, they would suffer the sanction of being cut off from its facilities—this taking the place of the present arrangements by which their remedy is to leave the Fund. There is something to be said for this change on merits. But apart from that it might help to convince Parliament that our discretion in this matter is now sufficiently safeguarded.

IV(2) of the Plan, which now runs as follows:

Subject to 5, below, no change in the par value of a member's currency shall be made by the Fund without the country's approval. Member countries agree not to propose a change of parity of their currency unless they consider it appropriate to correct a fundamental disequilibrium. Changes shall be made only with the approval of the Fund subject to the provisions below,

would have to be amended by the omission of the first and third sentences. The second sentence might then become part of Clause IV(3). Some such provision as that proposed by Lord Catto could then follow after what is now Clause IV(4).

Should the British Delegation press for this change?

4. (b) *Our Transitional Difficulties*

The solution of this primarily concerns the Americans and the Americans alone. But it concerns not only the U.S. Treasury, but the State Department and F.E.A. As a matter of timing, it is obviously impracticable to fix up even the outlines of any solution for the transition, before we have to decide upon our general line at the Conference. Moreover, we certainly want to avoid discussing this matter in general company. It is therefore recommended that whilst the opportunity might be taken of a private discussion with the Americans, the solution of our transitional difficulties should form no part of what the British Delegation put before the Conference.

5. (c) *The transitional arrangements in the scheme and the date at which the scheme is to come into effect*

The Joint Statement of Principles at present embodies two safeguards:

(i) No country is required to undertake the obligations of convertibility until it is satisfied as to the arrangements as its disposal to facilitate the settlement of the balance of payments differences during the early post-war transition period, by a means which will not unduly encumber its facilities with the Fund. No terminal date is attached to this safeguard.

45

(ii) During the transition, exchange regulations, etc. can be continued. To this also no definite terminal date is attached. But the members undertake to proceed as soon as possible by progressive stages and the position has to be reconsidered after three years, although no country is committed to a withdrawal at that date.

The Joint Statement is silent on the question whether or not the Fund is to be established before the end of the war.

The question here is whether the above safeguards are sufficient. Further possible safeguards would be the following:

(i) We could say that while we shall co-operate in international monetary affairs with other countries and with the Fund, we cannot, because of the exceptional problems facing us after the war, even undertake to join the Fund at all until the nature of the transitional difficulties, and a possible solution of them, is more clearly visible.

(ii) We could avoid subsequent possible miunderstanding by making it clear to those concerned that whilst we shall aim at convertibility as soon as possible, we do not expect to reach it within so short a period as three years.

(iii) We might make a stand on the point that whilst various preparatory measures can be taken, we do not contemplate adherence to the Fund before the end of the war.

Lord Catto's memorandum of May 3rd, suggested as a principle for the Fund:

that its power and influence should grow gradually and be derived from its inherent right to control its facilities, rather than from rigid rules and fixed limits which are likely to impinge upon national rights—rights which our Government would find it difficult, if not impossible, to abrogate to a new and untried international body.

This would go a great deal further than (i) above, since our merely standing out of the Fund for an indefinite period would not, in other respects, alter its character. It is not clear what we should gain from standing out of the Fund. Obviously for us to do so would be a serious disappointment to the American Administration.

(i) therefore would be neither one thing nor the other and it is not recommended. On the other hand to act on Lord Catto's suggestion of May 3rd would mean entirely re-writing the Joint Statement from beginning to end. Is it a practical proposition to make such a suggestion at this stage?

On the other hand it is recommended that the British delegation should endeavour to act in accordance with (ii) and (iii) above.

6. Mr Morgenthau's invitation makes it clear that the Conference has no power to reach final decisions and that the Delegates are not plenipotentiaries. It is recommended that the British Delegates should also make it clear that so far as they are concerned any decisions will be *ad referendum* to their Government and Parliament, who must at this stage reserve the ultimate right to suggest amendments if they find it unavoidable to do so as a condition of adherence.

[copy initialled] K

7 June 1944

On 8 June, the Chancellor discussed the Delegation's instructions on the Fund with Keynes, Robertson and other senior officials. On the exchange clause, the meeting agreed that while accepting the existing draft 'the Delegation should press for an overriding proviso reserving to a country, in case of necessity, the exercise of its sovereign rights over the parity of its exchange in consultation with the Fund, subject to the right of the Fund at its discretion to suspend the member from continued use of the Fund's facilities if the Fund disagreed with the exchange policy proposed'. The meeting also agreed that the Delegation should remind the Americans that British acceptance of the proposed institutions would be conditional on prior arrangements to overcome Britain's transitional difficulties, that the convertibility clause should make it clear that the obligations entered into did not cover past accumulations of balances, that the Fund would start operations after 1 August 1945 when countries representing x per cent of the quotas had agreed to it,[10] and that the transition period should be five years from the end of the war in Europe.

[10] x would be chosen so as to make British and American accession necessary to start the Fund.

On 9 June, in the light of previous discussions and American replies to suggestions, Keynes turned to the proposed Bank for Reconstruction and Development.

To T. PADMORE, *9 June 1944*

THE BANK FOR RECONSTRUCTION AND DEVELOPMENT

Four papers are attached.[11]

1. The American draft giving a preliminary outline, dated November 24th, 1943.

2. A summary of the above, issued by the American Treasury after consultation with certain other nations, not including ourselves, which is not very helpful since it tends to cover up certain rather essential points.

3. A paper prepared in the Treasury after the Dominion talks, which has been communicated to the U.S. Treasury, laying down certain general principles which ought, we thought, to be followed if the new institution is to be based on sound principles.

4. The American Treasury's comments on this, lately received. This Memorandum does not offer to depart from the actual text of the original draft (No. 1 above), but it interprets it on lines very much closer to the principles laid down in Paper 3 above. This and other indications suggest that a compromise in which the principles of Paper 3 are substantially maintained, is well worth trying.

The importance, not only from the point of view of the European countries, but also from our own point of view, of a Reconstruction Bank in the position of being able to make or guarantee loans, being organised at as early a date as possible, scarcely needs stressing. Failing this, there will be the strongest pressure on us to make advances far beyond what we can reasonably afford.

---

[11] Not printed. The paper referred to under 3 appears in *JMK*, vol. XV, pp. 415–23.

The attached paper is an outline of a possible compromise, which, whilst conceding much to the American Treasury in form, would be sufficiently changed in substance, to meet our requirements. It is recommended that the British Delegation should be authorised to proceed on these general lines.

KEYNES

9 June 1944

I. Suggested Principles for the Bank

1. Capital Subscriptions to the Bank
The capital of the Bank should be about £2,500m. The United States would be expected to contribute 33 per cent of this. Our share should not exceed 10 per cent.

2. Not more than 20 per cent of this would be paid up, and the remainder would constitute a Surety Fund, not to be called on for the purpose of making direct loans, but only in the event of money being required to implement guarantees given by the Bank for loans raised outside its own direct subscriptions.

3. The proportion of the paid up capital contributed in gold shall be 20 per cent as a maximum; the proportion payable by a particular country being graduated according to a schedule which takes account of the adequacy of the country's gold reserve. In our case we should not agree to a gold contribution exceeding 10 per cent of our paid up subscription. That is to say £5m. It will be seen below that this is the only contribution towards direct loans made by the Bank which would be outside our own control.

II. The Operations of the Bank

1. The Bank would be authorised to operate in any of three different ways:

(*a*) by a loan directly provided out of its own subscribed funds;

49

(*b*) by selling its own securities on the market of a member country;

(*c*) by guaranteeing loans made by private investors.

2. The loans under (*a*) would be made by a procedure which can be illustrated as follows.

The Bank agrees to make a loan of £20m to the Government of China. The Government of China decides in which markets it wishes to purchase capital goods that the loan is intended to finance. It expresses a wish to place orders for £5m in Great Britain. It is then for us to say whether or not we are prepared to make these goods available for payment out of the sum which we have subscribed to the Bank. That is to say out of our initial paid-up subscription of £45 million (£50 million less £5 million in gold). If we are unwilling to agree to this, then China will have to transfer the order to some member country willing to allow it to be placed in the above manner. Thus the rate at which our £45 million will be spent, and the goods on which it will be spent, will remain in our control.

3. Broadly speaking, approved loans would have to be devoted to the purchase of specific imports, and would not take the form of free exchange. There would however be some elasticity in this matter, and provision for exceptional cases. Moreover if the £5 million on orders placed in Great Britain under the above example, involved us in purchasing raw materials from abroad, there would be provision by which the cost of such raw materials might be recovered by us from the Bank, which would have to meet this out of other resources. The gold holdings of the Bank would be available at the discretion of the Bank to finance the placing of orders in any country.

4. Loans under (*b*) would be guaranteed by the whole resources of the Fund. That is to say all countries, whether they were creditor countries or not, would participate in the guarantee. Obviously, however, the loan could only be placed in a creditor country, and it would be a condition that the

approval of the monetary authorities of any country would be required for the placing of a loan by the Bank in its market. Since the loan would be internationally guaranteed, it would have to be an absolute condition that the proceeds of the loan thus raised would be available for purchases, not only in the country in which the loan was raised, but in any member country; so that such loans would be completely untied, and might make an important contribution towards maintaining the equilibrium of the international balances of payments.

5. Loans raised under (c) would be the same in principle as loans raised under (b), and the proceeds of the loans would not be tied to expenditure in the country subscribing to the loans. The guarantee might either be a complete one, or less complete, or even restricted to the guaranteeing of particular risks, such as exchange risks. These loans also therefore would contribute towards the maintenance of international equilibrium, as well as to the provision of funds to countries requiring reconstruction or development.

III. The Guarantee Commission

1. The Bank should charge a fairly substantial flat rate commission to the borrowing country, payable annually, in addition to interest. It is essential that no attempt should be made to differentiate between the credit of different member countries. A flat rate commission of, say, 1 per cent per annum, might be suitable. Thus, the total charge to the borrowing country apart from amortisation would be the flat rate of commission plus a flat rate of interest, fixed by the Bank as the standard, or the rate at which guaranteed loans could be floated in the market. (Let us suppose for illustration purposes, that this rate is $3\frac{1}{2}$ per cent.) In addition the borrowing country would pay an annual rate of amortisation appropriate to the length of life of the loan. For example, 2 per cent if the loan is for about 30 years. It

follows that a 30-year loan would cost the borrowing country an annual annuity for interest, capital repayment and commission, of, say, $6\frac{1}{2}$ per cent altogether.

2. In the event of a borrowing country defaulting on the annual service, the Bank would first of all use its accumulated commissions, less expenses, as a means of meeting the guarantee. Since, in the above illustration, the commission would be $\frac{2}{11}$ of the service of the loan, the running commission, apart from any accumulated commissions, would be sufficient to meet the defaults, unless more than $\frac{2}{11}$ of the total loans outstanding were simultaneously defaulted. Since loans are not generally defaulted from the very beginning, we might, for convenience of illustration, assume that the commissions would look after defaults amounting to at least 20 per cent of the total. Let us suppose that the Bank had guaranteed loans to the full amount of its nominal capital, namely £2,500m, and in order to indicate the measure of risk in which we should be involved, assume that no less than one-half of these were simultaneously defaulted. The service on the defaulted loans would cost the Bank £65,250,000. The commissions on the loans not defaulted would bring in £12,500,000, leaving a deficit of £52,750,000. Our responsibility for this would be 10 per cent, namely £5,275,000 a year.

3. It would seem a very small price to pay for the vast benefits to international trade, of international loans amounting to £2,500m—mainly raised in the creditor countries and available to be spent in any country—that, in the very unlikely event of no less than half of these being defaulted, it would cost us £5,275,000 a year.

IV. The Planning of International Investment

1. It should be a primary duty of the Bank to secure that investment is not made haphazard, but that the more useful schemes are dealt with first; also to co-ordinate investment,

whether it is made or guaranteed by the Bank, or made otherwise; and in short to see that international lending is a more wisely conceived plan than it was after the last war, and is not the ill-conceived racket that it was on that occasion. It would also be the duty of the Bank to consider carefully the capacity of borrowing countries to meet the service of the loans, and to take pains not to make loans except where there is a reasonable prospect of the receiving country being in a position to develop after having received the loan, an adequate favourable balance to meet the service.

2. On the other hand a loan once having been made, if the borrowing country is in difficulties about the service of the loan, for reasons beyond its own control, it should be the duty of the Bank to help it to retrieve its position and not to impose any penalties, except where the borrowing country is at fault. In particular, in the event of an acute exchange scarcity, the Bank should accept local currency in paper for a limited period.

3. The sanctions available to the Bank to be applied to countries defaulting unreasonably, would probably be limited to suspending them from membership, supported by an engagement by the other members of the Bank that they would not extend financial assistance to the defaulting country without approval of the Bank, until the country had been restored to membership, thus cutting it off substantially from any outside financial assistance until it had mended its ways.

V. The Management of the Bank

1. A three-tier management, similar to that contemplated for the Monetary Fund might be appropriate.

2. The voting powers of members would correspond to their subscriptions, except that no member would be entitled to exercise more than 25 per cent of the total voting power.

VI. Essential Features

1. The essential feature of this plan is that apart from the small gold subscription, no country's subscription should be expended at a greater rate, or for different purposes, than it from time to time approves.

2. The bulk of the funds will be provided by creditor countries.

3. The proceeds of loans raised or guaranteed by the Bank, apart from loans made out of its own capital, will be completely untied, and available for expenditure anywhere.

4. Whilst the bulk of the funds will have to be found by creditor countries, it is reasonable that all members should contribute to guaranteeing the risks of international investment to an extent proportionate to their subscription, for they will all have obtained the benefit of releasing these large sums for the expansion of international trade.

5. The foreign exchange liabilities of members will be limited to their initial gold subscription and to any contributions required from them to implement guarantees. The amount thus required in any one year is not likely, except in extreme circumstances when there has been a general world-wide collapse, to cost them at the outside, more than $2\frac{1}{2}$ per cent per annum of their uncalled subscription.

On 16 June, Keynes, Sir Richard Hopkins and Sir David Waley met the Chancellor to discuss Keynes's Bank paper and the Bank of England's comments on it. The upshot of the meeting was that the Delegation[12] should concentrate on gaining a clear draft following Keynes's suggested lines, that loans should be untied, that the planning and co-ordinating functions of the Bank should find greater emphasis, that the potential foreign exchange liabilities of the U.K. under the scheme should be small, that the quotas for

[12] The British Delegation consisted of Keynes (leader), D. H. Robertson, L. C. Robbins, N. Ronald, R. H. Brand, R. Opie and Sir Wilfrid Eady. Its advisers were G. L. F. Bolton and W. E. Beckett.

William Eric Beckett (1896–1966); Second Legal Adviser to Foreign Office, 1929–45, Legal Adviser, 1945–53.

debtors' contributions to the guarantee fund were essential to reduce American dominance of the Bank and that the Bank would better be known as a Fund.

The British Delegation left London on 16 June, and travelled to America on the *Queen Mary*. It arrived in New York on 23 June. With the Delegation came representatives of India, Belgium, China, Czechoslovakia, the Netherlands, Norway and Poland. Mr Casaday of the American Embassy in London also travelled as an observer. On board ship, the Delegation held discussions both amongst themselves and with the others travelling with them.

The results of the Delegation's work at sea were two 'Boat drafts' which it passed to the Americans at the preliminary drafting meetings at Atlantic City. The first draft dealt with the proposed International Monetary Fund. It raised the problems of the exchange clause, as required by instructions, the meaning of 'gold convertible' currencies in the Joint Statement,[13] of gold subscriptions to the Fund, the Fund's transactions in any particular currency, the withdrawal of persistent debtors and the length of the transitional period.[14] The British also made a series of proposals concerning the management of the Fund. Although these were relatively straightforward, they carried the seeds of future discord, for they suggested that the working of the Fund would be 'largely automatic' and routine, and that the Fund would not require 'a very high-powered Directorate permanently in residence' at the site of the Fund nor 'a large and high-powered management'.

The second 'Boat draft' was a re-working of the American Bank proposals designed to emphasise the guarantee function more strongly, to allow the Bank to make currency stabilisation loans, to emphasise the Bank's role in co-ordinating and improving the channels of international investment, to ensure that loans were not tied, to allow for more adventurous lending on individual projects which might make a loss, despite the Bank's obligation to break even overall, to charge a flat annual commission on all loans, as well as a standard rate of interest on its direct loans, and to set up a central reserve fund to avoid calls on national subscriptions.

The Delegation travelled directly from New York to Atlantic City where work began in earnest. The first two full days, 24 and 25 June, were spent

[13] Research in London had suggested that no such currency actually existed. Therefore, the British suggested that convertibility be defined in the Articles of Agreement.

[14] The Joint Statement had made representations from the Fund on transitional period restrictions possible from the start of operations and required consultations between members and the Fund on all restrictions after three years. The British Boat draft suggested that the transition period should be indefinite, that drafting should take some account of the uncertainties surrounding the period, and that consultations should not be required until five years had passed.

in discussions with the Americans and reporting the position to Dominion representatives. On the afternoon of 24 June, the session concerned the Bank. Professor Robbins commented in his diary,

> In the late afternoon we had a joint session with the Americans at which Keynes expounded our views on the Bank. This went very well indeed. Keynes was in his most lucid and persuasive mood; and the effect was irresistible. . . . The Americans sat entranced as the God-like visitor sang and the golden light played around them. When it was all over there was very little discussion. But so far as the Bank is concerned, I am clear that we are off with a flying start.

In the late afternoon of 25 June, Keynes reported the results of the discussions so far to the Commonwealth representatives present.

INTERNATIONAL MONETARY CONFERENCE

Minutes of second informal meeting with Dominion and Indian representatives, held in Lord Keynes's room, Atlantic City, at 4.45 p.m. on Sunday, 25th June, 1944.

(Note: No record has been kept of the first meeting.)

PRESENT:
Lord Keynes (In the Chair)

United Kingdom	*Canada*
Sir W. Eady	Mr L. Rasminsky
Prof. D. H. Robertson	Mr A. F. W. Plumptre
Prof. L. C. Robbins	Mr J. J. Deutsch
Mr W. E. Beckett	
Mr G. L. F. Bolton	*Australia*
Mr H. E. Brooks ⎫ Secretaries	Mr L. G. Melville
Mr A. W. Snelling ⎭	Mr J. B. Brigden
	Mr A. N. Tange
India	Mr F. H. Wheeler
Sir J. Raisman	
Sir T. E. Gregory	
Sir Chintaman Deshmukh[15]	

1. The meeting was called in order to enable Lord Keynes to give an account of a discussion which he had had with Dr White.

[15] Sir Chintaman Dwarkanath Deshmukh (b. 1896); Secretary to Central Board of Reserve Bank of India, Bombay, 1939–41; Deputy Governor, 1941–3; Governor, 1943–9; President, Indian Statistical Institute, 1945–64.

Dr White's views in general

2. Dr White's general reaction had been that, from a technical point of view, many of the U.K. suggestions were acceptable, but that some of them were likely to be politically unacceptable in the U.S. Among the questions on which Dr White thought that there was a divergence of view between the U.K. and the U.S. were the following:

(i) How far the I.M.F. proposals amounted to a return to the gold standard? On this point, the U.K. tended to emphasise the importance of elasticity of the exchanges, and the U.S. the importance of exchange stability.

(ii) As regards disciplinary powers, the U.K. stressed the rights of individual countries as against the Fund, whilst the U.S. emphasised the importance of the powers of the Fund as against the individual countries.

(iii) On the size of the Fund, the U.K. was suggesting larger figures, whilst in the U.S., the Fund had been criticised for being so big.

(iv) As regards the transitional period, the U.S. wanted to make it as short and definite as possible, whilst the U.K. suggestions tended in the opposite direction.

Exchange Adjustment Clause

3. Dr White had taken strong exception to the first sentence of the new IV(4), which stressed the sovereignty of Governments in monetary matters. The question therefore arose whether the U.K. should withdraw this suggestion and if so, whether now or later. Dr White's view was that this sentence would give rise to great political difficulties in the U.S., and MR RASMINSKY said that, in his opinion, Dr White was right on this point. SIR T. GREGORY and MR MELVILLE both shared the view of the U.K. that it was desirable to emphasise the sovereignty of Governments in monetary matters, but MR BECKETT pointed out that from the legal point of view, the sentence left much to be desired. The general conclusion was that it would be desirable to withdraw this sentence and to replace it by something less provocative before any documents reached the Press. Lord Keynes had also agreed with Dr White that the U.K. proposals as regards exchange adjustments (Annex B of I.M.C. (44) (F) 11) should be reserved for the time being.

Transitional Period

4. The U.K. suggestions that 5 years should be substituted for 3 years and that the duration of the transitional period should be made less rather than more definite gave rise to difficulties, because the thoughts of the Americans

had been moving in the opposite direction. Dr White appreciated the reasons for which the U.K. wanted these changes, but foresaw trouble with the rest of his Delegation. SIR T. GREGORY thought that there ought to be room for compromise, but LORD KEYNES pointed out that public opinion in the U.K. was strong on this matter. MR RASMINSKY wondered whether it would be possible to devise an objective test of the conditions in which countries should accept the obligation of multilateral convertibility. LORD KEYNES thought that this would be impossible because of the existence of war debts to be paid off, and of the necessity for giving credit for current exports.

5. MR DEUTSCH drew attention to the new American suggestion that 'no member country should prejudice through the use of exchange restrictions which are authorised under this Agreement or requested by the Fund any existing or future international commitments regarding the non-discriminatory application of exchange restrictions or international under-takings for the progressive relaxation of barriers to trade'. It was agreed that there was a danger that this new suggestion would make nonsense of the provisions as to scarce currencies, and that the position needed to be explored thoroughly with Dr White. MR BECKETT thought that unless the international monetary convention explicitly over-rode the provisions of treaties such as the U.K.–U.S. Trade Agreement of 1938, relating to exchange restrictions, the latter would continue to be binding upon the U.K. LORD KEYNES thought that one solution might be to delete 'existing or' in the new clause quoted above.

Quotas

6. Dr White was anxious that the question of quotas should *not* be discussed at Atlantic City. LORD KEYNES thought however that, notwithstanding its unsatisfactory nature, discussions at Bretton Woods would probably start on the basis of the U.S. formula. He suggested, therefore, that the Dominion and Indian representatives should check the figures in the United States formula for each of their own countries.

Conference Procedure at Bretton Woods

7. Dr White had had it in mind to suggest that at Bretton Woods, each country should have one vote. LORD KEYNES pointed out that the UNRRA Conference showed that this procedure was undesirable, and he had therefore suggested to Dr White that it should be laid down that there would be no voting at Bretton Woods, but that the Chairman should get the sense of the meeting and be responsible for resolving any deadlocks.

25 June 1944

On 25 June, as well, Keynes set out the position to Sir Richard Hopkins. Lyttleton's gaffe, referred to below, came in a speech in London which was taken to mean that the Japanese attack on Pearl Harbour had been provoked by American aid to Britain.

To SIR RICHARD HOPKINS, *25 June 1944*

Dear Hoppy,

We had a most peaceful and also a most busy time on board. I have often had the ambition of doing work on a ship, but this is the first time it has really come off. The result was that we got down on paper every point we wanted to raise with White, and discussed nearly all of them with our Allied friends. We also produced a complete revise of the Reconstruction Bank according to our own ideas, and that also we put through the Allies, who greeted it with some enthusiasm. They were all very nice and helpful and there was no serious dispute on any matter whatever. I am sure we established most useful personal and technical links with them. I am afraid we kept the staff working like slaves. Brooks[16] managed to have a complete report of our proceedings stencilled out by the time we arrived in New York.

In spite of all the work, speaking for Lydia and myself, we enjoyed ourselves extremely, and I have not been in better health for a very long time. We are sufficiently experienced travellers not to eat too much.

At New York we were met by Brand and Lee and spent the morning with them. As you will have discovered, Brand had not seen Stettinius but will be seeing him with the Ambassador in the course of this week. I shall be surprised if they get very far. We agreed that it would be better to postpone any more definite discussion until Brand had joined us at Bretton Woods, where Acheson will be present as well as Morgenthau and Harry White. Brand is not at all happy about the trend of events in relation to Stage Two, and entirely confirmed the view that it

[16] H. E. Brooks, Assistant Principal, Treasury, 1938–9, Principal, 1940–5, Assistant Secretary, 1946.

is essential for us to make a new approach not later than August. Otherwise a trend on the American side in the wrong direction will have gained momentum and we shall be faced with unilateral decisions based on considerable ignorance and misapprehension both of our position and of our point of view. Both Brand and Lee strongly reinforced the view previously expressed that we must be far fuller and franker in our statements of our own present position and future intentions to the Americans. A policy of lying low merely means in practice that we abandon our influence on the course of events. I mentioned privately to Brand the possibility of a visit from the Chancellor, accompanied by Oliver Lyttelton. He thought this unquestionably a good plan, provided the position had been sufficiently prepared beforehand and there was at the last moment jet propulsion from the PM in the shape of a communication to the President coupled with the promise that the Chancellor would follow this up in person. Unfortunately, as you will know only too well, Lyttelton's position is made difficult in this country at the moment by his recent gaffe. Brand and Lee thought this would make it inadvisable for him to be one of the party, and it might be better for Sinclair only to accompany the Chancellor. I rather doubt if this is correct. It was a storm in a teacup and it is all over. As Brand himself said, the average American reaction is that it was an indiscrete remark but nevertheless perfectly true. As regards developments in Canada, Brand's impression was that the prospects were fairly good and that Clark was seriously considering the expediency of taking over certain military expenses which we have lately suggested to him.

Turning now to our proceedings here, everything at present is as smooth and friendly as it could be. Nothing worth mentioning had happened before our arrival, except perhaps that Harry had learnt that the procedure he was attempting was far too complicated to be practicable; the present programme is that on Monday an inter-leaved copy of the Statement of Principles is circulated with our suggestions, the American suggestions, and those of any other Delegations incorporated. The whole body of us in a single committee then work through this clause by clause, referring to smaller *ad hoc* committees of those specially interested any matter which is too intricate to deal with in the larger gathering and which is sufficiently discussed there for the general trend of opinion to be clear. White is anxious that not too many doubts and choices between alternatives should be finally settled here at Atlantic City, since it is important for him that there should be no appearance of asking the members of the American Delegation who are not here and the other powers not represented here to rubber-stamp something already substantially finished. At the same time he agrees that we and the Americans should reach as high a degree of agreement behind the scenes as to which of the alternatives we are ready to drop and which we agree in pressing. Thus to the largest extent possible White and I will have an agreed text, but on the surface a good many matters may be presented in alternative versions. How this will work out remains to be seen. Nevertheless taking the document clause by clause in a single committee, even though it consists of about 60 persons in a room where those at the back can hear nothing is much better than the previous practice of conducting everything first of all in four unrepresentative sub-committees which then bring their half-baked results to the full body, so that everything was done twice and half-baked conclusions reached the main committee with the real merits already prejudiced.

I greatly hope that the Chancellor has been making good progress with the Bank at the hands of his colleagues. I dare say we shall have heard the results of this before you get this letter. We prepared on the boat a complete revise on the lines of the provisional directive with which we have been furnished and were pretty well pleased with the result. This we discussed fully with the European Allies, who were clearly enthusiastic. Yesterday I expounded the substance of it to the Americans, who are now looking into it with more detail. The first reaction

61

of White himself, Pasvolsky, the Federal Reserve Board people, and the others present was as fully as favourable as we could have any reason to expect. My present impression is that if we have authority on the lines proposed, the Americans will agree. It would therefore be rather a disaster, though I daresay there is no real risk of it occurring, of our having to draw back.

We have discussed the changes we want to make in the Fund with the Dominion representatives. Rasminsky thinks that the Catto exchange clause will be difficult or impossible for the Americans in its present form. I am having a preliminary talk with White about this later today and will probably add a postscript to this letter.* I think this is the only matter likely to lead to real difficulty, though there are indications that the Americans, so far from wanting to make the duration of the transition period less definite, will make a proposal that it should be more definite. I doubt however if this will be pressed on their side. The worst that could happen is that it would be more difficult for us to get the still further loosening which we are aiming at.

On the general politics of the position, White seems pretty confident. All the Americans here seem to be quite confident that the President is going to be re-elected. But, of course, they all come from that camp. I have not been here long enough to form any opinion based on reactions from wider circles. It is, however, clear, merely from reading the Press, that the Republican attack is at present a very shapeless and feeble affair. Obviously they cannot decide what is the best issue to take their stand on, with the result that there is more bark than bite, and after barking they seem scared about actually biting any particular portion of the President's body. One would suppose that one could hardly expect to win an election of this kind by such method.†

* No time to add this; it will have to follow tomorrow.
† I am told by those outside the Administration camp that if the campaign in France goes well between now and November, FDR will be re-elected; if not, not.

As regards the particular reaction of politics on our own business, the *New York Times* is conducting a regular campaign against the Monetary Plan, the character of which you will easily see if you glance at the cuttings I am sending Waley. These are not really worth looking at. An effort is being made to get a plank of the Republican platform opposing international collaboration on the Monetary Plan. White expresses himself as not too much concerned at this. Indeed he thinks it might lead to the Democratic party taking a much more definite stand in favour. The staging of the vast monkey-house at Bretton Woods is, of course, in order that the President can say that 44 nations have agreed on the Fund and the Bank and he challenges the Republicans or anyone else to reject such an approach. I should say that this tactic is very likely to be successful. While it is likely, I should think, that the results of our deliberations will not be taken to Congress before the election, White told me he had not entirely given up the idea of earlier action.

Meanwhile, as you will have seen from the cutting which gives the President's letter to Morgenthau appointing the American delegation, he is as clear and decided as the Chancellor that the proceedings at Bretton Woods are without commitment and that the full future rights of Congress are preserved.

Pasvolsky provided us yesterday with a copy of the telegram which the State Department have sent to Winant inviting this party to go to Washington after Bretton Woods to resume in an informal way the Article VII conversations on commercial policy and commodities. Eady and I doubt whether there is any useful information on this which we can send you from this side. You will probably find it difficult to return a direct negative. The degree of affirmativeness will, I suppose, depend on whether the Chancellor has been able to make any progress in breaking the deadlock on commercial policy. If he has, an attempt might, I suppose, be made, not perhaps to make definite progress, but to exchange ideas and second thoughts so as to prepare the ground for the next stage. In this case I daresay you will want to add Liesching to our party at that stage. I think it is clear that the Americans are not thinking of anything formal or definitive, certainly not of anything public. They accept the position that the next stage should be in London. The idea is, I understand, that the State Department would send Dean Acheson, Pasvolsky and Harry Hawkins to London later in the year to resume serious conversations if the prospects look in the slightest degree promising. The suggested conversations in Washington at the end of July would have no further ambition than to exchange information concerning the lines on which the two parties have been thinking since the last conversations.

This is far too long a letter. Whether our communication arrangements are good enough for it to reach you in time remains to be seen. But as we are not proposing to send much in the way of telegrams at the present stage, I thought there would be no harm in giving you this background. Perhaps the most striking feature of the position so far is one which I have not mentioned. Harry White is wreathed in smiles and amiability, hospitable, benevolent and complacent. I doubt if Sigi would recognise him. He also seems extremely fit and happy, and inclined to agree with almost anything which is said to him. Heaven grant that it continues but it seems too much to hope for. I am sending Waley a spare copy of this letter. I am attaching to it, although copies will also be going through the usual office routine, the four substantial papers which emerged from our work on the voyage, namely, the report on our proposals about the Fund with its annex, and the report on our proposals about the Bank with a second paper incorporating these proposals in the American text.

Yours ever,

MAYNARD KEYNES

On 26 June the British and Americans met informally to discuss the points at issue. The exchange clause proved to be the central area of difficulty, as the British note of the meeting makes quite clear.

From Note of an informal meeting between the U.K. and U.S.
Delegations at Atlantic City, 26 June 1944

Exchange Adjustment Clause

1. LORD KEYNES explained the difficulties arising out of the debate in the House of Commons and from other expressions of public opinion in the U.K. about the present draft of the Exchange Adjustment Clause (IV in the Joint Statement). He said that the Chancellor of the Exchequer wanted to be able to go to Parliament and say to them that their sovereignty in money matters had been assured. He agreed that the aim of both the U.K. and U.S. Delegations was to reach arrangements where exchange rates would be as stable as possible, but Parliament had very much in mind the experience of the early thirties. He thought it possible that Congress might dislike, as much as Parliament, having its freedom of action in matters of exchange rates fettered by an international agreement.

2. DR WHITE explained the serious difficulties to which the first sentence of the new U.K. draft of IV(4) gave rise. These difficulties were absolutely basic. The idea of the Fund had been put across in America as something conducive to exchange stability. Already, the United States had made major concessions to United Kingdom views in order to ensure a reasonable measure of flexibility. He was convinced that he could not retreat any further on this point in view of the criticism to which he had already been exposed because the plan envisaged a right to depreciate by 10% at unilateral discretion and a further 10% at very short notice. Unfortunately, those people in the United States who stressed the sovereignty of Congress in monetary matters were also the strongest opponents of the plan who were prepared to block its progress on any pretext. His chief aim was to make sure of the support of the much larger group whose main desire was to see exchange stability. He thought, therefore, that Lord Keynes's criticisms and proposals went right to the root of the plan, and that if he insisted upon them it would be impossible to reach agreement.

3. MR W. R. GARDNER envisaged a situation in which a country had already depreciated its exchange by 20%, and wished to do so further. In this situation the consent of the Fund would be required and he thought that if a country did depreciate further in defiance of the wishes of the Fund, that would represent a grave step of such fundamental economic importance that the country ought not to do so except after the most careful deliberation. If that deliberation led to the conclusion that the step must be taken despite the views of the majority in the Fund, withdrawal from the Fund seemed

to be the only possible consequence. MR GOLDENWEISER[17] remarked that the international financial position of the United Kingdom had been built upon exchange stability and he hoped that the prospect of future stability would enable the idea of the Fund to be put across more easily in England.

4. MR ALVIN HANSEN remarked that American critics said that the Fund did nothing to prevent domestic inflations and suggested that some provision should be inserted about the necessity for the maintenance of internal stability. PROFESSOR ROBBINS thought that this would be dangerous because it would tend to encourage the Fund to intervene in domestic political issues. Those who were anxious to prevent inflationary tendencies would, he thought, find their hands weakened rather than strengthened if it could be represented that anti-inflationary steps were being taken at the dictation of an outside body of international financiers.

5. LORD KEYNES undertook to reconsider the U.K. draft and hoped to be able to prepare a redraft which would be of help to the U.S. authorities in securing acceptance for the plan in America, whilst enabling the Chancellor to meet Parliamentary criticism.

On the other points, suspension from the Fund and, more important, the transitional period, the British made more progress. During the rest of the week, discussions continued on both the Fund and the Bank. Keynes effectively summed them up in another letter to Sir Richard Hopkins.

To SIR RICHARD HOPKINS, *30 June 1944*

Dear Hoppy,

We have just finished our business at Atlantic City and are leaving for Bretton Woods in a few hours. So I take this opportunity of dropping a letter as we pass through New York to let you know how we fare.

In spite of the vast number of persons attending meetings, seldom less than 60, we have got through a surprising amount of business. All proposals and amendments relating to the Fund and the Bank have been considered and indeed fairly fully discussed. There have also been numerous meetings behind the scenes between White and myself, a daily meeting of the British

[17] Emanuel Alexander Goldenweiser (1883–1953), economist; Director, Division of Research and Statistics, Federal Reserve System, 1926–45; Federal Reserve Open Market Committee, 1936–45; Board of Governors, Federal Reserve System, 1944; member, Institute for Advanced Study, Princeton, 1946–51.

Delegation, and a number of joint meetings with the other British Commonwealth representatives. You can imagine, therefore, that we have been fairly busy and have scarcely ever left the hotel. But all has really gone very well indeed. There has not been a single moment of heat or serious dispute, and amiability has prevailed. White has proved an altogether admirable chairman. His kindness to me personally has been extreme. And behind the scenes he has always been out to find a way of agreement except when his own political difficulties stood in the way.

The technique has been not to reach formal agreement on any matters, since White is much concerned not to present Bretton Woods with anything like a *fait accompli* or dotted line. Theoretically, therefore, we have merely received various proposals which different Delegations want to make and arranged them in order in a dossier; though in fact, of course, we have, as indicated above, gone much further than that.

We have not spent nearly so much time on the Bank as on the Fund. But in fact that has largely been because there has been so little to debate. Whilst they have not said so in so many words, we are given to understand that the Americans are prepared to swallow our revise of the Bank practically as it stands, with no more than drafting amendments on small matters. Indeed, they are good enough to say that they think our version better than their own, even from their own point of view. I can fairly say, I think, that our version of the Bank prepared on the boat has met with genuine applause in all quarters. We still have no news as to how it has been received in the Cabinet. But we hope for the best and indeed will be in a position of some considerable perplexity if anything different arrives. (On the Bank I have just received today the note of the Chancellor's conversation with the Governor. That is practically the first document which has arrived from London in the course of the whole fortnight whilst we have been here. But communications from your side have been virtually non-existent, the considerable budget which arrived today having taken eight days, so that the fast bag is considerably slower than the slow bag is supposed to be. However, previous experience in Washington taught me to know that the inefficiency of our communication methods is past praying for.)

On the Fund, there have been three outstanding points of difficulty:

1. There was first of all the Catto clause on altering the exchanges, about which we have been communicating with you by telegram. Since no telegram sent you so far has received any answer, we can only infer that they reached you. But I should expect that this will all have been settled one way or the other before you get this letter. To the best of our belief, the revised draft which we telegraphed to you a couple of days ago is going to be acceptable to the Americans, though we have not got that from them in so many words, and there is still trouble about one important phrase. White and Bernstein have been brought over to our point of view, but they are having the usual trouble which always occurs in this country and is one of the causes of preventing anything sensible being done; that is that they have to consult their lawyers, who are proving difficult. In this lawyer-ridden country even more than elsewhere lawyers seem to be paid to discover ways of making it impossible to do what may prove sensible in future circumstances. However, we have every hope that something pretty good will result. We hope that you are agreeing with us that we shall have obtained in substance what the Chancellor wanted us to get. The essence of our plan is that there is no absolute obligation to obey the Fund in the matter of exchanges and that a member in the last resort has the power to take the matter into his own hands without having to go through the prior act of formally withdrawing from the Fund. White has accepted in principle the advisability of meeting us on this point of substance, and it is only a question, I think, of how it is to be expressed.

2. Whilst we have drafted a clause making the transitional period of more indefinite duration, the Americans have tabled an amendment in exactly the opposite sense, namely, that after

three years the continuance of the transitional arrangements would require the approval of the Fund. I have told White that this is utterly and finally unacceptable to us. They are not pressing the matter, and I think agreement will be reached substantially on our lines.

3. The third matter concerns quotas, and is at present unresolved. This affects other parts of the Commonwealth than ourselves. White has avoided any open discussion of quotas at this stage, and has reserved the matter for Bretton Woods. He has told me privately that the American absolute conditions are the following:

(i) The aggregate must not exceed 8 billions.

(ii) The Russians must have 10 per cent.

(iii) The Chinese must come fourth in aggregate amount.

(iv) The aggregate voting power of the British Commonwealth must not exceed that of the United States.

He declares himself open to argument within that bed of Procrustes.

Now 8 billions is a lower figure than the figure previously given us by the Americans. It means that the Indians and the Australians are likely to be presented with figures below what they think reasonable. We had a Commonwealth meeting about that this morning. It appears that India is much more concerned with equality or near equality with China than with the absolute amount, though they would like something extra. Australia's present quota is probably too low, but she demands a figure which is quite out of line with anyone else's, and is quite inconsistent with the limit of 8 billions for the aggregate. I gather that Melville has instructions which make it difficult for him to compromise; all the same, in the end he will have to. I am going to see White privately again shortly and put up to him a solution which I have reason to believe will satisfy India and help Australia a little. If Australia is still dissatisfied, we are all agreed she must fight her own battle. I have been very anxious to avoid horse-dealing arguments about this in public.

4. Perhaps I should add a fourth matter, namely, manage-

ment. Eady is chiefly handling this. At present the American lawyers are holding out for a system by which Directors directly represent their clients, which is quite ludicrous. We have not yet tackled White on the matter, this question having been relegated to a sub-committee and not dealt with as yet in the main group. It looks to us as if the right voting power on the Directorate will be six votes for America, three for U.K., two for Russia and one each for nine other representatives elected by the remaining members, making twenty votes in all. The other members of the Commonwealth will have sufficient voting power to obtain two or three seats, which will satisfy the American condition. On the Board of Governors we are not objecting to U.S. having slightly more votes than the combined Commonwealth.

America has been as usual in a heat-wave. But here at Atlantic City with a room on the tenth storey immediately facing the Atlantic and with winds generally blowing in from the sea it has been most comfortable and endurable. One day when I was in meetings continuously from 9.30 to 7 without, to Lydia's great indignation, even five minutes' rest, my system gave ominous signs of conking out. But apart from that I have really been on top of my form and have not felt better for a long time. Indeed, I think I may claim to have had considerably better health than the average of the Delegation, who having exposed themselves more than I have to the elements, the sea, climate and the food, are inclined to disappear from action for a short time now and then.

The plans for Bretton Woods are rather incoherent. You will probably know more about them than I do before you get this letter. We start on the Fund, White being chairman of the Commission and there being four committees. Subsequently we pass to the Bank, with myself as chairman of the Commission and again four committees. So much of substance has already been settled that the actual course of business should not offer much difficulty. The real issue is the Press. White has in mind frequent releases to them of everything that is going on, so that henceforth nothing will be confidential, and something like two Press conferences a day. He regards this as a God-sent opportunity to try and win the Press over, which at present is almost uniformly hostile. When we have made sufficient progress on the Fund, which is to be taken before the Bank, there is to be perhaps a plenary meeting at which public speeches will be made explaining what we are doing, with a primary eye to the American public and Congress. White's idea is that I should make a full dress oration on that occasion.

If I dictate any more Miss Macey will not have time to copy it out before we leave. I hope this finds you as it leaves me. Lydia sends her love to you and family. Please tell the Chancellor that we really have nothing to worry about at present. But lurking behind lie the much more formidable issues, which apart from one talk with Pasvolsky we have not as yet raised at all. Indeed, there has been simply no opportunity and not an ounce of surplus energy or a moment of surplus time for anything but the daily duty. As before, I am passing a copy of this to Waley.

Yours ever,
MAYNARD KEYNES

The Delegation arrived at Bretton Woods on 1 July to find the hotel that was to be the site of the Conference still semi-prepared following its wartime closure. Keynes took no formal part in the opening preliminaries and speeches. In the evening, he gave a small dinner party to celebrate the 500th anniversary of the Concordat between King's College, Cambridge, and New College, Oxford.

Sunday, 2 July, was spent in meetings with Commonwealth representatives who had not been at Atlantic City to report on the events there, Indian officials on sterling balances, and the Canadian Minister of Finance on Mutual Aid. It was only on the following day that the three Commissions of the Conference—on the Fund, the Bank and other measures for international financial co-operation—started their proceedings. As chairman of Commission II[18] on the Bank, Keynes began the sessions.

[18] H. D. White was chairman of Commission I on the Fund.

OPENING REMARKS OF LORD KEYNES AT THE FIRST
MEETING OF THE SECOND COMMISSION ON THE BANK
FOR RECONSTRUCTION AND DEVELOPMENT

It is our hope that the institution of the Bank for Reconstruction
and Development, to which this Commission is to devote its
work, will serve the purpose of increasing the health, prosperity
and friendship of the participating countries in two main
respects.

In the first place, it will be authorised in proper cases and
with due prudence to make loans to the countries of the world
which have suffered from the devastation of war, to enable them
to restore their shattered economies and replace the instruments
of production which have been lost or destroyed. It is no part
of the purpose of UNRRA to provide funds for reconstruction
as distinguished from the necessary relief and rehabilitation in
the days immediately following liberation. There is, therefore,
at present a gap in the proposals of the United and Associated
Nations which is not yet filled, and to fill which there is no
proposal in view except the institution of this Bank. Yet this is
a matter of the utmost urgency and importance where we should,
therefore, press forward to reach agreement on methods and on
details. We do not know the date of the complete liberation of
the occupied countries of Europe and Asia. But we are now
entitled to hope that it will be not unduly delayed. We should
be bitterly failing in duty if we were not ready prepared for the
days of liberation. The countries chiefly concerned can scarcely
begin to make their necessary plans until they know upon what
resources they can rely. Any delay, any avoidable time lag will
be disastrous to the establishment of good order and good
government, and may also postpone the date at which the
victorious armies of liberation can return to their homelands.

I cannot, therefore, conceive a more urgent, necessary and
important task for the Delegates of the forty-four nations here
assembled. I am confident that the members of the Commission

of which I have the honour to be the chairman will devote themselves to their work in a spirit of full responsibility, well aware how much depends on their success.

It is likely, in my judgement, that the field of reconstruction from the consequences of war will mainly occupy the proposed Bank in its early days. But as soon as possible, and with increasing emphasis as time goes on, there is a second primary duty laid upon it, namely, to develop the resources and productive capacity of the world, with special attention to the less developed countries, to raising the standard of life and the conditions of labour everywhere, to make the resources of the world more fully available to all mankind, and so to order its operations as to promote and maintain equilibrium in the international balances of payments of all member countries.

These two purposes deserve particular emphasis, but are not exclusive or comprehensive. In general, it will be the duty of the Bank, by wise and prudent lending, to promote a policy of expansion of the world's economy in the sense in which this term is the exact opposite of inflation. By 'expansion' we should mean the increase of resources and production in real terms, in physical quantity, accompanied and facilitated by a corresponding increase of purchasing power. By 'inflation' on the other hand, we should mean the increase of purchasing power corresponding to which there is no accompanying increase in the quantity of production. The Bank will promote expansion and avoid inflation.

Under the proposals to be brought before you, the Bank will be free to operate along three different lines.

A certain part of the Fund's [Bank's?] subscribed capital will be called up and will be available for direct lending by the Bank for approved purposes in the currencies of the contributing members.

But the greater part of its subscribed capital will be held as a reserve fund with which to guarantee two other types of operations.

The first type of loan eligible for such guarantee will be loans for suitable purposes and on suitable terms issued through the ordinary channels of the investment market where on account of the risks involved there would be difficulty otherwise in placing the loan on terms which the borrowing country could afford to pay.

The second type of loan secured by the assets and subscribed capital of the Bank will also be placed through the ordinary channels of the investment market but will be offered on the Bank's behalf in its own name. The proceeds of such loans will then be re-lent by the Bank to borrowing countries on terms and for purposes to be directly agreed with them.

The proceeds of both these types of loan would be freely available for the borrower to make purchases in any member country, with due regard to economy and efficiency.

Let me now explain the nature of the proposed guarantee, for this is of a novel character which may be regarded as marking in a particularly significant way the international character of the proposed institution.

It is evident that only a few of the member countries will be in possession of an investable surplus available for overseas loans on a large scale, especially in the years immediately following the war. It is in the nature of the case that the bulk of the lending can only come from a small group of the member countries, and mainly from the United States. How then can the other member countries play their proper part and make their appropriate contribution to the common purpose?

Herein lies the novelty of the proposals which will be submitted to you. Only those countries which find themselves in specially favoured positions can provide the loanable funds. But this is no reason why these lending countries should also run the whole risk of the transaction. In the dangerous and precarious days which lie ahead, the risks of the lender will be inevitably large and most difficult to calculate. The risk premium reckoned on strict commercial principles may be beyond the capacity of an impoverished borrower to meet, and may itself contribute to the risks of ultimate default. Experience between the wars was not encouraging. Without some supporting guarantee, therefore, loans which are greatly in the interests of the whole world, and indeed essential for recovery, it may prove impossible to float.

Yet, as I have said, there is no reason in a case like this, where the interests of all countries alike, whether lenders or borrowers, or exporters, are favourably affected, why the unavoidable risks should fall exclusively on the lenders, for example, the investors or the government of the United States, if it turns out that they are the chief source of available funds.

The proposal is, therefore, that all the member countries should share the risk in proportions which correspond to their capacity. The guarantees will be joint and several, up to the limit of any members' subscription, so that the failure of any member to implement his guarantee will not injuriously affect the lender, so long as the Bank has other assets and subscriptions to draw upon, resources which will, according to our proposals, be of considerable dimensions. Moreover, it is proposed that every member country should undertake to provide gold or free exchange up to the full amount of its subscription, in so far as it is called upon under its guarantee. Therefore the quality of the bonds thus guaranteed should be of the first order; at any rate they will be a great deal better than in the case of many borrowing countries there would be any hope of offering otherwise than under the auspices of the new institution.

The bonds will be good for several different reasons. In the first place, they will have behind them the vast resources of the Bank available in gold or free exchange. In the second place, the proceeds will be expended only for proper purposes and in proper ways, after due enquiry by experts and technicians, so that there will be safeguards against squandering and waste and extravagance, which were not present with many of the ill-fated loans made between the wars. In the third place, they will carry the guarantee of the borrowing country; and this borrower will be under an overwhelming motive to do its best and play fair, for the consequences of improper action and avoidable default to so great an institution will not be lightly incurred.

But there is also a fourth safeguard of great importance to the guaranteeing countries as well as to the lenders. There are two reasons for hoping that the guarantors will not find themselves under any insupportable or burdensome liability. In the first place, a guarantee will relate to the annual servicing of the loan for interest and amortisation. Its implementation will, therefore, be spread over a period corresponding to the term of the loan and cannot fall due suddenly as a lump sum obligation. In the second place, there is an interesting and essential feature of the proposals in the shape of a commission payable by the borrower in return for its guarantee. It is suggested that for long-term loans of the normal character this commission should be at the rate of 1 per cent per annum. This rate of commission should be the same for all members alike, for it would be a mistake, and worse than a mistake, to attempt the invidious task of discriminating between members and assessing their credit-worthiness in what is really a mutual pool of credit insurance amongst a group acting in good faith—indeed in the old language of insurers consecrated by tradition, in the spirit of *uberrima fides*, of good faith, complete, abundant and overflowing.

This commission should not be an excessive burden on the borrower; 1 per cent added to the interest appropriate to a loan guaranteed by the Bank will not be onerous. On the other hand, the annual receipts from the commission will greatly augment the free reserves of the Bank available to meet its obligations before calling on the guarantors. The Bank should aim at so conducting its business that there would be a good hope of the pool of commissions being sufficient by itself to carry it most of the way.

Here are the broad outlines of the proposals which you will

be asked to consider. There are other aspects and much detail for you to work out. For the Bank has not enjoyed so much discussion as has the Fund prior to this Conference.

But I believe that we have before us a proposal the origins of which we owe primarily to the initiative and ability of the United States Treasury, conceived on sound and fruitful lines. Indeed, I fancy that the underlying conception of a joint and several guarantee of all the member countries throughout the world, in virtue of which they share the risks of projects of common interest and advantage even when they cannot themselves provide the lump sum loan originally required, thus separating the carrying of risk from the provision of funds, may be a contribution of fundamental value and importance to those difficult, those almost overwhelming tasks which lie ahead of us, to rebuild the world when a final victory over the forces of evil opens the way to a new age of peace and progress after great afflictions.

3 July 1944

The next day Keynes wrote to Lord Catto.

To LORD CATTO, *4 July 1944*

My dear Governor,

Today is the first breathing space I have had in which to write you a gossipy letter. Until now from the first hour we stepped on the boat one has had to be continuously occupied one way and another. We have reached now a point where much spade work has been done behind the scenes and the material is being consigned to small committees (a small committee is a meeting at which from 50 to 200 people attend), and for the time being at least I am sending the other boys to the meetings and staying away myself.

Hitherto we have been spending most of our time trying to get, so far as possible, a version agreed with the Americans

77

behind the scenes. Over a very broad front this has been successful. Harry White is fighting various battles in his own camp and in his own Press and is most disinclined to take on any issue with us if he can possibly help it—which, of course, makes it very much more easy for us to obtain satisfaction. Perhaps I might run through three or four of the main points.

What I call the Cobbold clause, that is to say, the difficulty which Cobbold brought to light shortly before we left London, we have obtained complete satisfaction, not only in drafting the clause, but also in its removal to the section dealing with obligations.

The Catto clause, on the other hand, that is to say, your suggestion for a redraft as to how we are to deal with the exchanges, has been much more difficult going. It was quite clear from the outset, as you will have seen in a telegram, that a forthright statement reserving discretion to a country to change its exchange without any breach of obligation would be politically impossible for them. But at an early stage I persuaded White of the wisdom of trying to find a way of conceding the substance of this to us. Since then there has been a very prolonged battle of drafts, with the American lawyers making it much more difficult than it need be. At the moment of writing the final t's have not been crossed or the i's dotted, but it seems practically certain that we have at least secured the substance of your proposal; that is to say, a country is entitled in the last resort to alter its exchange rate without a breach of obligation and without having to leave the Fund, provided it is prepared to be cut off from the privileges of the Fund, and in the case of a prolonged dispute, being called upon to withdraw. The final version is not very different from the one which we cabled at a half-way stage. But in so far as it differs it is, in my judgement, better rather than worse. The changes in language proposed in a Treasury telegram have been substantially accepted. The important parts of the new draft looks like running as follows, though I expect you will have had this by telegram before the arrival of this letter: 'The Fund shall concur in a proposed change if it is required to correct a fundamental disequilibrium. If the Fund considers that the proposal has not been shown to be required to correct a fundamental disequilibrium and is unjustified, having regard to the proper working of the Fund, the Fund shall object to the proposed change. If a member alters the par value of its currency despite the objection of the Fund in cases where the Fund is entitled to object, the matter shall be subject to the provisions of Article VIII section...' Article VIII then provides that in the case of a disagreement of this character, the Fund may declare a member ineligible to use the resources of the Fund and may, in the last resort, if it so desires, after an interval and after further discussion, call on the member to withdraw.

The trouble was not really between us and White, but between White and the rest of his Delegation, since the Congressmen and bankers have been pressing him for changes in precisely the opposite direction. He has really been fighting manfully to keep faith with us.

The next problem is that of the transitional arrangements. Here also White, under outside pressure, was proposing an amendment in precisely the wrong direction. But here also, though not at the date of writing with absolute 100 per cent certainty, we believe that the Americans have accepted our version.

Lastly, there is the question of quotas. Here, I am afraid, our proposals for something larger for the smaller people cannot be managed, since White would be under irresistible attack in his own Delegation if he were to agree to go beyond 8 billions for the aggregate; much smaller figures are being pressed upon him. On the other hand, I am hopeful that I have persuaded him to make a sufficient concession to India to keep them moderately satisfied, and enough for Australia to meet their desserts though not their demands.

Brand, Eady and I have had one long preliminary talk with

the Indian representatives on things in general, and Raisman expressed himself as well satisfied with the result. We shall have another talk shortly. My impression is that Deshmukh will be, as Raisman said he would be, 'loyal' and a good civil servant. Chetty[19] seems very amenable and sensible. Shroff is clearly, as Raisman says, a snake in the grass, trying to catch us out and filled with suppressed malice. Gregory, who has joined us, declares that he is fed to the teeth with the prevailing Indian attitude on everything and his only idea is to escape as soon as he can do so without disloyalty to Raisman. Raisman, I fancy, feels much the same; so do we all. If only some heavenly power would apply almighty shears and cut the painter. However, I do think we shall succeed in preventing them from making any extra trouble here or in India in connection with the monetary plan as such.

As you will have heard, we had a very important conversation with Ilsley, Clark and Towers. I have no idea what the way out is, or how Canada can help us on an adequate scale. But at any rate we did our duty in creating a very considerable impression on them and sent them away wiser and sadder men. I think we must give them a breathing spell to think over the situation in the light of what we told them. Nothing could have been more friendly and understanding than the way they received what it was our duty to tell.

I do not think one will be in a position to give any worthwhile advice about a visit from the Chancellor before the end of this week. My provisional feeling is still that it is very desirable for him to come at an early date. Meanwhile the position is going to be bedevilled by a visit from the Beaver. To send him here at this juncture is a crime for which all the members of the War Cabinet ought to be executed (if you happen to see any of them, please pass this on). It would be fatal for the Chancellor's visit to overlap with the Beaver's, and I do not yet know exactly what

[19] Sir Shanmukkam Chetty (1892–1953); Indian Delegate at Bretton Woods; Minister of Finance, India, 1947–8.

the dates of the latter's visit are. Theoretically the Conference about World Organisation will follow immediately after that. But there seems considerable likelihood of a postponement there. In that case there might be room for a visit from the Chancellor very early in August. The trouble is, however, that we have been too much occupied in other directions to be able to take the necessary soundings, besides which it was a bit premature to take them anyhow.

One remarkable bit of news. For the first time in my life I am really getting on with Morgy. In all the years I have known him there has never been a moment which was not sticky. Now all that is changed. Why, I do not suppose he knows any more than I do. But there is no stickiness at all and we can chat together like cronies by the hour. Of course, I have not yet tried any difficult subjects. The atmosphere was altogether too good to risk spoiling it! As for Harry, he has been all smiles, kindness and geniality. The position definitely is that we are allies and the common foe is from without. In spite of the immense volume of criticism in the Press and great doubts expressed by bankers and Congressmen, my judgement is (and I think Harry shares it) that the real position is extremely good. There is a lot of Republican politics in the position. But the Republican Congressmen here were already converted by the second day. My belief is that there is no steam in the opposition, and if the 44 nations come into what purports to be agreement, there is more danger than profit to be obtained by trying to sabotage it.

The case of Senator Tobey[20] is a good illustration. He is a Republican, formerly isolationist, an alleged anti-British Senator, who had claimed to be on because of his membership of the relevant Senate Committee. Owing to his general attitude the Administration fought hard to keep him off the American Delegation; they did not succeed. But the second day he had come round completely and on the third day he delivered a

[20] Charles William Tobey (1880–1953); Republican Member of House of Representatives, 1933–9; Senator for New Hampshire, 1939–53.

public oration, at which the Press were present, calling down the blessings of God on the Conference and saying that we should be untrue to Christ if we did not put these plans through, since the countries to be succoured had also been suffering from a crown of thorns (he is, by the way, as you will see, of good old non-conformist type). All the above was delivered through a microphone in a voice which shook the largest room, with raised arms and fists and intense conviction and genuine belief. We have met him at tea, where he was all friendliness and told us that it was quite definitely the duty of everyone concerned to see this matter through. What a strange country!

It is not off the map that the President will make the Plan a part of the Democratic plank and challenge the Republicans to oppose it. If this happens, the odds are, in my opinion, that they will funk it. As I have said above, there is really no steam in the opposition. This is such a boring subject that no public enthusiasm can be roused by discussing the details, whilst it would be frightfully dangerous to be open to the challenge of sabotaging the first international scheme. Anyone with isolationist origins will think twice before doing so.

Bolton has been most helpful in many matters and has taken charge of various sides of our discussions. There have been a number of issues where we should have been considerably at a loss without him, so thank you again very much for letting him come. Also a word to Bernard for being so kind in firmly saying that I should have Miss Macey, who, as you may suppose, is producing this letter here and now.

The climate both at Atlantic City and here has been very kind, and there has been no real heat. Eady has been a little seedy for a good part of the time,—partly, I should imagine, as a reaction from the pressure of previous over-work. Lydia and I are very well indeed. Though we worked very hard indeed on the boat, it was nevertheless a rest. Except on one day when I went on for more than ten hours without even a five minutes' rest, I have not had any heart symptoms whatever. Indeed, I believe I have to confess that so far as my heart is concerned, whatever other parts of the body, mind and spirit may think, the American climate does suit it.

Love to all friends. No chance I am afraid of my being back for the Bank celebration,[21] which is a great disappointment.

Yours ever,
[copy initialled] M.K.

For the first week of Bretton Woods, the Fund was the centre of attention and Commission II did not meet until 11 July. Throughout the week, Keynes and Dennis Robertson bore the main brunt of the work as the various Committees on the Fund inched their way through the draft articles of agreement. The week also brought rumblings of discontent from the Indians and Egyptians over the future convertibility of wartime sterling balances. By the end of the week, Professor Robbins reported,

Keynes is showing obvious signs of exhaustion and we are all very worried about him. He is not the easiest of men to control, and the eagerness of his mind is such that it is intolerable for him to go slow.

Everyone was by then beginning to show signs of wear and tear.

The next day, after a week of continuous discussions, largely carried on by E. M. Bernstein and D. H. Robertson, an exchange clause suitable to the delegation went before Commission I. The same day, Keynes reported to Sir Richard Hopkins.

To SIR RICHARD HOPKINS, *8 July 1944*

Personal for Hopkins from Keynes.

The British Press is reported here as expressing pessimism about the outcome of Bretton Woods Conference. I believe that this is a misreading of the position though a natural one. In fact great progress on most contentious and difficult issues is being made behind the scenes. In open Committee 44 nations are of course capable of wasting as much time as is at their disposal. But in the course of coming week I believe we shall be in a

[21] The celebration of the 250th anniversary of the founding of the Bank of England in 1694.

position to crystallise quite suddenly on concrete and agreed conclusions.

2. We are only now beginning to work seriously on the Bank. But that appears surprisingly free from controversial issues. There are several improvements needed to make set-up really workable from a practical point of view; but nothing so far as I am aware controversial between Delegations. It is confirmed that the Americans are accepting practically the whole of our suggested amendments. They are proposing that location of the Bank as well as of Fund should be in United States. We shall be tabling the same amendment as in the case of Fund namely to postpone the choice of location until the new organisation is actually set up.

3. My personal belief is that we shall probably be able to reach completely agreed [grp. undec.] both on the Fund and on the Bank by 19th July.

4. For ourselves we are all thoroughly enjoying life in this wonderful climate and in good comradeship of this place but all are greatly concerned for you in London and continuously worried by lack of news. The communication arrangements have proved so grotesquely inefficient that I am giving up writing letters to you. If however communications from this side reach you much more rapidly than yours to us, so that my letters arrive soon enough to be of any interest, please let me know.

By 8 July, Professor Robbins noted in his diary. 'Keynes...is now very exhausted and has to rest whenever he can.' Nevertheless, he still found time the next day to take part in Mr White's daily Press conference, with the result that he was misquoted in *The Economist* and had to write to the editor.

To the Editor of The Economist, *29 July 1944*

Sir,

In your issue of July 15th which has just come to my notice, you report me as having said in a Press conference at Bretton Woods that 'The real purpose of the Monetary Fund is to bring back gold as a fundamental reserve money'. In fact I said nothing of the kind. In case the matter is of any interest, the following is an extract from the report of the Press conference in question, published in *The New York Times*:

Lord Keynes said the modified form of gold standard being considered here was not inconsistent with his denunciation of the old gold standard in 1933 as 'a barbarous relic'. The old standard was so 'rigid', he explained, that it could not stand the strain of crisis and finally broke. Under the proposed standard, all currencies would have a 'link' with gold, but it would be 'flexible' enough to permit orderly changes in exchange rates when necessary to avert the breakdown of monetary systems, competitive currency depreciation and similar measures of economic warfare...

British sentiment is strongly opposed to a return to the 'rigid' gold standard, he went on, adding that the present 'scheme', as he called it, was 'quite different' in its flexibility. 'It retains the link with gold, but it can be adapted to changing circumstances from time to time', said Lord Keynes. 'It provides the machinery of consultation and agreement by which orderly changes can be made. I have never argued that gold was "a barbarous relic" in this sense. When I was criticising the old gold standard, I made various proposals for retaining the link with gold. I proposed that gold be made a "constitutional monarch", so to speak, which would be subject to the constitution of the people and not able to exercise tyrannical power over the nations of the world.' He said it would be very 'foolish' to propose 'departure from the gold link'. With the United States and certain western European countries holding large quantities of gold, and with the British Commonwealth and Russia producing large quantities of the precious metal every year, he went on, 'no one in his senses would want to make the gold resources of the world useless or throw the gold mines of the world out of employment'.

Yours, etc.

KEYNES

On 10 July, the sterling balances issue reached a head when the Indians pressed the case for the Fund's involvement in the post-war settlement of the issue through its making a portion available for multilateral settlement. Keynes, supported by the French and the Americans, successfully scuttled the matter as far as the Conference was concerned with the following remarks.

STATEMENT BY LORD KEYNES ON BEHALF OF THE
DELEGATION OF THE UNITED KINGDOM AT MEETING OF
COMMISSION I

Since the United Kingdom is the only country here represented
which has incurred large-scale war debts to her Allies and
Associates also here present, these alternative amendments must
be assumed, as Mr Shroff had indeed made clear, to relate
primarily to her.

The various members of this alliance have suffered in mind,
body and estate from the effort and exhaustion of war in ways
differing in kind and in degree. These sacrifices cannot be
weighed one against the other. Those of us who were most
directly threatened and were nevertheless able to remain in the
fight, such as the U.S.S.R. and the United Kingdom, have
fought this war on the principle of unlimited liability and with
a more reckless disregard to economic consequences than others
who were more fortunately placed. We do not plead guilty to
imprudence; for in the larger field of human affairs nothing
could have been less prudent than hesitation or a careful
counting of the cost.

But as a result there has been inevitably no equality of
financial sacrifice. In respect of overseas assets the end of the
war will find the United Kingdom greatly impoverished and
others of the United Nations considerably enriched at our
expense. We make no complaint of this provided that the
resulting situation is accepted for what it is. On the contrary,
we are grateful to those Allies, particularly to our Indian friends,
who put their resources at our disposal without stint and
themselves suffered from privation as a result. Our effort would
have been gravely, perhaps critically, embarrassed if they had
held back from helping us so wholeheartedly and on so great
a scale. We appreciate the moderate, friendly and realistic
statement of the problem which Mr Shroff has put before you
today. Nevertheless the settlement of these debts must be, in

our clear and settled judgment, a matter between those directly concerned. When the end is reached and we can see our way into the daylight we shall take it up without any delay, to settle honourably what was honourably and generously given.

But we do not intend to ask assistance in this matter from the International Monetary Fund—beyond the fact, as the American Delegation has pointed out, that the existence of the Fund and the general assistance it will give to the stability and expansion of trade may be expected to improve indirectly our ability to meet other obligations. We concur entirely in the view which has just been expressed by the American Delegation that the Fund is not intended to deal directly with war indebtedness.

Since we do not intend either to ask for, or to avail ourselves of, any special treatment from the Fund, it appears to the United Kingdom Delegation that this amendment could be of no practical effect; and is therefore better discarded if misunderstanding is to be avoided about the role which the Fund can expect to play.

10 July also saw the beginning of hard bargaining between the British and the Americans over the location of the Fund and the Bank. The Americans, thinking that both should be in the United States, proposed that they be in the country with the largest quota. The British thought that the problem should be solved at the first meeting of the Fund and the Bank, that meeting to be held in the country with the largest quota. Keynes warned White that he could not agree to the American alternative without the Chancellor's further instructions and successfully put off the issue for the time being.

The next day Commission II began its work by setting up a series of sub-committees to deal with the Bank's articles of agreement. Within a day there were complaints about Keynes's chairmanship. As Dean Acheson told Mr Morgenthau,[22]

The first problem about the Bank is that the Commission meetings on the Bank, which are conducted by Keynes, are being rushed in a perfectly impossible and outrageous way. Now that comes from the fact that Keynes is under great pressure. He knows this thing inside out so that when

[22] *Morgenthau Diaries*, Vol. 753, pp. 143–4.

anybody says Section 15-C he knows what it is. Nobody else in the room knows. So before you have an opportunity to turn to Section 15-C and see what he is talking about, he says, 'I hear no objection to that', and it is passed.

Well, everybody is trying to find Section 15-C. He then says, we are now talking about Section 26-D. Then they begin fiddling around with their papers, and before you find that, it is passed.

Mr Morgenthau, as President of the Conference, agreed to raise the matter with Keynes, with some success.

On 13 July, as well, the location of the two institutions, an issue which had been the subject of several Anglo-American discussions, came forward, as Keynes wrote to Mr Morgenthau.

To H. MORGENTHAU, *13 July 1944*

Dear Mr Secretary,

The United States Delegation have proposed that the principal office of the Fund shall be located in the United States. You will be aware that the United Kingdom Delegation have tabled an alternative to the following effect:

'The location of the principal office of the Fund shall be decided by the Fund at the first meeting of the Board of Governors, which will take place in the territory of the member having the largest quota.'

I was under instructions from the Chancellor of the Exchequer not to recede from this alternative without his express authority. When therefore during your absence a few days ago I learned from Judge Vinson that it was the view of the United States Delegation that their proposal should be pressed, I immediately communicated the position to the Chancellor of the Exchequer and asked him for further instructions.

His reply has now arrived. I am asked by the Chancellor to convey to the United States Delegation that it is the strongly held view of my Government that, whether the location of the Fund is determined during this Conference or at a later date, the decision is a political matter and therefore to be decided by Governments.

You will, I am sure, agree that the location of the headquarters of the Fund is a matter of high policy. It is not merely financial or economic factors that have to be taken into account: the question raises important issues of political, international relations. The question where the headquarters of the Fund should be situated cannot be considered without reference to the location of the other international bodies with which the Fund will have to co-operate. Among the most important of these international bodies will clearly be the projected over-all World Organisation. Until it is known what other international bodies are likely to be established within the framework of this World Organisation, and where they and the World Organisation are to be located, it would be premature to take any final decision about the Fund's headquarters. After all, it is only by accident that the Fund is to be—or perhaps I should say, looks like being—the first international body with extensive executive functions to be established. It seems to us that it would be more prudent without, of course, in any way prejudicing the claims of this or any other member country to be the seat of the Fund, that our two Governments should suspend judgment until they see more clearly where the seats of the other main organisations can most suitably be fixed. This would put them in a position, before taking a final decision, to weigh the many important political factors which will have to be taken into account.

If the alternative which the United Kingdom Delegation have tabled be adopted, it would be our hope that before the Board of Governors can hold their first meeting a decision could in fact be taken between Governments. But I must particularly emphasise in this letter that in the opinion of my Government it would not be a proper course to settle a political matter, such as this is, by equal voting of the financial or technical Delegates from the wide variety of nations here assembled. No one can suppose that the more difficult matters relating to post-war World Organisation, where the major powers are not for the time being in full agreement, ought to be settled in such a way.

I should add that the Chancellor's telegram is supplemented by a further telegram from the Foreign Office, which indicates that the Chancellor and the Foreign Secretary are acting in agreement. The Foreign Office is in fact closely engaged on the whole question of World Organisation at this very moment and expects, as you are aware, to discuss it at an early date with the State Department.

The particular manner in which the issue is reserved for subsequent decision is, of course, for us a secondary matter. The Chancellor also wishes me to make it clear to the United States Delegation, though this is not a major consideration, that the considerable opposition to the Fund which he will have to face in London would be gravely augmented if this issue were to be forced through here and now.

I should be grateful if you would be good enough to let me have an expression of your views on this matter in order that I may communicate them to my Government as soon as possible. I am, of course, at your disposal at any time for a talk.

Sincerely yours,
[copy initialled] K

Keynes saw Morgenthau the next morning and reported to London.

To SIR JOHN ANDERSON, *14 July 1944*

For Chancellor from Keynes.

After receiving Camer 44 I wrote to Morgenthau as in the next following telegram.[23] This morning he came up for a private talk at which he asked me to transmit the following to you as a personal message.

2. He has laid my expression of your views before the full American Delegation. All Congressmen present were emphatic that Congress will not accept Fund unless it is located in the United States. The proposal that settlement of this issue should

---

[23] See above, pp. 88–90.

be postponed for decision either by Governors of the Fund or by the Governments subsequent to this Conference would not be understood. In their judgement there must be no doubt on this matter when recommendations of this conference are published for the consideration of Congress. In any event he considers that the ultimate decision must be regarded as a foregone conclusion.

3. It is not easy to make clear to Congressmen connexion of this issue with other matters of which at present they know little or nothing or to persuade them that this ought to be settled by the Governments over their heads. Morgenthau who was as friendly and conciliatory as possible explained that his problem arose out of the peculiar relationship of Administration to Congress. He has regarded it as essential to bring considerations of Congress into close contact with the Conference and detailed drafting of the Convention. He has pursued this technique more boldly than it has ever been used hitherto. So far he has had an extraordinary and indeed miraculous success. All Congressmen here present, who include not only Republicans but one time Isolationists and hostile critics, have been brought round to enthusiastic support both of the Fund and the Bank. You will have seen Senator Taft's denunciation of the Fund published two days ago. The Republican Senators here are telling Taft in the sharpest terms that he does not speak for the Party and that they are now convinced that proposals under discussion are to the advantage of the United States. Morgenthau believes that a position has now been built up which makes the approval of Congress highly probable indeed almost certain. He begs you not to press him to upset the present mood of his difficult team and pleads that you should appreciate special nature of his problem which arises wholly from relationship of Congress to the Administration irrespective of politics.

4. Alternatives are:

(1) to acquiesce and withdraw our amendment;

(2) to argue strongly for our amendment in the Commission

and press it to a vote which would lead to a Press sensation and inevitable defeat. Whatever the other quarter may think they will give us no public support at the Conference;

(3) to argue for our amendment in mildly general terms saying that in our view the problem of the locations of international organs should not be settled piecemeal but not press the matter.

5. I believe that we are on a losing wicket here and hope that I may be instructed on lines either (1) or (3) in previous paragraph. Eady, Brand and Ronald reluctantly concur. An answer by Sunday night is essential.

6. If another view is taken I do not know any way in which it can be successfully pressed for at this Conference and the matter would have to be raised either at the highest level or through State Department. Whether this could be achieved in time is very doubtful and even if it were attempted I believe that Morgenthau's account of the situation here would influence Administration at all higher levels to support him. For his success with his Delegation here will have achieved an important result for the Administration.

7. Formally of course this is not your last opportunity to raise the issue. Nothing is in question except a recommendation by this technical conference in which neither Cabinet nor Parliament need concur. You would be perfectly free to re-open the matter in connexion with a later settlement of the question of location of international organs generally, even though prospect of an agreeable change in this particular case is remote.

The same day, Keynes, following the Chancellor's instructions, confirmed the exchange clause understanding with the Americans.

To SIR DAVID WALEY, SIR RICHARD HOPKINS *and* T. PADMORE,
14 July 1944

Our right to modify the par value of the exchange. I attach a copy of a letter which I have sent to Mr White in pursuance of the Chancellor's instructions in CAMER 43. I thought it better to put the statement in this more positive manner, since an enquiry in the form of a question might suggest that there could conceivably be some doubt about the matter.

In this connection the minutes of one of the committees of the Conference which discussed this clause may be helpful and should be put on record before we forget it. You will see that the Canadian Delegate is recorded as stating in forthright terms 'that these sections as approved allow a member country to change its rate without the approval of the Fund and yet remain a member in good standing'. He added that he thought the provisions in this respect 'had provided a happy compromise between exchange rigidity and exchange flexibility'. This was very handsome of him, because the Canadian point of view has been closely lined up with the American on this particular matter. Indeed, that has been one of our obstacles in reaching a satisfactory draft.

14 July 1944

My dear White,

You may like to know that I have had a telegram from the Chancellor of the Exchequer in which he tells me how well satisfied he is with Article IV 'Par values of currencies' in its revised form. He greatly appreciates the extent to which the American Delegation has been able to meet our views in the matter, which was for him from the Parliamentary point of view of a good deal of importance.

The Chancellor will feel able to defend this text in Parliament as recognising an inherent right on the part of members to modify their exchange rates despite the objection of the Fund.

He will, of course, attempt to do so in the manner which is least likely to provoke criticism from the other angle, but in a certain measure he will almost certainly be called upon to defend the text from this point of view.

Yours sincerely,

KEYNES

When the Chancellor replied to Keynes's suggestions concerning the location of the Fund, Keynes wrote to Mr Morgenthau.

To H. MORGENTHAU, *17 July 1944*

Dear Mr Secretary,

After my conversation with you the other day I communicated with the Chancellor of the Exchequer and have received his final instructions.

When the clause about the location of the Fund is reached at the Commission, he authorises me to withdraw the British amendment, but in doing so to place it on record that in the view of His Majesty's Government the question where the headquarters of the Bank should be situated ought not to be considered without reference to the location of other international bodies.

He also asks me to let you know that in his view I was understating his difficulties when, in mentioning in my previous letter the risk of increasing opposition to the Fund in London, I added that this was not a major consideration. The Chancellor asks me to tell you privately that he expects public and Parliamentary opinion to be very sensitive on this point. He is anxious, therefore, for me to explain that, apart altogether from the wider considerations which I have already emphasised to you, His Majesty's Government must not be considered as debarred hereafter from making a condition of acceptance of the plan that the headquarters of the Fund shall be in Europe or such other location as may be decided to be in the best interests

IT CAN'T BE OURS! IT'S GOT GOLDEN HAIR!

Cartoon by David Low by arrangement with the Trustees and The London Evening Standard.

95

of the Fund. All the work of this Conference is, of course, *ad referendum*. What the Chancellor asks me to make clear is that this correspondence must not be understood to affect that general understanding in its application to this particular issue.

I should add that the Foreign Secretary has been consulted by the Chancellor of the Exchequer and the above represents his views as well as those of the Chancellor.

Sincerely yours,

KEYNES

When the issue came up on 18 July Keynes, after further consultations, proceeded as he had proposed.

Although the Conference was to have finished on 19 July, after Keynes initially raised the matter with Mr Morgenthau a meeting of senior delegates agreed to a postponement to 22 July. The extra time was designed to reduce the strain on the delegates, who were proceeding quickly enough on the principles of the agreements underlying the Fund and Bank, but were finding the pressures on the draftsmen very serious.[24] At the same time, 17 July was declared a day of rest as far as formal meetings were concerned.

Two days later came another crisis for Keynes. Norway and other European countries had put forward a proposal for the rapid liquidation of the Bank for International Settlements. Working with the Americans, Britain informally agreed to a milder proposal to achieve the same ultimate end. However, when it came to the appropriate meeting of the Commission III committee, the Americans put forward an additional resolution making membership of the proposed Fund incompatible with membership of the B.I.S. This passed over British and Dutch objections.

Keynes immediately went to Mr Morgenthau, with whom he was to dine, and accused him of double crossing the British. Mr Morgenthau appeased Keynes by saying that they would leave the matter off the agenda of the evening meeting of the full Commission III and discuss it the next morning. After dinner Keynes wrote to Mr Morgenthau.

---

[24] Despite the delay in finishing the Conference, there were still not complete copies of the Articles of Agreement ready when the delegates signed them at the end.

To H. MORGENTHAU, *19 July 1944*

Dear Mr Secretary,

The B.I.S.

I was able to have a brief word with some of the members of my Delegation this evening. We are perfectly ready to accept the draft resolution which was before Committee 2 of Commission III until late today when a new text was surprisingly presented.

The text which we are prepared to accept runs, I understand:

'The United Nations Monetary and Financial Conference recommends that at the date of the constitution of the Board of the Fund the necessary steps will be taken to liquidate the Bank for International Settlements.'

We are entirely in accord with the general purpose in view and the form of words above, or something on similar lines, will be quite acceptable to us.

What we cannot manage is a recommendation from Commission III to Commission I to write some specific agreement into the International Monetary Fund. For technical reasons this, whatever our wishes might be in the matter, would inevitably prevent us from participating either in the Fund or in the Bank until after the expiry of an indefinite period.

Thank you very much for dealing with the position so promptly.

Sincerely yours,

KEYNES

After dinner, Keynes was the subject of worried Press reports that reached England.[25] Keynes related their origin three days later in reply to a telegram hoping he was well.

[25] Professor Robbins' diary, however, shows the strain of the Conference on Keynes, for after reporting the incident he continued: 'But, of course, throughout the Conference we have all felt that as regards Keynes's health we were on the edge of a precipice. There was one evening of prostration at Atlantic City, two the first week here, three last week, and I now feel that it is a race between the exhaustion of his powers and the termination of the Conference.'

From a letter to LORD CATTO, *22 July 1944*

It was very nice of you to send me that telegram. It was the first news I had that I was supposed to be unwell. What happened was that one evening after a very full day, and dinner with Morgenthau, I clean forgot my disability and ran upstairs to keep my next engagement, for which I was late. Of course, as usual this knocked me out for about a quarter of an hour. And Lydia, of course, was a little depressed, so seeing a lady journalist with whom she had struck up an acquaintance, she complained of what had happened. That acquaintance was the mother of a lad who is correspondent for Reuters, and he thought fit to send off the erring telegram. In fact I have been exceptionally well, and have managed to last out under almost overwhelming pressure of work without any injury at all.

At mid-morning on 20 July, Keynes, Ronald and Bolton met with the Americans on the issue. They agreed the following form of words: 'The United Nations Monetary and Economic Conference recommends the liquidation of the Bank for International Settlements at the earliest possible moment.'[26]

At a meeting later that day, Keynes again met the Americans on the problem of Australia, who was threatening not to sign the Final Act of the Conference owing to the absence of suitably loose arrangements for exchange flexibility and the smallness of her quota, and the problem of the reservations of many other countries to particular clauses of the draft Articles of Agreement. On the former matter they agreed to wait, in the hope that the Australian Delegation could convince the Government of the *ad referendum* nature of the proceedings and the lack of commitment in signing and hence gain a reversal of its instructions not to sign.[27] On the latter matter, Keynes agreed to speak at the Executive Plenary Session of the Fund after Mr Rasminsky had reported the work of Commission I.

[26] The B.I.S. is still in existence.
[27] The Australian Delegation did not receive instructions to agree to the Fund until the last day of the Conference. However, Australia did not join the Fund until 1947.

STATEMENT BY LORD KEYNES AT THE EXECUTIVE
PLENARY SESSION OF 20 JULY 1944

I am sure that I shall be voicing the sentiments of all here present if following our President I express our appreciation of the illuminating and valuable record of our work and the explanation of the merits and advantages of the plan which our Reporting Delegate, Mr Rasminsky, has given us, and associate the whole Conference with the more than well-deserved tribute which he paid to the invaluable work and the admirable determination of Dr White and to his conduct of our business in the Chair.

May I, however, return to the list of reservations which he began by reading us.

I venture to wonder whether there is not a possibility of some misunderstanding in the minds of the Delegates who wish to make reservations on particular points. So far as the U.K. Delegation is concerned we, in common with all other Delegations, reserve the opinion of our Government on the Document as a whole and on every part of it. The whole of our proceedings is *ad referendum* to our Governments who are at the present stage in no way committed to anything: we have been gathered here to put our heads together to produce the most generally acceptable document we could frame. We do not even recommend our Governments to adopt the result. We merely submit it for what it is worth to the attention of the Governments and legislators concerned.

Now I suggest to those Delegations who are proposing to make reservations that this procedure will suggest that there is some difference in commitment in respect of the points specially reserved compared with the rest of the document; and, therefore, that the *rest* of the document is in some sense accepted.

Is it not better that we all of us make clear the entire absence of commitment on the part of our Governments and that the particular points of reservation be merged in the general reservation and be not particularly recorded? Only in this way can misapprehension be avoided. Otherwise the position of those of us who are making no particular reservations may not be understood.

I would therefore urge this course on the Delegations interested in the particular matters which the Reporting Delegate has brought to our attention; and I propose to them that those reservations, by general agreement and in the light of the above; be retained in the minutes of the Commission where they are already recorded but are not made part of the Final Act.

The next day, at the Executive Plenary Session on the Bank, Keynes seconded the report.[28]

In seconding this motion I need add little to the eloquent report of our Reporting Delegate, the Delegate of Belgium, M. Theunis. But perhaps I may be excused the mention of a personal memory not irrelevant to this occasion. A quarter of a century ago at the end of October 1918, a few days before the Armistice, M. Theunis and I travelled together through Belgium behind the retreating German Armies to form an immediate personal impression of the needs of reconstruction in his country after that war. No such Bank as that which we now hope to create was in prospect. Today after a quarter of a century M. Theunis and I find ourselves brought close together again and engaged in making better preparation for a similar event.

Perhaps M. Theunis and I are the only members of this Conference—I am not sure—who were closely concerned with that earlier experience.

After the last war the most dreadful mistakes were made. It is with some emotion that I find myself today collaborating with my old friend to try to bring to birth an institution which may play a major part in restoring the devastation of a second war, and in bringing back to a life of peace and abundant fruitfulness

[28] In the published Press release, the words 'Mr. President' replace 'In seconding this motion'.

those great European and Asiatic parents of civilisation to which all the world owes so much of what is honourable and grand in the heritage of mankind.

21 July 1444

At the closing Plenary Session of the Conference, Keynes moved the Final Act.

SPEECH BY LORD KEYNES IN MOVING TO ACCEPT THE FINAL ACT AT THE CLOSING PLENARY SESSION, BRETTON WOODS, 22 JULY 1944

Mr President

I feel it a signal honour that I am asked to move the acceptance of the Final Act at this memorable Conference.

We, the Delegates of this Conference, Mr President, have been trying to accomplish something very difficult to accomplish. We have not been trying, each one to please himself, and to find the solution most acceptable in our own particular situation. That would have been easy. It has been our task to find a common measure, a common standard, a common rule applicable to each and not irksome to any. We have been operating, moreover, in a field of great intellectual and technical difficulty. We have had to perform at one and the same time the tasks appropriate to the economist, to the financier, to the politician, to the journalist, to the propagandist, to the lawyer, to the statesman—even, I think, to the prophet and to the soothsayer. Nor has the magic of the microphone been able, silently and swiftly perambulant at the hands of our attendant sprites, the faithful Scouts, Puck coming to the aid of Bottom, to undo all the mischief first wrought in the Tower of Babel.

And I make bold to say, Mr President, that under your wise and kindly guidance we have been successful. International conferences have not a good record. I am certain that no similar conference within memory has achieved such a bulk of lucid, solid construction. We owe this not least to the indomitable will and energy, always governed by good temper and humour, of Harry White. But this has been as far removed as can be imagined from a one-man or two-man or three-man conference. It has been teamwork, teamwork such as I have seldom experienced. And for my own part, I should like to pay a particular tribute to our lawyers. All the more so because I have to confess that, generally speaking, I do not like lawyers. I have been known to complain that, to judge from results in this lawyer-ridden land, the *Mayflower*, when she sailed from Plymouth, must have been entirely filled with lawyers. When I first visited Mr Morgenthau in Washington some three years ago accompanied only by my secretary, the boys in your Treasury curiously enquired of him—where is your lawyer? When it was explained that I had none,—'Who then does your thinking for you?' was the rejoinder. That is not my idea of a lawyer. I want him to tell me how to do what *I* think sensible, and, above all, to devise means by which it will be lawful for me to go on being sensible in unforeseen conditions some years hence. Too often lawyers busy themselves to make commonsense illegal. Too often lawyers are men who turn poetry into prose and prose into jargon. Not so our lawyers here in Bretton Woods. On the contrary they have turned our jargon into prose and our prose into poetry. And only too often they have had to do our thinking for us. We owe a great debt of gratitude to Dean Acheson, Oscar Cox, Luxford, Brenner, Collado, Arnold, Chang, Broches and our own Beckett of the British Delegation. I have only one complaint against them which I ventured to voice yesterday in Commission II. I wish that they had not covered so large a part of our birth certificate with such very detailed provisions for our burial service, hymns and lessons and all.

Mr President, we have reached this evening a decisive point. But it is only a beginning. We have to go out from here as

missionaries, inspired by zeal and faith. We have sold all this
to ourselves. But the world at large still needs to be persuaded.

I am greatly encouraged, I confess, by the critical, sceptical
and even carping spirit in which our proceedings have been
watched and welcomed in the outside world. How much better
that our projects should *begin* in disillusion than that they should
end in it! We perhaps are too near to our own work to see its
outlines clearly. But I am hopeful that when the critics and the
sceptics look more closely, the plans will turn out to be so much
better than they expected, that the very criticism and scepticism
which we have suffered will turn things in our favour.

Finally, we have perhaps accomplished here in Bretton
Woods something more significant than what is embodied in this
Final Act. We have shown that a concourse of 44 nations are
actually able to work together at a constructive task in amity and
unbroken concord. Few believed it possible. If we can continue
in a larger task as we have begun in this limited task, there is
hope for the world. At any rate we shall now disperse to our
several homes with new friendships sealed and new intimacies
formed. We have been learning to work together. If we can so
continue, this nightmare, in which most of us here present have
spent too much of our lives, will be over. The brotherhood of
man will have become more than a phrase.

Mr President, I move to accept the Final Act.

With the end of the Conference, Keynes and White made statements for
the BBC evening news on the Bank and Fund. Keynes's ran as follows.

I will not say that the establishment of the Bank for Reconstruction and Development is more important than the Monetary
Fund but perhaps it is more urgent. UNRRA will provide funds
necessary for relief and rehabilitation in the days immediately
following liberation but it will not provide finance for more
permanent reconstruction and the restoration of industry and

agriculture. To fill this gap is one of the main purposes of the Bank which we have been working at in Bretton Woods. Its other main purpose is the development of the less developed areas of the world in the general interests of the standard of life, of conditions of labour, and the expanse of trade everywhere.

The capital which we are aiming at and which we hope eventually to attain is £2,500 million. I can say with confidence that the initial capital of the Bank will not fall short of two thousand million pounds. This is a vast amount in terms of international lending and should be adequate for all proper requirements for some time to come. The Bank will have some novel principles. In the early days after the war only a few countries and chiefly the United States will have the necessary surplus resources available to invest overseas. How then can the rest of us help and how can the Bank become a genuinely international institution, whilst only the more fortunately placed countries can find large sums for investment during these early days?

The proposal is that it is up to the rest of us to stand behind the credit of the devastated and undeveloped countries and take—each of us—our share in guaranteeing the lenders from ultimate loss. There are many careful provisions to safeguard the guarantors from excessive loss, but the whole world will join together in a mutual credit insurance pool, as I would describe it, to shoulder risks which private investors might be unwilling to run with future prospects so uncertain and precarious.[29] [As a rule the Bank's loans will not take the form of free cash in the hands of the borrower, which he could use and squander as a free addition to his income, as was so often the case in the past. They will be tied to overseas expenditure—on specific projects, which have been carefully examined and approved. The term specific project will be widely interpreted and any proper scheme for the reconstruction of industry in Liberated Europe

---

[29] The passage in square brackets was deleted by the BBC from the advance script before the broadcast was heard.

or for fresh development will be eligible. The place of expenditure of the loans thus guaranteed will not be tied to the country
in which the loans are raised, but will be available for purchases
in any part of the world from the manufacturers best able to
supply the demand.] I can scarcely exaggerate the vast benefits
which may flow to the world from this great scheme. Resources
will be available to reconstruct the liberated areas. Buying power
will be available for the output of manufacturers in every
country physically capable of meeting the demand. A powerful
means will be provided to assist the maintenance of equilibrium
in the balance of payments between debtor and creditor
countries. There has never been such a far-reaching proposal
on so great a scale to provide employment in the present and
increase productivity in the future. We have been working
quietly away in the cool woods and mountains of New Hampshire
and I doubt if the world yet understands how big a thing we
are bringing to birth.

After the Conference, Keynes reported to London. His letter to the
Chancellor, parts of which also dealt with Stage II matters appears first,
followed by a shorter letter to Sir Richard Hopkins.

From a letter to SIR JOHN ANDERSON, *21 July 1944*

This letter is getting much too long. So I must wind up with
a few words about Bretton Woods.

I said near the beginning of this letter that I thought our
failure to approach the Americans on any topics outside those
immediately in hand had turned out fortunately. There is a
further reason for this. The fact that we have been able to work
in such intimacy and for so long a period with the Americans,
and more especially with the American Treasury, more as
colleagues on the same side of the table, helping them to
common ends and to make a good job of a piece of work, than

trying to get something for ourselves has, as I think all of us agree, produced a relationship of intimacy and confidence which has never previously existed. We have tried most scrupulously to be reasonable and not to be greedy. We and we alone of the other Delegations have spent 90 per cent of our time trying to help them and not make trouble for them. This is deeply understood and appreciated. At the end of the Plenary Conference yesterday which finally adopted the plan for the Fund, some of the junior American people came forward and told me how much they wanted us to know their intense appreciation of the help they had had from every member of the British Delegation. As I have already reported, one of the surprises has been the intimate and friendly relations with Morgenthau personally. As you know, I myself have now known him for a considerable time. But until Bretton Woods I had never spent a minute with him that was not sticky. Now all that is completely changed. I have seen a good deal of him, and increasingly as time went on. Most of the interviews have been *tête-à-tête*. For the first time I have been able to discuss serious matters of business with him in quite long interviews without his getting into those moods which used to be so obstructive to proper relations. He could not have been more consistently kind and friendly, and even expansive. As for all of the members of the U.S. Treasury, from Harry White downwards, we really have been in much the same relations with them as if we were all members of a single office in Whitehall. Now all this has, I am sure, been aided by the fact that we have not been at this early stage trying to bother them unduly with our own special problems. Not that these have been absent from the thoughts of either party. There have been many occasions when they have been apropos and we have not concealed our position. But the atmosphere has been developing naturally without our in any way trying to force it.

The pressure of work here has been quite unbelievable. It is as though, in the course of three or four weeks, one had to accomplish the preliminary work of many interdepartmental and Cabinet committees, the job of the Parliamentary draftsmen, and the passage through several Houses of Parliament of two intricate legislative measures of major dimensions, all this carried on in committees and commissions, numbering anything up to 200 persons in rooms with bad acoustics, shouting through microphones, many of those present, often including the Chairman, with an imperfect knowledge of English, each wanting to get something on the record which would look well in the Press down at home, and one of the most important Delegations, namely the Russian, only understanding what was afoot with the utmost difficulty and expense of time. On the top of this the Press which is here in full force has had to be continually fed and guided. And each of the Delegations expects some measure of social and personal consideration. Well I need hardly say more. We have all of us worked every minute of our waking hours practically without intermission for what is now four weeks. I have come off best because under the iron rule of my medical attendant I have resolutely refused to go to any committees after dinner (except once only against orders which promptly led to a heart attack, so that I suffered from guilt not less than from bodily discomfort!); whereas the others have been sitting in committees night after night up to 3.30 a.m., starting again in the committee at 9.30 a.m. next morning. How people have stood it at all is a miracle. At one moment Harry White told me that at last even he was all in, not having been in bed for more than five hours a night for four consecutive weeks. The climate has, however, been on the whole excellent and there is something in the air here that allows one, most dangerously in the long run, to use up one's reserves. So no one has actually broken down. But all of us from the top to the bottom, not least the secretaries and Gambling and his staff, are all in. You provided us with a magnificent team and every one has played his or her part. Typing and mimeographing half through the night has been all in the order of the day. The official papers of the Conference, some of them of great length, number nearly 500; and in addition much written matter has passed between ourselves, not to mention telegrams to and from home.

Our personal relations with the Russians have been very cordial and we have seen quite a lot of them socially. We like them exceedingly and, I think, they like us. Given time we should, I believe, gain their confidence and would then be able to help them a good deal. They *want* to thaw and collaborate. But the linguistic difficulties and very poor interpretation are a dreadful obstacle. Above all, they are put in a most awkward, and sometimes humiliating, position by the lack both of suitable instructions and of suitable discretion from Moscow.

Well we have survived. In my opinion the final products are clear and even aesthetic in presentation. I hope you will like the substance and will feel that we have protected your position not too badly. I have never forgotten your Parliamentary difficulties and in every little detail of phrasing have tried to take care of that aspect of the problem as much as was possible without becoming unreasonable or tiresome. I am despatching copies of the final documents by the fastest means. Brand and Eady have seen this letter and agree in substance.

To SIR RICHARD HOPKINS, *22 July 1944*

My dear Hoppy,

I despatched through Ronald yesterday an immense letter to the Chancellor, which I expect you will have seen. So I need not repeat what I have said there. This is just a personal line to yourself. If I have time I shall enclose one or two other letters on special topics.

Well it is all over and we are still alive. Nothing left but a final banquet and some speechifying. I suppose it will be prudent to assume that when you see our results in London some people at any rate will look on them sourly. But all of us here have the greatest sense of elation. All in all quite extraordinary harmony has prevailed. As an experiment in international co-operation the Conference has been an outstanding success, in spite of fearful muddle and inefficiency in detail. Apart from one or two tussles with the Russians, the atmosphere has never been heated. And we shall all be dispersing feeling that friendships and intimacies have been created running round the whole world. So forgive us if in this love feast we have done anything imprudent.

For myself I am hopeful that we have not. On the matters in the Fund to which the Chancellor attaches particular importance we have been at the greatest pains to secure not only the substance but also language that would help him, and to a very large extent the Americans have met us. The Bank, in my judgement, has quite extraordinary possibilities. We are not taking on any liability which need frighten us. On the other hand, the Americans are virtually pledging themselves to untied loans on a vast scale, which can be expended in whatever appears to be the cheapest market. They showed no inclination whatever to get back to the tied loan philosophy, and genuine liberalism in this matter seems to be part of their conviction. I suppose they are coming to realise that the only possibility of equilibrium in the balance of payments depends on their furnishing credits for exports from third countries. There is certainly much more to maintain equilibrium in the Bank than in the Fund. All the Americans here are convinced that they will be able to sell the Bank's bonds at a very fine rate of interest.

Everyone in our team has played together splendidly. If anyone is picked out I think it would have to be Dennis, whose help has been absolutely indispensable. He alone had the intellectual subtlety and patience of mind and tenacity of character to grasp and hold on to all details and fight them through Bernstein (who adores Dennis), so that I, frequently occupied otherwise, could feel completely happy about the situation. Eady took complete charge of the sections on management and associated matters. Some of the Americans told me that they had particularly appreciated his work and Dennis'. But really it is unjust to pick out anyone. I should certainly not leave out Beckett, the Foreign Office lawyer, who put in the longest number of hours' work of anyone. His only fault was that his love of perfection was perhaps sometimes out of proportion to the time at our disposal and upset the Americans a bit. But he really did a magnificent job of work. I should say that in due course he will become one of the finest Parliamentary draftsmen of our time. You ought to keep an eye on him.

Gambling and his girls have been trojans. There seemed to be no time in the day or night when Gambling was not on duty, and he has kept the machinery going with perfect smoothness in spite of considerable difficulties. One has never seen such a flood of papers.* Brooks and Snelling simply could not have been better. They are such particularly excellent lads in that whilst they are perfectly capable of the highest work you can give them, they are also more than willing to undertake the lowest without feeling that they are being put upon. With such sterling and beautiful qualities the civil service can really be proud of them.

In spite of the grossly excessive work, I think the team has in a sort of way enjoyed itself, and it has certainly been a remarkable experience for a good many of them. Up here in the hills there has been no heat to bother us. Today for example is rather like a typical coldish July day in England. My only real complaint has been the grossly excessive number of cocktail parties. I am decidedly of the opinion that they do no good and that the British Delegation should set a good example on future occasions by having few or none. The flow of alcohol is appalling, and they cost from about £30 to £50 each, with about half a dozen of them going on every evening. It does no one any good. The Americans set a perfect example by giving none whatever, though as hosts of the Conference they are, of course,

---

* I believe that the number of separate documents he has distributed to our Delegation is not far short of 10,000.

providing the final banquet. In my opinion we should follow their example.

Thank you very much for the telegrams and other communications you sent to my complaints about correspondence. I still cannot help feeling that this has been a bad business. People here are quite ready to assume that their wives and other relations are alive so long as they do not get telegrams to the contrary.[30] But obviously one needs a little more than this. Several people know that although their families are quite uninjured they are suffering inconvenience and worse, and will be greatly comforted by receiving personal letters telling them just how things are in detail. If one's wife is going through a trying time it is not sufficient just to be assured tht she is still alive. Moreover, we were quite definitely promised other arrangements. Everything we were told before we started was a fib. It always is. Every visit a delegation makes to Washington is treated as if it had never happened before and would never happen again. In fact, red tape at its bloodiest and most inefficient. Quite apart from people's human feelings, the unnecessarily long time which it takes to exchange correspondence is the greatest impediment to the efficiency of British Missions in Washington, and must cost in the aggregate vast loss and innumerable departures from the best possible. But I know by long experience that this is the sort of subject that it is impossible to do anything to persuade anyone who has power to take sufficient interest to do it. When by way of explaining the justice and efficiency of the arrangements one is told that the Ambassador himself is not allowed a copy of *The Times*, nor even the Prime Minister when he happens to be in Washington, one is surely left wondering.

I wish we could have heard a little more of how you yourself are getting on. We have a feeling that you must all be getting steadily under the weather and feeling the strain and worry, on top of what one has gone through already, almost too much to

[30] On 15 June the German V1 raids on London had started.

bear. I hope this is not so. At any rate our love and sympathy goes out to you, from those of us who may have had to work pretty hard but are here in this land of flowing abundance, infinitely remote from trouble, where there is no sense of strain, nothing but grilled steaks as big as your plate and ice cream.

Yours ever,

MAYNARD KEYNES

P.S. Since I wrote the above we have had our final banquet and celebration. The love feast was completed by the two black sheep, the Australians and Russians, receiving their telegrams just in time. Melville was able to sign the Final Act and the Russians raised their subscription to the full figure of $1,200m. This was a great triumph for Stepanov[31] who had clearly been advising Moscow along those lines. All the previous passages were promptly forgotten and amidst loud and continued applause, and embraces all round, the erring sheep were received into the fold. Stepanov said to me, 'So you see, after all we do really want to come in and be co-operative with you all'. Inevitably he had a somewhat appalling job to make clear to Moscow what it was all about.

The final scene went off in a blaze of enthusiasm. I enclose a copy of the speech I made. [above, pp. 101-3] I simply could not bring myself to produce any more hot air about the Bank and Fund, and a somewhat lighter vein did go off all right.

K

Keynes's role during the Conference was the subject of comments from two members of the Delegation. Professor Robbins recorded in his diary,
At the end Keynes capped the proceedings by one of his most felicitous speeches, and the Delegates paid tribute by rising and applauding again and again. In a way, this is one of the greatest triumphs of his life. Scrupulously obedient to his instructions, battling against fatigue and weakness, he has thoroughly dominated the Conference...

[31] M. S. Stepanov; Deputy People's Commisar of Foreign Trade and Chairman of Russian Delegation.

R. H. Brand wrote to Sir Richard Hopkins,

I hope you will think the Conference was a success. I must tell you that Keynes was without doubt quite the dominant figure. He certainly is an astonishing man. Frail in body but will-power and mental brilliance and flexibility enough for 10. I feel like the stupid boy in school in his company. He got thro' much more real work than any of us.

Keynes then proceeded to Ottawa by car for discussions with the Canadians on Mutual Aid. On 27 July, the day after his arrival, he held a dinner party to celebrate the 250th anniversary of the Bank of England. Afterwards he cabled the Governor.

To LORD CATTO, *28 July 1944*

Our birthday party was a great success. Eighteen of us—five each from the two Banks and the rest representing British and Canadian Treasuries. I ventured a short discourse on the Bank's history suitably and acceptably indiscreet, Gordon and Clarke replying in most flattering terms, the evening ending on a sentimental and friendly note. We all hope your celebration was happy and undisturbed by the enemy. I look forward to seeing you introduce the old Governor into the House. Congratulations! To him last night was his evening and any Canadian who could not bring out some tale or reminiscence of Monty Norman felt badly out of it.

MAYNARD KEYNES

The Bretton Woods Conference was hardly over before questions began to arise as to the exact meaning of the Articles of Agreement of the International Monetary Fund.[32] Much of the impetus for subsequent discussions came in a note which D. H. Robertson sent to Keynes in Ottawa.

[32] The articles that were the subject of discussion appear below in the Appendix.

From D. H. ROBERTSON, *31 July 1944*

A NOTE ON THE INTERNATIONAL MONETARY FUND
(AN ESSAY IN RABBINICS)

1. What is the exact nature of the 'convertibility' obligations to be assumed (after the close of the transitional period) under Article VIII, and what is the exact relation between these obligations and the rights and conditions of recourse to the Fund as set out in Articles V and VI?

2. As I understand it, the main and over-riding obligation is expressed, very briefly, in VIII 2(a). After the transitional period, and except in the case of a currency having been declared scarce, 'no member shall, without the approval of the Fund, impose restrictions on the making of payments and transfers for current international transactions'. It is on this section that the Americans and Canadians, for example, are undoubtedly relying as the embodiment of the promise that the proceeds of American and Canadian exports to England, whether invoiced in sterling or in the currency of the exporting country, can be remitted to the country of origin.

There are three points in particular to be noted about this obligation:

(i) While it can be suspended with the approval of the Fund, it is not contingent on the country concerned—England in the above example—being in possession of unexhausted rights of recourse to the Fund.

(ii) While the proceeds to be remitted must originate in a 'current transaction' (e.g. a recent export of goods), there is no limitation on the *purpose* for which remittance is required—the Canadian exporter (and through his person the Canadian economy) can take his (its) money away for investment at home or in some third country, and does not have to show that he (it) needs it for the purpose of buying goods or making other 'current' payments.

(iii) On the other hand there is no element of 'multilaterality' in the obligation itself—the Canadian exporter to England is assured of obtaining Canadian dollars, but not of obtaining United States dollars or Argentine pesos.

3. The obligation embodies in the much longer and more complicated Section VIII 4, is both narrower and wider than that embodied in VIII 2(a).

(i) It has reference only to a particular mechanism—that under which the export of goods etc. from one country to another results in the accumulation in the hands of a 'member' (i.e. a Government or central bank) of the currency of another member.

(ii) The obligation lapses if the member on whom it rests has exhausted (temporarily or permanently) its rights of recourse to the Fund.

(iii) On the other hand the obligation to redeem is not confined to balances which are strictly the result of 'current transactions' but is extended by VIII 4(a)(ii) to balances which are the result of transactions effected in the (post-zero-hour) past, provided that the conversion of such balances 'is needed for making payments for current transactions'.

4. There are two points in particular to be noted about the supplementary obligation described in Section 3(iii) above:

(i) It is on the face of it inconsistent with the unconditional right of members asserted in Article VI 3, to 'exercise such controls as are necessary to regulate international capital movements'. For such a removal of 'old' balances is unquestionably a movement of capital. Hence it has been found necessary to state explicitly in VIII 4(b)(i) that the right asserted in VI 3 overrides the obligation assumed under VIII 4(a)(ii). This takes a good deal of the sting or the honey (according to which way you look at it) out of that obligation.

(ii) From the fact that the obligations under VIII 4 lapse if the member on whom they rest has exhausted its rights of recourse to the Fund, it might seem at first sight to be a legitimate inference that, provided it has *not* exhausted its rights, a member can confidently have recourse to the Fund for the purpose of fulfilling its obligations under VIII 4, including the supplementary obligation to redeem 'old' balances. I am not, however, at all clear that this is the case. It seems to me that the Executive Directors, faced with an application for foreign exchange for such a purpose, would be on equally strong ground in conceding it, on the ground that the mention of such payments in Article VIII canonises them as 'payments which are consistent with the provisions of this Agreement' (Article V 3(a)(i)), or in rejecting it, on the ground that such a payment constitutes a 'large outflow of capital',—a thing which, while it may be perfectly legitimate and consistent with the purposes of the Fund, must not be financed out of the Fund's resources (Article VI 1(a)).

Thus neither a member's obligation under VIII 4(a)(ii), nor the means at its disposal for meeting this obligation, turn out on examination to be quite so solid as they appear at first sight.

5. It remains to say something about the companion piece to the obligation under VIII 4(a)(ii), namely the obligation under VIII 4(a)(i) to redeem balances 'recently acquired as a result of current transactions', regardless of the use to which the money paid over in redemption of such balances is to be put. Telegrams received from London at Bretton Woods criticised the assumption of this obligation as unnecessary and dangerous,

and suggested that such balances, like those of longer standing, should only be redeemable if the redemption-money was needed for making payments for current transactions. This criticism and suggestion seem to me misconceived. The obligation to redeem central bank balances accruing as the result of current exports is merely the form taken, in connection with the particular mechanism which is under discussion in VIII 4, by the general obligation not to restrict payments for current transactions, which has already been set out in VIII 2(a) (see point (ii) in Section 2 of this Note). That general obligation could not have been cancelled or whittled away merely by refraining from setting out, or by setting out in a restricted form, the particular application of it which is appropriate to VIII 4.

There are however two points in particular to be noted about the obligation set out in VIII 4(a)(i):

(i) It follows from what has just been said that the clause exempting a member which has exhausted its rights of recourse to the Fund from its obligations under VIII 4, is of very doubtful value so far as the obligation under VIII 4(a)(i) is concerned, since, as just stated, this obligation is already implicit in the master-obligation set out in VIII 2(a), which is subject to no such let-out.

(ii) There is no compulsory element of 'multilaterality' in the obligations in VIII 4, any more than in those of VIII 2. Thus under VIII 4(a)(i) England, for example, engages (after the transitional period) to redeem India's accruing sterling balances with rupees, which (provided her rights of recourse are not exhausted) she can obtain from the Fund for the purpose. But she does not engage to redeem those balances with dollars.* If India wants dollars, she must obtain them from some other source with rupees; and if she merely wants them as an investment, i.e. if she is merely attempting to shift her reserves from England to the United States, it is by no means clear that she can obtain them from the Fund, since such a transfer of reserves clearly constitutes a capital movement which the Fund may well deem to fall outside the margin of tolerance permitted under Article VI 1(b)(i). Thus the right to withdraw currently accruing balances regardless of the purpose for which withdrawal is required does not necessarily put the withdrawing country in a position to accomplish its purpose.

6. Both the original drafting of Article VIII 4, and the discussions and expositions thereof at Bretton Woods, were undertaken with the problem of the Indian sterling balances particularly in mind. It may therefore be well to recapitulate the two respects in which, when they study the final text at leisure, the Indian experts may be expected to find it (apart altogether from

* She has the *option* to redeem them with gold, in which case of course the gold can probably be exchanged by India for any currency desired.

its treatment of the pre-zero-hour balances) less satisfactory than they had hoped.

(i) The obligation to redeem 'old' balances under (a)(ii) turns out to be unilaterally revocable by the United Kingdom by the simple process of declaring such balances restricted under the general right of control of capital movements set out in Article VI 3.

(ii) The obligation to redeem 'new' balances under (a)(i) does not of itself ensure that these balances can be turned unconditionally into dollars.

It is my belief that, so far as we can be said to have formed any definite intentions about the post-transitional period, we do not in fact intend to limit the obligations assumed *vis-à-vis* the Indian and other holders of sterling balances in either of these two ways; and I was, I am afraid, myself guilty of assuring the Indian delegates, with Mr Bolton's approval, in the course of debate, that the effect of VIII 4(a)(i) was to make currently accruing balances, after the Transitional Period, unconditionally convertible into dollars.

I suggest that, when conversations take place with the Indians (and Egyptians) on the more pressing subject of the treatment of their sterling balances in the transitional period, opportunity should also be taken to confirm that our intentions as regards the post-transitional period are not in fact restricted in the ways in which a literal reading of the final text of Article VIII 4, would appear to justify.

31 July 1944   D.H.R.

Keynes replied to Robertson from Ottawa, sending a copy to Sir David Waley in London for information.[33]

To D. H. ROBERTSON, *9 August 1944*

My dear Dennis,

I am most grateful for the Essay in Rabbinics, for it has given me an excuse for using a day in which we were marking time to divert the mind to something interesting away from the barren fields and waste lands of financial diplomacy.

The result is the attached. You will see that I have a fairly big bone to pick with you. I am sure both of us dogs will find

[33] In the letter to Waley, Keynes added after the word 'diplomacy' in his first paragraph '—the meanest occupation known to man'.

it nourishing, whichever ultimately succeeds in getting hold of the big end of it. I await your rejoinder with enthusiasm.

Yours ever,
[copy initialled] MK

A NOTE ON A NOTE ON THE I.M.F.
(AN ESSAY IN METARABBINICS)

D.H.R.'s *Essay in Rabbinics* seems to me to be accurate and exact in so far as it deals with the obligations between members, i.e. between central banks. But on one matter of fundamental importance I claim that the Talmud has been misinterpreted.

This misinterpretation arises in what D.H.R. in his paragraph 2 calls 'the main and over-riding obligation' under VIII 2(a). This clause does *not* involve an obligation of convertibility; and I do not accept his 2(iii) for which I see no authority whatever in the text, as I endeavoured more than once to explain at Bretton Woods when this heresy occasionally raised its head. Where on earth, in particular, does D.H.R. discover in VIII 2(a) an obligation of convertibility into the holder's own currency but not into others?

As I understand this clause, it involves an obligation not to kill convertibility; but there is no obligation 'officiously to keep alive'; it is a prohibition against blocking where a current transaction is concerned. If a non-resident owner of sterling can find a purchaser for it in exchange for foreign currency within the permitted range of parity, then he may not be forbidden to sell his sterling; but there is no obligation under this clause actually to provide him with the foreign exchange he desires, whether his own or another country's. 'Convertibility' only comes about, if at all, through the combination of this clause with VIII 4. Indeed if D.H.R. were right there would be an obligation on a central bank in *all* circumstances to intervene continuously in its own free market to support its exchanges with all other member countries, an obligation which, if it existed, would render unnecessary, and indeed make nonsense of, the elaborate provisions of VIII 4.

The above carries with it a rejection of the defence in D.H.R.'s paragraph 5 against London criticisms where I agree with his conclusion but not with his reasons. I return to this below.

The above is closely connected with a fundamental characteristic of the scheme which D.H.R. appears to overlook. A leading peculiarity (and a leading cause of obscurity of interpretation) in I.M.F. is that, apart from VIII 2, the obligations all apply as between central banks and not as between a central bank and a non-resident individual.

Apart from VIII 2, which, as has been pointed out above, does not involve an obligation of convertibility, an individual has no rights at all and is at the mercy of his own central bank. A non-resident owner of sterling can only dispose of it, as a right against the British Control, through the kind offices of his own central bank, which is entitled, but not obliged, to buy it off him for the foreign exchange he desires. The British Control can, of course, if it chooses, maintain a free exchange market open to dealings by individuals through market support of all foreign exchanges, thus enabling anyone to transact business within the permitted range of parity; but it is not compelled to do so. Its only obligation is to take sterling off another central bank in exchange for that central bank's own currency; and this obligation is , of course, subject to the various qualifications set forth in D.H.R.'s note. All an exchange control is compelled to do in relation to private persons is to prohibit private transactions outside the permitted range, and to allow them within it if they are of a current character.

This vital distinction between the rights of individuals and the rights of central banks has the effect both of obscuring and of clarifying the practical consequences of the qualifications relating to 'capital transactions' and to 'scarce currencies'. The following is the best account of the matter I can give, taking 'capital transactions' for purposes of illustration.

If a non-resident individual, having acquired sterling as the result of a current transaction, transfers it to his central bank, can his central bank demand its own currency in exchange for it from the British Control? Or does the individual's transaction lose its identity amongst the other transactions of his central bank, so that the criterion depends on whether his central bank holds a net balance of sterling acquired from current transactions? It seems to me that it is the second alternative that is correct.

If, on the other hand, he has acquired the sterling by, e.g. selling Consols, then the proceeds can be blocked by the British Control even though the individual needs the proceeds for a current transaction, for there is no provision in VIII, 2(a) providing for unrestricted transferability by individuals in such cases, and the only let-out relates to central banks. There is not even a right to an individual to transfer the proceeds to his own central bank. It is only resources already belonging to the foreign central bank as, for example, currency reserves, which obtain the benefit of the let-out in VIII 4(a)(ii).

It follows, if the above is correct, that the 'convertibility' opportunities of an individual are limited to the proceeds of current transactions, and even in those cases, to those opportunities which the foreign central bank whose currency he holds chooses voluntarily to offer him, and, failing that, to those which his own central bank chooses voluntarily to offer him.

The effective obligations are all between central banks, and the criteria (e.g. of scarcity, of capital character, etc.) apply to a central bank's transactions taken as a whole.

As I see it, therefore, the philosophy of the whole scheme depends on the distinction between the rights of an individual and the rights of a central bank. The *only* right accorded to an individual is that his sterling, if currently acquired, shall not be blocked;—he is free to transfer it to his own central bank or to anyone else, provided he does not deal at a rate outside the permitted range. Rights of *convertibility* relate solely to the balances of central banks and are hedged round precisely as described by D.H.R.

It follows from the above that I cannot accept as valid D.H.R.'s answer to the London criticisms summarised by him in his paragraph 5. The right defence against these criticisms is, it seems to me, that, e.g., the current proceeds of sales of tobacco by U.S. in U.K. is from U.K.'s point of view a current transaction and cannot justifiably be blocked, because U.S. is on balance in a current creditor position *vis-à-vis* the world at large, and therefore *has* to use her net favourable balance for a capital purpose; to which, it may be added, that it is impossible to say of any given transaction in a given country whether or not it is part of a country's *net* favourable balance *vis-à-vis* the world as a whole. To provide that the *whole* of a creditor country's current receipts could be blocked merely because she was a creditor country in the world at large would surely be unreasonable and absurd.

One final point, namely, D.H.R.'s reference to his discussions with the representatives of India in his paragraph 6. I wonder if D.H.R. really spoke of 'convertibility into dollars' and did not merely say 'convertibility', which in the Bretton Woods context clearly meant convertibility into the other fellow's currency. For it was always clear to all of us that no country ever undertook to provide on request all the currencies of the world *à choix*. Whether our obligation to make India's own sterling 'convertible' meant in practice 'convertibility into dollars' must, to anyone who understands Rabbinics at all, depend on the status of the rupee *vis-à-vis* the dollar in respect of the particular transaction in view. I did not take part in the later conversations with the Indians after the full subtleties had been deployed. But in my earlier conversation with them I certainly spoke of 'convertibility' (i.e. in the Bretton Woods Pickwickian sense), and never of 'convertibility into dollars'. However this may be, we should certainly not give assurances to the Indians, or to the Egyptians, or to anyone else, of an unrestricted convertibility into dollars quite outside the ambit of I.M.F. If there is any misunderstanding on this matter in the minds of the Indians, then the right course is to explain the position to them forthwith before they have finally committed themselves. I much doubt, however, whether there is in fact any misunderstanding in their minds.

KEYNES

9 August 1944

In a subsequent letter to Robertson, Keynes raised another strand of discussion, when replying to Robertson's report of a conversation with Professor J. H. Williams. In their discussion, Williams had raised the problem of the use of other countries' currency subscriptions to the Fund when these countries moved into surplus, given the amount of world trade denominated in sterling and dollars.

To D. H. ROBERTSON, *14 August 1944*

My dear Dennis,

Thanks for your letter of August 4th from New York reporting a conversation with John Williams. There is one point on this which I should like to note down whilst it is fresh in my mind.

I am not myself clear that there is any real difficulty in making effective use of the currency subscriptions of members other than U.S.A. which may develop a creditor position. Are you not assuming that exchanges are always maintained by supporting the free market, instead of by forcing member banks to operate through the machinery of the Fund? Suppose, for example, that the Argentine has a favourable balance. The natural, and according to the philosophy of the Fund, I should say the desirable situation resulting from this would be that sterling would accumulate in London in the hands of the Bank of the Argentine, and that there would be no means by which the Bank of the Argentine could convert this except by calling on the Bank of England, which would liquidate the position by obtaining Argentine currency from the Fund. It is only if the Bank of England supports the private market in sterling *vis-à-vis* all the other currencies of the world that your problem arises.

I suspect therefore that this point is connected with the point I have made in my Essay on Metarabbinics, which may perhaps have reached you by now. I sent the top copy to you at Washington not knowing you had left; if it has not yet reached you, nevertheless you may have seen a copy I sent at the same time to Sigi.

I think the Americans were always rather confused as to whether they wanted central banks to support the private market in exchanges, or whether they wished to concentrate transactions in the hands of the respective central banks. In my view the former is mere conservatism and cuts right across the philosophy of the Fund. With the other alternative, the general structure of the Fund begins to make sense.

As soon as Bretton Woods was over the Treasury gave instructions that no papers of any kind were to be forwarded to Eady and myself. Thus nearly three weeks have passed since we received any communication whatever from London, and we are quite out of touch. Indeed nothing whatever arrives either of comfort or instruction, except a direction from time to time 'to keep ourselves fluid'. As we look like finishing our job here tomorrow the only thing seems to be to come straight home, which we are now trying to organise. I suppose just as we are stepping on our ship or our Clipper, as the case may be, some contrary instructions are just as likely as not to arrive.

This means that I shall probably only get the barest time in New York, if any time at all. I shall, however, make a point of getting into touch with Williams if he is still in New York and I can fit it in.

I fancy that the thermometer has not been much lower here than in Washington, and of course we are not air-conditioned.

On the other hand one can get cool by motoring to one of the lakes, and on the whole we have enjoyed ourselves. Today, however, really is the knock-out, with the thermometer climbing to or above 100. It knocks out the Canadians as much as ourselves, and thus seriously restricts business. You will have heard the result of our endeavours before you get this letter.

Yours ever,
[copy initialled] M

Robertson replied to Keynes's letter of 14 August and his memorandum on 29 August, referring at the same time to an article by Paul Einzig in *The Financial Times* of 23 August which concerned the possibilities of exchange arbitrage under the scheme.

From D. H. ROBERTSON, *29 August 1944*

My dear Maynard,

I.M.F.

I attach my rejoinder, which deals also with Einzig's article.

On convertibility, my recollection of what happened at Bretton Woods is this. When the two clauses now numbered VIII (2)(a) and VIII (4) were put cheek by jowl (having previously been separated by several pages) it became plain that the relation between them needed further consideration. The Americans slipped into VIII (4) a sentence, which I resisted, saying that nothing in VIII (4) qualified the obligation in VIII (2)(a), and we in turn added VIII (4) to the two sections mentioned in VIII (2)(a) as being sections to which VIII (2)(a) is 'subject'. Rasminsky meanwhile delivered a frontal attack on the 'let-out' sentence, now (b)(v), in VIII (4)—an attack which you resisted. An impasse developed, and we had rather a heated meeting, at which matters were further complicated by Gardner raising the question of *trade* restrictions; and we dispersed in danger of a break. Thereafter the trade restriction red herring was put to bed with Berny's [Bernstein's] help, and on the main issue the Canadians and Americans withdrew their attack on VIII (4), on the ground that they had no direct interest in this clause, and concentrated on demanding that the statement that VIII (2)(a) was 'subject to' the provisions of VIII (4) (including of course the 'let-out' provision now (b)(v)) should be eliminated. I put this to you and received your consent verbally via Eady; and I then felt—apparently wrongly—that the whole position was as clear and as satisfactory to everybody as it could be made, having regard to the fact that we had to keep to the Joint Statement as a basis and were not free to rewrite the whole thing from the start in the most lucid possible manner.

I should like to deal in this letter with two other points about I.M.F.

1. Your reference to the redemption of Argentine sterling balances in your letter to me of August 14th does not dispose of the difficulty which I was discussing, and which may be illustrated as follows. Peru and Chile are trading together, all trade between them being invoiced in U.S. dollars. The balance in a given year is favourable to Peru, and adverse to Chile, by 10 million dollars. Chile, according to rule, finances this adverse balance by parting with 5 million dollars of her own and obtaining 5 million dollars from the Fund, i.e. the Fund's holding of dollars is reduced by 5 million dollars and its holding of Chilean currency increased by the equivalent of 5 million dollars. Peru simply pockets the 10 million dollars, and the Fund's holding of Peruvian currency remains unchanged.

Article V (7)(b)(ii) was intended to deal with this situation by forcing Peru to part with the dollars to the Fund in exchange for its own currency, and in an earlier draft it did so. But as it now stands it does not do so, since the let-out in V (7)(c)(ii) has—in the course of the quest for simplicity—been made too generous. As the text stands it prevents a *debit* country from accumulating dollars by means of third country trade, but it does not prevent a *credit* country from doing so. In other words it does not prevent the Fund's supply of dollars from being denuded to finance adverse balances with countries other than the United States.

The Americans have a strong interest in getting this right, and I believe that Berny, Deutsch and I (who were the only people who really had any idea what all this was about) could easily agree on an improved text; but I fear that there is no constitutional way of effecting that, and that it will have to wait for the first meeting of the Directorate!

2. I have flagged in the Treasury file a minute which, while not a very lucid piece of reporting, confirms my recollection that what Rasminsky said about the 'changes in par values' section was that the provisions *in the Joint Statement had* seemed to him a happy compromise between rigidity and instability. He did not attempt to conceal his misgivings that the *new* text went too far in the latter direction. He repeated to me in private his fears that our success in getting this and other points past the American Delegation would materially increase the difficulties of the latter in getting the scheme past Congress.

I am sending a copy of this letter and enclosure to Eady, and of the enclosure to Rowe-Dutton, who has seen the previous papers.

Yours ever,

D.H.R.

A NOTE ON A NOTE ON A NOTE ON THE I.M.F.
(AN ESSAY IN COMMON SENSE)

1. I am afraid I find it impossible to take as narrow a view as you do of the obligations to be assumed under VIII 2 by a member who proposes (as I have always understood that we propose) to continue to exercise a Government monopoly of exchange dealings.

Under such a regime an American citizen (or his banking representative) who comes into possession of sterling through (e.g.) the sale of goods or the receipt of a dividend warrant, cannot go out into the free market in London and buy dollars, for there *is* no free market. The very existence of the Government monopoly constitutes the imposition of a 'restriction on the making of payments and transfers for current international transactions' to the United States, unless the monopoly is in fact so operated as *not* to hinder the making of such payments and transfers, i.e. unless the Control stands ready to sell dollars against sterling to anyone (whether British or American) who desires to make such payments or transfers.

In point of fact the Control is so operated at present, and it seems to me inconceivable that we should be claiming the right, on the great Zero Day on which sterling is at last declared Fully Convertible, to withdraw from the Americans facilities which we have accorded them even during war.

All our discussions with the Americans have proceeded on the basis of 'Live and Let Live' as regards systems of exchange management. The provisions of I.M.F. must accordingly be interpreted as guaranteeing (after the close of the transitional period) freedom of remittance of the proceeds of current transactions,

(*a*) between countries both of which centralise exchange dealings

(*b*) between countries neither of which centralises exchange dealings

(*c*) from a country which centralises exchange dealings to one which does not

(*d*) from a country which does not centralise exchange dealings to one which does.

I need only add that I entirely agree with the positive statement on page 4 of your note of the reasons for according unconditional convertibility to

126

the current receipts of creditor countries—our only difference is that I regard these reasons as having a wider applicability than you do.

2. If we are not demanding that the Americans should change their system, neither are they demanding that we should change ours. I took no part in the negotiation of IV (4)(b), but I certainly do not regard it, as Einzig appears to do, as obligating any member to set up or permit a free market in exchanges. In my view it simply states that where such a free market exists, dealings in it shall not take place outside the prescribed range.

I must admit that the clause, as now amended, seems to me of little value. The clause in the Joint Statement (IX 2) from which it is descended ran 'Not to allow transactions in its market in currencies of other members at rates outside a prescribed range based on the agreed parities'. The intention of this clause was that the Americans should undertake to lighten the task of supporting the pound, the franc etc. against depreciation in terms of the dollar by forbidding anybody to deal in those currencies at a discount in the New York market: but the clause as amended specifically exempts them from giving any such undertaking. While however I am inclined to think that the clause, having failed of its object, might as well have been dropped, I certainly do not read it, and am pretty confident the Americans do not read it, as conveying the implications which Einzig reads into it.

3. As regards our obligations to the Indians under VIII (4)(a)(i), I have not so far been able to find any record of my remarks (which were made in full committee, not in private conversation). My own feeling is that we should not in fact be likely to tie up such use as we make of the Fund with redemption of Indian sterling, but should go to the Fund for dollars and redeem Indian sterling, if called upon to do so, in gold. But I agree that the legal position is as stated in my last note, and I think that an early opportunity should be taken to explain this to Raisman.

29 August 1944   D.H.R.

On 21, 22 and 23 August, *The Times* published three articles by a special correspondent (in fact Mr T. Balogh) entitled 'World Monetary Policies'. On reading the third of these Keynes wrote to the editor.

To the Editor of The Times, *23 August 1944*

Sir,

In your issue to-day you publish an article from a Special Correspondent, who asks (in more words than the following) whether, in a case where matched bulk purchasing is impracticable, the Bretton Woods plan would be consistent with our requiring a country from which we import to take in return a stipulated quantity of our exports. The answer is in the affirmative.

The most effective means of carrying out such a policy would be to supply the country taking our exports with a certificate which importers from that country would be required to produce as a condition of receiving an import licence into the United Kingdom. If such a policy were to commend itself to us and if it were consistent with any commercial agreements we might have signed, there is nothing in the Bretton Woods plan to prevent it. Equally there is nothing to prevent other countries from requiring us to take their imports as a condition of receiving our exports.

I limit myself in this letter to answering the question of fact. Your Correspondent has tried hard in a long string of rhetorical questions to suggest (if he remembers his Latin grammar) that they should properly be preceded by *Num*. I am sorry to have to disappoint him by asking him to substitute *Nonne*.

Yours, &c.,

KEYNES

This letter led to questioning letters from Mr Balogh and others and a further reply from Keynes.

To the Editor of The Times, *29 August 1944*

Sir,

The Bretton Woods proposals are concerned solely with currency and exchange and not with commercial policy.

128

They are consistent equally with the more moderate methods of planning foreign trade which we are likely to need, at any rate so long as we have balance of trade difficulties; with more elaborate measures about the advantages of which it is not so easy to make up one's mind; and also with the more extreme proposals which, if applied all round, would be destructive of trade. Whether we adopt any of these methods, and if so which, will have to be determined by our own common sense and by the commercial treaties which we find it to be in our interest to sign because they offer compensating advantages. All this falls outside the ambit of the Bretton Woods discussions.

Some of your correspondents press me to admit (*a*) that forms of commercial policy, permissible under the Bretton Woods currency proposals, may nevertheless be very foolish; (*b*) that forms of commercial policy, permissible under the Bretton Wood currency proposals, may be so destructive of multilateral trade that, if they are adopted, Bretton Woods will have been rather a waste of time. Both of these contentions are, in my opinion, correct.

Yours, &c.,

KEYNES

Keynes also entered into correspondence with Joan Robinson on the issues raised by the Articles of Agreement in a note she had written for Robert Boothby.

To J. V. ROBINSON, *9 September 1944*

My dear Joan,

BRETTON WOODS

Thanks for letting me see the note you have furnished to Boothby. I agree with the major part of your comments but there are certain matters, some of them important, where I should like to urge a different judgement.

1. I do not think we need regard this as a U.S.A. dominated

system. The voting power of the U.S.A. will be virtually equal to that of the British Commonwealth.

2. I do not like the new provision for charges in V (8). But I think you seriously overstate the consequences. Except in flagrant cases, there is no intention, I should say, to make charges penal or to go beyond 5 % in any normal circumstances. You have to remember that this matter will be settled, if necessary, by voting and that the debtor or potentially debtor countries will probably have the majority of the votes. China and Russia are both potential debtors and have heavy voting power. In so far as these charges make the Fund the place of last resort, there is something to be said for them.

3. I do not agree that the onus of restoring equilibrium is thrown entirely on the debtor and the value of the scarce currency clause has been impaired. It seems to me you have arrived at your conclusion by treating 'may', which is the third word in VII (2) as though it was 'must'. It is only if the majority of the Fund think it advisable to borrow the scarce currency, that borrowing will occur. What I have just written above about the voting power of the debtors and potential debtors has an important application here. The scarce currency country is not entitled to borrow. Moreover, there is a further mitigation which has entirely escaped notice. The quotas are a minimum, not a maximum. The U.S. representatives were always eager to explain to us that that is strictly how they regarded them. There is nothing to prevent the Fund from allowing debtor countries to borrow more than their quotas. All this appears in V (4). Most people have not realised, I think, that this is the main purpose of that section. This also can be done by a majority vote. Thus, if the Fund were to decide to borrow a scarce currency, it could at the same time, increase the borrowing power of members under the section just mentioned. Thus the act of borrowing does not necessarily lead to an exhaustion of quotas. In fact, I should expect the Fund to be very chary of borrowing scarce

currencies, except to give the scarce currency country a breather to find another way out.

4. The obscure IV (5)(e) is a Russian clause. We none of us quite knew what it meant. It is to change the internal value of the rouble which is not allowed to be used for foreign exchange transactions without altering their effective foreign exchange rates. It is all nonsense, in my opinion, since Russia has no foreign exchange rate, anyhow, and is thereby automatically contracted out of these provisions. We put this funny little clause to please them, believing that it made matters no worse than they were already.

5. VI (3)—I should agree that the effective control of capital movements is difficult without complete exchange control. We contemplated that those countries intending to control capital movements strictly, e.g. ourselves, would retain the complete apparatus of exchange control.

6. I agree that V (8) tends to make the accommodation of the Fund only temporary or at any rate, as I said before, the place of last resort, though a country can always start again by paying off temporarily. On the other hand, that is not, I think, the purpose of V (7), which is a method of re-capturing gold from countries which have more gold than their quota, or whose gold is increasing.

More generally, I do not follow why the Monetary Agreement has to wait for the Commercial Policy. As regards the Commercial Policy, there are really two alternatives. The one is that we do nothing, or the equivalent to nothing. The other is that we enter into a multilateral convention consistent with Article VII. If the Monetary Plan is in itself a fairly good plan, it would be required whichever of the above alternatives emerges. I appreciate that outsiders want to have their curiosity satisfied. But when it is satisfied, I doubt whether it will be relevant to this particular issue. You are like the investors who refuse to buy railway shares because they do not know whether the railways are going to be nationalised or not, yet nevertheless are prepared to agree that if they are nationalised, the shares will be worth more, and that if they are not nationalised, the shares will be worth more. All the same, they will not buy until they know for certain which alternative is going to come to pass.

Yours ever,
MAYNARD KEYNES

From J. V. ROBINSON, *14 September 1944*

My dear Maynard,

Very many thanks for your letter. I much appreciate your sparing the time to write. On various points of detail I agree that the Fund could act sensibly in the various circumstances, but I don't see that it has any particular bias in favour of sense. Have you got to the bottom of Einzig's point about buying weak currencies? The drafting is very queer on that.

Your remarks about railway speculation leave my withers unwrung, because if I thought that we had, or were going to, sign up on an Article VII non-discriminatory trade agreement, I should be very strongly anti-Bretton Woods.

My idea is that G.B. has two problems: (1) quasi-permanent, to run full employment with a weak balance of trade position; (2) at some point in the future—to weather thro' the next great U.S. slump with as little loss as possible. Both problems require trade planning if there is to be even a hope of partially solving them. If we are committed to non-discrimination in currency it becomes all the more necessary to keep a free hand on commercial policy. If we are tied up on commercial policy, then we must be free to wangle it *via* currency. I do not like the second alternative (here I think I agree with you?) but to give up both seems to me to be asking for trouble, not only for this country, but for the world in general, as a new free trade (using this expression in a broad sense) system would break down and then seven other devils would come in.

Bob Boothby says the House learned from you to hate gold and you can't de-bamboozle them now.

Yours,
JOAN

To J. V. ROBINSON, *16 September 1944*

Dear Joan,

Einzig's point about buying weak currencies is based on the assumption that Article IV (4)(b) which says: 'Each Member undertakes through appropriate measures consistent with this Agreement, to permit within its territories exchange transactions between its currency and the currency of other Members only within the limits prescribed under Section 3 of this Article', does not mean what it says, but means that each Member undertakes to facilitate or provide the necessary counter-party, or whatever the right phrase is. This is entirely unfounded. The only meaning of that clause is that each member undertakes to prevent a black market in its territories, either by rendering a black market illegal or by some other means. I agree that this was rather clearer in the earlier version of the draft which read:

A Member undertakes not to allow exchange transactions in its market in currencies of other Members at rates outside a prescribed range based on the agreed parities.

When the wording was changed by the Americans to what they considered a tidier expression, there was no intention to alter the meaning. Thus this discovery also by Einzig is a mare's nest.

On the question of whether we should refuse to sign a non-discriminating trade agreement, I must have a word with you when we next meet. I think I can persuade you in two minutes to see the whole issue in a different light. I am doing my best to see that too much further time does not elapse before the public get the necessary illumination in the matter.

Yours ever,
[copy initialled] MK

The upshot of these discussions was a paper Keynes circulated within the Treasury and to other members of the Delegation.

I have now carefully re-examined the text and am of the opinion that, on all the main points which have been raised as doubtful, the strict interpretation is what I intended and thought it to be, and that, therefore, all is well. I am, however, disturbed that on the most important point of all that Professor Robertson takes a different view. If Professor Robertson's interpretation is correct, then, in my opinion, the draft is not one which the Chancellor is justified in commending to the House of Commons.

There are three questions at issue, of which the first two are connected. It is on the first that Professor Robertson and I differ.

(1) Article VIII (4) is headed 'Convertibility of foreign held balances'. Under (a) of this clause there is an obligation between central banks, each to take its own currency off the other if requested to do so in exchange for the other's country or (at its option) for gold, thus ensuring convertibility between the two currencies. In (b) of the same clause a number of circumstances are recited in which the above obligation of convertibility is suspended. The final version of this sub-clause was the outcome of prolonged controversy and discussion. Under it we are adequately protected. So far, so good.

Article VIII (2), which is headed 'Avoidance of restrictions on current payments' reads:

Subject to the provisions of Article VII Section 3(b) and Article XIV Section 2, no member shall, without the approval of the Fund, impose restrictions on the making of payments and transfers for current international transactions.

Article VII (3)(b) is the scarce currency clause and Article XIV (2) is the temporary transitional clause. I, therefore, understood this clause to mean that, except in the above two sets of circumstances and except for transactions which do not fall under the definition of 'current', there is an obligation *not to block balances*; that is to say, no legal impediment shall be put in the way of a non-resident holder of sterling to prevent him from using this sterling to make sterling payments or to buy foreign currencies, other than the impediment under Article IV (4)(b) not to deal in foreign exchanges outside a permitted range (this, however, is subject to the doubt discussed next below). It does *not* carry with it any obligation of convertibility. The obligation 'not to impose restrictions' does not carry with it an obligation 'to provide positive facilities'.

Professor Robertson, however, disputes this interpretation. He considers that this clause carries with it an over-riding obligation to *provide facilities* to convert sterling, whether held by residents or by non-residents, into any desired foreign currency in all circumstances, subject only to the exceptions specified in the sub-clause itself. He agrees that this entirely destroys the effect of VIII (4), on which we spent so much time and heat, rendering it unnecessary and valueless. More particularly, it renders nugatory the safeguard of VIII (4)(b)(v) which provides that, when a country is for any reason cut off from the facilities of the Fund, the obligation of convertibility lapses. This is a safeguard to which I have always attached primary importance. Indeed, without it I do not see how any country can safely sign. For in that case a country would be promising to maintain convertibility in circumstances in which it had been deprived of the power to do so.

There is another respect in which this interpretation cuts at the whole philosophy of the Fund as I have understood it. The obligation of convertibility under VIII (4)—in my opinion the *only* obligation of convertibility we undertake—is between pairs of central banks and relates only to convertibility between the currencies of the pair in question. It gives no rights to private persons, who can only obtain convertibility through the good offices of their own central bank. According to Professor Robertson, on the other hand, VIII (2)(a) imposes on our Exchange Control an over-riding obligation to provide any private person on request with any currency in the world.

I cannot discover this in the language of the text. I had better give Professor Robertson's reasons in his own words:

I am afraid I find it impossible to take as narrow a view as you do of the obligations to be assumed under VIII (2) by a member who proposes (as I have always understood that we propose) to continue to exercise a Government monopoly of exchange dealings.

Under such a regime an American citizen (or his banking representative) who comes into possession of sterling through (e.g.) the sale of goods or the receipt of a dividend warrant, cannot go out into the free market in London and buy dollars, for there *is* no free market. The very existence of the Government monopoly constitutes the imposition of a 'restriction on the making of payments and transfers for current international transactions' to the United States, unless the monopoly is in fact so operated as *not* to hinder the making of such payments and transfers, i.e. unless the Control stands ready to sell dollars against sterling to anyone (whether British or American) who desires to make such payments or transfers.

In point of fact the Control is so operated at present, and it seems to me inconceivable that we should be claiming the right, on the great Zero Day on which sterling is at last declared Fully Convertible, to withdraw from the Americans facilities which we have accorded them even during war.

All our discussions with the Americans have proceeded on the basis of 'Live and let Live' as regards systems of exchange management. The provisions of I.M.F. must accordingly be interpreted as guaranteeing (after the close of the transitional period) freedom of remittance of the proceeds of current transactions,

(*a*) between countries both of which centralise exchange dealings

(*b*) between countries neither of which centralises exchange dealings

(*c*) from a country which centralises exchange dealings to one which does not

(*d*) from a country which does not centralise exchange dealings to one which does.

I would comment on this that it is primarily his second paragraph which I dispute. The third paragraph is misleading because the present facility is granted subject to a system of discriminatory import licensing not allowed after the great Zero Day, by which we can prevent Americans from acquiring sterling in the first instance. The facilities for convertibility in his fourth paragraph *are* duly accorded by VIII (4) subject to the qualifications of that clause and provided that his own central bank is willing to oblige him.

What is to be done? I did not become aware of this difference between Professor Robertson (who was the British Delegate representing us on the Committee which dealt with this clause) and myself until the Conference was over. If his interpretation is held to be correct, I think we must ask to have the matter re-considered. If the interpretation is merely held to be open to reasonable doubt, I suggest that I should write personally to Dr White to discover how the Americans understand it. If my interpretation is held to be correct, then we can leave the text alone, though it might be advisable to put this interpretation on record.

(2) The second dubiety has been raised by Dr Einzig, and, if admitted, it would have much the same effect as Professor Robertson's contention. It arises out of Article IV (4)(b) which runs:

Each member undertakes, through appropriate measures consistent with this Agreement, to permit within its territories exchange transactions between its currency and the currencies of other members only within the limits prescribed under Section 3 of this Article. A member whose monetary authorities, for the settlement of international transactions, in fact freely buy and sell gold within the limits prescribed by the Fund under Section 2 of this Article shall be deemed to be fulfilling this undertaking.

Dr Einzig reads this passage as though the word 'permit' means 'facilitate', and he thus arrives at the same (or, perhaps, a more far-reaching) conclusion as Professor Robertson.

His argument is that this clause cannot merely mean (as I shall argue it does) that dealings outside the permitted range may and should be made illegal, because Article VIII (2)(c) forbids exchange restrictions, and to render a black market illegal would be an exchange restriction. Therefore the only way of preventing dealings outside the permitted range is for the Exchange Control itself to provide convertibility to all comers in terms of all currencies within the permitted range.

He goes on to argue that, under the second sentence of the clause, the United States is allowed to contract out of the first sentence, which is correct. He infers, therefore, that only in the U.S. is a black market to be allowed in a weak currency, which is also correct (and is an oversight on our part). And he infers further that *we* shall be under an overriding liability to absorb weak currencies in order to prevent them from depreciating in our market (and here his contention goes beyond Professor Robertson's), even in circumstances when we cannot pass them on to the central bank to which they belong. If his initial contention is granted, this also seems to be correct and is, indeed, its *reductio ad absurdum*.

Now there can, I think, be no doubt that this interpretation never occurred to anyone at Bretton Woods. The only purpose of the clause was to require members to make black markets in weak currencies illegal, whereas, according to Dr Einzig, Article VIII (2)(a) has done just the opposite—it has put members under an obligation to keep black markets legal.

The history of the matter is as follows. The clause originally ran as follows:

A member shall undertake not to allow exchange transactions in its market in currencies of other members at rates outside a prescribed range based on the agreed parities.

We, then, weakly and illogically and mistakenly, allowed the Americans to contract out by the addition of what is now the second sentence, because they wanted to avoid having to bring before Congress a special law such as would be required to make black markets illegal. But they and we failed (inexcusably) to notice that this addition only prevented dealings in the dollar outside the permitted range and would allow black markets in other currencies. But we all assumed that the other members would forbid black markets by law. Finally the lawyers altered the language, as being more tidy and in better form, to what it now is.

No one noticed that to make the intention of IV (4)(b) fully consistent with VIII (2)(a), certain words should have been added at the end of VIII (2)(a), namely, 'within the range permitted under Article IV (3)'.

It would be sufficient here to call the attention of the United States Treasury to this inadvertence of drafting which is easily remedied.

(3) The third point relates to Article XI 'Relations with non-member countries'. This Article was hastily compiled at the last moment without adequate discussion. No one paid much attention to it because it was regarded as affecting only a few recalcitrant or objectionable countries which declined, or were not admitted to, membership when, or shortly after, the Fund is set up. It occurred to no one, so far as I am aware, that 'non-members' obviously includes 'ex-members'.

The question is now raised whether, in its application to ex-members, this Article has the effect of depriving a Member, exercising his right of withdrawal under Article XV (1), of that immunity from the subsequent jurisdiction of the Fund which that Article was supposed to confer on him. For example, if a member has left the Fund because it cannot agree its exchange rate, does Article XI (1) require the remaining Members to outlaw it after its withdrawal on the ground that by maintaining an exchange rate of which the Fund disapproves it is acting 'contrary to the provisions of this Agreement or the purposes of the Fund'?

My own reading is that the above interpretation is *not* correct. The purpose of Article XI is to prevent *members* from acting in a manner 'contrary to the provisions of this Agreement or the purposes of the Fund' in their relations with non-members. It is not intended to prevent non-members from acting 'contrary to the provisions of this Agreement or the purposes of the Fund', which would indeed be absurd. For example, a member may not buy gold from non-members for its own exchange except at the agreed parity of its exchange, but there is nothing in IV (3) to prevent it from dealing with a non-member in the non-member's exchange at a rate with which the Fund disagreed so long as the non-member was a member. There is nothing 'contrary to the provisions of this Agreement and the purposes of the Fund' in a *non-member* having any exchange rate it likes. Perhaps the lawyers will offer an opinion. If they do not confirm my reading, the text may require re-consideration.

17 September 1944   KEYNES

The paper brought replies from J. E. Meade (Professor Robbins being away on leave), Mr Beckett, the legal adviser at Bretton Woods, Mr Bolton, Professor Robertson, Sir Hubert Henderson and Mr Brooks. On receiving these, which saw Messrs Beckett and Bolton support him on all three questions, Mr Brooks support him on the second and third but admit ignorance on the first, and Meade support him on the second and third but question his logic on the first, Keynes wrote to the Chancellor's private secretary.

To T. PADMORE, *20 September 1944*

INTERNATIONAL MONETARY FUND: TEXTUAL DOUBTS

I attach various comments on my paper entitled 'The I.M.F. Drafting Queries'. I doubt if the Chancellor will wish to spend the time and trouble necessary to look through this tangled story. But I attach the collection in case he would like to glance at it.

The most important note is that by Mr Beckett of the Foreign Office, who was the Legal Adviser at Bretton Woods and our principal draftsman. You will see that he supports my interpretation throughout.

The next paper is by Mr Bolton of the Bank of England. This appears to support my view in principle on the matter where I differ from Professor Robertson, but it is not sufficiently precise on drafting points to carry the issue much further.

The third document is a rejoinder from Professor Robertson. The fourth is a note by Sir H. Henderson which, in my opinion, is built on a mare's nest, as I attempt to show in the fifth paper attached.

Professor Robbins and Sir W. Eady are both on leave and I have not been able to get their comments.

My own suggestion after reading these papers is that I should be authorised by the Chancellor to discuss the matter in the first instance orally with Dr White, suggesting two necessary drafting changes, one on the first point and the other on the second point (the third point I am firm in believing we can safely leave alone), taking advantage of the procedure referred to by Mr Beckett by which the Secretariat has authority to correct errors in the text. If Dr White accepts these changes as mere corrections restoring the meaning of the text to what we intended it to be, that will settle the matter. If, however, he is more difficult about it, then I shall have to report further from Washington.

I still feel that Professor Robertson's interpretation, if correct, makes the document unacceptable for the two reasons already mentioned: (1) that it puts us under an inescapable obligation of convertibility even in conditions where we cannot fulfil it, a defect from which the text as I understood it, is entirely free, and (2) because it runs quite contrary to the philosophy of the whole set-up by giving private non-residents rights against our Exchange Control; the only obligations we should accept are those between pairs of central banks, for it is only if we have the option to invoke that procedure that the various qualifications to which I think we ought to attach importance, can be operated.

20 September 1944   KEYNES

I also append as document (b) a note from Mr Brooks who was one of our representatives on the Drafting Committee.[34]

The result was two meetings with the Chancellor on 21 September. In the end, the discussion centred on VIII (2) and Keynes was instructed to

[34] Not printed [Ed.].

approach H. D. White and E. M. Bernstein on the matter, as well as the exchange support obligation, during the Stage II discussions in Washington. During the voyage to America, Keynes prepared a letter to White. After an initial conversation on Bretton Woods, which was very desultory owing to Morgenthau's and White's greater interest in de-industrialising Germany,[35] Keynes put his letter in to White.

To H. D. WHITE, *6 October 1944*

Dear Harry,

THE BRETTON WOODS DRAFT OF I.M.F.

Two questions of interpretation have been raised in London, each of them leading to a possible doubt as to the acceptability of the scheme, which are of sufficient importance to make it necessary for us to get the matter cleared up before the discussion in Parliament which the Chancellor of the Exchequer contemplates. He has, therefore, asked me to take the opportunity of my present visit to Washington to discuss them with you, and, if possible dispose of them.

(1) The first relates to IV 4(b), which is about permitting exchange transactions only within the prescribed limits. All of us who were at Bretton Woods believed the intention of this clause, and its only intention, to be that those members, who were not in a position to contract out under the second sentence of the sub-clause, were authorised, and indeed required, to render illegal dealings outside the prescribed range. Some critics have argued, however, that this would be inconsistent with VIII 2(a) about the avoidance of restrictions on current payments. For it is said that to forbid a black market would be a restriction on current payments. Much capital has been made out of this by Paul Einzig who, as perhaps you know, is one of the chief thorns in our flesh. Strictly speaking, it seems to us that there has been a slip in drafting, and that words should be introduced at the end of VIII 2(a) such as the following:—

'Within the range permitted under Article IV (3).' This

[35] see *JMK*, vol. XXIV, pp. 130–1 and 153–4; below pp. 375–82.

would make it clear that restrictions on dealings outside the prescribed range are, as was intended, in order.

Do you agree that the intention is as described above and that the draft should be tidied up accordingly?

I take this opportunity to point out that the second sentence of IV 4(b) by which, in effect, the U.S. contracts out of this clause, is in fact illogical. For, whilst gold convertibility prevents the dollar from depreciating, it does not prevent *other* currencies from depreciating in the New York market. Thus unless you legislate to the contrary, New York will become, as Einzig has been eager to point out, the chartered black market where all dubious transactions and weak currency deals will be concentrated. Let us hope that in spite of the Statue of Liberty pointing to New York as, under the Constitution, the proud home of black markets as the symbol of Freedom, you will in fact legislate!

(2) The other point is more serious. It is concerned with the relationship, and possible inconsistency, between VIII (2)(a) which deals with 'Avoidance of restrictions on current payments' and VIII (4) which deals with the obligation of 'Convertibility of foreign held balances'.

On the face of it, VIII (2)(a) has nothing to do with convertibility and is limited to prohibiting the internal blocking of balances, the phrase 'making of payments and transfers' being, in fact, a piece of jargon taken over from the British Exchange Control regulations where it relates to internal transactions only. In particular, there is no suggestion in this sub-clause of any obligation on the monetary authority positively to support the exchanges or to stand ready at all times with an offer to provide any foreign currency to any private applicant. In practice, of course, a monetary authority is *entitled* to be as obliging to all comers and as sparing of red-tape as is convenient to it. But the obligation of convertibility comes in, not here, but only in VIII (4) where it appears as an obligation as between pairs of monetary authorities or central banks.

On another interpretation of the clause, however, this conclusion is thought to be unduly *simpliste*. Our view is, as you know, that we cannot conveniently maintain an effective control of capital transactions except by a monopoly of all foreign exchange dealings by an official exchange control. It is argued that such a monopoly would be a 'restriction' within the meaning of VIII (2)(a), and would, therefore, be disallowed, unless, perhaps, the practical effect of the monopoly was offset by the exchange control standing ready at all times with an offer to all-comers of any desired foreign exchange at a rate within the prescribed range, though even then it is not clear on a strict reading that the monopoly would be in order.

If this is correct, a very paradoxical result ensues. A country which sets up an official monopoly of exchange dealings becomes subject to a very much more stringent obligation of convertibility than a country which does not. The latter country has no such obligation whatever except under VIII (4), and can, in particular, take advantage of the let-out under VIII (4)(b)(v). The former country, on the other hand, has a less justified obligation from which it cannot escape under VIII (4)(b)(v), and one moreover which is not towards other central banks but to any private applicant. Thus, as I have said, the purpose of VIII (4)(b)(v) would be wholly frustrated. Difficulties would also arise in the interpretation of other criteria, for example in connection with the use of the Fund for capital movements, if there are obligations to individual private applicants and not merely an over-all obligation to other central banks.

I suppose that we might get round the difficulty by some technical device. For example, all proposed exchange transactions might be required to pass through the central machine which would not then handle them itself but would grant licences (*inter alia*) to *all* requests relating to 'current' transactions allowing them to be dealt with by the open market, leaving the applicant to take his chance whether or not the open market can find a counter-party for him at a rate within the prescribed range. This would have the same practical effect as an official monopoly of exchange dealings, but in a more clumsy and less convenient way.

It appears, therefore, that in our own case, we should be forced either to use what we believe to be an inferior technique, or accept an obligation of convertibility going far beyond what the provisions of the Fund appear to require, or, in fact, do require in general. This would have to be explained to Parliament and would be, almost certainly, inacceptable. I may add that the application to Russia of VIII (2)(a), as at present drafted, scarcely bears thinking about.

If it is agreed that this dilemma is not intended but is the result of inadvertent drafting due to the unavoidable haste with which we were working, then it is a question of finding the neatest way of tidying it up. I suggest that the following would meet the case:

Amend VIII (2)(a) so as to run—

(a) No member shall, without the approval of the Fund, impose restrictions on the making of internal payments and transfers arising out of current international transactions, or on foreign exchange transactions which are inconsistent with or frustrate the obligation of convertibility of foreign held balances under VIII (4) below.

(3) In conclusion, on the assumption you agree that the above two drafting amendments are necessary to secure the consistency of our intentions at Bretton Woods, there is the question how most conveniently to get them incorporated in a revised text.

I suggest that these are cases where we should be entitled to take advantage of the authority specifically entrusted by the Conference to the Secretariat to correct errors in the text, because we all knew that there would be, inevitably, drafting errors and inconsistencies in the text such as the above owing to the haste in which a most complicated piece of work had to be done. Your Delegation originally suggested that this power should be given to the U.S. and U.K. Delegations, but our memory is that in the end it was given to the Secretariat, this being more in accordance with the general practice at international conferences.

Yours sincerely,

KEYNES

In the weeks following, Keynes heard nothing from White on the matter. On 9 November he reported to Sir Wilfrid Eady,

You will have had the letter which I fired in to Harry White on our difficulties of interpretation in the Bretton Woods document. He has, of course, not even acknowledged it. Early next week I shall start to agitate. Sitting next to Bernie at lunch the other day, I found, as expected, that they had no difficulty in putting the first point right but were bothered about the other. I shall not desist from pressing the matter.

Keynes and R. H. Brand finally met the Americans on the matter on 18 November. Keynes reported the results on his return to London in a memorandum, dated 29 December, which also took account of an attempt at a re-draft of VIII (2) by Rowe-Dutton and Cobbold.

THE INTERNATIONAL MONETARY FUND

I

On October 6 I sent Mr White a letter on two questions of interpretation, copies of which have been circulated. This was not discussed until November 18, when Mr Brand and I (having had, meanwhile, no reply to my letter, or even an acknowledgment of it), sought an interview with Mr White, who was accompanied by Mr Bernstein and Mr Luxford, the upshot of which is reported below. On the following day I sent Mr Bernstein a letter of which a copy is attached (Appendix A). No reply to this has been received. At my last meeting with Mr White (on other matters) before I left Washington, he promised a reply in writing to the questions I had raised, to reach me after my return to London. No such reply has been, or is likely to be, received. American autographs are very rare.

146

Mr Morgenthau's present intention is to bring both the Fund and the Bank before Congress at the earliest possible date, perhaps February. As will be seen below, Mr White will try to railroad both plans through as an indivisible whole incapable of amendment. Nevertheless he will not, I think, be able to by-pass some weeks of committees during which all and sundry, bankers and economists and *per impossibile* much worse than either, will be invited to give evidence, create prejudice and make unpleasant remarks about ourselves as the case may be. Almost certainly, the line taken by the responsible opposition will be to support the Bank as an immediate necessity and to urge that the Fund should be postponed until we can see our way more clearly, some of its proposed functions being exercised meanwhile by the Bank. If I was in the place of Mr Morgenthau and Mr White, I should accept this compromise. But that is not their present intention, and I do not believe they will ever accept it, except under political orders from above. When I left Washington Mr White believed that he could railroad it through all right. Since internationalism is, for the moment, in a temporary trough in Washington, his chances may not now be quite so good. Indeed some delay in bringing the proposals forward may easily be the result—the President's sense of timing may now find itself offended by the time-table which was in view when I left Washington.

I think it is odds on that Mr White will succeed in (i) rail-roading both plans through Congress. But (ii) a temporary delay and (iii) a compromise on the above lines are also very possible. We should, therefore, in our own plans, take each of these possibilities seriously.

I suggest that Mr Brand should be asked to obtain the latest ideas about the time-table. If there is not to be a delay, the question of the right way of handling the matter in Parliament seems to me rather difficult. It would, for obvious reasons, be undesirable to have a debate *during* the discussions in Congress. Presumably the Chancellor will not wish to ask Parliament for formal approval until *after* Congress has declared. To have no debate at all until then may, however, give rise to criticism and impatience. To have a preliminary, non-committal debate before Congress means early action—unless there is to be a delay on the other side.

III

I now return to the issues raised in my letter of October 6 to Mr White.

On the first point relating to IV 4(b) they agreed with us immediately that my letter correctly interpreted the intention of all concerned, and Mr White offered to state this to us in writing (autograph not yet received). They promised to vote in favour of an interpretation to this effect as soon as the Fund was set up. I think that we can safely disregard this particular difficulty henceforward, and that our interpretation could, if necessary, be given in debate without fear of contradiction.

The second point, however, namely the suggested inconsistency between VIII (2)(a) and VIII (4) gave rise to much more trouble. It was obvious that Mr White, like myself, had not had his attention called to this issue during the Bretton Woods Conference, and it took some time to make him appreciate what it was. Mr Bernstein and Mr Luxford, on the other hand, knew all about it and strongly supported, in substance, the interpretation sprung on us (or, at any rate, on me) after our return by Professor Robertson.

Mr White, when he had grasped what the point was, remarked that personally he attached very little importance to it from the practical point of view (which shocked Mr Bernstein who evidently attached considerable importance from the doctrinal point of view) and would readily have compromised if we had drawn his attention to it during the Conference. But in face of the advice given him by Mr Luxford, his legal adviser, and

Mr Bernstein, his economic adviser, he could not now agree to *interpret* the clause in the sense I was putting forward. At the same time no procedure existed for *amending* at this stage this (or any other) clause of the plans. Moreover this was better so. For, if the plans could be amended, every legislature concerned would amend them in a different way; and, above all, his own project of offering them to Congress to be accepted or rejected *as they stand* would fall to the ground. He, therefore, urged us to accept, from the other angle, his own view that the practical importance of the matter was small and might be overlooked.

To this I replied that if the matter had not been already raised publicly, this might have been at least considered. Unfortunately the question had been raised prominently by the critics of the scheme; the Chancellor could not possibly avoid explaining to the House of Commons what he understood the clause to mean; and I, at any rate, could not advise him to defend on its merits the meaning put on it by Mr Bernstein, nor could I take it on myself to say or imply, which would not be true, that I had consciously accepted at Bretton Woods a clause having the effect which Mr Bernstein claims for it. I added that I believed most of the other signatories would be extremely surprised if the alleged effect of what they have signed were to be pointed out to them. (We, all of us, had to sign, of course, before we had had a chance of reading through a clean and consecutive copy of the document. All we had seen of it was the dotted line. Our only excuse is the knowledge that our hosts had made final arrangements to throw us out of the hotel, unhouselled, disappointed, unanealed, within a few hours.)

Well, said Mr White, we must take time to think over what can be done, and I will let you know later; upon which we broke up after a very exhausting afternoon. Even that man of iron, Mr White, enquired sympathetically as we went out, whether *we* were such men of iron that we did not find such a discussion tiring.

IV

Is Mr White in fact right that the issue has small practical importance? Even if he is, the doctrinal importance is, in my opinion, too great to be disregarded; and also the inner inconsistency of the document. Let me rehearse the matter again, beginning with the merits, before passing on to the intention or to the legal interpretation of the text.

The essential point is this. If a country gets into exchange difficulties two types of remedy are open to it. It can depreciate the rate of exchange; or it can restore the limited and discretionary convertibility of its currency into foreign currencies such as we have now. We took great pains to ensure that our discretion to use the former should not be unduly fettered. I thought that we had taken equal pains to retain discretion in emergency to use the latter also, by accepting under Article VIII 4 an obligation of free convertibility which was limited in the sense that the obligation accepted in VIII 4(a) lapsed in the event of any of the circumstances set forth in VIII 4(b). This limitation of obligation was only obtained with a considerable struggle and after prolonged discussion. I attached particular importance to VIII 4(b)(v). For this meant that our obligation lapsed as soon as we had run through, or had been deprived of, our right of drawing on the Fund; so that we were not compelled to go on accepting convertibility until we had run down our own gold reserves to the level at which the Fund might choose to let us off. I argued that there were reasons of politics and war which made it both reasonable and essential that we ourselves should retain the discretion to decide at what point we should call a halt to the further depletion of our gold reserves.

We are now told, however, that what was secured in VIII 4(b)(v) after so much open debate has been quietly removed and cancelled out in VIII 2(a). I had assumed that VIII 2(a) was qualified by, and subordinate to, VIII 4(b). And so it very nearly is. VIII 4(b) provides for five let-outs. VIII 2(a) recapitulates three of these, but omits (iii) and (v), of which (v) is important. There was, as I have said, no opportunity to read the draft carefully for small drafting omissions of this kind.

Now the substantial question is—Are we prepared to hand over to the Fund the discretion to decide to what point we have to reduce our gold reserves (having already run through, or been cut off from, the resources of the Fund) before the obligation of free convertibility for all current transactions is suspended?

I say, on merits—No. The matter is important because, if we do get into difficulties, we are much more likely to want to suspend free convertibility than to depreciate. In addition to which, the Chancellor would be in a poor position if he had to explain the above to the House of Commons (as he would have to) and tell them that the apparent let-out under VIII 4(b) is a pure deception, because our representatives at Bretton Woods had not been wide enough awake to notice that the necessary cross-reference to this in VIII 2(a) had been omitted. I do not see how the Chancellor can successfully defend the omission of a reference to VIII 4(b)(v) in VIII 2(a).

V

I now turn to the question of intention and legal interpretation. Intention cannot be considered important. It could only relate to four or five individuals at the most. The question was never raised in a main Committee, and nine out of ten delegates will be found, I am sure, as innocent of all knowledge of the matter as were Mr White and myself.

On legal interpretation two points arise:

(i) VIII 2(a) certainly does not impose on a member a positive obligation to provide any foreign exchange required for current international transactions. The most that it does is to forbid certain means of preventing it. For instance, it forbids interference between a willing buyer and a willing seller of foreign exchange (provided they deal within the permitted range of parity) and it, therefore, rules out a type of exchange control which involves such interference. Thus centralisation of all foreign exchange transactions through the Control, such as we now have, would be disallowed; but it would not be difficult to devise a system of control, which fell far short of free convertibility, yet did not obviously infringe this clause. Thus, on strict interpretation, I should argue that the clause has a nuisance value, particularly to us, but cannot be interpreted as the U.S. Treasury seek to interpret it.

(ii) It is, perhaps, of more decisive legal importance that VIII 2(a) and VIII 8(b)(v) are in certain circumstances directly contradictory, if the American interpretation of the former sub-clause is accepted. For the latter says that the obligation to buy sterling from another member shall not apply in the circumstances of VIII 8(b)(v), whereas it is alleged that the former requires that the obligation shall apply. What the lawyers do when two clauses of an instrument contradict one another I do not know. But I should have supposed that they would give the benefit of the doubt to any interpretation which avoided the contradiction.

Mr Bernstein defended the language from being directly and merely contradictory on the ground that VIII (4) covers two types of transactions, namely those specified in VIII 4(a)(i) and (ii), whereas VIII 2(a) only covers transactions of the VIII 4(a)(ii) type. I am not sure that this is true. But if it is, it does not prevent a contradiction arising in the case of the latter type of transactions.

Mr White defended the practical effect by arguing that we could always dodge Mr Bernstein's intention by import controls. There is something in this; but such controls in peace-time would fall a good deal short of covering all types of current transactions as defined in XIX (i).

VI

I let matters drift during my last days in Washington and did not attempt to reach a more definitive conclusion because, shortly after the above interview on November 18, I received a telegram from London instructing me to hold my hand pending receipt of a further letter, since doubts were felt in London whether the re-draft I had suggested to Mr White in my letter of October 6 was the best way out. This letter did not reach me until I was about to sail.

The letter does not seem to me to make any material difference to what is set out above. It points out that, in normal circumstances and before special difficulties had arisen, we should in our own interest act in conformity with VIII 2(a) in practice,—with which I entirely agree. Secondly it suggests a revised draft (given below in an appendix) for attaining the purpose I was aiming at, which I accept as a considerable improvement on my own proposal. The only objection to this re-draft is that it is, admittedly, a drastic change of wording in the interests of clarity. If one is free to re-draft, I greatly prefer this text just because it is quite clear. I was trying to find the minimum change of wording which would serve the purpose, in the hope that this change could be accepted as a mere interpretation.

I still think that we might be wise to content ourselves with the minimum change of words. Indeed I now feel that a smaller change will serve than that proposed in my letter of October 6, namely the addition of a reference to VIII 4(iii) and (v) in VIII 2(c), so that the first words of the latter read:

Subject to the provisions of Article VII Section 3(b) and Article XIV Section 2, or except in the conditions of Article VIII 4(b)(iii) or (v)...

which could be put more shortly

Except in the conditions of Article VIII 4(b)...

Nevertheless the other, more drastic re-draft, should also be offered to the Americans as an alternative.

Time is running out. Would it not be advisable for the Chancellor to write a letter to Mr Morgenthau calling attention to the discrepancy between the provisions of the above two sub-clauses as drafted; explaining that Lord Keynes, who signed for the U.K., was depending on the protection of VIII 4(b) and, in the haste of the concluding days, failed to notice that VIII 2(a), by a confusion of the draftsmen, was not in full conformity with VIII 4(b) but could be read in a sense in certain circumstances contradictory to it; saying that he is being asked to explain which clause, if either, prevails over the other; and concluding that he proposes to inform Parliament that there is here a plain error of drafting and that our adherence must be subject to the difficulty being cleared up in due course on the lines of one or other of the above re-drafts? We cannot be expected to sign an instrument which is either self-contradictory or hopelessly obscure.

KEYNES

29 December 1944

Appendix A

Dear Bernstein,

This letter is a footnote to our conversation yesterday. If you could let me have a quick reply it might help us to get on.

As I understood yesterday's discussion, you and Luxford based your argument primarily on VIII Section 2(a). Could you provide me with a paraphrase of this which you consider to be its legal equivalent, and which clearly bears the interpretation you place on it?

This interpretation, if I understood rightly, was that this imposed on a member a positive obligation to provide at the par of exchange any foreign exchange required to make payments and transfers for current international transactions.

Suppose a country had no exchange control, and merely a law

rendering illegal exchange transactions outside the prescribed range, how would this clause apply to them?

The main object, however, of this letter is to get from you the paraphrase of this section which would plainly carry on the face of it the interpretation which you wish to give to it.

19 November 1944   Yours sincerely,

                                                                KEYNES

Appendix B: Re-draft by Mr Rowe-Dutton and Mr Cobbold

VIII 2(a) to read as follows:

Subject to the provisions of Article VII Section 3(b), Article XIV Section 2 no member shall, without the approval of the Fund, impose restrictions which

(i) prevent the making of payments in its own currency by persons in its territory to persons outside its territory in respect of current transactions, or

(ii) prevent the transfer of currency paid to persons outside its territory in accordance with (i) immediately above to the central bank or other fiscal agent operating in the territory of such persons.

We suggest that if a wording on these lines were adopted Article VI 3 could, and we believe should, end at 'capital movements', since the new VIII 2(a) suggested above covers the point with which the latter part of VI 3 is concerned.

With the New Year, Keynes's document became involved in the preparations for a possible Parliamentary discussion of Bretton Woods. A meeting with the Chancellor on 10 January, which Keynes attended, discussed Keynes's 29 December memorandum and the Parliamentary position. On the Parliamentary problem, the Chancellor agreed to investigate the strength of feeling for a debate in the Commons before the American Congress considered the Bretton Woods documents. Such a debate would, in effect, be of the 'second reading' type, to get approval to await formal Congressional action yet avoid a rush after American approval. The Chancellor sent a memorandum to this effect to his Cabinet colleagues on 22 January 1945. The Cabinet decided not to discuss the issue in the Commons until after Congress had acted, largely as a result of continued Cabinet disagreements over other aspects of Article VII.

The meeting of 10 January also agreed that Keynes should prepare a draft letter to Mr Morgenthau on the outstanding points and that Britain should consider either a new conference to clear up the matters at issue or a redraft of the offending clauses before accepting the obligations of convertibility.

BRETTON WOODS (INTERPRETATION OF ARTICLE VIII):
DRAFT PREPARED BY LORD KEYNES

Dear Mr Morgenthau,

A question has arisen of the interpretation of a certain clause in the Final Act of Bretton Woods which is causing me some difficulty and perplexity. It arises out of a possible conflict or inconsistency between Section 2(a) and Section 4(b) of Article VIII of the Fund. This has been already the subject of some discussion between Lord Keynes and Mr White.

On our view of the matter the only obligation of convertibility should be the obligation between members clearly arising out of VIII 4(a) as qualified by VIII 4(b). VIII 2(a) should, in our view, relate only to the internal blocking of currency, or, if it is held to go beyond this, should be read in conjunction with VIII 4 and subject to the same qualifications.

If you could agree with us that, in due course, this is the interpretation which should be adopted, I would be well content. If not, certain questions arise, to which, my advisers tell me, I ought to seek, an answer. I give these in an annex to this letter.

The truth seems to me to be that we have here a piece of inconsistent, ambiguous, faulty drafting, which is not surprising in view of the inevitably hurried work of the last days of the Conference.

It is believed that up to a late stage of drafting VIII 2(a) actually included a reference making it subject to VIII 4(b); so that all was well. This was dropped out in the final version without the omission having been explained to, or debated by, the main Committee. Hence all this trouble. The result is that no clear meaning emerges; and at some stage this will have to be tidied up. I only wish that the fundamental point at issue was sufficiently trivial for us to overlook it at the present stage. But that unfortunately is not the case. Critics of the plan have already fastened on the point, and I shall probably be expected to give Parliament some clear guidance as to what obligation in this respect they are being asked to assume.

The essential point is this. The obligation under VIII 4(a) lapses under VIII 4(b)(v) if the member has exhausted his facilities with the Fund. In such circumstances, therefore, he resumes his discretion how far and for how long he shall continue to exhaust his ultimate gold reserves by maintaining *de facto* convertibility. I shall be expected to explain whether this is in any way undone by VIII 2(a), so that, in the above circumstances, the discretion is given to the Fund, instead of to the member, to decide up to what point the member shall be required to deplete his gold reserves, which represent a country's iron ration for many purposes including war, before being allowed a relaxation. I am not prepared to advise either the Cabinet or Parliament to be content with a lesser safeguard in this respect than that which appears to be given by VIII 4(b). Nor is it likely, if I gave such advice, that it would be accepted. Furthermore, the critics of the Fund, who are none too friendly, would be given an opportunity to claim that it is a regrettable piece of deception to allow what appears to be a clear safeguard in one sub-section to be taken away by what is a far from clear, and indeed dubious, interpretation of another sub-section of the same clause.

Nevertheless an attempt to secure an amendment here and now is, I agree, inadvisable, as well as difficult, since it would open the door to other changes. It seems to me, therefore, that unless our two Governments can agree that this is a matter which must be put right in due course, so that no greater obligation is required than clearly appears, we here must put ourselves on public record, not only with you but with all the other participants in the Conference, that in our opinion VIII 2(a) is faultily and inconsistently drafted unless it is read as implicitly qualified by VIII 4(b); and that we shall regard the satisfactory clearing up of this matter in the meanwhile as one of the essential conditions pre-requisite to our being in a position to accept eventual convertibility under Article XIV.

I still hope that we can, between us, find some way to avoid this. Do you not share my feeling that, in the case of a document prepared so hastily as the Final Act yet so difficult to amend, it would be a bad and dangerous precedent to seek by subtle interpretation to impose any obligation which did not appear, clearly and unambiguously, on the face of the document, or which had not been understood or accepted by those who signed it?

The above has now become a matter of some urgency in view of forthcoming debates. I should be very grateful if you could keep me informed through Mr Brand of your time-table with Congress. How long do you expect the debate to last? Will the examination of witnesses in Committee be public? I am contemplating a preliminary debate in the House of Commons before Congress has pronounced, but I should not ask for a positive commitment at this stage. There are some obvious inconveniences and dangers in a more or less simultaneous discussion in our two legislatures, which I should like to avoid if, which appears doubtful, the time-table would allow it.

Annex

(1) Could your advisers tell us exactly what obligation of convertibility, if any, VIII 2(a) imposes on a member in their view? Would they furnish us with a paraphrase of this sub-section which clearly bears the desired interpretation and is held by them to be its legal equivalent?

(2) VIII 4(a) imposes an obligation of convertibility only between *members*, i.e. between central banks or treasuries. Is

it held that VIII 2(a) imposes an obligation of convertibility between a member and private individuals (including both its own nationals and others)? If so, how is this consistent with the view that whether a country is or is not exporting capital depends not on isolated, individual transactions, but on its over-all debtor or creditor position?

(3) Does VIII 4(a) impose an obligation of convertibility with *any* currency, whether the national currency of the applicant or not? If the obligation is not thus unlimited, by what words in the text is it limited?

(4) VIII 4(b) expressly relieves a member of certain obligations in certain contingencies. Is it held that VIII 2(a) re-imposes obligations which VIII 4(b) has expressly removed? If so, is there not a direct inconsistency between the two sub-sections?

(5) If a member declares exchange transactions illegal except within a permitted range but has no exchange control, is it free from any obligation under VIII 2(a)?

Keynes sent a copy of his draft letter and December paper to D. H. Robertson, who by then had returned to Cambridge as Professor of Political Economy in succession to Pigou and was, therefore, not a recipient of official papers.

From D. H. ROBERTSON, *January 1945*[36]

My dear Maynard,

B.W.

Thank you for your letter. You must do as you think wise about keeping me in touch. But if I *do* see papers, I must comment on them freely without being deterred, as I have been so far, by fear of adding to your difficulties (a paper on which one can't comment is like a tick under the skin!). If you think there is any risk of the latter, please tear this up unread.

[36] This document is a Treasury transcription of effectively Robertson's letter to Keynes. At the top of the document the Treasury added the words 'rough draft altered in places'. The top copy has not survived.

(1) *History*

(i) There is no doubt, I think, that the intention of the Rasminsky–Bernstein proposal to omit the reference to VIII (4) from VIII (2)—a reference which I had stuck in myself to hold the position—was *not* to cancel the protection of VIII 4(b)(v) in the class of cases held to be dealt with in VIII (4) (e.g. Indian or Brazilian sterling balances); but *was* to d[efine] that protection in the class of cases (i.e. *in primis* the £–U.S. $ and £–Can $ exchange) held not to be dealt with in VIII (4). (Bernstein ought to answer NO to question 4 in your questionnaire.)

(ii) There is equally no doubt, I think, that (after a rather stormy little meeting on the subject of convertibility to which I had summoned you, and which ended in impasse) the proposal to omit the reference was put up by me to you through Eady; that I received your assent through the same channel: and that thereafter I explained, in the sense which you repudiate, the mutual relation of the two clauses to some major body (whether 'Commission I' or 'Committee I of Commission I' I do not remember). I do not think there was any debate.

(iii) All this, of course, does not alter your personal position. It clearly remains true that, as you say in your memorandum of Dec. 29 you did not consciously accept a clause knowing that interpretation and are not only entitled but bound, if your judgment so directs, to repudiate it. But it *does* mean that the Americans and/or Canadians are in a position, if they wish, to explode any notion of a last-minute drafting slip, and that you may have to proceed by way of a more definite statement (for which he is quite prepared!) that the U.K. delegate on Committee I misinterpreted his instructions.

(iv) I cannot remember whether my put-up of the proposal was or was not accompanied by a copy of a note which I had prepared (against a possible meeting of the Delegation to discuss the matter) giving the arguments against making this a breaking-point. But in any case I made a great error of judgement in not deciding when I received your assent, that I must see you myself to make sure you had understood its implications. There were so many other thorny questions pending that the assent did come to me as a gift-horse; but it was [one] which should have been looked firmly in the mouth!

(2) *The Future*

My real feeling now, especially in view of the activities of the 'key-currency' school, is that it will prove very difficult to defend the plan in either country—sooner or later there will occur some frightful gaffe—unless it is possible to give a clear account, the same in both countries, of how under the plan it is proposed to administer the dollar–sterling exchange *in normal times*—i.e. *after* the transition and in circumstances when we have *not* run through our money with the Fund. The question of the let-out, though I won't attempt to dispute its importance, either really or politically, seems to me (logically at all events) to be secondary to this.

What troubled me frankly about your memorandum of Dec. 29 was that your mind seemed to be working in two opposite directions on this question. On p. 6 you say that under VIII 2(a) 'centralisation of all foreign exchange transactions through the control, such as we now have, would be disallowed'. But on p. 8 you express approval of the Rowe–Dutton–Cobbold redraft. Now the effect of the latter, so far as I can see (but you must remember I haven't heard the discussions) is to put the U.S. Government under notice that if they want to make sure of their exporters being paid they must adopt just such a centralised system as you say on p. 6 that we must abandon,—they must instruct their traders to invoice exports to the sterling area in sterling, exports to France in francs etc., and they must instruct the Federal [Reserve] to stand ready to buy up all these foreign currencies claims. I am not sure whether in your letter to Morgenthau you are in effect asking him to accept this interpretation: but I believe if you are, and if he realises that you are, he will refuse, whatever he may agree to about the let-out. For I do not see how, in view of all that has been said about the Fund not affecting the procedures of the ordinary traders and bankers, he could put any such proposal across Ed Brown, let alone Congress.—Anyway, I repeat such a development would be in the *opposite* direction to that indicated on p. 6, where you seem to be thinking in terms of a universal return to free markets, albeit apparently somewhat phoney ones.

I do therefore agree with your conclusion that the Chancellor must know what the convertibility obligation means, especially as regard the dollar exchange; but he must know what it means for ordinary times as well as in the case where we have run through our borrowing powers with the Fund, and he must know the same thing as Morgenthau knows, or sooner or later there will be trouble.

The floodgates being opened, I will end by trying to give my own answers to your examination paper.

(1) I have not got my lawyer with me!

(2) Yes. I don't see the force of the objection about capital. Surely a member is entitled, and indeed in some circumstances obliged, to stop *individual* capital transactions, e.g. the shift of a big bank balance from London to New York, without waiting to know what the national balance of payments for the quarter is going to look like.

(3) No,—but this is a nasty question for I don't think the 'key currency' question has been cleared up even now. The Americans are assuming that Chile can get U.S. $ from the Fund to pay Peru,—hence the provision (such as it is) for 'recapturing' Peru's dollars. And I think that is right,—e.g. if we find that we (i.e. either H.M.G. or the private trader, according as our policy may develop) have to go on paying for Cuban sugar in U.S. $ if we want to get it, we want to be in a position [to] get such $ from the Fund. But we must also be in a position, as we are now, to say to the private English importer from India 'you must not pay for Indian exports in U.S. $'. If that is not clear it should be made so.

(4) No.

(5) Such a member is discharging its obligations under VIII 2(a) and IV 4(b) respectively. But it has also a more general obligation under IV 4(a) to promote exchange stability and maintain orderly exchange arrangements; and a situation in which people cannot pay their debts because they *cannot* buy foreign currency at par and *must not* buy at a premium is not orderly or stable. I.e. such a member would have to be prepared to support its currency in the market, police action would be no more than a useful auxiliary.

From D. H. ROBERTSON, *21 January 1945*

My dear Maynard,

BRETTON WOODS

I wrote to Hoppy telling him you had sent me a copy of your memorandum as a friendly courtesy, but that I did not take this as giving me either the right or duty of comment. I received no answer, but on ringing up Jack Robertson next time I was in London I obtained confirmation that this was indeed the position. (In my letter I had said that I must make one exception, viz. that I felt I ought to remind him of the prominent part played by the Canadians in this affair; and Robertson told me this had been noted).

This suited me all right, for I need not say I am very sorry for my share of responsibility for the misunderstanding which occurred at B.W., and that my chief desire now is not to do or say anything which will hamper you and the Chancellor in clearing up the situation. But in applying this criticism I am put into a new dilemma by receipt of your draft letter to Morgenthau. For it contains one historical statement which I think he may be able to disprove by reference to the complete records of the conference, and which therefore may prove an embarrassment; and I am uncertain whether you would wish this pointed out or not (perhaps the letter has already gone anyway).

Unless I hear from you I shall leave it at that, in pursuance of the official ruling that in respect of B.W., as in all other respects, I am now dead; and in view of the same rulings it will be best that you shouldn't send me any more documents.

Yours,

[D.H.R.]

From a letter to D. H. ROBERTSON, *23 January 1945*

Dear Dennis,

BRETTON WOODS

Thank you for your letter. I am cutting out the sentence to which you refer. I was not too sure about it and was already thinking that it might be better away.

I should like, in spite of what you say, to keep in touch with you on this matter from time to time. The letter to Morgenthau I am toning down slightly. The Economic Section would like us not to make such heavy weather about it. I wish I could see how to fall in with that advice. White, in a conversation with Brand, is taking the line that, if only we will not make a fuss now, they will try to see that this is cleared up later.

Nevertheless, it is not easy to see how the Chancellor can fluff so fundamental a matter in Parliament. He is assuming a great responsibility in accepting the convertibility obligation and can scarcely take the line, when pressed, that he does not know exactly what the obligation is, but hopes to discover it in due course.

Yours ever,

[copy initialled] MK

To D. H. ROBERTSON, *8 February 1945*

Dear Dennis,

BRETTON WOODS

As I said, I like to keep you up to date with this for your purely private and personal information. So here is the letter from the Chancellor to Morgenthau as it eventually went off; also a letter of mine, following it a week later, to Harry.[37]

[37] See below, pp. 175–82.

The proposal of the bankers is pretty awful, especially in what they propose about the American representation on the Bank. Their idea is that every single operation of the Bank ought to be brought down to the lowest level of American politics and vetted by every Congressman. Really bankers are past praying for. This has, of course, had the effect of making us rally round Bretton Woods.

A campaign of education is now to start. The Chancellor will be seeing various members of Parliament, and so shall I, and I shall be giving a discourse next month at Chatham House. Meanwhile the obligation of convertibility sinks temporarily into the background, and I only hope that we shall have a chance of re-drafting it properly. After all, the obligation of convertibility is a serious thing, and it is an awkward matter to bring it before Parliament in a form which is certainly unintelligible and maybe inconsistent.

We appointed Roy [Harrod] editor of the *Economic Journal* in my place at the meeting of the Council yesterday.

Yours ever,
MAYNARD KEYNES

From D. H. ROBERTSON, *12 February 1945*

Dear Maynard,

I.M.F. ARTICLE VIII

I must not be a bore about this, but the more I think about it the more it appears to me that interpretation on something like the rejected Bernstein–Robertson lines is not only necessary to make the whole contraption work, but is specially in the interests of the U.K.

This is because we export in terms of our own currency to a very wide range of countries, hereafter called 'Brazil', who hold balances with us, while we don't, to any extent, hold balances with them. Hence 4(a) is precious little good to us *as a means of getting payment for our exports*; and if this is ruled to be the only convertibility obligation, i.e. if 2(a) is not held to impose any obligation on a member to ensure (by one means or another) that private persons are paid for current transactions, it will be open to 'Brazil' to refuse at any time to release sterling to her importers to pay our exporters with, even though she may still be holding large sterling balances obtained from her own exporters. She can tell us that if we want to ensure our exporters being paid we must instruct them to invoice in 'cruzeiros' and must instruct the Bank of England to buy up the 'cruzeiros' and present them for conversion. Surely we don't want to be put in that position *vis-à-vis* the whole range of countries here called 'Brazil' any more than the Americans do.

I doubt if, by accepting the Bernstein interpretation of 2(a), we should let ourselves in for doing anything for the Americans and Canadians which we shouldn't *in practice* have to do anyhow; while by rejecting it we should be giving *carte blanche* to 'Brazil', consistently with their obligations under the Fund, to play all sorts of tricks against us—a *carte blanche* which sooner or later many of them wouldn't scruple to use.

If it *be* agreed that there is an obligation under 2(a) additional to that under 4(a), the question remains whether it should be made subject to the same let-out. I know your mind is made up that this is necessary; so I will only say that it must be remembered that this too is a double-edged weapon. For it gives *carte blanche* to 'Brazil' to run through her borrowing powers with the Fund and then impose every kind of exchange restriction against us even though she may still have plenty of sterling left. On the present text she can't do this, while if *we* get into trouble we *can*, under 4(b)(v), impose restrictions against her. This is unsymmetrical and apparently unfair, but unfair if at all in our favour, and really defensible as a special concession to the position of a member whom everyone wants to see continuing as a custodian of international balances though she is not really in a strong enough position to be one (that, I think, is how the Americans have always regarded (4)). To generalise the let-out, through extending it to countries which are not custodians of balances, may increase, on paper at least, our ultimate protection against being drained of gold and dollars; but it may also, I think, appreciably impair the efficacy of the whole plan as a prop for our export trade to the world at large.

Perhaps all I'm saying is that everything cuts both ways!*

Yours,
D.H.R.

---

* But that, after all, is the chief argument for preferring the plan itself to the insidious sweets of bilateralism.

To D. H. ROBERTSON, *14 February 1945*

My dear Dennis,

I.M.F. ARTICLE VIII

In my opinion there is great force in the argument of your letter of February 12th. But it is exceedingly difficult to get the issue sufficiently clear. My notes on your letter are as follows:

(1) As a normal procedure, apart from exceptional occasions of difficulty, I am inclined to agree that what you want to discover in 2(a) would be to the general advantage. My difficulty is that it is not clearly or unambiguously there; indeed, I do not think it is there at all. What you are really saying is that we have overlooked a critical point in the drafting of 4(a). It is that which really needs amendment. 4(a) ought to be so expressed that it works both ways and compels Brazil, if she holds sterling balances, to release them to her importers. That is where it belongs in the general structure of the plan.

(2) This would have the advantage that the same let-out applies as that already provided for in 4(b).

(3) You cannot bring in this piece of machinery, which I agree is necessary to make the whole scheme water-tight, by a side-wind in a clause which purports merely to prohibit exchange restrictions.

(4) If your point is brought in in Section 4, that preserves what I still think an important part of the philosophy of the scheme, namely, that the obligations are between members and not between members and private individuals.

I conclude after reading your letter even more forcibly than I had concluded before reading it, that the only way to clear up this matter is to re-draft Article VIII, so that it makes clear and unambiguous sense. I do not disagree with you as to what one wants as the normal procedure. But I still maintain that, when the criterion of exceptional conditions is satisfied, the discretion as to how to handle them must remain with the country and not be handed over to the Fund. I would point out that in the case of a small country the Fund can very likely retain a measure of authority by making further assistance conditional on accepting such authority.

I enclose a copy of the full text of the bankers' counter-proposals [to Bretton Woods]. You will, I think, find the general approach disappointing and nothing like as good as Williams's article or Burgess's conversation. In particular, the provision on page 17 for a United States Directing Committee in regular consultation with Congress, which brings the participation in any loan right into the middle of American politics, is unbelievably wicked. The bankers must well know how wicked it is and have inserted it entirely by way of pandering to Congress.

Yours ever,
MAYNARD KEYNES

From D. H. ROBERTSON, *17 February 1945*

Dear Maynard,

I.M.F.

(1) Article VIII. Yes, I agree that the convertibility obligations, whatever they are decided to be, would be best drafted as a continuous whole, and expressed as obligations of members to one another or to the Fund (i.e. one couldn't have private importers suing their central bank, or another member's central bank, on the strength of municipal legislation establishing the Fund.

But I should foresee great difficulty in setting down in black and white that a member must release 'convertible currencies' to its importers without setting down the same thing in black and white as regards gold (you will remember that XIX(a) lumps the two together as 'monetary reserves').

(2) I am glad to have the bankers in full, and will keep the copy you sent unless you say you want it back. Yes, after the pious words about 'political' lending on p. 10, the bumsucking of Congress is very bad.

Where I have some sympathy with them is in their desire to know (top of p. 15) what U.K. is prepared to borrow from U.S., and through what machinery, before tying themselves up to general schemes!

Yours,
D.H.R.

Keynes also sent copies of his draft letter to J. E. Meade and Professor Robbins, as well as to other officials in the Bank and Treasury. In their replies, both Sir Wilfrid Eady and Professor Robbins gave Keynes more information on the origins of the difficulties.

From SIR WILFRID EADY, *24 January 1945*

I am afraid that the scraps of documents relating to the period have not helped me to remember exactly what happened on this point or whether and when the safeguard which you regard as important appeared and then disappeared from the text. In all the circumstances I can only comment on what seems to me the present, not the historical, merits of the position.

There is an obvious contradiction between VIII (2)(a) and VIII (4). Indeed (a) and (b) of VIII (4) are not both reconcilable with the American interpretation of VIII (2)(a). But I think Meade is right in believing that if we want to get the position beyond the power of a Fund which does not understand the facts to intervene to the damage of a country, more amendments may be required. Rowe-Dutton's point, which has always troubled him and the Bank, is a difficult one, but you will remember the unexpected and absurd attitude which the Americans produced about IV (4)(b).

Despite these contradictions I doubt the wisdom of an approach to Morgenthau even in the modified form of your letter, for I doubt whether anything would come of that letter which would really help the Chancellor. Either Morgenthau will not reply, which is most probable, or he will not reply in time. If he does reply, and it is a point on which he will simply sign a letter prepared for him by Bernstein and White, I think that he, as Bernstein, will find unexpected virtues in VIII (2)(a) to which he will attach importance. He will argue that the main objective of the Fund is to achieve convertibility, an obligation not to be lightly undertaken, and still less to be lightly thrown over, either in the case of a country whose currency is a key currency in international trade, or in the case of other countries. One purpose of the drawing power provided by the Fund is to enable convertibility to be undertaken and maintained, and the waiver conditions give the Fund discretion to make those drawing powers somewhat elastic in a good case. In other words it would not make sense of the international obligation if a country could depart from that obligation, possibly after having obtained all the facilities of the Fund, without consulting the executive instrument charged with supervising the obligation. He would urge that it must be assumed, if the scheme is to work at all, that the Fund management will have a sense of reality and that it will not withhold its approval in a proper case.

168

And also that there is nothing to make it necessary for a country to put its reserves in danger before it approaches the Fund for approval for temporary or partial or conditional restrictions. In this sense the reciprocal responsibilities of the Fund and the member are not essentially different from IV (5)(c)(ii). It is true that the Fund is obliged to concur if the change in the exchange rate is required to correct a fundamental disequilibrium, but we wisely and judiciously have not attempted to determine the criteria for a fundamental disequilibrium, or to say who, in the end, judged whether the situation had arisen.

All this is pretty plausible. Indeed, if we could be dead certain about the management of the Fund, there is, on balance, a good deal to be said for it on merits. Here, however, we open up a misgiving which we can scarcely make public. The management of the Fund might be partially staffed by pedants, like some of the members of the present Federal Reserve Board, fortified by American lawyers, or at best might be both geographically and in understanding, remote from the real difficulties that were overtaking a country or a group of countries. *We* might, for example, have an instinctive feeling that a depression was coming, or might feel that the European situation as a whole was so overcast that it was essential for us, even at the cost of disturbance to international trade, to build up our liquid reserves. That is your argument of the war chest, but I cannot believe that either Morgenthau or White could possibly appreciate the European instincts that are contained in those two words.

On the other hand I agree with you that we ought to go on record with Morgenthau about the obvious conflict of intention between VIII (2)(a) and VIII (4)(a) and (b), and about the gap in VIII (4)(b).

For this purpose I think it would be sufficient to say that this situation would create such obvious difficulties that before the Fund came into being the necessary steps would have to be taken to put the matter beyond reasonable dispute.

I should have thought that a unilateral declaration by us in these terms, which did not flurry Morgenthau by making him consider the great awkwardness of an amendment at this stage, might serve our purpose best. If this rather subtle point is taken in Parliament, then the Chancellor at any rate has the answer that he has put the British Government on record about it, and he will not be handicapped by a reply from Morgenthau.

Moreover, if, as we now think possible, Congress may make some amendments, then those amendments can only be dealt with I believe by a further Conference, and once one amendment has been accepted of course the doors are open. We could make up our minds what amendments we wanted without attempting to re-write the draft, for none of us could survive another Bretton Woods!

W.E.

24 January 1945

From SIR WILFRID EADY, *25 January 1945*

Dear Maynard,

The mystery of what happened about VIII (4)(v) and VIII (2)(a) is, I am afraid, insoluble. The crucial time was the 11th July. At that time the British Delegation was divided functionally so that Brooks was looking after the general stuff, and except for seeing us anxiously running through the corridors, had very little knowledge of what we were doing. The general documents, both our own Delegation documents submitted to the Americans, and the American Secretariat documents, give no clue. Everything important at that stage was being referred to an Ad Hoc Committee, and then the records simply gave up the unequal struggle. For 5 days there is silence in his documents!

The only exhibit I have been able to obtain which I should like to have back is the attached.[38]

You, I think, were tied up at that time with some other anxiety. The crucial question is, when I gave you Dennis Robertson's note of the 11th July, did you tell me that Dennis and the Americans and the Canadians could go to hell, or did you say 'Oh, all right then'. You think you said the former. Dennis thinks you said the latter. And I cut the inglorious figure of being completely blank, except that I do know that whatever you did say became a directive.

I am very sorry to be so useless even in my own defence. The trouble was that at that time I was terribly preoccupied with the issues in IV (4)(b). I had always assumed that every signatory country would make it an offence against domestic law for its residents to deal in exchanges outside the approved parities. When the Americans said that they would not do that I was very shocked, because it seemed to me that under our ordinary procedure for supporting the exchanges by leaving an open order with the Bank's agents in New York, if there was any evidence that our exchange was moving to a discount on an individual transaction of importance, or possibly as a temporary trend, the agent would use the reserves to support the exchange. I was fighting against the soothing suggestion of the Americans that if they made black market transactions unenforceable they would in fact have done the trick, and that combined with their own *de facto* practice of buying and

---

[38] Not printed [Ed.].

selling gold freely, was enough. In the end, after delivering a horrified lecture to the Americans about New York being the Black Market centre of the world, you thought I was making too much bother about the point, and that as the Americans would not in any case do anything to meet us we had better do the best we could. Out of that wreckage I saved IV (4)(a) which of course means nothing.

I am not reviving this *infandum dolorem* merely in self-defence. I think the material point is that if the Gods are propitious, and we get a chance of making any amendments, we must attack IV (4)(b) as well as VIII (2)(a). I suspect we must also attack the charges under V (8)(c), for if a country is genuinely struggling with adversity, and is looking to the Fund to help it through, the load mounts up rather steadily. We must therefore pray for sweet reasonableness on the part of Morgenthau in going to meet Congressional criticism.

Yours,

25 January 1945   WILFRID

From L. C. ROBBINS, *17 January 1945*

Dear Maynard,

Thank you very much for sending me your draft letter on the interpretation of Article VIII of the Bretton Woods Agreement. I have been reviewing the various papers which have been circulated on this point during the last few days, and have a number of observations to make.

(1) To begin with a personal matter—the position of Dennis Robertson. As you know, I was engaged on other matters during the Conference; and in the later stages, in common with the rest of us, was not in a position to follow closely the evolution of drafting in sections other than my own. But I have certain distinct recollections which, without clearing up the mystery, do, I think, go far to vindicate the propriety of Dennis's conduct. I recollect very distinctly that, some days before the end of the Conference, he informed me that you were very worried about the line the Canadians were taking on the question of convertibility, and had even suggested that this might be a breaking point. He said that negotiations were still proceeding and that, although he saw great difficulty, he did not think that we should yet abandon hope. Some days after I enquired again what was happening, and he said that he thought a suitable compromise had been reached, but that he had been unable to see you, and was, therefore, not in a position to close with the Drafting Committee. Later on, either on the afternoon of that day or next morning, we met and he said that, although he himself had not been able to see you, the point had been put to you by Eady and satisfactorily

cleared. The nature of our meeting, which, so far as I remember, was outside the Committee Room, was not such as to enable me to enquire what the nature of the compromise was. But it was clear to me that Dennis was completely sure of your concurrence.[39]

All this is very unimportant at this time of day. But I think it does establish that there was genuine misunderstanding somewhere—very comprehensible in the appalling circumstances under which we were working—and that Dennis did, at every stage, imagine that he was acting with your authority. It must, therefore, have been as much of a shock to him to discover that you did not agree with the interpretation he put on Article VIII as it was to you to discover that he took a different view.

(2) Coming to questions of the policy, I am inclined to agree with you that it would be *desirable* that we should have the right to impose exchange restrictions once we have ceased to be eligible to draw on the Fund—although, for reasons given below, I do not regard it as *essential*. And, while I think there might be difficulty in getting the Canadians to accept this view (for I certainly remember Rasminsky expressing himself strongly in the other direction before the controversy had been raised in committee), I do not believe that the Americans would find it so difficult to swallow; for, in the outline of the proposed Commercial Convention which Hawkins has given us orally, there is mention, under the balance of payments let-out, of the possibility of either regulating imports or rationing exchange. Thus, Article XXII, paragraph 1, provides that 'in any period when the Monetary Fund determines that a country is in serious balance of payments difficulty, it may limit either *the exchange made available in payment for goods* (my italics) or the imports of goods'. (A.S. (U.S.) (44) 2nd Meeting.) It is true that this invokes the authority of the Monetary Fund; but if we were negotiating with a clean sheet I should have thought it would have been quite easy to shift the emphasis to some sort of objective test.

(3) But, of course, we are not negotiating with a clean sheet, and I do not think that our position is altogether a strong one. Quite apart from the fact that, as you point out, the Americans will strongly resist any alteration of the text at this juncture, they could point out that we did not claim the liberty in question in earlier discussions. Paragraph 38 of the Clearing Union, which states that 'in any case it should be laid down that members of the Union should not allow or suffer among themselves any restrictions on the disposal of receipts arising out of current trade or "invisible income"' might well be taken to be evidence of a different frame of mind. Furthermore, I

---

[39] Professor Robbins' diary from Bretton Woods for the period was silent on the issue in question, although there are repeated references to the general difficulties of drafting during the period and the yeoman services of Robertson. [Ed.]

am bound to say that I think, myself, the imposition of import restrictions, which is not touched by the Bretton Woods document, and which certainly loomed large in our own domestic discussions, is a sufficient and effective instrument, and one, moreover, which is more in line with our own practice than the imposition of exchange restrictions would be.

(4) Hence, I believe that it ought to be possible to meet public debate with insistence on the sufficiency of this instrument. I have seen your note to James [Meade] on this matter, but I cannot altogether share your view. I cannot believe that there is any objection to the Chancellor insisting very heavily on our freedom to impose import restrictions. Nor do I believe that Hawkins or the State Department would be in the least embarrassed if the Chancellor went out of his way to say that, in any commercial conversations that we entered into, we should certainly insist on reserving the right to impose such restrictions if we were in balance of payments difficulties. On the contrary, indeed, it has always seemed to me that unless somehow or other this point could be made plain in the House of Commons debates on the monetary scheme, we are fighting with one arm tied behind our backs. For, confronted with the scarce currency provision in the monetary draft, the critics of the scheme are apt to reply that this may be an efficient safeguard against general unbalance of the world *vis-à-vis* America, but it is far from being a safeguard against particular unbalance on our own part *vis-à-vis* the rest of the world. And, unless we make it plain that we shall insist on a let-out on this score in other instruments, they are in a position to make debating points which, if our full intentions were divulged, would not be open to them.

(5) On the tactics of the negotiations with Morgenthau, not having recently sniffed the atmosphere, I do not feel particularly competent to express an opinion. I do not feel sure that it would be helpful, at this stage, to put our dissent on public record, as suggested in the last paragraph of your page 2; and I am inclined to the view that perhaps the best thing would be to confine ourselves to telling the Americans privately that, once the Fund is set up, we shall ask for clarification of the ambiguities of Article VIII. I cannot help thinking that, in any case, something will have to be done to put that indefensible muddle in order. But I am not sure that we should admit that we regard it as indefensible while the main issue of the Fund's existence is still in doubt.

James [Meade] tells me that he is writing to you on certain technical issues arising from your annex. If I have understood rightly the points he proposes to make, I am in agreement with him.

I am sending a copy of this to Eady.

Yours sincerely,

L.C.R.

173

Keynes replied to Robbins as follows.

To L. C. ROBBINS, *19 January 1945*

Dear Lionel,

BRETTON WOODS

Thanks for your letter of January 17th.

On your (1), I remember Eady coming to me about some drafting point near the end, but no memory or consciousness that it was this one. If it was, we neither of us, I fancy, understood it.

On your (4), see my further letter to James, of which I enclose a copy. I greatly doubt the advisability of defending Bretton Woods by reference to what is going to be in a commercial agreement. Something it may be necessary to say. But, if you admit that the acceptability of Bretton Woods is linked up with our getting a particular kind of commercial agreement, then surely the opposition is entitled to say, which is just what they are wanting and trying to say, that the two things must be taken together.

On your (5), I am much attracted by what you advise here. I will put it up for further consideration. Nevertheless, it does seem to me extremely awkward for the Chancellor to have to tell the House that he does not understand the meaning of clauses so fundamental as those which determine our obligation of convertibility, and that he is signing something ambiguous or meaningless, in the hope that, at a later date, the meaning attached to it will be one which he will find satisfactory. It is the extreme importance of the obligation of convertibility, at any rate in the public mind, which makes it difficult to fluff the point in a way which would be quite easy on something more trivial.

Yours ever,
[copy initialled] K

P.S. Since writing the above, I have been reading the Minutes of the 8th meeting of the Hawkins Conversations. This seems to make it even more difficult than I thought to refer to what may or may not be in a commercial agreement. In some respects Hawkins appears to go beyond Bretton Woods, though in other respects to fall short of it. For example, Article XXII appears to provide that, if the Monetary Fund agrees that a country is confronted with serious balance of payments difficulties, it can then take action, either on the line of quantitative regulation or of exchange restriction, or both, apparently, for all that is said to the contrary, at its own discretion. This would be permitted on my interpretation of Bretton Woods, but on Bernstein's only with the agreement of the Fund. I am afraid we get into difficulties if we try to relate Bretton Woods to the problematical wording of a commercial agreement which does not yet exist.

After receiving the comments, Keynes re-drafted the letter to Mr Morgenthau to the form in which it finally went to Washington under the Chancellor's signature.

To H. MORGENTHAU, *1 February 1945*

My dear Mr Morgenthau,

A question has arisen of the interpretation of a certain clause in the Final Act of Bretton Woods which is causing me some difficulty and perplexity. It arises out of a possible conflict or inconsistency between Section 2(a) and Section 4(b) of Article VIII of the Fund. This has been already the subject of some discussion between Lord Keynes and Mr White.

The truth seems to me to be that we have here a piece of ambiguous, and probably inconsistent, drafting, which is not surprising in view of the inevitably hurried work of the last days of the Conference. The result is that no clear meaning emerges; and at some stage this will have to be tidied up. I only wish that the fundamental point at issue was sufficiently trivial for us to overlook it at the present stage. But that unfortunately is not the case. Critics of the plan have already fastened on the point, and I shall probably be expected on a matter so important as the obligation of convertibility to give Parliament some clear guidance as to what obligation in this respect we are being asked to assume.

The essential point is this. The obligation under VIII 4(a) lapses under VIII 4(b)(v) if the member has exhausted his facilities with the Fund. In such circumstances, therefore, he resumes his discretion how far and for how long he shall continue to exhaust his ultimate gold reserves by maintaining *de facto* convertibility. I shall be expected to explain whether this is in any way undone by VIII 2(a), with the result that, in the above circumstances, the discretion is given to the Fund, instead of to the member, to decide up to what point the member shall be required to deplete his gold reserves (which represent a country's iron ration for many purposes, including war) before resuming liberty of action. I do not see how I could advise either the Cabinet or Parliament to be content with a lesser safeguard in this respect than that which appears to be given by VIII 4(b). Nor is it likely, if I gave such advice, that it would be accepted. Furthermore, the critics of the Fund, who I am sorry to say are none too friendly, would be given an opportunity to claim that it was a regrettable deception of public opinion to allow what appears to be a clear safeguard in one sub-section to be taken away by what is a far from clear, and indeed dubious, interpretation of another sub-section of the same clause.

I expect you will share my feeling that, in the case of a text prepared so hastily as the Final Act yet so difficult to amend, it would be a bad and dangerous precedent to seek by subtle interpretation to impose any obligation which did not appear, clearly and unambiguously, on the face of the document, or which had not been understood and accepted by all those who signed it.

Nevertheless an attempt to secure an amendment here and now is, I agree, inadvisable, as well as difficult, since it would open the door to other changes. I propose, therefore, to assure Parliament, when the time comes to seek its judgement, that they are not being asked to accept any obligation beyond what clearly appears on the face of the document, and that we shall have to regard a satisfactory clearing up meanwhile of any possible ambiguity in the drafting as one of the essential conditions prerequisite to our being in a position to accept eventual convertibility under Article XIV.

You may be interested to know that my colleagues have recently been discussing whether or not it would be advisable for the Government to initiate an early discussion in Parliament on the general principles of the Final Act, before Congress has pronounced. We have decided that it will be better that Congress should have spoken before we bring matters to a head here. In any case, the Parliamentary time-table does not leave room for a debate here before the Congressional discussions begin, if our latest news about the date of these is correct. Since a debate here, in which some critical and hostile remarks may be made, simultaneously with the discussions in Congress might be inconvenient or embarrassing, this is an additional reason why it may be better to postpone, though I shall probably be seeing privately some groups of members of Parliament for the purpose of elucidation of the proposals.

With very kind regards,

I am

Yours sincerely,

JOHN ANDERSON

Keynes also raised the issue directly with Mr White.

To H. D. WHITE, *6 February 1945*

My dear Harry,

Since I came back we have been worrying our heads a good deal over the interpretation of Clause 2(a) and Clause 4(b) of Article VIII of the Fund, the question, that is to say, which I discussed with you and Bernstein and Luxford. The Chancellor has written a letter to Mr Morgenthau, since he had to make up his mind just how he would handle this tiresome matter in Parliament. He does not in that letter go into any of the technical or legal conundrums, and doubts if there is any convenient way of settling these at the present time. Nevertheless, it may be better, I think, that I should send you a brief note of some questions which were drawn up here with a view to bringing the issue to a head, if it had been practicable to pursue it along the lines of obtaining an interpretation here and now. I enclose this as an Annex to this letter. Beckett, who was, as you will remember, our legal representative, is of the opinion that no consistent meaning can be extracted from the text which clearly and unambiguously supports either view and that there is nothing whatever to be done except to take some opportunity of re-drafting.

The Chancellor has also been giving thought to the right Parliamentary handling of the Final Act. There would, of course, be no question of putting a formal resolution of approval to Parliament until after Congress has passed on it. There might, however, have been some advantage in having a preliminary debate in the near future, based on a resolution asking for general approval of the principles. This would have met the critics, who are demanding an early opportunity to make their views known. It would also have given Parliament the opportunity to express a general opinion at this stage rather than later on.

On the other hand, this course also had its inconveniences. The Parliamentary time-table would not allow such a debate to come on until after the hearings in Congress have commenced. Highly incomplete reports cabled backwards and forwards might lead to some embarrassment. A debate over here at the present time would meet with heavy attacks and, quite possibly, a very bad Press. Nearly all our responsible economists are, as you know, in Government service, with lips more sealed than would be the case on your side. Thus, there has been a lamentable absence of serious defence of the proposals, not only against the quite crazy ideas of some out-and-out bilateralists, but also against intelligent and responsible comments. The result is that a large part of the Press—not merely the *Daily Express*, but *The Times* and the *Economist*—are either hostile or so luke-warm as to be no use. To correct this we need some time. I myself, as you know, returned to Washington after a very brief visit here last autumn, just when I was thinking of doing a little work of education.

After taking account of the above, and also other, considerations, the final conclusion has been, as you will have learnt from the Chancellor's letter to Mr Morgenthau, not to facilitate a debate during the period of the Congressional discussion. At the same time, this does not mean that we shall remain passive. Indeed, one of the purposes is to allow time for further education. The Chancellor is intending to see groups of members of Parliament in the near future, from whom he will be able to hear comments, and to whom he will be able to give clearer explanations of the nature of the plan. I shall be doing the same with various members of the House of Lords. We shall also, I expect, be talking to some of the more responsible writers in the press. Furthermore, next week I shall be addressing privately a small group of publicists and others at Chatham House. It would, I am sure, have been very unwise to bring matters forward without more preparation on some such lines as the above.

The fact that the Report of the American Bankers has just come out and received a good deal of prominence in our Press will lend further interest to the above impending private discussions. So far the bankers have had a poor Press over here. The general view seems to be, even amongst the critics of Bretton Woods, that they decidedly prefer Bretton Woods. Whatever the effect may be on your side, I am sure that the effect here will be to help the Final Act.

If there is anything you can tell us about the time-table you anticipate for Congress, it would be rather a help in making our own arrangements. In particular, what do you consider the chances of rail-roading the whole Final Act through without having to concede any modification or compromise whatever? I know that it was your original plan to insist that it was a question of taking or leaving the Final Act just as it stands. If you had our procedure, by which nothing more was required than a one-day debate followed by a general resolution, that would be practicable. But one wonders (though perhaps this is only because one knows so little about Congressional procedure) whether that can really be possible if a document is to be examined in Committee line by line and with expert witnesses over a period of weeks. Some reasonable or, at least, plausible suggestions are sure to be made. I am perfectly certain that on this side pure stone-walling tactics would meet with defeat. In similar conditions on this side one would find it inevitable, in order to save the main fabric, to make some concessions here and there, especially on the question of the date at which finality is reached in relation to other parts of the post-war programme.

It might make a difference to our right tactics here, if we knew whether to expect with high probability that Congress will approve the Final Act exactly as it stands, or whether, on the other hand, there will be a further round of international discussion; in other words, another international conference, though one would hope and pray that this would not be with the intention of making any drastic changes or re-opening most of the matters already settled. The great objection to this is that the Bank is really urgent.

One is anxious to form an opinion about this because prospects here might be improved if it were so to turn out on your side that we could take things here slowly and have a little more time. The main force of opposition here is not concerned with technical detail at all, but is based on a preference, and sometimes a fanaticism, for some version, mild or extreme, of bilateralism. Now, in my opinion, most of our bilateralists are just talking nonsense. They are envisaging as practical politics an alternative which simply does not exist. The trouble is that they are able to bring together a variety of sentiments and emotions, whilst many of the countervailing facts it is not easy or convenient to express publicly in a clear and emphatic form. Nevertheless, given time, I am sure that these mists will clear away.

Ever sincerely yours,
[copy initialled] K

P.S. Since writing the above, a fuller report of the Bankers' Proposals has arrived from Brand. One knows that bankers will be bankers. But surely this oversteps even that limit.

I am afraid that they made a considerable mistake in the passage in which they alleged that their proposals 'would be accepted as readily by other countries'. When our press gets hold of the full details, I am sure that their strictures will be

even stronger than they have been so far. There is no school
of thought in this country to which the Bankers' Proposals will
commend themselves. I am sure it would be safe to say that they
would be entirely unacceptable here.

All this makes me feel more strongly that we must not risk
losing the main fabric of the Final Act. You will be the judge
of your own tactics. But it seems to me that in your own minds
you ought not to rule out too strictly the possibility of a further
conference, though I hope some means will be found of keeping
the attendance down to a relatively small number. It seems to
me that, if you could adopt a conciliatory attitude to such
reasonable and responsible criticisms as may be made during the
Congressional discussion and could say that an opportunity
would be taken to consider these and other matters at a further
meeting of the principal nations concerned, you would have a
very much easier tactical task. In practice we could give just as
much or as little attention to the suggestions as they might
deserve. It might be much easier to resist the bankers to the
utmost if it was not necessary to be intransigent and unconci-
liatory on every detail. Mr Morgenthau could make it quite clear
that he would expect to bring back from any further discussions
substantially the same fabric as at present conceived. Certainly
not anything on the lines of the bankers. But he thought some
interesting and useful comments had been made and that he was
sure that all those concerned would be glad of an opportunity
to take advantage of them. When you next came back to
Congress it might be much easier to avoid a prolonged debate
and simply put forward a resolution such as we shall content
ourselves with here. It may be better to face a short delay like
this rather than risk the whole matter,—unless, indeed, the state
of opinion is such that you feel fully confident. If this course
proves inevitable, then I think we ought to get on forthwith in
getting down to the full details in respect of the Bank, so that
there will be no further delay in bringing that into immediate
operation once the two schemes have been approved.

Annex

(1) What obligation, if any, does VIII 2(a) impose on a member in your view? Could you furnish us with a paraphrase of this sub-section which clearly bears the desired interpretation and is held by you to be its legal equivalent?

(2) VIII 4(a) imposes an obligation of convertibility only between *members*, i.e. between central banks or treasuries. Is it held that VIII 2(a) imposes an obligation of convertibility between a member and private individuals (including both its own nationals and others)? If so, how is this consistent with the view that whether a country is or is not exporting capital depends not on isolated, individual transactions, but on its over-all debtor or creditor position?

(3) Does VIII 4(a) impose an obligation of convertibility into *any* currency, whether the national currency of the applicant or not? If the obligation is not thus unlimited, by what words in the text is it limited?

(4) VIII 4(b) expressly relieves a member of certain obligations in certain contingencies. Is it held that VIII 2(a) re-imposes obligations which VIII 4(b) has expressly removed? If so, is there not a direct inconsistency between the two sub-sections?

(5) If a member declares exchange transactions illegal except within a permitted range but has no exchange control, is it free from any obligation under VIII 2(a)?

The Chancellor's letter to Mr Morgenthau continued to have repercussions throughout the spring of 1945. Messrs Brand and Opie met with Messrs Bernstein and Luxford on 27 February and 1 March. As a result of these, the origins of the misunderstanding became clearer. The issue had never been openly and fully thrashed out at Bretton Woods, owing to lack of time. Keynes himself had not seen the final text when he agreed to it, as it had not emerged from the drafting committee in time for the circulation of a full text. The state in which matters remained is best summed up by Mr Morgenthau's eventual reply to the Chancellor's letter and Keynes's comment on it.

From H. MORGENTHAU *to* SIR JOHN ANDERSON, *8 June 1945*

My dear Sir John,

This is in reply to your letter of February 1, 1945, inquiring about a possible inconsistency between Section 2(a) and Section 4(b) of Article VIII of the Fund.

I can see no inconsistency whatever in these sections. Article VIII Section 2 is designed to assure people engaged in international business that no member of the Fund will prevent their being paid for the goods they export and for other current obligations. The section states, subject to specified qualifications, that 'no member shall, without the approval of the Fund, impose restrictions on the making of payments and transfers for current international transactions'. With this provision international business can proceed without the restrictions that would result from the imposition of exchange controls on current transactions.

The exceptions to the general principle of Section 2 are enumerated very clearly and in unmistakable terms. If a currency should be declared scarce, a member may impose restrictions in accordance with Article VII, Section 3(b); and any country covered by the transitional arrangements may during the transitional period maintain and adapt to changing circumstances wartime restrictions on payments and transfers for current international transactions. No other exceptions to the general principle of Section 2 are specified because, I believe, no other exceptions were intended.

Section 4 of Article VIII deals with a different problem. Under this section each member (or its central bank) is obligated to buy balances of its currency held by another member (or its central bank) if the balances have been recently acquired as a result of current transactions or the conversion of these balances is needed for making payments for current transactions. There then follow the conditions under which the obligation does not apply, all of the exceptions being specifically listed.

In our view Section 2 and Section 4 have different obligations to meet different problems. Section 2 is concerned to see that an exporter is assured of payment for his exports in his own currency. Under Section 4, the exporter no longer owns the foreign currency, for it has been acquired by his central bank. Under Section 2, the currency represents the accruing proceeds of current trade and is being presently acquired or will be acquired in the near future by a private trader. Under Section 4, the currency balances have already been acquired by a central bank, and they may represent balances resulting from recently completed transactions or even balances long accumulated from past transactions.

The financial obligations contemplated by the two sections are of a different order. By their nature, the sums involved in Section 2 are moderate in amount; the sums involved in Section 4 may be enormous in amount, for they can include the accumulated balances of years. As a practical matter, a country can be asked not to restrict payments and transfers to traders for current transactions. On the other hand, the burden of converting large accumulated balances held by foreign central banks may be too great for a country when it cannot secure the help of the Fund.

These are the reasons why restrictions on current payments may not be imposed without the consent of the Fund except in the two cases specified in Section 2, although the convertibility of balances held by foreign central banks can be restricted when a country no longer has access to the Fund and under the other conditions specified in Section 4.

As you are aware the distinction between these sections of Article VIII do not become significant until the end of the transitional period and may not be of consequence then.

We have explained these points in greater detail some time ago in conversations with Mr Brand and Mr Opie.

Sincerely yours,

H. MORGENTHAU JR

To SIR WILFRID EADY, *21 June 1945*

This all turns on the meaning of the phrase 'impose restrictions'. If the Chancellor is to reply to this letter, I suggest that he should stick to this point, as in the draft below.

But, quite apart from this, I agree with you that the U.S. Treasury doctrine is unworkable. The letter repeats what Bernstein had explained to Brand, namely that Section 4 allows a country which has lost access to the Fund to block all existing balances absolutely but it must continue to provide foreign exchange for all future current transactions. Coupled with the resumption of import licensing which we should no doubt take care to retain in case of such an eventuality, this is probably all the protection *we* could need. All the same it makes no sense, regarded as an interpretation of Section 2.

184

A reply, if desired, could include some such passage as the following:

It all depends on the interpretation given to the words 'no member shall make restrictions on the making of payments and transfers for current international transactions'. Our interpretation is that these words forbid a member to impose legal restrictions which would prevent a holder of its currency from spending it to pay for goods or to buy any foreign currency, provided the price of the foreign currency is within the permitted range and the currency he offers in exchange represents the accruing proceeds of current trade. Section 2 does not mean, in our view (to give a concrete example), that the U.S. monetary authority is under an obligation to buy for dollars any foreign currency arising out of a current transaction which may be offered to it or to provide in return for dollars any foreign currency which a trader may desire to cover a current transaction. In our view the obligation of the U.S. monetary authority to provide foreign currencies arises solely out of Section 4.

I agree with you that the question cannot arise immediately. It may be that there is no substantial difference between us. You can rely on me not to raise the matter unnecessarily. But if it is necessary to allay doubts, I may have to tell Parliament that if, at some future time, the question were to arise in any practical way, we should ask the Governing Body for an interpretation to the effect that the only obligation of a member's monetary authority to provide foreign currency is that which arises out of Article VIII, Section 4, under the rubric *Convertibility of foreign held balances*.

[copy initialled] K

The first few months of 1945, as noted above, also saw informal briefings in London preparing the ground for the eventual debate of the Bretton Woods proposals. Keynes set out the proposed tactics in a letter to R. H. Brand early in February.

From a letter to R. H. BRAND, *8 February 1945*

For the last week or two I have been on the point of sending you a letter of report about the attitude here to Bretton Woods. But something fresh kept on arising for which it was worth while to wait, and you will now, I think, have had most of the essential news by telegram.

The letter to Morgenthau from the Chancellor will have reached you for delivery before now. I enclose the pendant to this, namely, a letter from myself to Harry White (and also a carbon for your own use). You will see that the Annex of technical questions, which in an early draft was to be attached to the letter to Morgenthau, is now included with this letter to Harry. You will see that I have also ventured to stray a little into the realm of tactics.

There is here a bit of a dilemma. So far as the Bank is concerned, it is obviously essential to start it as soon as possible. On the other hand, without wanting to make any radical changes, we all think that it would be helpful, if there was time, to take another look at the actual drafting of the Fund. After all, the obligation of convertibility is a very serious affair, and it is exceedingly awkward to bring a version before Parliament which is largely unintelligible and probably inconsistent on this vital point. If, however, this point stood by itself, I think we should leave it alone. But there are two other considerations.

The first one is whether Harry really has a sound hope of thinking that he can rail-road all this through Congress without conceding a comma. To us at a distance it looks, in the present state of Congressional opinion, exceedingly improbable. If this is so, we feel that the wisest thing, in both our interests, is that he should not be too intransigent. If, without promising to concede anything vital, he could tell Congress that we should all have a look at it again, he might then be able to bring it back a little simplified perhaps, but essentially unchanged, into a better atmosphere. One is afraid that if he and his master are unduly undiplomatic they might lose the whole thing. We are all the more clear about that after getting your summary of the Bankers' Proposals. They seem to have slipped a good deal since I was in Washington. The proposal for the American representation on the Bank, which would bring every important transaction straight into American politics, seems to us one of the silliest and wickedest things ever. Moreover, it seems also their idea to bring under the same régime the exchanges of all the countries involved without giving these countries the slightest motive for coming in. All this shows what I have long expected, namely, that no reliance whatever can be put on those bankers, and that we are very much more happily placed with Morgy and Harry.

The second reason is that, just as one more stage in the evolution of the Fund might help Harry with Congress, so undoubtedly a little delay would help us here. I should say that the atmosphere is a little better than it was. But a good deal of education is still necessary. The Chancellor, I think, has reason to congratulate himself on the turn things have taken. He thought it would be dangerous not to offer the critics in the Cabinet an immediate, semi-non-committal debate, since, if we wait until Congress has pronounced, it is really impossible for us to back out. Thus, to put off as long as that might be deemed in doubtful faith. His colleagues, however, under the leadership of the Prime Minister, decided that it would, for a variety of reasons, be better to wait until after Congress had spoken. The result was, therefore, exactly what the Chancellor wanted, namely, that he should have given an opportunity for a debate to the critics and that they should have rejected it.

Now we are released to go ahead with an educational campaign.

The Chancellor saw Pethick-Lawrence a day or two ago and will shortly be meeting a group of Labour M.P.s privately. He will also see the Birmingham group led by Hannon, and probably also another group collected by Hammersley. Meanwhile, I am free to do much the same in the House of Lords. I shall be seeing a group assembled by Nathan and, either at the same time or separately, some from the opposite benches, such as Balfour of Burleigh. Next month I shall be talking privately on the subject to a group at Chatham House, and, in due course I shall talk to Crowther and other journalists.

I feel perfectly confident about the final outcome. But nothing happens right unless one takes trouble.

Keynes also briefed the Chancellor for the meetings with M.P.s.

NOTES FOR THE CHANCELLOR ON BRETTON WOODS

(1) Members might be interested to have brief information about the procedure contemplated in Washington. This is outlined in the attached telegram.[40] Copies of the bankers' counterproposals have now been supplied to the Press over here and could be made available to any other interested (we could have a few copies in the room).

(2) The Bank for Reconstruction deserves more lime-light than it has yet received in this country. It achieves two purposes of the first importance.

(a) It enables American loans to become available, which might in the limit approach £2,000 million in all, which are entirely untied and are available for expenditure in the cheapest market. Without the Bank it is rather likely that American loans, particularly to Europe, will be tied to expenditure in U.S.A. and will, therefore, be of no assistance towards reaching equilibrium.

(b) The Bank is the only instrumentality yet projected for providing reconstruction funds to Europe as distinct from relief through UNRRA and otherwise. There is no reason why the Bank should not be in effective operation reasonably in time for this purpose. Without this provision individual countries will be put entirely in the financial power of the United States and will have to pick their way piecemeal as best they can.

In addition to these purposes, the Bank provides methods and standards for international loans guaranteed by Governments, which should be relatively free from the great abuses which attended such loans between the wars.

(3) In the case of the Fund, too much attention has been paid to the obligations into which we enter and too little to the important safeguards which it secures for us. It is of great

‖   [40] Not printed.

importance that we should have secured these safeguards before entering on negotiations with U.S.A. in respect of post-war finance. In particular, the following safeguards deserve emphasis:

(*a*) During the transitional period we retain our full liberty of action.

(*b*) Freedom from exchange rigidity is secured, whilst we are protected from competitive currency depreciations and other objectionable practices, which we are most unlikely to adopt ourselves, but from which we have suffered severely in the past through their adoption in other quarters.

(*c*) The scarce currency clause commits the United States to finding a way out in the event of the balance of trade turning obstinately in her favour, whether from her failing to maintain full employment or for any other reason. The business of finding a solution is placed clearly on her shoulders, and she formally abjures the right to drain gold out of the world in such circumstances.

It would be a great thing to get all this settled in an atmosphere of equal influence and authority and with relative freedom from the pressure politics which may very easily ensue if we leave all these matters unsettled until after the war and the period of firm alliance is over.

(4) The bankers' counter-proposals are objectionable from our point of view in two respects. They quite deliberately throw all the international loans to be made by the Bank into the American political arena, encouraging Congressmen to express opinions and to advise the American representatives on every separate occasion, so as to take away both from independent representatives and from the administration the power of decision. This is a shameless pandering for Congressional support by making a concession which the bankers well know to be disgracefully wicked. The bankers also throw into the melting pot all the above safeguards, implying that they will be re-drafted in what form we do not know, but without any of

the inducements and aids to sustaining them which are provided by the Fund in the shape of a substantial volume of credits, thereby making it most unlikely that the other countries which participated in the Bretton Woods discussion would come in.

(5) The question is raised whether this agreement commits us prematurely and unduly to a multilateral system of international trtading. The agreement itself relates to currency and not to those matters which would be covered by a commercial agreement. Our commitments at this stage, therefore, relate entirely to currency matters and not to commercial matters. This does not mean, however, that the agreement does not point the way to a multilateral policy. It certainly does. Nevertheless, it leaves us with a free hand in this respect during the transitional period. There are many reasons why, thereafter, a system of discriminatory blocking is quite impracticable and seriously to the disadvantage of our exporters. If a non-discriminatory trade and currency policy breaks down in the long run, we shall all have to think again, and we shall all be free to do so. But it would be an entirely different matter to fall back by common agreement on some alternative and probably inferior policy after having tried what is most to the advantage of the world, than in a cowardly spirit to assume defeat from the first and embark on a policy likely gravely to lower the standard of life in this country in the period immediately after the war.

(6) Not only would the full bilateral policy be a bad policy in itself, but it would also involve most serious consequences as follows:

(a) We should have to repudiate the Mutual Aid Agreement which we have signed with the United States, by which it is agreed that the ultimate settlement of lend lease shall not be such as to cause any burden on trade. In other words, the present satisfactory basis of lend lease would be destroyed, and we should become liable for payments in the equivalent of cash, from which at present we are free.

(*b*) We should have to denounce our existing commercial treaties with U.S. and a number of other countries.

(*c*) This, however, would not be enough by itself. We should have to induce the countries with which we proposed to enter into bilateral arrangements to denounce their treaties with the United States.

(7) The proportion of the world which would be prepared to gang up with us against the United States along these lines would not be large. We should be extremely lucky if it covered anything like 25 per cent of our trade.

(8) We should throw Canada economically, and perhaps even politically, into the arms of the United States. Canada attaches enormous importance to our giving the multilateral approach at least a serious trial.

(9) A satisfactory economic and social settlement of the post-war world depends above all on our working intimately with the United States. An attempted policy of self-sufficiency by which we ruptured our trade relations with a great part of the world would mean that this intimacy of collaboration must necessarily come to an end. The immediate effect on the standard of life in this country scarcely bears thinking about, and the political, economic and other reactions throughout the Empire and the world at large would be such that surely no responsible person could contemplate them.

(10) The idea that there is some bilateral system which would weld the Empire more closely together is a pure delusion. Nothing would be more likely to break up the economic relations within the Empire and destroy the primacy of London in the sterling area system than a wanton rupture with the currency and commercial systems of North America before there was any proof that the alternative system, so much better for all concerned if it would work, must necessarily break down.

(11) No-one can feel confidence that the United States will solve the problem of maintaining full employment over the next five or eight years. The Administration and its advisers are,

however, acutely conscious of the problem in a way they have never been before and are deeply concerned with finding a solution. It may be they will half fail and half succeed. We cannot rule out the possibility that an acute international situation may arise. If so, we shall all have to take counsel together. But it would appear to be a complete delusion to suppose that we in any way save ourselves from the consequences of such a situation by refusing to enter into the Bretton Woods Agreement. So far from aggravating our difficulties, this plan makes at least some provision for mitigating them. The scarce currency clause in particular permits us to return to discriminatory practices against U.S.A. as soon as they have failed to solve their balance of trade problem. There appears to be no particular in which the Bretton Woods plan puts us in a worse position in the event of severe unemployment in U.S.A., and some important respects in which it protects us against such a contingency.

(12) In short, it would be a counsel of madness to organise an economic and financial rupture with the United States and a large part of the rest of the world immediately at the end of hostilities, when we shall be in the weakest position ever to sustain a position of economic isolation and attempted self-sufficiency, along with the very few others whom we might be able to persuade to join us in so futile an enterprise.

15 February 1945   KEYNES

At the end of March, after the series of meetings was over for the time being, Keynes concluded 'that there is no steam in the opposition and, if the plan is accepted by Congress, it is safe to assume that it will be accepted by Parliament'.

As the plans moved through Congress, Keynes commented on the results both domestically and to his American counterparts.

The American in question was E. M. Bernstein. He had written to Keynes on correcting an earlier attribution to him by Keynes of a particular clause in the Articles of Agreement as follows.

From a letter from E. M. BERNSTEIN, *15 May 1945*

I have worked rather closely with White on the Fund and the Bank since he first began to put his thoughts on paper. There were innumerable meetings of the Treasury group and the American technical group to discuss the projects White prepared. But I can think of nothing of any consequence in the two projects the Treasury presented that didn't come from White's own fertile mind.

Because White gave me the task of carrying much of the discussion, there seems to be an exaggerated notion of my part in the work. In fact, I was only a Levite serving the Priests in their holy work.

I have been attending the House Committee hearings regularly. You will enjoy reading the Record. Keynes is quoted more at these hearings than Mohammed is in Mecca. Yesterday, one of the Congressmen quoted you, as follows: 'I believe Keynes said that in the end we are all dead.'

White did a remarkably good job in his testimony. His answers were clear and to the point. He was exceptionally convincing on the scarce currency question. Throughout his testimony he was careful to say nothing that might in any way add to your difficulties in Parliament. He was the special target of the Keynes quotations. He supported and defended them, and I think I can say you both came off with highest honors.

Keynes replied.

To E. M. BERNSTEIN, *29 May 1945*

My dear Levite,

Thank you for your most charming letter of May 15th. I will only comment in reply that perhaps Priests cannot get on without Levites any more than the Queen Bee without her workers. On the particular question of the re-purchase clauses I was not so much thinking of the original conception as the much more elaborate working out of them which caused them to take their final shape in the eventual plan.

The Record of the House Committee hearings reached me about the same time as your letter, and I had, as you may suppose, quite a lot of fun in looking them through. I thought White managed magnificently and I could only feel apologetic that he was so much pestered and, indeed, bombarded with my

193

name and words. He certainly said nothing which could be of the least embarrassment in the subsequent discussions on this side, and I was, indeed, very grateful to him for the handsome way in which the whole difficult issue was handled.

And how much I enjoyed Mr O'Neal's evidence, with his refrain from time to time that the bankers are lousy with money!

Well, it is a great triumph for all of you in the Treasury to have got the Plans through so triumphantly when it came to the final show-down. I do not know quite how seriously we have to take the amendments which were apparently the price of it. In part they seem to us entirely unexceptionable, but there are certain aspects of them we do not altogether like. Let me take the four of them in order.

(1) That the American Directors of the two organisations should be the same man is obviously a domestic matter where we have no right to object. All the same, it seems to me a thoroughly bad idea. Different qualities are required, and the range of activities of the two would be widely divergent. It must be doubtful, therefore, whether one man can efficiently perform both functions. I should like to see the Board of the Fund composed of cautious bankers, and the Board of the Bank of imaginative expansionists.

(2) The proposal to make the American Director subject to an advisory council is also, of course, a purely domestic matter, to which we cannot object. Some of us, however, had been hoping that the officials of the two bodies would, in the course of time, come to regard themselves as primarily international officials, taking a world, objective outlook, and only where clearly necessary grinding their own national axes. So one would have wished to minimise, rather than maximise, their national representative character and their position as delegates from outside authorities. However, if there is to be such a council, one would be greatly comforted if, as I gather is suggested, it consists of the heads of the American Departments concerned and is not of a political or Congressional character.

(3) The interpretation that the Bank is free to make stabili-

sation loans is entirely unexceptionable from our point of view. It is just how we have always understood it.

(4) I understand from a telegram recently received that there was a fourth amendment, put forward by Wolcott, to the effect that Congress interprets the Agreements as 'not authorising the Fund to use its resources for relief, construction development or long-term stabilisation or for a large or sustained outflow of capital'. We assume that this does not mean any actual amendment of the text of the Final Act, but merely gives the sense in which the American representation would interpret certain provisions in any case in which a doubt were to arise. If the Wolcott amendment is to be regarded as no more than high-lighting what is already written in Article XIV (1), clearly there is no harm in that. If, however, the amendment were taken literally as limiting the rights of a country in using the Fund, it would, I should have thought, be impracticable. It is impossible to ear-mark money, and when a country, which in fact is in the course of reconstruction or getting straight after the war, uses the Fund, it is impossible to say in any particular case exactly to what purpose that particular dollop of money is devoted. Take, for example, the case of Greece or of Poland.

Pigou has just called my attention to a passage in Marshall's Evidence before the Gold and Silver Commission—Q. 10,006, more than fifty years ago (have we yet asked more than 10,000 questions about Bretton Woods?) as follows:—

I think that there is a real, though very slow-moving, tendency for national interests to overrule provincial interests, and international interests to overrule national, and I think the time will come at which it will be thought as unreasonable for any country to regulate its currency without reference to other countries as it would be to have signalling codes at sea which took no account of the signalling codes at sea of other countries.

So once more we may hope the old man has been right, with not much more of a time-lag than it is reasonable to expect, at least in international affairs.

Ever sincerely yours,
[copy initialled] K

When the Bretton Woods Bill passed the House of Representatives, Keynes wrote a longer comment for his colleagues.

BRETTON WOODS

By accepting a fairly drastic re-draft of the Bill, the U.S. Treasury have successfully effected a compromise with the bankers and with the Republican dissidents, led by Congressman Wolcott, which has enabled them to carry it through triumphantly with only three extreme die-hards left in the opposition. Since the bankers and the Republicans now express themselves as satisfied, we can safely assume that the Bill will pass through the Senate in the same form and perhaps with less delay than was previously expected.

In the Press comments and in the Weekly Economic Summary from Washington (258 Saving) the revisions in the Bill are regarded as no more than window-dressing to save the face of the bankers and to obtain the withdrawal of Mr Wolcott's opposition, whilst avoiding the necessity of a further international conference. Mr Morgenthau took the same line in his Press communiqué, declaring that

The amendments made by the Committee are not of a character which will require another conference. They are constructive, chiefly clarifying in character, and are acceptable in the Treasury.*

This seems to me a correct description of the bulk of the amendments, but there is one of them which requires more careful attention. The following is an attempt to analyse what the changes in the Bill amount to in practice.

I

(1) It is provided that the United States shall appoint the same individual to be their representative as a Governor of the Fund

---

* Sever 990 tells us that the U.S. Treasury fought the amendments; Remac 453 that they drafted them. Probably both statements are true.

and as a Governor of the Bank. This was to meet the view of the bankers that there should be one rather than two institutions. An examination of the actual text shows, however, that the least possible harm has been done. The above provision applies to the Governors representing the U.S. and not to their Executive Directors. The Governors of the two Institutions are, so to speak, ornamental personages, who receive no salary and only function on the occasions, which may be no more than once a year, when the Board of Governors representing the whole number of the United Nations is assembled. The operative officials in both Institutions are the Executive Directors. The American Executive Director for the Fund will be a different individual from the American Executive Director for the Bank. Here, therefore, there has been no more than window-dressing.

(2) There is to be set up 'a National Advisory Council on International Monetary and Financial Problems'. The bankers had suggested that the American representatives on the two Institutions should be subject to a Committee directly responsible to Congress. This point also has been met in a harmless way. The National Advisory Council will not be of a political or Congressional character,* but will consist of the Secretary of the Treasury as Chairman, the Secretary of State, the Secretary of Commerce, the Chairman of the Federal Reserve System and the Chairman of the Export–Import Bank. It will be concerned with the general, external financial policy of the United States in all its aspects. That the U.S. should set up such a body is obviously unobjectionable, is a matter properly within their domestic control and may be entirely for the good. No harm, therefore, done here. The Council has to make a report to the President and to Congress as least every six months 'with respect to the participation of the United States in the Fund and the Bank' and shall also make special reports as to whether the Fund and the Bank are achieving the purposes for which they

---

* Sever 990 tells us that the U.S. Treasury consider the avoidance of direct Congressional representation to have been a great triumph.

were established, the first of which shall be made within two years.

(3) The third amendment provides that the American representative on the Bank shall ask the Executive Board of the Bank, as soon as it has been brought together, to give an official interpretation whether the Bank has authority 'to make or guarantee loans for programmes of economic reconstruction and the reconstruction of monetary systems, including long-term stabilisation loans'. If it is ruled that the Bank has no such powers, then the Americans will ask that the constitution be amended so that it has such powers. There can, however, be no doubt that an interpretation should be given in accordance with the American wishes. Whilst the language was deliberately made obscure because at that time Mr Wolcott took the opposite of the view he now holds as to what would commend itself to Congress, there can be no doubt that the Bank both has, and was intended to have, the necessary authority. We could without hesitation support the Americans, both in the matter of interpretation and also in voting for a change in the constitution, should it come to that.

(4) The fourth amendment similarly requires an interpretation, or alternatively an amendment, in relation to the Fund. This involves much greater difficulties, and I reserve the discussion of it for the next section of this paper.

(5) The only other change of any apparent significance relates to the obtaining and furnishing of information asked for by the Fund. The Bill gives the President powers to collect such information, provided that 'no information so acquired shall be furnished to the Fund in such detail that the affairs of any person are disclosed'. No doubt we ourselves will wish to have a similar provision, which seems entirely suitable.

II

The only issue which requires further examination is, therefore, the proposed interpretation relating to the Fund. The American representatives are directed to obtain an official interpretation—
'(i) whether the Fund's authority to use its resources extends beyond current monetary stabilisation operations to afford temporary assistance to members in connection with seasonal, cyclical and emergency fluctuations in the balance of payments of any member for current transactions, and (ii) whether it has authority to use its resources to provide facilities for relief or reconstruction or to meet a large or sustained outflow of capital on the part of any member.'

Let us take (ii) first. V 3 (i) of the Bretton Woods Plan requires that a member desiring to use the Fund's facilities shall represent that its request is for a payment 'consistent with the provisions of this agreement'. XIV (1) states that 'The Fund is not intended to provide facilities for relief or reconstruction or to deal with international indebtedness arising out of the war.'

Now I have little doubt that 'the provisions of this agreement' for the purpose of V 3 (i) did not include *in any obligatory way* XIV (1). That, at least, was not the intention. XIV (1) was meant to be no more than a statement of fact, inasmuch as the resources of the Fund would not be sufficient to deal with relief and reconstruction and war indebtedness, this being a suitable preamble to the rest of Article XIV since it provided a ground why the transitional provisions could be considered reasonable. Nevertheless, XIV (1) obviously lends colour to the proposed American interpretation. One would not be gravely straining the language if the American interpretation were accepted. Moreover, if this was operated in a fairly loose sense, meaning that members must not use the Fund habitually or on a large scale in order to provide for reconstruction and must rather go to the Bank if they want funds for such purposes, the position could be defended on its merits. On the other hand, if it was intended to be interpreted strictly so that no country which was engaged in relief or reconstruction or was re-paying war indebtedness was entitled to use the Fund at all unless these purposes were fully covered from some other source, then it would scarcely be workable. For it is impossible to say of any given transaction whether or not it has arisen in such a context. The meaning might be, of course, that the Fund must not be used to finance a particular transaction for the purchase of capital goods for reconstruction. But that interpretation would be quite inoperative.

I conclude that an interpretation to the effect that, during the transitional period, a country must find other means of financing a substantial adverse balance directly caused by relief or reconstruction imports would not be seriously against the language of the document or seriously objectionable on merits.

The other question, however, gives rise to much more difficulty. Here it is impossible to find any words in the draft which support the American interpretation. On the contrary, the purposes of the Fund, as set forth in Article I, directly imply that it is legitimate to use the Fund when a country is in difficulties, irrespective of the precise cause of those difficulties. For example, I (ii) says that the purposes of the Fund are to facilitate the expansion and balanced growth of international trade; (iii) says that it is to promote exchange stability; (iv) that it is to assist in the establishment of a multilateral system of payments; above all, (v) declares that the purpose of the Fund is

to give confidence to members by making the Fund's resources available to them under adequate safeguards, thus providing them with opportunity to correct maladjustments in their balance of payments without resorting to measures destructive to national or international prosperity.

Clearly these words are much wider than the words in the American Bill, and I do not think that any honest lawyer could affirm that the authority of the Fund is limited in the manner in which the Americans desire that it should be. The only loop-hole would be to regard 'emergency fluctuations' as covering every kind of fluctuation which had not been provided against in advance. Sever 990 reports Bernstein as defending the U.S. proposal on the ground that the use of the Fund in connection with cyclical fluctuations 'envisages the use of these resources for operations which may be of considerable duration'.

Except with the help of this loop-hole, the criterion would be almost impossible to apply in practice. A cyclical fluctuation would arise either as a result of a local boom or inflation not equally shared by the outside world, or by a slump in the outside world not equally shared at home. The criterion would mean, therefore, that a country would only have access to the Fund if it could demonstrate one or other of these states of affairs. Who knows beforehand whether a cyclical fluctuation has begun? Moreover, an unfavourable balance might be partly due to such a cause and partly due to other causes, and no-one in the world could separately quantify the two causes.

Apart, however, from the difficulty of applying the criterion, it is essentially unreasonable. A country may be running an adverse balance because its exchange is too high or because of its domestic policies or because of inadequate import control or because of an unexpected loss of markets for certain of its exports or because of excessive domestic investment. The purpose of the Fund is to give it some elbow room and an interval of time within which to make the necessary adjustments. A country can scarcely be expected to accept convertibility if it only has a right to apply to the Fund in the special set of circumstances which are described by the word 'cyclical'.

Newspaper reports show that the word 'cyclical' was only accepted by the opposition after a struggle by the U.S. Treasury. No doubt, on the part of the bankers this amendment is a subtle attempt to sabotage the Fund by making its resources virtually unavailable. For it might be made to mean that the resources of the Fund are not accessible to anyone unless the Governing Board has declared that there exist cyclical fluctuations (I omit 'seasonal' from the discussion, for this would only apply to very short-term assistance, and I have already mentioned the possibility that a very wide interpretation of 'emergency' might afford a let-out).

Enough has been said to show that this amendment runs the risk of losing the last vestige of the central idea of the Clearing Union and also of destroying the unqualified accessibility of the Fund to members, to which in previous negotiations we have attached fundamental importance.

I conclude, therefore, that we could not honestly interpret the Fund as already meaning what the Americans wish. Nor could we, on merits, vote for an amendment in this sense. If the Americans were to take the line that, unless the amendment is carried, they would withdraw from the Fund, that situation would have to be considered when it arises. There is, however, no hint of this in the Bill. There is no provision in the Bill requiring the United States to withdraw in the event of their failing to get either the interpretation they wish for or, in the absence of that, the necessary amendment.

III

There is, moreover, a further difficulty in the American amendment. If a country is precluded from the use of the Fund on the ground that it is not suffering from a seasonal or cyclical fluctuation, then presumably the provisions of VIII 4(b)(v) come into force. If a country is cut off from the facilities of the Fund whenever it is not suffering from a seasonal or a cyclical fluctuation, then under the above section (unless 'emergency' covers everything else) the convertibility clause is suspended. It follows that the Americans would indeed have poured out the baby with the bath-water and, by limiting access to the Fund, have lost the obligation of convertibility. That is to say, this would have happened unless we were to accept the American interpretation of VIII 2(a), which was the subject of the Chancellor of the Exchequer's letter to Mr Morgenthau, namely, the contention of the Americans that the promise to avoid exchange restrictions on current payments in itself involves a positive obligation of convertibility. It is not necessary that I should enter in this place into that argument all over again. It is necessary, however, to point out that the new provision increases its importance.

It also increases the reasonableness of our view of the matter. The new American version in its entirety would require members to accept convertibility in respect of current payments which were not eligible to be made out of the resources of the Fund; that is to say, they would have to accept the obligation and be at the same time deprived of the means of meeting it. It seems to me likely that a number of countries would object if they understood that they were being asked to accept a convertibility obligation far more comprehensive and less quali-fied than they had previously supposed, whilst at the same time they were being deprived of any access to the Fund for the purpose of satisfying this obligation, except in certain special circumstances.

Nevertheless, it might be fairly easy to give some purely verbal satisfaction to the Americans. The spirit of the Fund is that it should not be used for permanent loans but is to provide a reserve against temporary fluctuations. There would be no harm in an express declaration to this effect, together with authority to the Fund to suggest to a member that it should apply to the Bank for any credits which looked likely to become, or actually had become, of a quasi-permanent character. We have provided already various deterrents against quasi-permanent loans, more particularly the provision which auth-orises a very high rate of interest when a loan has run more than a certain time. But to try to go further than the above and use such limiting words as those of the American interpretation would deprive the facilities of the Fund of any measure of certainty and would, therefore, strike at the whole conception.

IV

It will be observed that in a sense the Americans put themselves at the mercy of the other members of the Fund. They can obtain a favourable interpretation by a bare majority. Failing this, they can only obtain a change in the constitution by a vote supported by three-fifths of the number of members and four-fifths of the number of votes. Thus, there is no harm perhaps in allowing matters to take their course. When the time comes, probably some verbal compromise will be vamped up which may meet the case.

Nevertheless, the Chancellor may be expected to declare his attitude to the American amendments. My advice would be that he should speak in general terms, confirming the American view about the Bank and agreeing that the purpose of the Fund is to meet temporary fluctuations and not to grant permanent credits, though deprecating any attempt, which must be vain, to go behind the causes of a temporary fluctuation. If he is asked to go beyond this, he can point out that it is not for him to prejudge a quasi-judicial decision of the Executive Board. As for what happens if the decision of the Board is unfavourable to the American view, that is a hypothetical question which it would be premature to consider. I think that is probably the line which the U.S. Treasury would wish him to take. If the Fund once gets set up, probably some way round all this will be discoverable.

V

The technique adopted by Congress deserves attention in case we wish to imitate it. On the particular matter which has been the subject of correspondence between the Chancellor and Mr

Morgenthau we could similarly provide that we should seek an interpretation in the sense we desire. There may be other cases where this technique can be used to affect a compromise with the opposition. For example, Mr Bevin's recently revived opposition on the ground that sterling is being tied to gold might be covered by our seeking an interpretation, the language being carefully chosen, that this is not the case.

VI

I call attention to the fact that under the terms of the Bretton Woods plan we have to signify our adherence not later than December 31st of this year. Moreover, unless by that date members representing 65 per cent of the quotas have adhered, the plan falls to the ground. The latest news from Washington (273 Saving of June 3) indicates that, as a result of the July/August recess, Congress may not be finished with the Bretton Woods Plans before September.* Thus, there will not be much time after the assembling of the new Parliament. We may also be reluctant to give our last word until after there has been some progress in the Stage III discussions. Perhaps we should approach the U.S. Administration with a view to their proposing to all the Bretton Woods participants an extension of the date beyond December 31, 1945—say, to March 31, 1946.

VII

The emphasis placed by the Americans on the inapplicability of the Fund to the problems of the financial *sequelae* of the war may help us in asking for special arrangements, outside the Fund, for Stage III. According to their present view the Fund shall not be used for such purposes. Nor would our particular problems appear to be in any way suited to the Bank for

* A later message indicates that the Administration will do their best to get the plan through *before* the Summer Recess.

Reconstruction and Development or to the Export–Import Bank. In this context, therefore, the line taken by the bankers and the opposition may have done us a good turn. The influential Committee of Economic Development is also taking this line by urging 'the broad expansion of foreign commerce ...through a prompt and final settlement of war debts and other international obligations which would be a source of uncertainty to post-war trade',—this, it is emphasised through-out, in the interests of preserving the system of private enterprise. We are now in a stronger position than before for representing our Stage III proposals as a necessary complement to the Bretton Woods Plans for freeing trade and providing a general convertibility of money for current transactions.

14 June 1945   KEYNES

From June 1945 onwards, however, Stage III problems naturally pre-occupied Keynes and he spent little time on Bretton Woods until after the passage of the Anglo-American Loan Agreement and Bretton Woods' institutions and Britain's accession to the Articles of Agreement.

At that stage, Keynes began to prepare for the inaugural meetings of the new institutions which he expected to attend as the British Governor. One of the outstanding issues, in addition to the one concerning its location, remaining for the meeting was the actual role of the Executive Directors of the Fund and Bank. On this R. H. Brand reported a conversation with H. D. White.

From a letter from R. H. BRAND, *23 January 1946*

I am afraid this question of the Executive Directors may be a somewhat difficult one. From every conceivable point of view, except one, your picture is, of course, undoubtedly the right one. Nobody in their senses would think of setting up any national organisation, or any organisation inside a nation, on any such basis as having twelve Executive Directors. But this is not a national organisation; it is an international one. And it is here that the difficulty arises. The Fund is concerned with forty nations or so, and deals with matters of vital import to them. No Managing Director will be regarded by each of these forty nations as an expert authority on its affairs, save possibly the country of which he is a national. I much doubt, therefore, whether the nations concerned are going to allow one Managing Director to run the Fund as freely as you suggest. You may reply that important questions will not arise, and, when they do, the Executive Directors can be called together. I am inclined to think, with so many nations concerned and so many possible problems—exchange rates, etc.—that important occasions will be pretty frequent.

I think I differed from you before, when you thought it so monstrous that Congress should show its intention to follow closely such an institution. But, with all the dollars involved, they *will* follow it closely, and they will look to the Executive Director to keep them informed. It may be all very sad that nations are going to behave like this and not trust, rather, to the appointment of a first-class man who will run the show for the benefit of each nation. But I fear national sentiment is not sufficiently international for this. I doubt if you yourself would assume that Harry White, for instance, was sufficiently knowledgeable on all sterling area problems for you wholly to trust his sole judgement. I feel sure, when any question touching some vital interest of the United Kingdom is on hand, the House of Commons will expect the Executive Director to be and to have been right on the spot, even in the event of the Managing Director being an Englishman. It is, perhaps, stretching my argument too far to ask you to consider how far the Secretary-General is likely to be allowed to run U.N.O.

Harry White lays great stress on what he considers to be one of the great merits of the Fund, namely that the Directors of different nationalities should be in close consultation and discussion, and should learn as much as they can about *all* the problems of the Fund, since they will be responsible for all decisions or recommendations. They are not merely concerned with their own country's interests, but with all countries' interests and must learn to know what the problems of all are. Each Executive Director is a representative, not a delegate. If he is only a quarter-time man, does it not indicate on the contrary that he is to be regarded as by no means concerned with *all* the Fund's problems, but merely with the special ones of his own country, in fact that the only man representing the Fund as a whole is the Managing Director, the Executive Directors each being concerned only with special interests? This, I think, would be a bad mistake.

Keynes replied on 8 February, after commenting on the fact that he had heard nothing of the progress of the informal preliminary discussions for the inaugural meetings conducted in Washington by C. F. Cobbold and Sir Wilfrid Eady.

From a letter to R. H. BRAND, *8 February 1946*

I am sorry you do not agree about our point of view on the Executive Directors; or perhaps the better way to put it is you do not think our conception practicable. For I still feel it very fundamental to the success of the new institution. You will have learnt by now from Eady and Cobbold how strongly we feel about this.

We do not, of course, dispute the constitutional position, which is indeed indisputable. The constitutional responsibility and ultimate control is, of course with the Directors. The analogy is with the General Manager or Managing Director of a great institution. The fact that it is essential in practice that he should run the show so long as he has the confidence of his Board does not mean that the Board do not keep in close touch or that they surrender in any way their constitutional responsibility. Could any Managing Director be so gifted as to be capable of running with efficiency any institution with twelve polyglot directors with divergent interests, most of them interested in grinding their own axes rather than in running the institution, who are in his office every day and on top of him and dictating his day-to-day policy?

I agree with Harry White that one of the greatest benefits that can be obtained will be from the frequent and close consultation and discussion between the directors of different nationalities. But this good object will be defeated unless the directors are of the highest calibre their countries can provide and are in close touch with their own central banks and Treasuries. Would Harry White be inclined to be Executive Director if this involved continual residence in Buenos Aires? On our conception you will get a body consisting of very responsible people in the heart of their own institutions. On Harry's conception the Executive Directors will be retired Indian Civil Servants rather than Deputy Governors of central banks. Harry's purpose can, therefore, only be achieved our way.

By 13 February he was able to set out his views more fully on his prospective programme.

To SIR EDWARD BRIDGES, *12 February 1946*

SAVANNAH

If I am to reach Savannah by March 8th, I must sail by the *Aquitania** on February 25th. I remain dreadfully divided in mind about going, but perhaps lean a little more to the affirmative than when I saw you the other day.

On the one hand—

(1) Having spent so much of myself on Bretton Woods and its preliminaries in the last four years, it would be a satisfaction to be in at the official birth.

(2) A great deal will turn, I think, on getting the role of the Executive Directors settled right. Eady's telegram, Remac 69, suggests that there is still a reasonable hope of achieving this by good, stiff fighting. Unfortunately Brand does not much sympathise with our point of view here and regards the U.S. Treasury doctrine as inevitable.

(3) Our Delegation must be reasonably strong in relation to the American and Canadian (which will be in full force) and possibly others.

(4) My doctor is very insistent that it would be good for me to get into warm weather in March, and my wife, on the whole, agrees with him. The work will certainly not be strenuous and the month's absence will be in the nature of a holiday.

On the other hand—

(1) Apart from the point mentioned above, the rest of the business will not be important.

* Or, much better, the *Queen Mary*, if, as now looks likely, she is delayed until at least the 24th.

(2) There is a great deal of interest going forward here—Budget, loan programme, sterling area, reduction of political and military expenditure, where even a trifling contribution may be more useful than Savannah, the Bank's appointed day, etc., though I regard the sterling area as something we want to handle as *slowly*, not as fast, as possible.

(3) It is easy to make the excuse to the Americans that we had always told them the early date would not suit.

If I go, I should like to take either Rowe-Dutton or Brooks. For the Bank, Eady suggests Bolton and Bridge[41] (relatively junior) who is already there. If Rowe-Dutton goes and not Brooks, Bridge could be Secretary of the Delegation.

If I do not go, Brand could be Governor pro-tem. and Bolton Executive Director. In this case I think it would be very desirable for Rowe-Dutton to be of the party.

Alternatively, Eady might stay over (which I know he does not want) or fly back again after a few days here. (Cobbold plans to be back on February 20th; Eady was, I believe, thinking of leaving a few days later—and he may easily be kept in Canada longer before he is finished—and he would have to be off again by March 4th.)

Sorry to bore you with all this. I will look in on you when you have given it the brief necessary thought.

KEYNES

12 February 1946

On 19 February, Keynes was officially appointed the British Governor of both the Fund and the Bank. He travelled to New York on the *Queen Mary*, arriving there on 1 March.

On his way to Savannah, Keynes stopped in Washington for preliminary discussions on the proceedings with Secretary Vinson as well as meetings with old friends. After meeting with Mr Vinson on 6 March, he reported to London.

[41] Roy Arthur Odell Bridge (b. 1911), banker; Bank of England 1929–1969, Deputy Chief Cashier 1957–63, Adviser to the Governors 1963–5, Assistant to the Governors 1965–9.

To THE TREASURY, *7 March 1946*

1. In the course of a long talk with Vinson yesterday the following points emerged concerning the line the Americans will take at Savannah.

2. Somewhat shamefacedly and at the end of our talk as I was leaving, he told me that the Americans will be proposing that both the Fund and the Bank should be situated not at New York as we had been assuming but at Washington. I reacted very vehemently, declaring that in that case these bodies could not be regarded as international institutions but were being treated as an appanage of the American Administration, which was just what the critics had declared them to be. I told him that I should report this to London, but that I felt confident that this proposal would be viewed with the utmost dismay. I could not say how other countries would feel since we have all been assuming the choice of New York. Vinson indicated as politely as he could that we must take this as a more or less final American decision and that they would use all their influence to rail-road it through. When I asked him to give some explanation of so objectionable and, as it seemed to me, indefensible a proposal, he replied that in the American view the institutions would be fatally prejudiced in American opinion if they were placed in New York, since they would then come under the taint of 'international finance'. I interpret this, however, as partly a move in the struggle for position between the Federal Reserve Board and the New York Federal Reserve Bank, but perhaps as primarily a reflection of the abiding suspicion of New York bankers on the part of the Administration. I may add that I pointed out emphatically but with little effect that to place the two bodies in New York would greatly facilitate their co-operation with United Nations Organisation.

3. A rumour to the above effect had reached us from another source the previous evening. It is apparently a formal decision of the National Advisory Council, which is playing an increas-

ingly important part in these matters. This is the body set up under the Bretton Woods Act, consisting of the Secretaries of State, Treasury and Commerce Departments and the Chairmen of the Federal Reserve Board and Export–Import Bank, which has now become in effect the Cabinet Committee for all questions of foreign finance and lending. I am told that it has a session every week, generally prolonged, and is acquiring a small staff of its own. The importance of this body is, of course, a further reason against the location of the Fund and the Bank in Washington, since they would then be under the immediate eye and subject, through the American Executive Directors, to the daily instruction of this body. All of us here, therefore, feel that the new development should be viewed with the deepest concern. No doubt we shall find sympathisers in other countries, but with so many potential claimants for American favours still unsatisfied, the power of the Americans to rail-road their proposals through if they so determine is probably considerable. Vinson claimed, however, that so far they had used their power and influence moderately and one can hope, though without much confidence, that they may be open to reason on this matter. May we have your instructions?

4. On the question of the position and authority of the Managing Director and President as against the Executive Directors, the position looks more promising. I think I thoroughly convinced Acheson of the rightness of our point of view at any rate as regards the Fund. I believe he has already supported our arguments with Clayton and Vinson. Clayton I have not yet seen. Vinson was non-committal but showed considerable sympathy with our standpoint but considered our arrangements not so strong in relation to the Bank. It is not impossible that a workable compromise may be reached. On the other hand, if the institutions are placed in Washington we expect that some of the European Governments will insist on whole-time Executive Directors so as to be always present as a check on the American Administration.

5. Vinson told me that they were thinking of $50,000 subject to tax as the appropriate total renumeration for the Managing Director and the President. This is very nearly equivalent to what we had in mind, though we were thinking in tax free terms. Vinson also seemed to accept the idea that the Executive Directors should be paid on only a moderate scale but we did not get down to figures.

6. On the question of personnel, we have heard from several quarters that the idea of making Harry White Managing Director of the Fund has now dropped out and Vinson confirmed this to me. I found, however, that the only reason for this is as follows. Vinson agreed that White would be ideally suited for the position and would receive his warm support apart from the consideration which follows. He was, as he expressed it, a 'natural' for the job. The difficulty is that the Americans have come to the conclusion that the President of the Bank should be an American on the ground that only in this way could the confidence of the American investment market be secured. Whether they have a candidate in view we do not know. We believe Ned Brown of Chicago was approached but has refused. Since they did not think it would be proper to have Americans as the heads of both bodies, this rules out White for the Fund. The American candidate is Graham Towers.

7. Vinson remarked to Brand this morning just before continuing his evidence before the Senate Banking Committee that if there were going to be great difficulties between American view and ours perhaps it would be better to postpone Savannah meeting. Brand did not take the suggestion as seriously meant and replied that postponement now was obviously impossible. But I mention Vinson's remark as confirmation of paragraph 2 above, and as a hint of the strength of their feeling.

The next day he proceeded to Savannah. On arrival, he wrote the following, presumably for the local Press.

This is my first visit to the South. I find one need not be here many hours to experience the warmth of the Southern hospitality as well as of the climate. To come from the cold, grey damp of an English March to the balmy air and bright azalean colour of Savannah refreshens the body; I foresee a gay and kindly reception which will cheer the heart; and I am expecting that the Conference itself may provide some interesting stimulus to the ingenuity and devices of the brain. For we are assembled here to carry a stage further a great project of international co-operation at which some of us have been at work for what is now quite a considerable time. My own countrymen in England are exceedingly tired and sometimes irritable; we feel an acute need of more colour and variety and relaxation in our lives than we are able to get just yet; we are disappointed that the return to former easements and amenities has to be so slow. In short, what we want is a break. But behind that there is a pulsation of latent energy, which may easily be overlooked or underestimated abroad, to re-shape and re-form peaceful and profitable ways of life at home and abroad. We, with our close links with many nations and communities overseas, are supremely conscious that the world to-day needs to be shown more than ever before that the representatives of many different nations can join together successfully in a constructive, peaceful enterprise.

Driving to-day through the streets of Savannah I did not see citizens above the age of about 17 nearly enough to account for the great cheerful crowds of juniors. It seemed to be a city of children. Driving out a little further and seeing for the first time in my life the festoons of Spanish moss, I became aware that I was seeing in this city a beautiful woman, the mother of many hopefuls, but whose face was concealed behind a veil of delicate lace. The British delegates for whom I speak eagerly anticipate their brief sojourn in this gracious place.

At the opening session of the Savannah meetings, Keynes spoke after Secretary Vinson and the representatives of China, Czechoslovakia, France and Russia.

LORD KEYNES'S SPEECH
AT INAUGURAL MEETING OF GOVERNORS
OF FUND AND BANK
SAVANNAH, 9 MARCH 1946

Mr Secretary Vinson, Governors, Alternates, Advisers—and Observers.

Like several others here present, I have been intimately concerned with what will, I think, always be known as the Bretton Woods plans. The gestation has been long; the lusty twins are seriously overdue; they will have put on, I hope, as a result, a weight and strength which will do credit to their mixed and collective parentage. At any rate it is a privilege I would not have readily forgone to be present at the hour of birth, in some capacity whether as Governor or governess, along with the midwives, nurses, doctors and parsons ready to christen (and I shall always hold to the view that the christening has been badly done and that the names of the twins should have been reversed).

Hidden behind veils or beards of Spanish moss, I do not doubt that the usual fairies will be putting in an appearance at the christening, carrying appropriate gifts. What gifts and blessings are likely to be most serviceable to the twins, whom (rightly or wrongly) we have decided to call Master Fund and Miss Bank?

The first fairy should bring, I suggest, a Joseph's coat, a many-coloured raiment to be worn by these children as a perpetual reminder that they belong to the whole world and that their sole allegiance is to the general good, without fear or favour to any particular interest. Pious words exceedingly difficult to fulfil. There is scarcely any enduringly successful experience yet of an international body which has fulfilled the hopes of its progenitors. Either an institution has become diverted to be the instrument of a limited group, or it has been a puppet of sawdust through which the breath of life does not blow. Every incident and adjunct of our new-born institutions must be best calculated to emphasise and maintain their truly international character and purpose.

The second fairy, being up-to-date, will bring perhaps a box of mixed vitamins, A, B, C, D and all the rest of the alphabet. The children may faithfully wear their many-coloured raiment, yet themselves show pale, delicate faces. Energy and a fearless spirit, which does not shelve and avoid difficult issues, but welcomes them and is determined to solve them, is what we must demand from our nurslings.

The third fairy perhaps, much older and not nearly so up-to-date, may, like the Pope with his cardinals, close the lips of the children with her hand and then open them again, invoking a spirit of wisdom, patience and grave discretion, so that, as they grow up, they will be the respected and safe recipient of confidences, of troubles and of perplexities, a reliable and prudent support to those who need them in all times of difficulty. If these institutions are to win the full confidence of the suspicious world, it must not only be, but appear, that their approach to every problem is absolutely objective and oecumenical, without prejudice or favour.

I am asking and hoping, you will see, a great deal.

I hope that Mr Kelchner has not made any mistake and that there is no malicious fairy, no Carabosse, whom he has overlooked and forgotten to ask to the party. For if so the curses which that bad fairy will pronounce will, I feel sure, run as follows:—'You two brats shall grow up politicians; your every thought and act shall have an *arrière-pensée*; everything you determine shall not be for its own sake or on its own merits but because of something else.'

If this should happen, then the best that could befall—and that is how it might turn out—would be for the children to fall into an eternal slumber, never to waken or be heard of again in the courts and markets of Mankind.

Well, ladies and gentlemen, fairies or no fairies, this looks like being a very pleasant party and a happy christening and let the omens be good.

As the meetings continued, Keynes became more pessimistic. Thus he wrote to R. F. Kahn and Sir Edward Bridges.

From a letter to R. F. KAHN, *13 March 1946*

The climate here is very delightful and the business so far not severe. On the other hand, we look like running into plenty of snags. The Americans have no idea how to make these institutions into operating international concerns, and in almost every direction their ideas are bad. Yet they plainly intend to force their own conceptions through regardless of the rest of us. The result is that the institutions look like becoming American concerns, run by gigantic American staffs, with the rest of us very much on the side-lines. I am sure that when they get down to operations things will not work out as they are expecting. Perhaps it is only at that stage that criticism will become effective. At present I can only say that I am pretty pessimistic. The Americans at the top seem to have absolutely no conception of international co-operation; since they are the biggest partners they think they have the right to call the tune on practically every point. If they knew the music that would not matter so much; but unfortunately they don't.

From a telegram to SIR EDWARD BRIDGES, *13 March 1946*

5. We cannot pretend to be satisfied with the atmosphere here. Vinson has enough stooges, more particularly China and Mexico with a scattering of smaller powers, such as Ethiopia, Egypt, Honduras and Guatemala who have been prominent, to feel able

to act independently of the views of the rest of us who are moreover unorganised, although Canada, France, Belgium, South Africa, India and ourselves are generally found in agreement.

The Savannah meetings saw the American view that the new institutions should have headquarters in Washington prevail, Keynes's instructions in the end being to give way gracefully. On the issue of the duties of Executive Directors and Alternates, Britain and the United States compromised with a form of words that did not require them to give their full-time attention to the Fund. However, on the question of salaries, which brought the problem of the role of the Executive Directors of the new institutions to the fore again, on the instructions of the Chancellor, Keynes made the following statement. It was the only occasion at Savannah when a negative vote was cast.

After consultation with the Chancellor of the Exchequer, I much regret that I am unable to support the paragraph in the Report of the Committee which relates to the remuneration of the Executive Directors and their Alternates. We feel that it would lead to severe and well-justified public criticism to load the budgets of these new bodies with such high emoluments for so large a body of officials. It is all the worse at a time before we have even begun to consider the costs of their actual staffs, who will, we hope, be mainly responsible for the burden of daily business, and when the available income for such expenditure is still uncertain.

It is not uncommon to find that one mistaken decision leads to another. If we had foreseen at Bretton Woods what was going to happen—and it has turned out widely different from our expectations—we should certainly have proposed that the remuneration of the Executive Directors and their Alternates, who, as distinct from the staff, are National Delegates, should be provided or shared by the Governments appointing or electing them and not by the institutions themselves. This would have allowed the necessary elasticity for adjustment to the widely differing levels of official salaries in different countries. Unfortunately that course was not followed. The difficulty facing us has been greatly increased by the decision to provide for whole-time service by Alternates, not merely in the absence to be inconsistent with the best efficiency of the institutions; and still further aggravated through the wholly unexpected provision for whole-time services by Alternates, not merely in the absence of their principals, but in addition to them. Nor do we believe that most countries can wisely spare from their own pressing problems the services of so many individuals of the calibre indicated.

These decisions, however mistaken in our opinion, have nevertheless been made. The difficulty of the resulting dilemma which faces us is obvious. A more unpleasant duty than that which falls to me today I have seldom experienced. I do not wish to deprive any man, especially old and respected friends, of their due and proper reward. But, in our view, so large a body of persons cannot properly be remunerated on the very high level proposed, which equals or greatly exceeds the highest remuneration available in most countries for public service.

My country feels, therefore, that they cannot share in any way the responsibility of this decision.

16 March 1946

On his return to London after a difficult journey,[42] Keynes reported to the Chancellor under a tentative covering note.[43]

[42] See Lord Kahn, 'Historical Origins of the International Monetary Fund', in A. P. Thirwall (ed.), *Keynes and International Monetary Relations* (London, 1976), pp. 26–9. Keynes drafted his report on board ship, as he reported to R. H. Brand on 3 April 1946.

[43] Differences between this initial report and the version given wider circulation—some of a drafting character, some reflecting issues on which the Treasury wished to make up its own mind—are indicated in the footnotes.

To H. DALTON, *29 March 1946*

Reading this through, I feel that Section I is too long and has the effect of giving a greater emphasis of discontent than I really intend. I think I could profitably rehash the document before it received wide circulation.

I have marked a passage on page 7 [below, pp. 235–6], which it might be thought advisable to keep at the present stage for private discussion in the Treasury rather than give it premature wider circulation.

The truth is that my own reactions to the Conference changed with further reflection, and the result is that the document needs a certain amount of abridgment and rearrangement before the emphasis will be just where I want it to be.

KEYNES

THE SAVANNAH CONFERENCE ON THE BRETTON WOODS
FINAL ACT

I

The time of this conference was largely occupied with formalities. Of the three substantial issues which arose we were defeated on one (the site of the Fund and the Bank) without previous warning that it would arise; on the second (the rôle of the Executive Directors) we had to be content with useful, but inadequate, concessions; on the third (the rôle of the Governors) we were, in substance, successful.

Our object when we set out was to secure a form of organisation for the Fund which would give it a good chance of becoming an international organ and focus of the central banks and Treasuries of the world, in which they would feel confidence and to which they would bring their doubts and technical troubles. We conceived its daily business, its research and the preparation and digestion of the raw material of decisions as being managed and conducted by a staff of international Civil Servants under a well remunerated Managing Director of the highest possible qualifications, all of them owing their duty to the Fund and not to its individual members. Superimposed on the staff and constitutionally responsible for decisions of policy, there would be the Board of Executive Directors, composed of individuals highly placed and active in their own central banks and Treasuries, who would meet together at intervals, partly to pass on the recommendations of the Managing Director, and, scarcely less, to interchange confidences, information and counsel with the Managing Director and amongst themselves. This, if it went well, might furnish a truly international body for consultation and co-operation on monetary and financial problems which would serve the purpose which some had hoped, but had been disappointed, from the B.I.S. The concourse of Governors (forty for each body) we thought of as ornamental rather than executive. We contemplated a similar set-up with the necessary differences for the Bank for Reconstruction and Development.

We had not conceived it as possible that either institution would be placed away from New York. In New York they would be in the daily contacts which can be provided by a great centre of international finance; they would be sufficiently removed from the politics of Congress and the nationalistic whispering gallery of the embassies and legations of Washington; and they would probably be sufficiently near to the seat of U.N.O. to be able to co-operate closely on the economic and statistical side of their work with the Economic and Social Council.

Passing through New York on our way to the Conference we discussed these ideas at the Federal Reserve Bank of New York, and found them in complete sympathy. No rumour had reached them of any site other than New York. No rumour reached us until a day or two before we left Washington for Savannah, when Mr Vinson told me that the American Delegation had decided that both institutions should be placed in Washington and that this was a final decision the merits of which they were not prepared to discuss. The United States Administration, he said, were entitled to decide for themselves what location within the United States was to be preferred.

At Savannah we soon found that a majority of the other Delegations (China, Poland and perhaps some South Americans were on the other side) shared our view that this was an unfortunate, indeed a very bad, decision. It also appeared that it was primarily a personal decision of Mr Vinson supported only by the Federal Reserve Board (which would find itself strengthened against the New York Federal Reserve Bank by the Washington location), and not supported on its merits by the rest of the American Delegation. Unfortunately Mr Vinson, before warning us or seeking our views, had thought fit to take his proposition direct to the President and to obtain his authority to make this an absolute instruction to the American Delegation from which they were not to be free to depart in any circumstances. This made it impossible for Mr Clayton, for example, to listen to our arguments, however much he recognised their force.

Mr Vinson had no great difficulty in rail-roading this decision through the Conference, vocally supported (as became usual) by a pathetic procession of stooges, of which Ethiopia (represented by an American banker), Salvador, Guatemala, Mexico and China were prominent, with most of the rest discreetly silent but Canada and the Western Europeans supporting our views with greater or less tenacity. My concluding speech in opposition is given in an Appendix.[44]

These methods, however, were felt to be distasteful by many, including several of the Americans, who sympathised with and apologised to us behind the scenes, and created for a time a disagreeable atmosphere, though the cloud gradually lifted towards the end.

On the second main issue, the rôle of the Executive Directors, we never had much hope of full success, though the final

[44] This sentence did not appear in the later version. The speech is not printed.

outcome, which in one respect was worse than we had foreseen, did embody a partial compromise. We were aware that the Americans wished to shift the centre of gravity of both institutions from the staff of international Civil Servants to the Executive Directors who are national delegates of their own Governments. Instead of expecting from the Executive Directors part-time duty only with the Fund and the Bank, thus leaving them free to take an active part in work for their own Government, the Americans proposed that they should be whole-time officers of the institutions, always on the spot, though with the prospect of very little to do unless they took over what ought to be the jobs of the regular staff. But worse than that (and of this further development we had had no previous warning), the Americans also proposed that each Executive Director should be supported by a whole-time Alternate. Thus, for the two institutions together, there would be forty-eight whole-time Executive Directors and Alternates over and above the actual staffs. All these individuals were to be paid at a level as high as or much higher than any civil servants in any of the member Governments, including the American. Starting at a higher figure, the Americans would in the end accept no salary less than $17,000 for a Director and $11,500 for an Alternate *free of all taxes in every country*; if an individual is liable for any taxes under the law of his own country, the Fund or the Bank will pay them for him by increasing his salary to whatever figure is necessary to yield the above result free of taxes. I think that the above works out, on the basis of British taxation, to about £15,000 for a Director and £7,500 for an Alternate subject to tax.

Nevertheless, by hard fighting and considerable support from other Delegations, two mitigations were obtained. In the first place, it has been agreed that it is not compulsory that *both* a Director *and* his Alternate should be present together or that either of them need be whole-time. It is optional to them how they divide their duties provided that one is always available.

It is also agreed that the above scale of salary is for whole-time service, proportionately abated for part-time service, and is a ceiling up to which an individual is entitled to claim, so that an appointing Government may make it a condition of appointment that he shall claim less than the ceiling. The Canadians made it clear that they would not allow their officials to take the maximum amount. The French also were particularly insistent on this arrangement. M. Monick, the Governor of the Bank of France, explained that he might find it convenient to suggest a promising young official of his Bank for an Executive Directorship, and that it would be scandalous and demoralising to pay him four or five times his own salary, and what would be, on the basis of French taxation, a higher remuneration than will be received by the President of the Republic (just as in our case an Executive Director, though only one member of two bodies of twelve each, would receive more than the Prime Minister).

We voted against this decision to the end and the Chancellor is free from any responsibility for it. The final expression of our standpoint is given in the Appendix.[45] But we voted alone. We could scarcely hope to prevail against two obstacles, one of them respectable, the other less so.

The salary proposed for a Director is higher than will be received by any American civil servant, even when President Truman's proposals for higher civil service salaries have been passed by Congress, and the salary for an Alternate will be about equal to the top level. But they do not correspond to anything like so high a gross salary on the basis of American, as on the basis of British or French taxation. Furthermore, there is a steady drift of Americans out of official posts into private employment, and the figures proposed probably do not exceed what the individuals in view could earn in private employment. In the case of the American appointees who are leaving the civil service on appointment (this argument may not apply to many

[45] The letter C was added in the later version. The speech appears above, pp. 218–19.

other countries), the jobs are non-pensionable and probably temporary. Moreover, life in Washington is becoming increasingly and fearfully expensive and any British official appointed to work there hereafter will deserve a more substantial allowance than has prevailed hitherto. Thus for the American appointments, treated as the Americans intend to treat them, the proposed salaries, though handsome, can be justified.

The less respectable obstacle to successful opposition lay in the fact that the majority of the individuals taking part in the salary discussion were expecting to receive these jobs. It was noticeable that the French representatives, who were thus placed, refused to take part in the discussion, but others were less delicate.[46] Moreover, political and financial patronage was being created of the first order of attraction for South American (and other) countries—life in Washington with no defined or onerous duties and a grand, tax-free salary.

On this basis and with the staffs, still to be appointed, as contemplated by the Americans, the budget of each institution looks likely to reach $2,500,000 to $3 million annually for working expenses with no secured source of earnings, particularly in the case of the Fund and in the early years, from which these sums can be met.

Indeed, it is the *total* expense involved, rather than the scale of remuneration in individual cases, which justifies severe criticism. The Americans have reached a *reductio ad absurdum* of their own conception of management by applying it to a body of persons who could amount at the maximum to a mob of forty-eight. There can be no adequate work for this number of eminent experts, and such a number of very highly qualified persons, who can be spared from the pressing problems of their own countries, simply do not exist. If, however, the other horn of the dilemma is accepted and most other countries appoint one, rather than four, whole-time representatives, the American influence on the Board is dangerously over-weighted. This is

---

[46] This sentence did not appear in the later version.

aggravated by the fact that in the case of *elected* members, who represent more than one country, several deals have been carried through, notably in the case of the Latin-American countries, by which four countries or more pool their votes, on the basis of each being entitled to appoint *one* Director or Alternate, immediately or by rotation, so that the full number of four is always filled up.

On the third issue, the rôle of the Governors, we had more success. We had thought of the Governors as being more ornamental than executive, meeting once a year to hear a report from the Executive Directors and to deal with constitutional questions, but not taking much initiative. Early in the Conference a steering committee of twelve Governors was appointed, called the Executive Committee, of which Mr Vinson was Chairman and I was Vice-Chairman, the functioning of which, most of us supposed, was limited to the Savannah Conference. Subsequently we learnt (from the Press) that Mr Vinson intended that this body should continue in existence between sessions, available for him to summon and consult whenever he might think it necessary. This would have made it possible for Mr Vinson, in his capacity of Chairman of both Boards of Governors, to butt in to the work of the Executive Directors whenever he felt inclined, with most of the other Governors not available in Washington and having hurriedly to appoint some available Alternate. The French, the Canadians and ourselves reacted so vehemently, however, against this conception, that it was dropped. The Executive Committee was re-named the Procedures Committee and its functions were limited to the members being available for consultation by post or cable concerning future business of the Governors as a whole and to meeting a day or two in advance of future Board Meetings to prepare the agenda—functions which are harmless and perhaps useful. The first regular annual meeting was provisionally fixed for late September 1946 with subsequent meetings at annual intervals.

I I

Nevertheless, the outcome, though discouraging to our previous hopes and a doubtful augury for the efficient working of the new institutions, must be viewed in its right perspective. No specifically British interest has been injured. In the judgement of the members of the British Delegation, the strength of the new institutions has been impaired, both for effective action and for unwise interference alike. The outfit of expensive whole-time Directors and Alternates was imposed by the Americans because they wanted their own representatives to be of the highest calibre and to be free to play a significant, and perhaps decisive, part in the management. But they overlooked the extent to which the activity and authority of the Fund (and the Bank) would be frustrated by so great a dispersal of decision and what an infernal nuisance the polyglot mob of Directors and Alternates may prove in practice. This set-up will make the effective interference of these bodies in the affairs of the members more, and not less, difficult. In the case of the Bank, moreover, the Americans will come to regret, as in the case of UNRRA, a form of management which increases the influence of a body largely composed of potential borrowers.

The outcome, therefore, is not such as to confirm the fears of the critics, although it may hamper the new bodies in the fully effective exercise of their constructive functions.

By the time that the Conference was coming to an end, the Americans were becoming increasingly conscious of the force and justice of our criticisms. Dr Harry White was eager to explain to me in private that he had spoken against us more strongly than he felt, and that, if experience confirmed our views, he would be the first to move to undo what has been done (which will not be so easy). They nearly all confessed, in private, to cold feet about the effect of what they had been doing on the daily efficiency of the young twins.

It would be a mistake to suppose that the Americans have

227

far-sighted plans, whether good or bad. Mr Vinson is a shrewd and ambitious politician, aiming (some say) at running for the Vice-Presidency in the next Election, interested in immediate power and patronage, in personal publicity, and in the appearance of successful Americanism; but it is unlikely that he has given ten minutes thought to what he would like the institutions to be doing two years hence—they will have passed out of his field of vision before that. Mr Vinson has appeared hitherto as a conservative friend of the New Deal. But the boys of the New Deal are now being eliminated and not one is expected to survive. One was conscious of personal frustration behind the scenes and of a glimpse into the labyrinth of American political and official life, but *not* of a far-sighted, deliberate design to our, or to anyone's disadvantage. Indeed, the trouble is that, after a brief initial period, when there should be plenty to occupy them, the Americans have no clear idea what work is to be found for the Executive Directors, especially in the case of the Fund. Mr Rasminsky of Canada had a night-mare of the Directors and Alternates studying trends (which, we were told, might be one of their more chronic duties) *and voting on them.*

Moreover, there were some important developments on the credit side which deserve to be emphasised.

The actual appointments of Executive Directors, which have been made so far strike us as excellent. A list, and the voting power of each, is given in an Appendix.[47] For the Americans Dr Harry White, as Director of the Fund, and Mr Collado, as Director of the Bank, could not be improved upon. The Canadian appointments are both first-class. Several of the Europeans are highly competent, reliable and experienced; and the Latin Americans are providing the very best experts at their disposal. Both Boards will be, broadly speaking, honest, internationally-minded and knowledgeable.

The next point for emphasis is that the United States Treasury and State Department (under Mr Vinson the Treasury

[47] Not printed.

now deserves to be mentioned first in this context), intend to pass on their impending headaches to be treated by the new institutions. No harm in this. It means, for one thing, that we can pass on our headaches too (and a good many headaches we have in common). The following are examples:

(*a*) Italy's application for membership will be made the occasion for the Fund and the Bank to join in working out a general plan of financial and economic reconstruction.

(*b*) In the same way China's applications to have an initial exchange rate approved and to receive a stabilisation loan will lead to the preparation of a comprehensive economic plan for China.

(*c*) The tied loans of the Export–Import Bank are to be confined in the main to the early transitional period of 1946–47, when they will be no serious obstacle to our own exports, and thereafter countries will be referred to the Bank for Reconstruction of which the main resources, even when they are raised (as they will be) in the United States, will be wholly untied and equally free of use in our markets.

(*d*) Generally speaking, the problems and perplexities of foreign countries, which reach the United States Treasury and State Department, will be promptly passed on by them to the Fund or the Bank or to the two conjointly. The Americans hope in this way to remove international economic and financial affairs a stage further from Congress, whilst retaining a decisive American influence over the decision and maintaining unimpaired the authority of the new National Advisory Council under Mr Vinson's chairmanship, which will give direct instructions to the American Executive Directors, such as they could not give to the international staff.

All this seems to us to be mainly to the good. We do not want to become directly responsible for the reconstruction-pangs of Italy or China or Austria or any other countries. Nor do we wish these applicants to become sole clients and preserves of the United States State Department and Treasury. Yet their problems cannot be evaded. Nor can American influence be other than dominant. Nothing can suit us better, therefore, than that international institutions, where we are free to play a very important part, should administer what will be largely American funds for the succour of these regions. Nor is there any obvious ground why we should not refer to these bodies in the same way the difficulties of other regions, such as Malaya and Burma, where the initial responsibility is primarily ours.

There is also another aspect of the Savannah Conference which may, perhaps, be justifiably mentioned on the credit side. All the members of the British Delegation have come away, I think, with the feeling that, although our views did not prevail on the issues discussed above, we did not impair, but on the other hand, improved, our moral leadership and the intimacy and confidence of our contacts with the British Commonwealth and European Delegations. We were never fighting for a British interest, but solely for the future efficiency and usefulness of the new institutions, and many of those present heartily agreed with us on the merits of the case. The fact that we spoke out frankly on matters about which others felt obliged, for one reason or another, to keep silent or hesitant, enhanced—we make bold to believe—the prestige of our country even though we did not prevail. Increasingly through the Conference we felt ourselves to be moving in a sympathetic atmosphere; and on the personal side old contacts and friendships were strengthened and deepened, and new ones established. Mr Rowe-Dutton and Mr Bolton circulated through the Delegations more widely than I did, and won a measure of confidence and intimacy with representatives of many countries, the future value of which to us should not be under-estimated.

It may be worth while to enlarge on this aspect a little further. With the Canadian Delegation, led by Mr Ilsley, we maintained the closest relations behind the scenes from the first day, and frequently worked together, though Mr Ilsley himself was inclined to take a weaker line than his officials. We had several intimate and friendly conferences with Mr Melville of Australia (who was, of course, only an observer) and Mr de Kock[48] of South Africa, though they were not in a position to play the same prominent part in public as the Canadians. The excellence and closeness of our relations with the Indian Delegation deserves special comment. Sir Chintaman Deshmukh handled his case with high dignity, ability and reasonableness; we always supported him on his interests and he always supported us on ours. There were happy and undisturbed relations with the Egyptians. Thus the sterling area stood together in solid agreement. To the Western Europeans, who were mostly old friends, we were naturally close and like-minded. I would particularly mention the happiness of our relations with the French under M. Mendés-France[49] (whom at Bretton Woods we had found difficult). In spite of the imminence of his Government's negotiations with the United States Treasury, M. Mendés-France, with whom we were in unvarying agreement on all matters under discussion, adopted throughout a noticeably courageous and highly independent line. We were much impressed by the ability and obvious desire for friendship and collaboration with us shown by M. Brozniak,[50] Governor of the Bank of Poland, one of the new Poles; we thought him better material than the old Poles, already well-known to us, whom he had, in a welcome spirit of compromise, agreed to bring with him as members of his Delegation.

I may seem to say too much. But I firmly believe that the whole of the British Commonwealth and the Sterling Area and of Europe stood closer to us than to the Americans and looked to us, rather than to them, for leadership.

In spite of the bad atmosphere of the early days, which I have

[48] M. H. de Kock, Deputy Governor of South African Bank; co-delegate at Bretton Woods Conference, 1944; Reporting delegate for Committee on Organisation and Management of International Monetary Fund.

[49] Pierre Mendés-France (b. 1907); Finance Minister, Provisional Government of France, 1943–4; Head of French Financial Missions, Washington and Bretton Woods, 1944; Minister of National Economy, 1944–5; Prime Minister of France, 1954–5.

[50] The name 'Drozniak' replaced the name 'Brozniak' in the later version.

mentioned above, the Conference mellowed, as generally happens, towards the end. My last memory is of Dr Harry White, with vine leaves (or were they cocktails?) in his hair, leading into the dining room a Bacchic rout of satyrs and Silenuses from Latin America, loudly chanting the strains of 'Onward Christian Soldiers'. So we must hope for the best.[51]

III

What of the future? We all came away convinced that we shall be making a grave mistake if we do not treat our participation in these institutions seriously and give them of our best. They are certain to be deeply involved in grave problems which are also our problems. The standing and quality of the appointments already made by others indicate that we cannot afford to be less adequately represented. We have a great opportunity for leadership and for guiding the new institutions—in spite of the initial mistakes which have been made—to a position of high usefulness and to becoming key bodies in the international institutions of the future. The Fund can scarcely be, at any rate in the early years, the nucleus of a super-central bank, such as we hoped. It will be a different kind of body, much more closely linked in its activities to the Treasury and other Whitehall Departments, and much less to the Bank of England, than we had been anticipating. But[52] it may prove none the less important.

Indeed, the main point for London to realise clearly is that the two institutions have become *different* from what we were expecting when we came away from Bretton Woods. For their former purpose, as we had conceived it, they have probably become less *efficient*. But their new rôle may be both *important*

---

[51] This paragraph did not appear in the later version. On its subject Rowe-Dutton recorded: 'The closing scene was when Lord Keynes left the dining-room on the last evening, when the whole company rose to its feet to sing "For he's a jolly good fellow". For once the conference showed complete unanimity.'

[52] The additional words 'though different in function and in opportunity' followed the word 'But' in the later version.

and *useful*. I fancy that the Americans themselves are only half self-conscious about the sea-change which has occurred. What has happened, as I see it, is like this.

The National Advisory Council, set up by Congress under the Bretton Woods Act, consisting of the Secretary of the Treasury (as Chairman), the Secretary of State (or his deputy), the Secretary of Commerce, the Chairman of the Federal Reserve Board and the Chairman of the Export–Import Bank has become (under Mr Vinson's chairmanship) much more of a reality than anyone had been expecting. It is, in effect, a Cabinet Committee in charge of all economic-financial international affairs, and is proving more effective and looks more likely to last than is usually the case with such Washington Committees. It meets every week and is collecting a small group of whole-time officials.

This Council has obtained or expects to obtain certain powers from Congress, namely—

   (i) A statutory position;
  (ii) The Bretton Woods Fund;
 (iii) The Bretton Woods Bank with powers to borrow on the American market without going to Congress;
  (iv) The Export–Import Bank with the substantial capital of $5\frac{3}{4}$ billions of which perhaps 2 billions is already committed but very little actually spent;
   (v) The British Loan.

The Council has to report to Congress once a year and must keep itself reasonably free from public criticism. But the idea and the hope is that a considerable time can be allowed to pass before it has to go to Congress again for any additional powers or additional finance. For the first time the Administration possesses an organ for international collaboration on economic and financial affairs which is relatively independent of Congress. That, for all of us, is a step forward, the importance of which is not to be under-estimated.[52]

[52] The word 'evident' replaced the words 'not to be under-estimated' in the later version.

It is through this Council that the Administration propose to participate in economic reconstruction in the outside world. Its main organs will be the Bretton Woods Fund and Bank. The predominance of the American position will be safeguarded. It is expected that the main provision of funds will be American. But we are invited to participate as senior amongst the other partners—Vice-Chairman, so to speak, to their Chairmanship. The new bodies will take over the functions of the Economic Committee of the League with far greater powers to operate; they will provide the guts of the Economic and Social Council of U.N.O.; and much more, too. It would be exceedingly misguided on our part to crab the new bodies, to cold-shoulder them, to stand aside. We must do our utmost to make them a success.

It is this change from technical to political tasks which explains[54] the Washington venue; and it is the character of the duties envisaged which explains the American determination for a team of whole-time directors and alternates of the highest calibre and correspondingly remunerated. It may have been rather stupid of us not to tumble to all this sooner. Some of our criticism and opposition may have seemed churlish and a little off the point. But we were not handled in a way which made apprehension easy. Moreover, as I have said, the Americans are only half self-conscious about the above.[55] And even, in so far as they are self-conscious, they do not want things talked about just yet on any such explicit lines as the above. They are still feeling their way.

IV

Our problem of staffing falls into two parts—our national representatives in the shape of Executive Directors and Alternates, and our contribution of manpower to the staff of the international civil service. I suggest that the Governor, who

[54] The additional words 'even if it does not justify' followed the word 'explains' in the later version.
[55] The words 'their purpose' replaced the words 'the above' in the later version.

could cover both the Fund and the Bank, should be, sometimes at least, a Minister.

We are bound to station at least one man continuously in Washington as Director or Alternate. He might act as alternate on both bodies. He might act as Director on both. He might act as Director on one and alternate on the other. At least two others will have to be available in Washington from time to time, but could be largely occupied on associated duties and interests in London. The indications are, therefore, that we need a team of, perhaps, the full four, two or three of whom would, however, be part-time, so far as work strictly appertaining to the Fund and Bank were concerned, and only intermittently resident in Washington. The practicability of such a plan will partly depend on whether the Fund and the Bank are prepared to reserve their more important business and major decisions of policy for periodic meetings, say once in three months, instead of taking them at any time when they happen to be ready. (In private conversation Dr White indicated his personal willingness to co-operate towards making something of this kind possible.)

Obviously this will need careful thought in the light not only of the duties required but of the men available.[56] I plunge into a first draft so as to afford a basis of discussion:

(*a*) A separate section of O.F. might be set up to which would be assigned all problems of international co-operation and reconstruction within the purview of the Treasury. At the present time this would cover UNRRA, the Economic and Social Council, the International Monetary Fund and the Bank for Reconstruction, and include the exchange problems of all *overseas* countries (but not our own exchange control) and relief and reconstruction advice and assistance overseas (but not loans made for strictly commercial purposes or, except secondarily, affairs within the British Commonwealth or the problems arising out of the liquidation of Sterling Area balances).

(*b*) This section would have attached to it a small inter-

---

[56] The sentences from here to the end of (*e*) did not appear in the later version.

departmental Committee representing the Foreign Office, the Board of Trade, the Economic Section and the Bank of England as well as the Treasury.

(*c*) The Executive Directors and Alternates would be drawn from the members of this Committee, including the Under-Secretary, Third Secretary or Second Secretary in the Treasury concerned with this field, as convenience and the importance of the current work might dictate. Apart from our representative continuously resident in Washington, or perhaps two from time to time if and when the briskness of the business afoot appeared to justify it, the others might take it in turns (not strictly and without prejudice to a particular individual serving for an appropriate period) to attend the more important meetings in Washington, so that there would be a group of officials with experience of Washington and cultivating wide international contacts.

(*d*) It would be the duty of any members of the above group, continuously or intermittently resident in Washington, to assist the Ambassador and the Treasury Representative in Washington on any matters where their special knowledge and experience would be helpful, and they would not be limited to work specifically connected with the Fund or the Bank. Similarly it might sometimes be convenient for the Treasury Representative in Washington to act as Director or Alternate. It would probably be advisable that the Washington resident should not so continue for more than two years at the maximum.

(*e*) Members of the group should continue, however occupied, to draw their normal civil service or Bank of England salaries. When in Washington, whether continuously or intermittently, they should draw in addition a living allowance from the Bank or the Fund. This allowance, whilst not reaching the permitted ceiling, should be substantial and liberal. The allowance will be inclusive of entertainment expenses and the economic position of the British representatives should not be markedly inferior to that of their colleagues. $40 a day for

Directors and $30 a day for Alternates *plus* travelling expenses might not be inappropriate for short visits, with three-quarters of this rate for a longer stay. (Governors will receive $50 a day and travelling expenses.)

The question of the international staff of the two bodies presents much difficulty. The Managing Director of the Fund and the President of the Bank will receive $30,000 free of all taxes, [57] which, on the basis of British taxation is the equivalent of about £120,000 a year subject to tax (which, personally, I can only regard as the *reductio ad absurdum* of our tax system for peace-time purposes), *plus* a substantial expense and entertainment allowance. These two officers will be appointed at the first meeting of the Executive Directors. With some difficulty I succeeded in getting this meeting put off until around the 1st May next, so as to give the Chancellor time to look round both for Directors and for staff. [58]

The Managing Director and the President will then appoint their own staffs, ideas about which are still very fluid. It is expected, I think, that each will have a Deputy with substantial emoluments. Some hold that the rest of the staff should start small and grow gradually. Others are thinking in terms of 150 to 200 economists and statisticians and the rest of the outfit in proportion. They will have to be reasonably polyglot. A fairly large staff is probable.

The Americans propose to nominate the President of the Bank. Mr Clayton was approached and has refused. There are no authentic rumours as to who it is to be. Mr Vinson is a poker player who holds his cards close to his chest. Some excellent names have been mentioned; others much less so, which would be of the nature of political patronage.

As Managing Director of the Fund the Americans, with our full approval, approached Mr Graham Towers, Governor of the Bank of Canada, but he refused. Thereafter several of us,

[57] The words 'which...peace-time purposes' did not appear in the later version.
[58] In the later version the words '(It has now been called for the 5th May)' were added here.

237

including, in particular, the Canadians, French, Dutch and Belgians, sounded M. Gutt. an old and trusted friend and a successful former Finance Minister of Belgium (though no longer young or very vigorous).[59] He is not disinclined to serve and proposes to arrive in London from Brussels on the 1st April to talk things over with us. When I last saw him, shortly before he left Savannah, he was somewhat disconcerted by the fact that no approach to him had been made by Mr Vinson.[60] I do not know if this was made good at their final meeting; but I heard subsequently that M. Gutt's candidature was not favoured by the Latin Americans. I am not aware of any other plausible candidate in sight.

If we cannot supply either the President or the Managing Director, then it is of the first importance that we should supply at least one of their Deputies and two or three other key men and economists and statisticians. The tax-free character of the stipends may facilitate an otherwise difficult task. I trust that those concerned with questions of personnel will give most earnest and early attention to this problem.

27 March 1946   KEYNES

[59] In the later version the words 'He is prepared to serve if invited to do so; but he lays stress on being supported by a well-qualified British deputy' replaced the words 'He is not...before he left Savannah'.
[60] The words 'at Savannah' followed the words 'Mr Vinson' in the later version.

Chapter 2

COMMERCIAL POLICY, DECEMBER 1941–DECEMBER 1945

From his 'Proposals to Counter the German "New Order"' (*JMK*, vol. xxv, pp. 7–16) onwards Keynes had taken an occasional part in discussions of post-war trade policy. In the course of his Washington visit in 1941 he had helped undermine the attempt of the Board of Trade to extend the Anglo-American Trade Agreement of 1938 and had played an important role in the early discussions of the form of the master Lend Lease Agreement. After his return to London, throughout the rest of 1941 and the early part of 1942 he continued to take part in the Lend Lease Agreement discussions, especially those surrounding Article VII (*JMK*, vol. xxiii, pp. 143–7, chs 4 and 6).

In December 1941 Mr Pasvolsky of the State Department completed a memorandum entitled 'Possibilities of Conflict of British and American Official Views on Post-War Economic Policy'. He passed a copy of this to Redvers Opie for transmission in confidence to London. On reading the memorandum, Keynes commented

My notes on Mr Pasvolsky's memo:

1. The bulk of this paper, which is a very able one within its own limitations, is a dogmatic statement of the virtues of *laissez-faire* in international trade on the lines familiar forty years ago, much of which is true, but without any attempt to state theoretically or to tackle practically the difficulties which both the theory and the history of the last twenty years has impressed on most modern minds. Mr Pasvolsky *looks* like Rip Van Winkle and evidently *is*, in fact, he!

2. He admits the difficulties in our post-war balance of payments problem in his Section II but he gives no hint anywhere how we are to solve it.

3. I infer that he expects our post-war difficulties to be due primarily to lack of export productive capacity, not of markets.

4. This leads him to misunderstand the nature of the

argument in favour of bilateral agreements which he regards as no more than a means of obtaining forced loans by means of blocked balances. He regards it as a dogma that *laissez-faire* must maximise *everyone's* trade, and the notion that trade might take place under a barter arrangement, which otherwise could not take place at all, would strike at the root of his philosophy. For example, we desire meat and will pay £110 for it; Argentine desires a motor car price £110 in U.K. and £100 in U.S.A.; U.S.A. does not desire the meat, has a tariff against it and will not pay more than £50 for it, if that; the Argentine has the meat and will gladly accept £100 for it rather than not sell it but cannot take less than £100; we, having no dollars, can only afford to buy the meat if we sell the car. Under *laissez-faire* the trade cannot take place; for if we pay for the meat in money, whether at £110 or £100, the Argentine will spend the money in buying the car in U.S.A., and we become insolvent. Some system by which our buying the meat is made contingent on the Argentine buying our car is the only way by which the trade can take place. Otherwise the Argentine's meat producers and our motor-car producers are both thrown out of work.

This possibility is excluded in Mr Pasvolsky's philosophy because of latent assumptions, assumed in his classical theory but not realised in practice, that, if you buy the Argentine meat for cash and the Argentines buy the American car for cash, it necessarily follows that America will buy from us some export worth £100. In other words, Mr Pasvolsky's fundamental philosophy has assumed the non-existence of the very problem we are out to solve.

5. He seems unaware that tariffs can be so operated as to defeat the purposes of M.F.N. He nowhere justifies greater hostility to preferences than to tariffs.

6. In all this Mr Pasvolsky is a long way below the level of responsible academic thinking in U.S.A. Prof. Viner, Prof. J. M. Clark, Prof. Hansen, Mr Currie, Mr Walter Stewart,

Mr Mordecai Ezekiel[1] (I name these because they all advise Government Departments) and many others would be ashamed to have this document regarded as representing the stage of economic education which U.S.A has reached.

For this reason I feel some hesitation about giving it widespread circulation in Whitehall. For this might lead to its importance being greatly over-estimated. Its significance is pathological, casting psychological light on some important elements in the State Department, elements the ultimate importance of which in moulding American policy we are already in danger of over-estimating. It is, indeed, a further piece of evidence (if we need more evidence) how desirable it is, if possible, to approach the Americans with a multilateral proposal,—and for that reason, to me at least, welcome. But advocates of bilateral clearing agreements and of sterling area solidarity cannot be expected to accept this as a fair or properly informed exposition of what they are driving at.

7. Nevertheless the upshot and final conclusion of the document about what subjects now need discussion is, as Sir R. Hopkins points out, entirely in line with what we ourselves look forward to. The chief moral I draw from this paper is the inadvisability (which I wish Lord Halifax could be made to appreciate) of our being asked to sign up ambiguous under-takings on the dotted line *in advance* of face-to-face discussion about the principles of future policy. Mr Pasvolsky seems on this point to be in full agreement *with us*. Our position could not be better stated than in the second paragraph of his p. 53 which I have marked in the text. I should like to pick up this paragraph, emphasise it back to Washington, express our agreement with Mr Pasvolsky's *agenda* and forget the rest of his paper.

8. The disadvantage of continuing much longer behind two sets of closed doors is emphasised by the extent to which Mr

---

[1] Mordecai Ezekiel (b. 1899); economist with U.S. Department of Agriculture, 1922–46; U.N. Food and Agriculture Organisation, 1947–62; U.S. Department of State, 1962–4.

Pasvolsky has got us wrong. See, for example, the reference to myself on p. 11 as the protagonist of bilateral clearings, which reads oddly in the light of our actual discussions. I never had a conversation with Pasvolsky on this subject whilst I was in Washington, since, although I saw him once or twice, he was away sick during most of my visit. He is depending on garbled accounts of my conversations with Stirling and Hawkins on the Trade Agreement, which were broken off incomplete and which Hawkins did not pretend to follow with understanding. I should like to send Opie a letter about this which he is free to 'leak' to Pasvolsky. Do you see any objection to this? I append a draft. Perhaps a letter like this might fill the bill for the time being so far as Washington is concerned.

[copy initialled] J.M.K.

5 January 1942

J.M.K. to Opie (through Lord Halifax with a covering note saying that he might confidentially let Pasvolsky have a copy of this letter):

Dear Opie,

We have been reading with very great interest a most able memorandum by Pasvolsky which has reached us confidentially through your hands.

I myself feel that he is inclined to slur over the necessary accompanying conditions of multilateralism, conditions which have not yet been specified with enough clearness. But there remains a wide area of agreement. I note the following points in particular:

(1) We appreciate his realisation of the difficulties we face in our post-war balance of payments. As regards the actual figures we have almost finished as careful a study of the prospects as the available facts allow.

(2) Pasvolsky's *agenda* (on pp. 54, 55) of the matters for discussion are in very close conformity with what we ourselves would like to put forward.

(3) His statement in the second paragraph of p. 53 about the advisability of preceding a declaration of general policy 'by a thorough exploration of, and agreement on, the specific policies which will need to be followed' could not be bettered. That is just what we are pleading for. The State Department are causing false alignments and dangerous misunderstandings, and the magnification of what may not turn out to be real divergencies, by their insistence that we should sign general principles on the dotted line before we have discussed the specific policies required to carry them out. Can't you persuade them what an error of tactics and psychology it is to press first and foremost for this signing on the dotted line business, even though coupled with assurances that the words do not mean quite what they say? It has, as I have said, the effect of magnifying out of all proportion differences which can only be resolved *by discussion* and would, one can hope, cease to exist altogether in a fuller and more detailed setting of policy.

(4) The disadvantage of our proceeding much longer behind two sets of closed doors is illustrated by his reference to my alleged attitude on p. 11, which reads very oddly (as perhaps Stirling will have told you) to anyone who has taken part in our domestic discussions where I have been perhaps the most ardent of all in advocating a multilateral solution. I didn't have the chance of a personal discussion on this with Pasvolsky when I was in Washington, for he was away sick much of the time. I expect he is depending on a misunderstanding of a very incomplete discussion I had with Hawkins, broken off as Stirling will remember half way through, in which I was emphasising the inadvisability of our signing away certain principles *before* the conditions necessary for multilateralism had been devised and agreed.

Yours sincerely,
[draft not initialled]

On reading Keynes's comment and suggested letter, Sir Horace Wilson minuted

From SIR HORACE WILSON, *23 January 1942*

I saw these papers on their way to the Chancellor, covering Mr Pasvolsky's memorandum, and I appreciate (and to a very large extent share) your desire to hit back. I am wondering, however, whether the advantages and pleasure of this procedure will, in practice, outweigh the disadvantage of seeming to take Mr Pasvolsky's opinions as worth quite that shot of ours, still less the disadvantage that 'by the nature of the beast' Mr Pasvolsky will feel bound to try to defend himself and to produce still more memoranda for which he will say that he has been provided with adequate excuse. In any event, ought we not to have advanced rather further, both in clearing our own minds and in securing some sort of ministerial acquiescence in our views, before disclosing to anyone in the State Department part of what may turn out to be our line of approach?

23 January 1942   H.W.

To this Keynes replied.

To SIR HORACE WILSON, *27 January 1942*

Would you object to my sending something to Opie embodying the substance of section 4 of my draft letter below which deals with my own position? Pasvolsky's document, which has probably had extensive circulation, attributes to me by name opinions the opposite of those which I hold. Having seen this document, I feel it is embarrassing to allow this statement to go on circulating without contradiction.

Rightly or wrongly, I rather favour the technique of the 'leak' in our relations with the Americans! They practise this themselves on an exaggerated scale, which it would be not only inadvisable but impossible for us to imitate. But, if we go too far to the other extreme and become complete oysters during all the preliminary stages of discussion, misunderstandings, not only of what we are after, but as to whether we are after anything at all and are not being merely obstructive, are liable to arise.

27 January 1942   J.M.K.

The result was Wilson's agreement to a letter to Opie.

To REDVERS OPIE, *13 February 1942*

My dear Opie,

Though it is all rather a long time ago and stale matter now, I should like to send you a line about that most able memorandum by Pasvolsky which reached us confidentially through your hands. I won't attempt to comment on this document, but I should like to say a word about the reference to myself somewhere in the course of it, where I am put forward as the protagonist of bilateral policies.

To anyone who had been present at the numerous discussions we have had over here since I came back from Washington this would read most oddly. In fact, exactly the opposite has been true. I imagine that Pasvolsky was depending on a misunderstanding of a very incomplete discussion I had with Hawkins, broken off, as Stirling will remember, half way through, in which I was emphasising the inadvisability of our signing away certain principles *before* the conditions necessary for multilateralism had been devised and agreed. If you get a chance of mentioning the substance of this to Pasvolsky very informally sometime, I wish you would do so. I should not like him to go on labouring under this misapprehension.

Since you went back we have been working intensively on the preparations and discussions about international post-war arrangements. It is a tremendous job to get a large volume of papers agreed by all the many Departments of Whitehall simultaneously. But we really have made rather remarkable progress, I think. Within two months at the latest we ought to be well on the way to being ready.

I have had a little talk about this with Winant, who is, I believe, going back to U.S.A. for a short visit in a week or two's time. He thinks that it might be undesirable at this early stage to have any formal conference which would be known to the Press and upset Congress unduly. Much the best plan would be for a small delegation of responsible U.S. officials to pay a visit here in the early spring with a view to picking up our atmosphere, exploring the ground and exchanging ideas pretty fully. I do not know if that will come off, but all of us here believe that it is a very hopeful development. The Chancellor will be seeing Winant before the latter goes home and will, I expect be welcoming a gathering of this kind in London early in the spring.

Yours sincerely,
[copy initialled] J.M.K.

All this very confidential at present.

Keynes's letter to Opie inevitably led to a further exchange of letters.

From L. PASVOLSKY, *27 April 1942*

Dear Mr Keynes,

Redvers Opie has communicated to me the contents of your letter to him concerning my memorandum. I am most grateful for the kind things which you said about it and I am extremely sorry that I misstated your position on bilateralism. My reference to you in that connection was based on the reports which I had of your conversations in Washington last summer and which, I now realize, gave me the erroneous impression that you favored a policy of bilateralism. I may say that I was never so happy to be corrected on any statement I have ever made as I was in this instance.

I am thoroughly satisfied that, whatever may be the difficulties and requirements of the transitional period, the acceptance by either your country or mine of bilateralistic ideas as the basis of post-war economic policy will lead to inescapable disaster. In this connection, you may be interested in a recent speech of mine, which incorporates some of the material contained in my memorandum. May I call your attention particularly to the passages marked on pages 18–20?

With kindest personal regards,
Sincerely yours,
LEO PASVOLSKY

To L. PASVOLSKY, *22 May 1942*

Dear Mr Pasvolsky,

Thank you very much indeed for your letter of April 27th and the pamphlet which you sent me with it. The confusion about the policies I advocate arose because I found it so necessary when I was in Washington to emphasise the degree of our post-war difficulties and to explain that, unless they were solved by some other means, there appeared to me to be nothing we could fall back on in the last resort except a policy of bilateralism.

This was misinterpreted to mean that I myself favoured such a policy. In fact my object was quite the contrary. I was arguing the importance of finding an alternative solution, but at the same time not blinking the difficulty of finding another and, as I should have said, the right way out.

The more closely I have examined the details of bilateralism since I came home, and the more I have looked at alternatives, the more firmly have I felt that the alternative line is the right one for all of us. Bilateralism may be all very well if one looks at it from the point of view of a single country pursuing it with enlightened self-interest. But as a world system with everyone playing at the game I am appalled at the complications and errors likely to arise.

So let us get busy on finding the alternative. I am hopeful from what I hear that the delays hitherto at getting down to this are coming to an end. No-one can foresee when the war will reach its conclusion. There is an immense amount of exchange of ideas to go forward and clarification of policies and the elaboration of new ideas before we shall be ready to face the new world.

Sincerely yours,
[copy initialled] J.M.K.

At the time Keynes wrote, James Meade was beginning to work up a series of proposals for post-war commercial policy which would go beyond the context of the 1938 Anglo-American Trade Agreement. By August 1942 these received limited circulation and Keynes suggested that Meade try them on Sir Arnold Overton of the Board of Trade. By the autumn, the Board of Trade had made Meade's proposals its own and the usual inter-departmental committee, this time under the chairmanship of Sir Arnold Overton, was at work. Although Keynes was not a Treasury representative on the Committee, he did comment on the Board of Trade's proposals as they came before it.

To SIR WILFRID EADY, *20 November 1942*

PROJECT OF A COMMERCIAL UNION

I have now dug out Meade's original draft of this, from which the President of the Board of Trade's document is believed to have sprung. You will see that it is a much more considered and careful document and not open to all the criticisms which we passed the other day on the version which had reached us. It will not be worth your while to read the original draft at the bottom of this file dated August 4th. You will see that in my letter of August 10th I suggest that he should try it on Overton, and I made some criticisms. Then comes his revised draft dated August 21, which is worth your attention.

But, although this is a much better document than the one officially before us, I believe that, in the preamble, at any rate, as distinct from the specific proposals for a Commercial Union, we should do well to break up the problem into its several heads on some such lines as the following:

1. *Means to avoid an unbalanced position of international payments*
   Bilateral barter agreements
   Import quotas and prohibitions
   Export subsidies

2. *Means to foster new industries or preserve old ones for domestic purposes*
   Tariffs
   Subsidies for domestic produce consumed at home
3. *Means to foster special political or geographical or racial intimacies*
   Preferences
   Customs unions
4. *International purchasing and selling combinations*
   (i) State trading
   (ii) Bulk purchasing either on long or short term contracts
   (iii) International cartels between private interests for manufactured or semi-manufactured products
   (iv) International quotas for primary products between private interests
   (v) Buffer stocks and international quotas sponsored by governments.

We could, in my opinion, comment on these various headings somewhat as follows:

(1) We are prepared to agree to the prohibition of these expedients subject to the safeguards set out in paragraph 38 of the Clearing Union scheme, by which, in certain circumstances, a debtor country is allowed an emergency exit.

(2) We could express ourselves in favour of a provision forbidding new tariffs or subsidies in excess of 30 per cent and providing for a gradual reduction down to that level of all existing tariffs and subsidies exceeding 30 per cent.

(3) Here we could argue that it is not reasonable to disallow all intermediate relationships between complete separation and complete federation. A number of cases may arise where even the outsider may agree that it is a good thing to encourage special intimacies, and, generally speaking, it might be agreed there is no sufficient ground to forbid them altogether. There might, therefore, be complete liberty to undertake customs unions,

provided that they are complete and provide for full free trade between the members. As regards preferences, we might agree that any new preferences should not exceed 15 per cent, and preferences in excess of that figure should be gradually reduced.

(4) We are prepared with proposals covering 4 (v). If this were accepted, 4 (iv) would not arise. 4 (i) and 4 (ii) raise difficult questions, especially in relation to Russia, about which we have reached no settled conclusions. We have some reason to believe that the United States is especially interested in 4 (iii) and would be interested to hear of any concrete proposals.

The whole of the above should be governed by safeguards relating to the transitional period.

The above leaves on one side one important concept of Meade's, namely, the project of the Commercial Union, all the members of which are entitled to the advantages of the standard rules of the Union, provided they are also prepared to accept its disadvantages. But what has been set forth above is intended to be an outline of what such standard rules might contain. Under Meade's proposals members of the Commercial Union would be free to make any arrangements they liked not conforming to the general rules with non-members.

[copy initialled] K

The Overton Committee's deliberations resulted in two reports, one from a majority of the Committee, the other from Sir Hubert Henderson, one of the Treasury representatives.[2] Keynes commented on drafts of both documents.

---

[2] Henderson's report later appeared as 'Great Britain's Post-war Commercial Policy' in *The Inter-War Years and Other Essays* (ed. H. Clay) (Oxford, 1955).

To S. D. WALEY *and others, 31 December 1942*

OVERTON COMMITTEE DRAFT REPORT

The general lay-out of this draft seems to me satisfactory. But I have the following comments, some of them important:

(1) The paper is well designed to call the American bluff that it is we who are the obstacles in the way of more free trade. But, looked at from another angle, I am a bit scared of it. It seems to me to go considerably further than the United States, or indeed any country other than ourselves, is at all likely to accept. We have to remember that the free trade element in the State Department, with whom we are in direct contact, represents almost nothing but themselves. If this document was to get into the hands of Republicans, it might prove, I fear, political dynamite,—a dangerous British plot and just what it would suit the Isolationists to accuse the State Department and ourselves of conspiring to produce. Thus, I should want to have the consensus of several wise heads in close touch with Washington conditions before letting it see the light.

(2) On the other hand, I am rather in the dark as to the magnitude of the changes in which those who accepted it would be immediately involved. Should there not be an appendix setting out the arrangements with a typical group of countries as they are now and as they would be if this plan were accepted?

(3) There is not a word on the rather important subject of local customs unions, whether amounting to a *Zollverein* or merely preferential arrangements. I mean Balkan Unions and the like. It seems to me that geographical groupings of this sort should be entitled to the same measures of preferences between themselves as we are claiming in the case of political groupings. At any rate, the matter needs discussion and ventilation.

(4) I find it difficult to interpret the relation of paragraph 16 to *future* tariffs and subsidies. 16B seems to be drafted on the assumption that there will be no new tariffs hereafter. Surely

that is impracticable. But, if there are new tariffs, what is the interpretation of B(ii)? I appreciate the reasons given in paragraph 22 for the introduction of B(ii). But, all the same, it does not seem to make much sense. If all future new tariffs are forbidden, this should be stated. If they are allowed, provision should be made for them.

(5) A maximum *ad valorem* duty of 25 per cent is not much use to an infant industry. That is a matter on which India and the Dominions and a good many other countries will be interested. There is no reference to the problem of infant industries. Apparently, they can be given unlimited subsidies under 16 C. But that is only a substitute where the Budget is in a position to do the needful entirely through the technique of subsidising.

(6) The clause 16 C(i), which forbids subsidies, seems to me to be drafted, either on purpose or by mistake, in a fashion which, to my mind, does not meet the case. Governments are allowed to give unlimited subsidies to exports, provided they subsidise their home consumer to the same extent. It had never occurred to me that this is what we meant by deprecating export subsidies. It would, for example, allow the United States to export cotton and wheat to any extent so long as the home as well as the foreign consumer was paying the same price. Moreover, it would allow a cotton producer, such as Brazil, or once again the U.S., to subsidise cotton used by the local manufacturer whilst charging a higher world price for export cotton and then allow the subsidised home producer to compete on the world textile markets. It allows the producer of a raw material to sell that raw material cheaper at home, even though it be for subsequent use in exporting, than the exported raw material. I should like to know whether all this is deliberate or inadvertent. Surely the subsidising of exports should be interpreted to mean their sale abroad at a price less than that received by the home producer.

(7) In 16 D(i) the same question arises as in the case of tariffs.

The draft seems to assume that no new quantitative import restrictions will ever be introduced. Does that make sense? If, on the other hand, they are introduced, how is that compatible with always reducing them below what they were at some past fixed date?

KEYNES

31 December 1942

To SIR HUBERT HENDERSON, *4 January 1943*

Dear Hubert,

You have written a magnificent document, which, in my judgment, knocks the Overton Report sideways. I attach a copy of a note on it, with some part of which you may not agree, for circulation to those interested.

Yours ever,
J.M.K.

To SIR WILFRID EADY AND OTHERS, *4 January 1943*

SIR H. HENDERSON'S CRITICISM OF THE OVERTON DRAFT REPORT ON POST-WAR COMMERCIAL POLICY

The most advisable course very likely lies between the Overton Report and Henderson's critical rejoinder. But Henderson's impresses me as the more fundamental line of approach. His is a most powerful paper, and he makes the majority report look superficial. It is undoubtedly up to them to come down to earth and answer, if they can, his very pertinent criticisms.

The majority draftsmen seem to be moved—(1) by a strong free-trade bias—too strong until we know more about the set-up of the post-war world. The greater the degree of planning, the more inappropriate obviously is an attitude, the intellectual support of which is so largely based on the assumption of *laissez-faire* conditions; and (2) by a desire to meet the supposed wishes of the United States—wishes, however, which are only those of a small (though at present influential) minority and are probably violently opposed to the majority policy in Congress. We can easily run the risk of appearing to affront Congress by taking the initiative along the lines proposed.

The Overton Draft, as Henderson points out, seems to give scarcely a thought to the question where our self-interest lies. Certainly it is entirely lacking in any considered calculation of the actual consequences of their proposals to our trade position. Ought we not to begin in a much more concrete manner? Should we not be considering what we are likely to want to do after the war and whether this frame-work is likely to fit it? For instance, we shall very likely have to decide that we cannot afford to import, e.g. motor-cars, aeroplanes, radio apparatus, refrigerators, agricultural machinery, manufactured paper, textiles, etc. except in insignificant quantities. How do we propose under this set-up to arrive at that result? We shall have to increase our exports to the British Commonwealth generally, and especially to the East and West African colonies, on a large scale. Do we think that these proposals will help us to do so?

I am inclined to agree with Henderson's criticism of the present version of the escape clause based on Clearing Union statistics. I should prefer to put it the other way round, *e.g.* that no country shall be required to limit either tariffs or import restrictions until it has been a creditor on the average of the previous five years, and that when once it has satisfied this condition it shall not reimpose these restrictions in excess of the maximum credit figure until it has been in debit by (say) a quarter of its quota on the average of two years.

Also, as I said before, I am not happy with the present definition of export subsidies. It would mean that Brazil and the United States could supply their own textile manufacturers with cotton at a cheaper price than they supplied the export market and then proceed to sell cotton textiles abroad on this subsidised basis, provided only that they allow their own consumers also the benefit of the subsidy.

*   *   *   *

It is essential that any preference concessions we make should be absolutely and clearly contingent on a multilateral scheme. The Draft Report does not point out the extraordinary difficulties in the way of Congress accepting this. It would not be possible for the Administration to enter into a multilateral arrangement on the basis either of the existing tariff legislation or of a projected extension of it. Such a plan would have to be expressly approved by Congress. And it would differ from anything Congress has ever passed hitherto in that it would tie their hands for the future. I should have thought, therefore, that the chance of the United States accepting these proposals was rather remote. It is equally unlikely, though for different reasons, that China or Russia or most of our European friends would accept them. The chief virtue of the paper is that it calls the American bluff that it is we who are the obstacles in the way of a movement towards free trade. But I do not believe that the Overton draft represents a scheme of things that can be expected to come to pass. It all becomes, therefore, very much a question of political tactics.

Looked at from this angle, I am finding Henderson's argument increasingly convincing, that it is wiser for us *not* to take the initiative. Surely this would be wise until there is more evidence as to whether, in connection with the prospective legislation, Congress encourages or rebuffs free-trade ideas. It would be a mistake for us to show our hand meanwhile.

Nevertheless, when we enter into discussions with the Americans we are bound in conversation to express views, and for this purpose we ought to be clear in our mind what we are prepared to say if challenged. I suggest that the following (which perhaps goes further than Henderson would himself agree) might meet the case:

255

(1) We are prepared to make all arrangements, apart from preferences, non-discriminatory.

(2) We are prepared to abate preferences gradually but substantially if there is a multilateral plan generally agreed for reducing tariffs, export subsidies and shipping subsidies* to an extent calculated to help us in putting our trade position in better balance.

(3) We are prepared to abate import restrictions in course of time, subject to some kind of an escape clause based on the Clearing Union.

KEYNES

4 January 1943

In the discussions which followed, during which the majority of the Overton Committee prepared a rejoinder to Henderson's document, Keynes made two more contributions, sending a copy of the second to Sir Arnold Overton.

POST-WAR COMMERCIAL POLICY

The Report of the Committee and the Note by the President of the Board of Trade

I

1. As I stand half way between Sir Hubert Henderson and the Committee, I venture to put forward a suggestion less rash than the recommendation of the Committee (for I agree with Sir Hubert Henderson that it is very rash indeed), but more constructive and forthcoming than Sir Hubert Henderson's. I begin with some general observations.

2. The conclusion that the general adoption of these proposals would help to restore our balance of payments rests too much

---

* Why does the draft report ignore shipping subsidies, which, from the point of view of our future earning power, are perhaps more important than any other single item?

on the *ipse dixit* of the Board of Trade and too little on a detailed survey. Nevertheless, subject to two qualifications to be mentioned in paragraphs 4 and 5 below, I am prepared to believe that the Board of Trade may be right, if a multilateral scheme on these lines was actually to be adopted by the greater part of the world.

3. But is there a reasonable chance of this? Unlike some of our other proposals, there is too much history and political background to commercial policy for the proposals to receive unprejudiced consideration anywhere. If the Board of Trade Report were to get into the hands of the Isolationist group in Congress, I believe that, so far from its assisting our position with the Americans, it would be used as a most dangerous weapon against us. I should doubt if there is any chance of India accepting these proposals, and I am not sure that the Dominions would consider that there was sufficient protection for their infant industries. They bear no reasonable relation to the set-up or prospective set-up in Russia or China. What about South America? They would be regarded almost throughout Europe as destructive of the existing agricultural system as well as exposing industries in a weak position to the full blast of competition. There is hardly any country in the world in which they would not provoke serious opposition. Unless we think that there is really a substantial chance of these proposals being acceptable to the world at large, it all becomes very much a question of tactics. I am fearful of prejudicing our other post-war plans by associating them too closely with something as full of dangerous political dynamite as this.

4. The point on which I am in unqualified agreement with Sir Hubert Henderson is in opposing the offer to begin giving up all quantitative import restrictions after two years, subject to an escape clause based on a country's position with the Clearing Union. There is nothing so objectionable in principle about quantitative import restrictions compared with tariffs that the former should go altogether and not the latter. Indeed they

are to be preferred to tariffs in many respects. But, above all, their abolition does not fit in at all with that degree of planning which is likely to exist in the post-war world. In our own case we are so unlikely to be in a position to afford to give them up that, as Sir Hubert Henderson points out, it is lacking in candour to purport to start giving up after two years a form of restriction which we shall most certainly be increasing rather than diminishing two years after the war is over. However successful other elements in post-war policy may be, I do not see the faintest chance of this country becoming altogether independent of quantitative import restrictions in the foreseeable future. It is not an overstatement to regard this part of the proposals of the Committee as irresponsible.

5.   The Overton Report shirks the question of shipping subsidies. Yet this is the form of subsidy from which we are most likely to suffer injury. Surely the exclusion of such subsidies, so far from being neglected, should be emphasised.

6. Nevertheless, it may be undesirable to appear to the State Department to be running away from Article VII or to leave undisturbed the atmosphere which has been created, in which we are made to appear as the principal impediment in the way of a movement towards greater freedom of trade. For, in fact, exactly the opposite is the case. There might be an advantage, therefore, in preparing a paper setting forth our general line of approach to be handed to the United States when it seems to be called for. But surely this paper should be much less detailed and particular in its proposals than the Overton Report. It must be premature to mention particular figures for the reduction of preferences or for ceilings to tariffs. Something on the lines of which a summary is given below might gain many of the advantages which could be hoped for from the Report of the Committee whilst avoiding some at least of the very great dangers to which the unguarded use of their Report might expose us.

II

(1) It is to be understood that the arrangements proposed are contingent on the successful establishment of some form of multilateral clearing and the adoption of a system which allows and encourages an expansive world economy.

(2) The proposals are also based on the assumption of a multilateral commercial policy agreement, embracing most of the major countries. It is impossible for this country to be put into a satisfactory trade position by any concessions which the United States alone is in a position to give to us, however liberal. On the other hand, we may have much to gain from a general policy of this kind covering our customers and suppliers generally.

(3) The United Kingdom, both by tradition and by experience, regards an increased freedom of trade as particularly in her interest. We shall join in any movement to secure it, and when it comes down to practice we are the least likely quarter in which to find opposition. Our sympathy is entirely with those who are seeking to extend the freedom of trade. Any qualifications we have to make are entirely due to the special difficulties of our position in the immediate post-war period and the present uncertainty as to what will in fact lie within our power.

(4) We will accept any ceiling for tariffs, however low, which is found to be generally acceptable for incorporation in a multilateral agreement.

(5) We are prepared to make all our arrangements, including particularly quantitative restriction of imports, non-discriminatory. Preferences, which we do not regard as discriminatory in a strict sense of the word, are dealt with below.

(6) Quite apart from our own position, a general plan should leave room for special arrangements between political and geographical groups, since these are likely to be asked for and can be properly conceded in many cases. We do not ask for any

lasting concessions in regard to Imperial Preferences not granted in other cases. We are prepared to reduce them progressively on more drastic lines than those which may be agreed for tariffs under (4) above, with a view to their ultimate elimination as and when the freeing of trade generally gives us reason to feel that our balance of payments is safe without this protection.

(7) We have no affection for the quantitative regulation of imports for its own sake. We are prepared to agree from the outset that such regulations should be entirely non-discriminatory. We shall gladly give them up altogether as soon as it is clear that we can afford to do without them. But we can see no likelihood, in the best of circumstances to be expected, of our becoming independent of them in the near future.

(8) We are prepared to agree to measures designed to prevent export subsidies and, more particularly, subsidies to shipping.

III

If we were to take the initative on the lines of the Overton Report, all the other parties concerned would then seek to modify the proposals to their own advantage. We should have already gone to the limit. We should have shot our bolt, leaving the rest of the world with its ammunition in hand. No-one will look after us if we do not look after ourselves. The solution of our balance of trade problem is the clue to our post-war economic prospects all along the line. It is not a thing to be handled so light-heartedly. Without a more robust—if you like, a more selfish—policy, we are sunk.

KEYNES

15 January 1943

Dear Overton,

You may like to see this note, which I wrote on your Committee's rejoinder to Henderson, and Waley's comments on it.

You will see that my only real difficulty is about the first sentence in (vii). This is mainly a question of degree. But it seems to me so important practically that it is better to have no ambiguity about it.

I do not like the appearance of special hostility to import regulation, since it seems to me to be, not merely temporarily, but permanently much the best technique open to us for the sort of things we are likely to want to do. I am not clear that it is yet fully appreciated how the growth of state trading and planning generally is likely to favour import regulation as the better technique compared with tariffs or subsidies.

Except possibly in the case of agriculture, I do not in fact want to use import regulations except to support the balance of trade. Thus, in a sense, I am protected by the words you use. But I doubt if it would be enough to satisfy me that we should be entitled to use such a technique if we had got into trouble with the Clearing Union. We shall need, it seems to me, quasi-permanent arrangements, not merely to rescue us from achieved disaster, but to prevent us from reaching that stage of things altogether.

The fact that what you propose is entirely evaded by your permission to allow state trading is an extra reason, I suggest, for not being too strict about import regulation, since it becomes merely a discrimination against those countries which are relatively averse to state trading.

In practice, with the possible exception of agriculture, I can probably get what I want under your rubric, either by state trading or by pleading balance of trade difficulties. But if, in fact, we are going to get round the rubric in one or other or both of these ways, is it wise to stress it in so emphatic a manner?

I still feel, after reading Waley's note, that we want to make up our minds just what we are going to do about our own infant industries before we commit ourselves too deeply. My example of agricultural tractors is a good one. But this is probably extensible to almost the whole of the engineering industry. And oil refining is another good example, where we need to make up our minds what we intend and what we shall have to do before committing ourselves too deeply to *a priori* principles.

Yours sincerely,
[copy initialled] K

To SIR DAVID WALEY, *1 February 1943*

THE REPORT OF THE OVERTON COMMITTEE ON COMMERCIAL POLICY

I naturally have little to quarrel with in Part I of your rejoinder. I do, however, still adhere to the only two points where you have made a material change from my own suggestions. I feel that the first sentence in (vii) about quantitative regulation of imports goes too far. I am also sorry that you have still omitted to refer to shipping subsidies in (viii). They are the kind of subsidy from which we have most to fear, and they can, of course, be used as a means of subsidising any kind of export.

My main criticism on the rejoinder as a whole is that it still seems to me to be unrealistic. It is so abstract and *a priori*. There is no sign that the Committee have figured out in any sort of detail the kind of thing we may find ourselves forced to do after the war, with a view to seeing how this would fit in to their theoretical plan.

Let me give you a leading example of this. I believe that, broadly speaking, there is no type of engineering product which cannot be perfectly well produced in this country if we set ourselves to do so. But no doubt there will be a period when we are not 100 per cent self-sufficient. In a case like that, quota import restriction, providing that we import no more than the excess of our demand over what we are in a position to supply, is surely much the most effective and sensible way of doing it. Before the war we produced no agricultural track-laying tractors. After the war it will be absurd for us, as a long-term policy, to import any such articles at all, we must make them all ourselves. Nevertheless, for a time at least a limited import may be in our interests. How does the Committee propose to deal with a situation like that? The object would be to have in general no engineering imports whatever. But some exceptions, temporary or permanent, would be advisable. Tell me how you propose to arrange this.

Suppose again that in the interests of the plastic industries we decide that a large proportion of the oil we import must be imported crude and refined in this country, so that we get the by-products. We set up refining plant on a large scale, but not so as to make us completely self-supporting. The quota import restriction would be the ideal way of dealing with this. How does your Committee propose to deal with it?

Again, have you faced the agricultural problem? There again, quota import restriction seems the ideal technique; if you reject this what is your technique going to be?

The absurd thing seems to be that by the method of state trading you get round the difficulty altogether, since with state trading you can import just the quantity you choose to import and no more. Thus, state trading automatically provides a complete system of quota import restriction. Is it the object of the Committee to make state trading the technique in these cases or what? For example, of the problems I have raised above, none would arise if state trading was introduced. If tractors were made a monopoly of the Ministry of Agriculture they would import just the number required to make up the balance above what would be provided at home. If the Ministry of Food continued to have a monopoly on wheat importing, they would import the excess of our requirements over what it was our agricultural policy to produce ourselves. If the import of oil was handed over to the Ministry of Fuel etc. no problem would arise.

If, on the other hand, you really are contemplating *laissez-faire* in these matters, I think you may be moving in a world which is not only dead for the time being, but will not be resurrected. One senses an excessive prejudice against autarky. A great many manufactured products can be produced with almost equal efficiency in any industrial country. Undoubtedly, if the rest of the world is going to be more autarkic than formerly, we least of all can afford to be cut off from this. I see that we were importing before the war over £m200 manufactured goods. Probably the vast majority of these we shall have to manufacture for ourselves. Though sometimes, as in the case of oil, this will require a larger importation of raw materials.

Another respect in which the Report is unrealistic comes from its failure to compare the consequences of the set-up it proposes with the pre-war position. The appendix, which has just reached me, indicates that the recommendations about tariffs, taking the world as a whole, will have little or no effect, except in the case of rayon and perhaps woollens. But you make no attempt to show the effect on the tariff systems of the Dominions, or of the effect on countries which have agricultural protection. One would have supposed that you would begin by a careful examination of what the tariff systems of the world are and what consequences they have, and would then show in what respect you proposed to change them. On the evidence at present produced, your proposals about tariffs could do very little to help our export trade, whilst your attitude towards the quantitative regulation of imports might stand seriously in the way of our balancing our trade.

If the Committee have invented this policy out of their heads, without considering in detail just how it will work out, they have gone the wrong way about it. If, on the other hand, their Report is the outcome of a careful, realistic study, they have failed to do themselves justice by suppressing the realistic study on which it has been based.

KEYNES

1 February 1943

§5 Subsidies do not increase *total* consumption if they are met out of taxes.

Overton's reply to Keynes's letter of 3 February led to further correspondence. Keynes and Sir David Waley met Overton on 18 February.

From SIR ARNOLD OVERTON, *9 February 1943*

Dear Keynes,

Many thanks for your letter of the 3rd February and enclosures about commercial policy. At Waley's suggestion we have altered the first sentence of (vii) and I hope this meets your difficulty.

In the present context, you are mainly thinking of the development of industries in this country, which you fear would be prejudiced by our proposals. I want to assure you that I have had this point very much in mind. We are, in fact, already beginning to study, in consultation with the Supply Departments—Ministry of Aircraft Production and others—how best to turn over at least the major part of the enormous capacity in the engineering &c. trades for peace-time products. I do not think our style should be seriously cramped by the limitation of protective tariffs to 25 per cent and the gradual removal of import restrictions over a period, which for purposes of argument, is put at five years. But if it were in certain cases, we are not of course precluded from direct subsidy if this should be necessary to get any industry on its feet; and there is the provision for extra tariffs or restrictions if agreed by the Clearing Union to be necessary for strategic reasons.

The general problem is essentially one of balance of interests and here what seems to be of importance is the relative make-up of our import and export trade. The great bulk of our imports is foodstuffs, raw materials and semi-manufactured goods used for further manufacture; and, if my memory is right, less than 10 per cent of our imports before the war consisted of finished consumer goods. On the other hand, the great bulk of our exports consists of finished manufactures which the importing countries would tend to manufacture for themselves if high protection is rampant throughout the world, or, at a pinch, could do without.

If you would care to have a talk with some of us here one day soon I should be very glad indeed to arrange it.

Yours sincerely,
A. E. OVERTON

To SIR ARNOLD OVERTON, *12 February 1943*

Dear Overton,

COMMERCIAL POLICY

Thank you for your letter of February 9th. The alteration you have made in the first sentence of (vii) sufficiently meets my point at this stage of things. But I still think we want to get clearer in our own minds just what technique it will be most advisable for us to use to achieve our necessary purpose. I shall be delighted to come over any day which may be convenient to you and others to talk a little more about such matters. Meanwhile, it may save time if I give an example in rather more detail of the sort of problem which is troubling me, if as a matter of principle we rule out import restriction.

I take two examples which represent major amounts in our semi-manufactured imports, namely refined oil and high-grade iron ore and steel billets:

(*a*) I am credibly informed that with modern processes all the by-products of refining oil are commercially valuable, so that the old argument that it saved waste of tonnage to import oil in the refined form no longer holds good. These by-products are the fundamental materials of the plastic and other synthetic industries. Hitherto the amount of oil which we have refined ourselves has been a small proportion of the whole. It very likely suits the existing big combines to continue refining in their plants abroad. Nevertheless, a continuance of this may be contrary to sound national policy, not merely on balance of trade grounds, but also if we are to foster certain new, growing and vitally important industries. Now it seems to me that the right way for us to approach this is for us to decide from time to time on what scale we will ourselves set up refining plants and on what scale we will import refined oil. Having arrived at a decision and having encouraged the sinking of a great deal of capital in refineries, surely it would then be reasonable to give the output of our own refineries the first claim on our domestic demand, importing the excess of our own demand over the capacity of the refineries. As time goes on, the proportion imported might tend to diminish or, if the game turned out not so promising as it looked, they might increase. Is not the restriction of import to the amount of the surplus of our demand over our capacity the sensible way of dealing with this problem? Having set up the plant, can there be any sense in not using it to capacity and importing instead, merely because of some, very likely temporary, price advantage? I should have thought not. Of course, one could get round the whole thing, and that may be in fact the best way of doing it, by making the importation of refined oil a state trading activity. We should then automatically follow the above principle, very likely averaging the price to the consumer. Your formula allows that way out. But, if we have something of this sort in mind and are doubtful whether state trading is the right technical means for reaching our ends, is it wise to cut off the alternative method?

(b) I am also credibly informed that with modern methods we can supply ourselves with all the iron we need out of our own relatively low-grade iron ore at a cost which is reasonably competitive. The Hermann Goering Works in Germany is using much lower grade ore than ours, and even that is said to have post-war possibilities. Unfortunately, however, the whole of the existing lay-out of our industry, geographically and otherwise, is based on the importation of high-grade ore. Here again we have to come to a decision, how far it is wise to develop our own ore and how far to go on depending on importation. Having made this decision, we shall have to encourage the sinking of a large amount of capital, both in the developing of the low-grade ore and in establishing our up-to-date iron and steel works in geographically convenient positions. Now, once we have sunk the capital, clearly we cannot afford not to use it to capacity (unless, indeed, the experiment turns out to have been a mistake and the iron ore is not as profitable to work as was hoped). Again, therefore, the right technique would be to limit the importation of high-grade ore to the excess of our demand, in the new circumstances, over our domestic supply.

In both these cases the old method of price competition looks to me silly and out of date. If it related to relative costs of one thing or another over a long period of time, that is another matter. In making one's preliminary decision, one has to reach the best judgement one can as to this. But, having reached one's long-run decision, and until there is sufficient reason for revising it, day-to-day price competition can only lead to a waste of the national resources. Tariffs and subsidies are merely a way of smothering price competition, but have other undesigned and inconvenient consequences and, if they are limited to 25 per cent, may not be consistently effective.

You will see that I am arguing in favour of import regulation, not merely on balance of trade grounds, but also on the ground of maintaining stability of employment in new staple industries.

I have not given you an example from agriculture for that, no doubt, is already fully familiar to you. My point at this stage is, not that the procedures suggested above are necessarily the right ones, merely that they may be; that we have not yet throughly thought our way through, and that until we have we ought to be careful about acting too precipitately on preconceptions which may belong more properly to the world that is disappearing than to the world ahead of us.

Yours sincerely,

[copy initialled] K

P.S. I should see no objection to a qualification of import restriction, that it must not lead to the home producer receiving a price in excess of what the foreign producer would ask by more than the ceiling, whatever it is, provided for in your tariff arrangements, subject to the following qualifications:

(i) an escape clause for balance of trade difficulties;

(ii) an escape clause for a new industry, with a limited number of years in which the infant has to grow up; and

(iii) that the foreign price is measured, not by the temporary or dumping price, which may prevail sporadically, but by the price on which one can rely for a period of years.

Keynes passed his second letter to Sir Arnold Overton on to a Treasury colleague, with interesting results.

From E. G. COMPTON,[3] *17 February 1943*

Seen, thank you.

I know nothing of the case for your first example of oil refining.

But on your second—steel production from home ore:

1. I should like to match your parallel of the Hermann Goering Works in Germany with a remark recently made to me by the Director-General of Weapon Production—that the secret of German weapon production lay in the Swedish ore available to the Ruhr steel industry and that we could double our gun production if we could dispose of the same raw material as the Germans. Is it not still technically true that neither the Germans nor the Allies can make high-grade acid or alloy steel out of high phosphoric pig iron—and all our native ores, except for the dying hematite deposits in Cumberland, are high phosphoric?

2. The ores of Lincolnshire, Northants and Oxfordshire are also lean, the iron content being 30% or less. The imported high phosphoric ores—e.g. from Newfoundland—are 60/70% iron content. There are limits to the process of compensating higher fuel costs with lower transport costs.

3. Apart from the Swedish mines, the foreign sources of high-grade ore have been largely developed by English capital—some of it derived from the

---

[3] Edmund Gerald Compton (b. 1906), K.B.E. 1955; entered Home Civil Service, 1929; Colonial Office, 1930; Treasury, 1931; Ministry of Aircraft Production, 1940; of Supply, 1941; Assistant Secretary, Treasury, 1942, Under-Secretary, 1947, Third Secretary, 1949–58; Comptroller and Auditor General, 1958–66; Parliamentary Commissioner, 1967–71.

Bank of England. They are: South Spain and North Africa; Sierra Leone; and Newfoundland.

4. The wholesale removal of steel works from the coast in South Wales and Middlesbrough to the Midlands would be a colossal task. Among them, you would be shutting down some of the most modern plants we have—e.g. the Port Talbot plant of Guest, Keen and Baldwins, where they unload an iron ore ship of 10,000 tons in two days. The blast furnaces alone cannot be moved as they are integrated with the rest of the steel works.

5. Finally, British steel production, like the American and unlike the Continental, is primarily on the open hearth system in which half the charge of the furnace consists not of pig iron but of scrap. (The current proportion of scrap to steel ingot for the British steel industry is 61%.) About half the scrap arises from the operations of the steel works itself. The other half is bought. Transport is a big factor in the cost. So economical open hearth steel production depends a lot on proximity to scrap supplies which are either imported or come from the industrial areas in which the works are at present located.

Forgive me for burdening you with this detail. But I am frightened that the Board of Trade may engage you in argument on the merits of your illustration at the expense of the issue which you want to illustrate.

16 February 1943   E.G.C.

To E. G. COMPTON, *17 February 1943*

Thanks for your note on the use of low-grade iron ore in this country. The credible authority I referred to was David Eccles at the Ministry of Production, who has been working at this lately with the iron and steel people. I am sending him your note to ask him whether he has got far enough in his enquiries to be sure whether or not he knows a good answer. It is a matter of which I myself have no knowledge whatever. I was merely passing on a story which was, I knew, current in the Ministry of Production.

[copy not initialled]

To DAVID ECCLES,[4] *17 February 1943*

My dear Eccles,

Have you got any further with your study of the question of using our own low-grade iron ore? I have used this recently as an illustration of the sort of matters we ought to consider closely before arriving at decisions on our post-war commercial policy and have received the attached riposte. (I send it in original; may I have it back?)

Do not bother to reply in detail, if you have not already reduced the general story to paper. But I should like to know whether, in your opinion, there is a satisfactory answer to this.

Yours ever,
[copy initialled] K

From DAVID ECCLES, *18 February 1943*

Dear Keynes,

The study of steel production in the U.K. is nearly ready. I don't know who your correspondent is, but what he says is beyond—well, wait until you see our paper.

Yours ever,
DAVID ECCLES

To E. G. COMPTON, *19 February 1943*

IRON AND STEEL

Eccles replies that he thinks he has a good answer to your note. The Ministry of Production's study of steel production in the U.K. is nearly ready, and he asks us to wait until we can see their paper.

[copy initialled] K

---

[4] David McAdam Eccles (b. 1904), 1st Baron 1962, 1st Viscount 1964; joined Ministry of Economic Warfare, 1939; Economic Adviser to Ambassadors at Lisbon and Madrid, 1940–2; Ministry of Production, 1942–3; Conservative M.P. for Chippenham, 1943–62; Minister of Works, 1951–4, of Education, 1954–7; President of Board of Trade, 1957–9; Minister of Education, 1959–62; Paymaster General, 1970–3.

From E. G. COMPTON, *24 February 1943*

IRON AND STEEL

Many thanks for your notes on 17th and 19th February.

I asked the Ministry of Production to tell me who was the author of the promised study of steel production in the U.K. I am told that it will not be a Ministry of Production paper but some notes from a representative of Messrs. Brassert.

As you know, this firm designed and built the iron and steel works at (*a*) Corby in Northants; (*b*) the Herman Goering Werke; (*c*) the Karabuk Plant in Turkey.

Brassert's views on further developments of this sort in this country will be valuable but, of course, *ex parte*. They make their living by encouraging developments of this sort but never take a financial stake in either the construction or the operation of them.

24 February 1943   E.G.C.

There the matter ended to all intents and purposes, although Keynes did send all the correspondence along with the completed Ministry of Production memorandum to Richard Kahn in the Ministry of Supply who commented on 13 May,

Prima facie I am inclined to say that although the memorandum emanates from a prejudiced source the arguments put forward in it are not arguments that can be ignored without further enquiry.

During the proceedings of the Overton Committee, Keynes also had an extensive correspondence with James Meade on import restrictions following an initial discussion on the subject after a meeting on reparations.

The correspondence opened with a short paper from Meade on which Keynes made the following comment.

To JAMES MEADE, *15 December 1942*

My dear James,

IMPORT RESTRICTIONS

My observations on your paper fall under three heads:

I. I have more sympathy than you have for the use of import restrictions for the second of the four purposes catalogued at the beginning of your paper.[5] The second seems to me to run into the fourth. Moreover, there is no reason why protection given in this way need be unrestricted. It can be subject to the same ceiling as is indicated in your paragraph 7. I feel that Henderson's theoretical argument in favour of import restrictions as against tariffs is particularly applicable to case (ii).

II. I believe you are contemplating that the Commercial Union should be in effect a multilateral settlement, to which the nations concerned should adhere. I doubt the feasibility of this. I believe it would be better to regard the provisions of the Commercial Union as something rather like Table A in company law, that is to say, a code which can be incorporated in bilateral agreements.

In the case of the United States you will be up against great constitutional difficulty in aiming at a multilateral agreement treaty. In practice there are very few bilateral commercial arrangements which will not have to take account of special circumstances not easily covered in a multilateral agreement. There might be good reasons for accepting some part of the general code and not all of it. It would also be possible to provide for alternatives, the choice to be according to taste. For example, some of the matters discussed in your III could be made alternative. For instance, either form of safeguard in relation to the Clearing Union could be adopted.

I believe you will be sufficiently ambitious if the Commercial Union includes a number of sections, some of them with alternative versions, ready to be lifted bodily into bilateral agreements. But the agreements themselves should be, as heretofore, bilateral.

---

[5] Following Henderson, Meade mentioned four grounds for import restrictions: (*a*) as a corrective for unbalanced international payments; (*b*) as a device for unrestricted protection; (*c*) as a device for discriminating between sources of supply to economise hard currency for balance of payments reasons or for bilateral commercial bargaining; (*d*) as a device for increasing the stability of particular industries.

Meade's paragraph 7 proposed that the proceeds from auctioned import proceeds could be used as a basis for comparing the effects of a non-discriminatory quota against a ceiling on *ad valorem* tariffs.

III. I now come to the main point. I do not feel that you really take up my challenge to produce a workable technique for non-discriminatory import restrictions. I was aware of the proposal for an auction as a general idea. My difficulty was to see how it could be worked out in practice. I certainly should not despair of devising a working model. Perhaps some of the following questions and the half-answers to them may supply some hints:

(i) Should those bidding at the auction be importers or exporters?

It would give a more non-discriminatory flavour if they were to be the exporters, but it would probably be much more convenient to deal with the importers, who would be on the spot, so that the authorities of a country would only be dealing with their own nationals. It is a weakness of this that it can easily become discriminatory in the case of state trading.

(ii) Would the bidding for an import licence be the equivalent of a specific or of an *ad valorem* duty, that is to say, would you bid for a licence to import a given number of cars, or would you bid in terms of an *ad valorem* percentage of a given value of cars?

Probably the latter. But perhaps sometimes one and sometimes the other, according to the nature of the commodity.

(iii) How is it possible to provide reasonable security to the exporter of continuity of trade? Take bacon: in the former system the Danish bacon factories knew a long time beforehand what quantity they would be allowed to send to this country and could make arrangements accordingly. When one is dealing with bulk purchases and a central body for each country, that may be feasible. Is it feasible in general?

You might have, I suppose, auctions at monthly or quarterly or yearly intervals, and the licences obtained at the auctions might have a year's validity or longer. Possibly a monthly auction, the licences having a year's validity, would be the best compromise. This seems to me the crux of the problem, namely, how to make import restriction consistent with reasonable security to the exporter. Since tariffs are not changed at frequent intervals, the exporter knows, under the tariff system, what he has to expect for a reasonable time ahead and is only caught out by occasional surprises. How, on the other hand, is he able to predict what an import licence is going to cost him? It is like a fluctuating tariff, about the fluctuations of which the exporter has no knowledge until the last moment. In the case of transactions between governments or between organised monopolistic bodies in each country it may be practicable to satisfy this condition by reasonably long-term arrangements. But how is the same object to be secured under conditions of genuine *laissez-faire*?

I do not put all these points in order to make difficulties. On the contrary, I should like to see them solved, since the non-discriminatory import regulation does appear to me a highly important and necessary technique. But it is these practical matters which need attention. I daresay there are other similar snags which have not occurred to me. I wonder if there is anything to be learnt from past experience. It is not a matter on which I have detailed knowledge.

Yours,
[copy initialled] K

Meade's reply to Keynes's letter set the stage for further correspondence.

From JAMES MEADE, *17 December 1942*

My dear Maynard,

IMPORT RESTRICTIONS

Many thanks for your letter. May I comment on each of your main points in turn?

I. On your first main point I do not believe that there is much real difference between us. All that I had meant to argue was that quantitative import restrictions ought not to be permitted merely as an instrument of getting round the tariff ceiling and of giving perpetual protection above the tariff ceiling level. I had intended to admit all arguments for them in so far as they were (*a*) non-discriminatory and (*b*) limited in their long-run protective incidence within the tariff ceiling level. I believe you would agree with this, and that any apparent difference on this point was really due to obscurities in my draft.

II. I recognise the force in your argument that the Commercial Union should provide a model for bilateral agreements rather than form an actual multilateral agreement. There is, however, one very strong argument on the other side. If we enter into a bilateral commercial agreement with, e.g., the U.S.A., we shall be obliged under M.F.N. rules to extend any benefits which we grant to the U.S.A. to many other countries, and in return we shall only get a reduction in the American tariff (which in any case may not be the major impediment to our export trade). If we try to get over this difficulty by scrapping the M.F.N. provision in bilateral agreements, we are likely to end up in a general discriminatory system as chaotic as anything which we have yet experienced. Moreover, any bargain which we make with the U.S.A. is bound to implicate the Dominions (since it will involve bargaining Imperial Preference for tariffs). If we are to consult our own interests, it should also help other countries, since we may hope to obtain advantages from the removal of barriers in, for example, European countries who in turn may obtain advantage from the removal of barriers in, for example, the Dominions and the U.S.A.

Is there not, therefore, a real dilemma? Either we proceed by way of bilateral negotiations with M.F.N. clauses, in which case we and other countries are in danger of giving more than they get in each bilateral agreement; alternatively, we proceed by bilateral negotiation without M.F.N. treatment, in which case we are in danger of ending up in a complete discriminatory chaos. It is for this reason that we should, I think, in the first place attempt to obtain a really extensive multilateral commercial agreement.

This attempt may, of course, fail and in particular it may fail because of the constitutional difficulties in the United States. If this is so we shall have to think again; and in my opinion what we should then do depends very much upon whether the United States has agreed to some monetary arrangement corresponding to the Clearing Union, or whether the failure to obtain American approval of a multilateral commercial agreement is combined with a failure of the United States to co-operate in other parts of more ambitious proposals for post-war economic arrangements.

In the former case we should, I presume, proceed in commercial policy by way of bilateral negotiations and should make use of any Commercial Union proposals in the way in which you suggest as forming a model for such bilateral agreements. We shall have in this case frankly to face the difficulty that such bilateral negotiations if they are not to lead to discriminatory chaos will need to be as closely co-ordinated with each other and made as dependent as possible upon each other so that we are not asked to make concessions to third parties for which we get no counterbalancing advantage.

In the latter case, i.e., if we cannot get any extensive economic cooperation with the United States, I think that we ought to proceed in a rather different way and to attempt to get a general multilateral agreement on something corresponding both to the Clearing Union and to the Commercial Union between ourselves, the rest of the British Commonwealth and the countries of Europe. Such an attempt would naturally mean that in many ways these proposals would have to be modified in order to give as little offence to the United States as possible.

It is not worth while exploring these various possibilities any further as we presumably hope to obtain extensive agreement with the United States, but for the reasons given above I think we should first attempt to get the Commercial Union proposals across in the form of an actual multilateral agreement and only failing that should we turn to the more limited use of such commercial proposals.

III. On your third and main point I think that the idea of auctioning import licences under import quota arrangements should really be practicable. You will probably have received already a short additional note which I sent you developing my ideas on this point. Perhaps I might repeat the main ideas again in this letter.

I would not propose any physical meeting for an auction but merely that anybody who wished to import any quantity of the commodity in question in a given future import period should be required to fill up an application form stating the total quantity which he would wish to import at various prices of the import licence stated on the application form. In other words, the authorities in the importing country would receive from each potential trader who wished to bring the commodity into the country a schedule showing for a wide range of possible prices for the import licence the number of import licences which each merchant would wish to purchase.

The authorities would then merely add up these quantities and obtain a combined schedule showing for each import licence fee the total number of import licences which they would sell. They would then fix the import licence fee at that figure which restricted the total demand for import licences just to the pre-determined total quota of imports for the commodity in question. This method should be convenient. It would be non-discriminatory and it would apportion out the permitted imports among the different qualities and different sources of supply in a reasonable and nondiscriminatory manner.

Starting on this basis of public tender it would be possible to meet the particular points which you raise in your letter:–

(i) I should not restrict the applicants for import licences either to importers or exporters but leave it entirely free to anyone to apply in the manner described above for these import licences. Such applicants might be importers or exporters or merchants or state trading organisations, or any other form of commercial concern. The whole process of application could be done by cable through agents by overseas exporters provided that a fairly short period of notice were given; and I see no reason, if we wish to make the process really non-discriminatory, for limiting the applicants in any way except according to some test of their credit-worthiness in taking up the import licences for which they have applied.

(ii) Again I should put no special restriction on whether the import licences should be equivalent to a specific or an *ad valorem* duty up to the tariff ceiling on a particular commodity, so I should leave it free to fix a quota in terms of the number of units of a commodity imported or in terms of the total value of the commodity to be imported at the discretion of the importing country.

(iii) I was vaguely aware at the back of my mind that I had not really dealt with the problem of providing adequate continuity of trade to particular exporters. In this connection I very much like your suggestion that import quotas might be sold for say an annual period, but at more frequent intervals than once a year. I should have thought that these intervals in most cases need not have been more frequent than once a quarter. This ingenious proposal of yours I think certainly deserves close consideration. For the moment I should not wish to introduce it into the general discussion as it appears to complicate a suggestion which to some people already appears somewhat over-complicated. But if once the general idea should receive any considerable support I am sure that this is a refinement which should be taken up at once.

Yours sincerely,

J. E. MEADE

P.S. I would also make the import licences a transferable commercial instrument, so that they could be sold by one merchant to another after their issue. This would make it still more possible for particular sources of supply to obtain continuity of supply in the market in question.

To JAMES MEADE, *18 December 1942*

Dear James,

IMPORT RESTRICTIONS:
YOUR LETTER OF DECEMBER 17TH

I. Agreed.

II. I had certainly assumed that M.F.N. rules would be abolished under the new regime or, at any rate, that they would only apply as between countries which had adopted bilateral agreements conforming in general to the multilateral model.

III. I like your postscript making the import licences a transferable commercial instrument. But I do not feel at all happy about your suggestion of public tender. Too complicated and too difficult, I should have thought, to work.

I have seen Hubert's letter to you of December 16th on the same subject. But, in effect, he is adopting the historical principle of the allocation of quotas for the first five years and passing the buck, which is the real problem, as to how one avoids crystallising the ancient situation permanently by referring it to 'discussion and, if possible, amicable agreement'. That hardly solves the problem.

Another variant has since occurred to me. I believe it would be better for the importing authority itself to fix the price for a specific number of licences. This would amount in effect to much the same thing as a tariff. The licences would then be sold at this price, being, as you suggest, transferable, to first-comers until they are all gone. The importing authority would then consider whether to put a further number on offer, perhaps at a higher price, with some condition that the second batch is not to be available for those who had been the buyers of the first batch until other buyers had been satisfied. There might conceivably be an interval between the first offer and the second offer, during which unsatisfied bids at the former price would be accumulated and would have priority as soon as a new offer is started, either at a higher price for the same importing period or at the same or a higher price for a later importing period. This may not look very clear and may seem more complicated than it really is. But you will easily see what it is I am aiming at.

Yours,

[copy initialled] K

From JAMES MEADE, *22 December 1942*

My dear Maynard,

IMPORT RESTRICTIONS

Your letter of December 18th.

II. I still see some difficulty in treating the Commercial Union proposals as a model to which bilateral agreements might be made to conform. May I give an example? Suppose that countries (*a*) and (*b*) adopt a bilateral agreement containing a tariff ceiling of 20%, while countries (*c*) and (*d*) reach a bilateral agreement containing a tariff ceiling of 30%. Is country (*a*) in these circumstances to have three rates of tariff, one of 20% which applies to goods imported from (*b*), one of 30% which applies to goods imported from (*c*) and a still higher rate of tax for other outsiders? If this is the sort of situation which you have in mind we should surely reach a discriminatory situation in which each country might have as many tariff rates as there were independent bilateral trade agreements.

If, however, your anwer to this is that the model agreement would lay down the same tariff ceiling for all bilateral trade agreements which claimed to conform to it, then it seems to me that you are in fact suggesting what amounts practically to a multilateral agreement. In other words, if the model agreement lays down as a necessary essential to all bilateral agreements all the main provisions limiting protection within a certain defined range, the bilateral agreements themselves have little scope for variation except in relatively unimportant detail. In this case any country which signs a bilateral agreement with another country which conforms to the multilateral model is in essence not so much signing a bilateral agreement as joining a multilateral commercial union.

I had also, of course, assumed that M.F.N. rules would be abolished under the new regime in the sense that they would apply only as between the members of the Commercial Union. Any member state would in these circumstances be free to discriminate against a non-member state. Indeed, the possibility of such discrimination would provide the main inducement for non-member states to join the Union.

The difference between us here is, when one examines it, largely one of degree. If the conforming bilateral agreements are very strictly defined by the multilateral model then your proposal approximates very closely to the proposal of a multilateral convention. It is only in so far as the degree of conformity of a bilateral agreement with the multilateral model grows smaller that your proposals diverge from mine. All I would add is that if we go too far on your road it is liable to end up in that type of discriminatory muddle which we desire to avoid.

III. The suggestion which you make about import licences has given me an idea which does, I think, limit the protective incidence of import quotas in a very much less complicated way than by means of the public auctioning of import licences. I enclose a short note which I have written developing this new method. It seems to me that it is now reduced to a process which is sufficiently simple to be a really practical proposition. I should very much appreciate your opinion on it.

Yours sincerely,

J. E.MEADE

THE PROTECTIVE INCIDENCE OF IMPORT QUOTAS

1. The purpose of this note is to describe a much simplified method of limiting the protective incidence of quantitative restrictions on imports, which does not require the complicated mechanism of a public auction of import licences. The suggested rules are as follows:

(i) The importing authority would sell import licences at a price which it would itself fix beforehand. This import fee (together with any other import duty) would lie within the limits fixed by the tariff ceiling.

(ii) The importing country would undertake to increase the total quota by at least 5% in any year, if in the previous year the total demand for import licences had been in excess of the total permitted quota, so that part of this demand had not been satisfied.

(iii) The importing country would undertake not to set a total quota in any year which was less than the actual imports of the previous year.

(iv) The importing country would undertake that, if the total demand for import licences could not be satisfied within the total permitted quota, the distribution of import licences between different sources of supply would be made on as non-discriminatory a principle as possible (e.g. on the basis of trade in some previous representative period).

281

(v) The 'escape clause' envisaged in connection with the Clearing Union to meet the needs of countries with specially acute balance of payments difficulties would take the form of a let-out from (ii) and (iii) above.

2. This type of provision should not present too great administrative difficulty. It would mean, on the one hand, that no country need ever allow its imports to increase in quantity by more than 5 % per annum, and would thus afford an effective instrument of stabilisation for particular industries; it would also enable countries to reduce the quota for any commodity for which such restriction was justifiable within the tariff ceiling limits of protection. Moreover, nothing would prevent the granting of additional protection by means of a direct state subsidy. On the other hand, it would mean that so long as the degree of protection afforded by the quota restriction was above the tariff ceiling level, there would have to be a gradual expansion of imports; and this is the essential point.

3. The above seems to me to be the essential minimum limitation on the use of import restrictions. Without something of this kind the Commercial Union is practically worthless, since otherwise quantitative import restrictions can be used to give unlimited protection.

4. It would be possible to refine on the above proposal by such suggestions as:

(i) The import licences might be made negotiable commercial instruments so that they could be sold by one supplier to another. This should introduce a desirable flexibility into the arrangement from the point of view of the suppliers.

(ii) The import licences might be issued, say, once a quarter for quota periods of, say, a year, so that at any one time there would be four overlapping quota periods current. This complication would again introduce an element of flexibility that would be helpful to suppliers.

(iii) The importing country might be free to issue 'specific' import licences (i.e., those giving the right to import a given amount of the commodity) or '*ad valorem*' import licences (i.e., those giving the right to import a given value of the commodity). Such a decision would turn on such questions as whether it was desired to encourage (for sumptuary reasons) or to discourage (e.g. because of low-cost competition) the cheaper qualities. These are, however, refinements. What is essential is contained above in paragraph 1.

22 December 1942   J. E. MEADE

There the correspondence appears to have ended.

The ensuing months were taken up with getting a set of agreed commercial policy proposals through the Cabinet so that they could, following discussions with the Dominions, form a part of the projected Anglo-American discussions on post-war economic policy. Eventually, the Cabinet allowed a series of proposals to go forward without commitment and these formed the basis for one of the areas of discussion in Washington during the Law Mission of the autumn of 1943.

At the conclusion of the discussions, the Law Mission reported to the War Cabinet. During the extensive discussions that followed, Keynes returned on several occasions to the problem of quantitative restrictions. Initially he did so in a note to Richard Kahn on the latter's comments on a memorandum by James Meade entitled 'The Post-War International Settlement and the United Kingdom Balance of Payments'.

To R. F. KAHN, *13 January 1944*

My dear Richard,

JAMES MEADE'S MEMORANDUM

I have only given this a quick glance through and have been carrying it about with me for several week-ends hoping, vainly, to get time to read it more thoroughly.

At a first impression, however, I was not at all happy about it, and the points which were troubling me were largely the same as those which have troubled you. In general, it seemed to me to weaken his case by seriously overstating it. In particular, he seemed to overlook very largely, as you indicate, the terms of trade side of the matter; and that caused him to exaggerate the efficacy of such rights as we possess to alter the sterling exchange. Obviously, there are occasions when it pays you to depreciate your exchange (provided, of course, other people do not), since there is no reason why the *de facto* rate should be the optimum level. I still believe that was the situation prior to 1930. On the other hand, I think it is very often the case that you worsen your position by depreciating the exchange, and I am strongly of the opinion that that is much more likely than the opposite to be the case in the early post-war years. We shall start with a very low value of sterling, and the optimum value is much more likely to be higher, rather than lower.

In the case of the power to regulate imports, we are up against a very deep-seated difference of opinion. There is obviously great force in your points, as I have always felt there was in Hubert's in this context. James seems to me to fail to give the only answer which carries any conviction to me, namely, that, if all the other countries in the world agree to fall in with the stipulations of his Commercial Union (which, in my judgement, is extremely unlikely), we shall gain more on the swings than we shall lose on the roundabouts. That we shall lose something on the roundabouts is, in my judgement, indisputable. Nevertheless, I am ready to be persuaded not to oppose the scheme, on the ground that our discretion is only restricted if others also are conforming to a strict code, and that the latter, if by a miracle it does come about, may be to our very considerable advantage.

Yours,

[copy initialled] J.M.K.

The second occasion was in a memorandum drafted in consultation with Meade.

QUANTITATIVE REGULATION OF IMPORTS

I have not found it easy to understand exactly what is proposed in the Commercial Policy paper about the quantitative regulation of imports, or how far it will still remain possible for us to attain the objects for which, in the absence of an agreed international policy, quantitative regulation might be the most obvious method. After discussion with Mr. Meade, I think that the statement below sets out the relevant points as clearly as possible. Since others besides myself may have found it difficult to see their way through all this, I am circulating this statement to some of those likely to be interested.

KEYNES

9 February 1944

A quantitative regulation of imports may be required for either of two reasons:

(1) To keep out goods, which we should be quite pleased to buy from abroad if we could afford them, in circumstances where, having to cut our coat according to our cloth, we need a method for keeping out less essential imports so as to make sure of being able to afford the essentials. There is also the case, which can be taken with this, where it is vital to have a positively favourable balance of trade and not merely equilibrium, so as to have means of financing the expansion of British business and investment abroad, *e.g.* it might be impossible for British enterprise to be in a satisfactory condition unless we have a favourable balance of trade of (say) £100 millions a year.

(2) In order to give security of outlet to the home producer up to a given amount without necessarily wanting to offer him more than the world price. To give an imaginary example,—we might come to the conclusion that British agriculture could supply half our wheat requirements at 55*s* a quarter and that, on an average of seasons, that would be to restrict imports to half our requirements.

I understand that a claim is made, and, as far as I can see, made legitimately, that the proposed commercial policy arrangements would allow both of the above purposes to be achieved satisfactorily.

So far as the first type of quantitative restriction is concerned, it is allowed without qualification during the transitional period. After the transitional period it continues to be allowed, provided our reserves have not risen above a stipulated figure or if they have fallen at more than a stipulated rate. Thus, if our stipulated figure of reserves, a fall below which allows us to use quantitative restriction, is our quota under the currency scheme, i.e. £325 million, then, if at the end of the transitional period our reserves do not exceed that amount, we can continue the quantitative regulation until they do. Thus, if we pay off our back debts or make new investments at the rate appropriate to keeping our reserves below the crucial figure, we can go on with the quantitative regulation indefinitely, although we should, after a period of years, be under an obligation to consult with such bodies as the Monetary Fund and the Commercial Policy Organisation, whether there were not a preferable alternative solution for our balance of payments problem.

It should be added that, if, during the later years of the transitional period, our reserves were above the crucial figure, we should only be under an obligation to take off restrictions gradually, and if the result of this was to bring down our reserves to the crucial figure, then at that point we should regain our freedom of action. Thus, in practice, our freedom of action would only be withdrawn from us in circumstances when we really had no need to employ it, namely, when the balance of payments, after we had made such foreign investment and such repayment of past debts as suits us, had been sufficiently improved to restore our reserves above the crucial level.

The proposed rules would not allow us to achieve the second of the two purposes above by quantitative regulation. But it is argued that there are two other means of achieving the same result, which would still be open to us, so that we do not really need the expedient of quantitative restriction. The first of these is the expedient of state trading. The state would be entitled to monopolise the importation of the wheat and to keep its importations of wheat at the same figure as would be allowed under quantitative regulation, provided that this mechanism of state trading was not used to raise the price to the consumer above the world price by more than the margin permitted under the tariff rules, any excess of the price paid to the home producer over and above this forming a direct charge on the Exchequer.

Alternatively, the state could buy from the British farmer at 55s the amount which he would have been in a position to sell under quantitative regulation of imports, and then dispose of it on the market by under-bidding the foreign importer to the extent that was necessary to keep imports down to what they would have been under quantitative regulation. The difference between the price paid to the British farmer and the price charged to the home consumer would be a subsidy such as is permissible under the proposed plan. Since, even with quantitative regulation, the British farmer could only be assured of a fixed price by the Government taking his crops off him the above technique would, from the practical point of view, come to almost exactly the same as under quantitative regulation.

The conclusion which I am inclined to draw from the above is that, so far as the quantitative regulation clauses are concerned, the draft agreement is probably more open to criticism on the ground that there are so many ways round that it becomes rather a mockery, than on the ground that it ties us up too tight.

The third occasion came in his response to a paper from J. M. Fleming,[6] entitled 'Quotas versus Depreciation', dated 14 February 1944.

To J. M. FLEMING, *13 March 1944*

Dear Fleming,

Your paper on quotas versus depreciation, sent me with your letter of February 14th, raises a very interesting question. But, for my own part, I am not one of the 'most economists', to whom in paragraph 2 you attribute the view that disequilibrium ought, so far as possible, to be corrected by movements in the rate of exchange rather than by controls over commodity trade.

---

[6] John Marcus Fleming (1911–76); member, Finance Section, League of Nations, 1935–7; Ministry of Economic Warfare, 1939–42; Economic Section, Cabinet Office, 1942, Deputy Director, 1947–51; Visiting Professor, Columbia University, New York, 1951–5; Chief, Special Studies Division, International Monetary Fund, 1954, Adviser to Fund, 1959, Deputy Director of Research Department, 1964–76.

There is, first of all, to the contrary the simple-minded argument that, after all, restriction of imports does do the trick, whereas movements in the rate of exchange do not necessarily do so.

Put in a more sophisticated way, there are two objections to movements in the rate of exchange, to neither of which you do justice. The first relates to the effect on the terms of trade. We all, of course, know about that. But you do not seem to recognise that, in certain conditions of the elasticities involved, a depreciation in the rate of exchange may actually worsen the balance of payments, and it is easy to imagine cases where, even if equilibrium is restored, it is at the cost of a serious and unnecessary reduction in the standard of life.

In the second place, in the modern world, where wages are closely linked with the cost of living, the efficacy of exchange depreciations may be very considerably reduced.

Apart, however, from these two arguments, the preference in favour of movements in the rate of exchange seems to me to be based on a vestigial belief in the way in which things would work under *laissez-faire*, which you have probably given up in other contexts. The trouble is that prices are not a satisfactory index, either to social utilities or to real social costs. Their divergence from real social costs becomes increasingly marked in a community which is subject to heavy rates of taxation, part, at least, of the incidence of which serves to increase costs.

I should agree that it would probably be foolish to establish a rate of exchange such that, in *laissez-faire* conditions, exports would cover no more than (say) half of the imports. But if, in such conditions, the rate of exchange would lead to the imports being covered to at least 75 or 80 per cent by exports, then I think there is a great deal to be said for picking and choosing as to how one brings about the 20 or 25 per cent of equilibrium. We can do better without some things than without others. And just to do without them, leaving the general price structure unchanged, may be far the most sensible thing to do.

I believe, therefore, that it is a positive merit of our proposals that they make it easier to obtain permission to impose quotas than to depreciate the exchange rate, and if the quotas remain semi-permanent, it is no worse than if the depreciated rates of exchange remain semi-permanent. I cannot believe that it is a course of prudence and wisdom to tear up one's prices and wages system because there is 20 or 25 per cent of one's imports which would come in under *laissez-faire* which one cannot afford. The right way is to decide which are the least essential imports and just not have them.

I have no sympathy with the idea, which, as I have indicated above, I regard as vestigial, that, if imports have to be restricted, it is in some way sounder to raise their prices by depreciation of the exchanges than by any other technique.

Will you pass this letter on to Meade and Robbins? I sometimes think that when a post mortem is carried out on you and James, all kinds of pockets of *laissez-faire* appendicitis will be found in unsuspected parts of the body!

Yours sincerely,
[copy initialled] K

Keynes's letter led to a confession of faith from D. H. Robertson and further exchanges with Fleming.

From D. H. ROBERTSON *to* SIR HUBERT HENDERSON *and* SIR DAVID WALEY, *16 March 1944*

My body being notoriously dropsical with pockets of *laissez-faire* (and proud of it), I have no shame in uttering a cry of sympathy with Mr Fleming's memorandum and dissatisfaction with Lord Keynes's rejoinder.

(1) I believe that Lord Keynes, having once over-estimated, now greatly under-estimates the *efficacy* of exchange depreciation as a restorer of equilibrium, as a result of concentrating entirely on the very short-run effects. Given time for consumers, merchants etc. to adapt themselves to the new situation, I see no reason to doubt that a fall in the foreign price of exports, especially of British exports, whether due to exchange depreciation or to any other cause such as a reduction in costs, will normally lead to an increase in total receipts.

(2) I agree with Mr Fleming that the cumulative effect of all the let-outs in the international plans, as they have now developed, is likely to be to make it too easy for countries to protect an over-valued exchange by import restriction, as the Gold-buy countries did in the late thirties. I regret very much the disappearance (I suppose in the sacred names of 'sovereignty' and 'passivity') of the original clause in the Clearing Union Plan empowering the Governing Board to *require* a reduction in the value of a member's currency as a condition of further support.

I find it hard to believe that if we, or any other country, really uses to the full the let-outs about import restriction with which we are now armed, there will be the slightest chance of securing any permanent reduction in tariff levels.

(3) 'We can do better', says Lord Keynes, 'without some things than without others.' There speaks, but thinly veiled, the voice of the Authoritarians and Totalitarians of all ages, knowing better than the common man what is good for him.

In war we bureaucrats have had to make these decisions declaring bacon and tobacco to be necessary and eggs and fruit, books and foreign travel unnecessary. In the transition period we have admittedly got to go on making them as best we can, though the task will be far more difficult as the legitimate diversity of human tastes and ends, on the one hand, and the power of pressure groups on the other, re-assert themselves. The equanimity with which Lord Keynes contemplates the indefinite continuance of this particular method of 'living within our means' scares me stiff.

(4) Mr Fleming, on the other hand, is perhaps tempted to under-estimate the disadvantages of exchange mobility. The plain fact is, of course, that we are all in a quandary owing to our rejection of the one method of adjustment—compression of the money-stream—which is so distasteful that there is no temptation to use it for fun. We have moved a long way from the brave words of the Clearing Union Plan 'The Governing Board may recommend to the Government of the member state any internal measures affecting its domestic economy which may appear to be appropriate to restore the equilibrium of its international balance'. In my heart of hearts I agree with Mr John Williams:

'I question whether a multilateral trade system can ever be attained along with adherence to a rigid internal cost–price structure... For the continuing operation of the system, once reasonably stable currency relationships have been found, cost–price adjustments must also play a part. Whether such adjustments are deflationary depends upon how they are combined with other policies... In Britain to-day... the development of a conscious state responsibility for social welfare... provides ample explanation why fears are felt of too rigid currency plans. But unless a reasonably stable multilateral trade system can be worked out the internal objectives will probably be jeopardised as well.'

16 March 1944   D.H.R.

From J. M. FLEMING, *6 April 1944*

Dear Keynes,

I am sorry not to have replied before to your letter of 13th March, but I was for some time incapacitated, not by '*laissez-faire* appendicitis', but by the spring fever now epidemic among economists and others known as 'writing a White Paper on employment policy'.

May I first make a few observations about '*laissez-faire*', the price system etc. Perhaps I am just a relic of a by-gone age, but I certainly retain a strong attachment to the price system, not because I think it works perfectly, but because the alternative appals me. In the past few years I have attended a good many meetings where people were engaged in allocating scarce resources between alternative uses; and no matter how high-minded and intelligent the allocators, I have always felt that the most imperfect of markets would have made a better and more sensitive job of it. However, I do not deny bias, for even if I believed in the superior efficiency of administrative allocation as compared with the market system, I should still prefer the latter, for reasons alluded to by Dennis Robertson in his Minute of 16th March, namely, that this is the only means by which decisions can be decentralised, and the common man retain his freedom, without producing chaos. I think that human wisdom can often rise to the point of saying that the decisions of [the] market err in this direction or in that; and therefore I am quite in favour of measures which seek by taxes, subsidies, and the like, to *influence* the decisions which find expression through the market mechanism. I also believe that the state has a useful role to play in maintaining an adequate flow of expenditure; in re-distributing money incomes; in speculating and counter-speculating in order to stabilise prices (cf. exchange equalisation account, buffer stocks, etc.); in securing, by public ownership if necessary, that firms act in a quasi-competitive non-monopolistic fashion; and in acting *in loco parentis* to special classes of consumers who cannot be trusted not to do themselves a mischief.

All these types of interventionism—with some of which your own name is prominently associated—can be carried out without prejudice to the market mechanism. But when that mechanism is itself discarded, I fear the worst. Even in such a case as the use of urban land, where admittedly the market does not work properly and some direct planning is inevitable, we

291

see all too plainly what crimes and follies are about to be perpetrated by the planners. The case for adhering to the market mechanism is, in my view, still stronger in the sphere of external than that of internal trade for two reasons:

(a) that the only way to curb the predatory manifestations of economic nationalism is by establishing international agreement on certain norms of behaviour; and

(b) that it is, in practice, as the Article VII discussions on Commercial Policy have shown, very difficult to establish such norms except in terms of a market mechanism, in which the existence or absence of discrimination and the observance or violation of tariff ceilings can be clearly ascertained.

Coming at last to the question of quotas *versus* exchange appreciation with which the controversy started, I confess myself unable to understand why credence is now widely given, particularly in the Treasury, to what seems to me an absurdly catastrophic view of the extent to which our currency would have to depreciate in order to rectify an initial deficit in the balance of current payments.

Of course, I realise that elasticities of demand and supply for our exports and imports are conceivable in which a decline in the relative level of British *vis-à-vis* foreign exchanges, whether brought about through an exchange depreciation or otherwise, would actually worsen the balance of payments. This is a far cry from saying that these elasticities are probable.

Last December I had occasion to work out the formula by which the shift in the balance of trade associated with a shift in the relative cost levels at home and abroad is expressed in terms of the relevant elasticities. It helped to confirm me in my incredulity about the danger of an incurable disequilibrium in relative cost levels when I found that, in the most adverse circumstances of supply (i.e. when the supply of exports from this country and particular imports from abroad are both infinitely elastic), a decline in our relative costs would have an adverse effect upon our trade balance only when the (weighted) sum of our elasticity of demand for imports and the foreigners' elasticity of demand for our exports falls short of unity. When the supply curves are less than infinitely elastic the demand curves may be even more inelastic than is indicated above without the possibility of a stable equilibrium being thereby destroyed.*

Admittedly, in the absence of any statistical measurement of what the elasticities of demand and supply for our exports and imports actually amount to, both in the long and in the short run, it is impossible to prove anything by such formulae. Nevertheless, I find it difficult to believe that

* I can furnish, if necessary, a long, and, (I hope) impressively mathematical, document in support of these assertions.

given a year or so's grace to elicit a fuller reaction to price changes, the elasticities of demand for our imports and exports are anything like as low as would be required to give rise to a radical disequilibrium, or even a very high degree of instability in relative cost levels.

It is significant, I think, that some of those who believe in the incurable disequilibrium of exchange rates and relative cost levels fail to draw the logical consequences of their beliefs. However inelastic the demand in this country for imported food and raw materials may be, no one would deny that a decline in our level of costs, prices and incomes in terms of foreign exchange (employment remaining constant) would bring about *some* reduction in the physical volume and the foreign exchange proceeds of our imports. If, therefore, the net effect on the balance of trade is adverse, it can only be because foreigners spend less of their own currencies on our exports the cheaper these become. But if people really believe that this is likely to happen, how absurd it is for them to worry about increasing the efficiency of our export trades, or about diverting raw material and other resources in the early post-war period for the building up of these trades. We should, on this hypothesis, gain more foreign exchange by leaving the export trades to wallow in their inefficiency, or even by stinting them of labour and raw materials. This doctrine will seem a paradox to many who are ready to swallow what, in reality, would be the still more paradoxical doctrine of the incurable disequilibrium of exchange rates.

This new fangled superstition makes an odd contrast with the theory of purchasing power parity, which was widely current after the last war. The two theories are, of course, at precisely opposite poles, for P.P.P. pre-supposed infinite elasticity of demand and supply for imports and exports, while the new doctrine pre-supposes a very high degree of inelasticity. (Nevertheless, some people, in defiance of logic, try to hold on to both beliefs at once and say that whereas to depreciate from an overvalued level helps the balance of trade, to depreciate beyond a certain rather mysterious 'parity' harms it). The course of exchange rates, internal prices and cost of living during the inter-war period showed that fairly substantial short-run variations in the relative cost levels of different countries can exist, particularly under the troubled conditions of inflation, with abrupt and chaotic capital movements. But I think it is a rather remarkable testimony to the elasticity of international demand that after the currency troubles were over, the relative cost levels of the different European countries had returned so near to their 1913 position, and that where a currency, e.g. sterling, was overvalued by this criterion, the effects were clearly visible both on the trade balance and on the level of employment of the country concerned.

It is also worthwhile repeating a point which James Meade has made with a great deal of force. In the kind of brave new world which the Article VII discussions have been aiming at—with multilateral trade, low tariffs, no exchange controls etc.—the elasticity of demand for British exports should be much higher than at any time during the inter-war period; which would make the remedial effect of a decline in our relative costs all the more prompt and easy. But, of course, if the advocates of quotas here are allowed to have their way and their example is followed in all countries—and if the balance-of-payments escape clause is abused, it will only be a matter of time before quotas are adopted everyhere—they will create that very inelasticity of demand for our exports which will deprive us of any alternative to the perpetuation of import restriction.

I am aware that all these arguments are open to the objection that they relate, not strictly to changes in exchange rates, but to changes in the relationship between cost levels in the different countries, and that the effect of exchange depreciation on relative cost levels may be wholly or partly offset by wage increases, if wages are linked to the cost of living. This, however, is not so much an argument against exchange depreciation as an obstacle which confronts any method of correcting an adverse balance of trade. Tariffs and quotas, like exchange depreciation, normally entail a reduction in real wages. If wages are linked to the cost of living, any method of correcting the balance of trade is liable to touch off an inflationary spiral of prices and money wages. The only way to avoid this, short of faking the cost of living index, would be by subsidising the cost of living. In view of the Treasury's interest in preventing inflation and in setting limits to cost of living subsidies, I cannot understand the equanimity with which they appear to regard these pernicious sliding scale arrangements. A great part of France's financial, economic, social and political troubles after 1936 are, in my opinion, attributable to the inclusion of a provision in the Matignon agreements, linking wages to the cost of living (at an impossibly high level of real wages).

I am not forgetting, in all this, the favourable effect which import restriction, as compared with exchange depreciation, would have on the terms of trade. But one must set against this the maldistribution of resources involved in protectionism. Whether the effect of the latter on this country's real income will outweigh that of the former will depend partly on the height of the initial level of protectionism and partly on the elasticity of the foreigner's supply of our imports and demand for our exports. It might be argued that, even if our import restrictions and tariffs are already at an 'optimum' level from the long-term point of view a further turn of the screw would have favourable *short-term* effects—assuming no retaliation—because of the short-period inelasticity of demand for our exports and supply of our imports. To this it might be answered:

(*a*) Is it certain that the *foreign* demand for our exports is unresponsive to a fall in price even in the short period? Does not the difficulty in equilibrating the balance of trade arise mainly from the inelasticity of demand and supply in the depreciating country owing to the difficulty of expanding production beyond the limits of capacity? But increased protectionism would rather aggravate than solve this problem.

(*b*) Even if, in a particular case, an increased restriction of imports were calculated to raise the real income of the country or to prevent it from falling as much as it would in case of depreciation, it does not follow that the effect on real (pre-tax) wages would be better than that of a depreciation. Tariffs and quotas act as a tax on the cost of living and as such tend to reduce real wages even if the proceeds are used to remit direct taxation.

(*c*) Import restriction is not the sole alternative to exchange depreciation. The appropriate remedy for a short-run disequilibrium in the balance of trade is neither of these but either an export of gold or an import of capital. International arrangements should ideally be such as to ensure that a country can always draw on international credit to fill in temporary hollows in its balance of payments provided that it is carrying out adjustments necessary to eliminate long-term disequilibria by exchange depreciation, or by internal money cost adaptation, and not by commercial policy. If the balance of trade is temporarily disturbed, e.g. by a falling off in exports, and if the disturbance cannot be removed at once by acting on the cause it is simply provocative of structural dislocation both at home and abroad to try to compensate for this by making temporary alterations in other items in the balance of trade. The dislocation is still worse if instead of trying to act on *all* the items in the balance of trade, one tries to effect the entire adaptation by imposing quotas or prohibitions on a few items in the import category.

I am surprised to see from your letter that you are prepared to contemplate the permanent—or 'semi-permanent'—retention of quotas to remedy a long-period disequilibrium. You say this is no worse than a semi-permanent retention of depreciated rates of exchange. This seems to imply that there is some particularly sacred rate of exchange by reference to which other rates, however permanent can be described as 'depreciated'. If one dismisses this idea one is left with the proposition that, other things being equal, the more a country restricts imports, the higher will be its rate of exchange (and the better its terms of trade). This is no doubt true. But it is simply the commonplace argument for protection. And if a country has already reached a certain 'optimum' level of protection further protection, even if it does improve the terms of trade, will not raise its real income. Besides, in the context out of which this discussion arose, other things will not remain equal. I believe that any attempt by one group of countries to retain permanent—or even 'semi-permanent'—quotas for balance of payments reasons, would lead to the breakup of the Commercial Union and to a general intensification of import restriction. The net effect of such a development on our terms of trade might be at least as bad as if, in a relatively free trade world, sterling had been allowed to find its level; and everyone would be impoverished by the decline in international trade.

No doubt, in the heat of the argument, in my paper and in this letter, I have been led to soft pedal the disadvantages of flexible exchange rates. These chiefly consist, I think, in introducing a new and disturbing speculative element into international capital movements. I agree with Lerner that the disturbing effect on international *trade* of uncertainty regarding future exchange rates is negligible, while the effect on the stability of the export trades of actual variations in exchange rates is certainly better than either of the alternative methods of making adjustments to changes in international demand, i.e. changes in commercial policy, and changes in the level of domestic employment. Even the difficulties raised by capital flight and 'hot money' are, I think, often exaggerated. It was only the prospect of very substantial exchange profits which gave rise to the large scale capital flight and exchange speculation of the '30's. If all currencies were kept, by frequent small exchange-rate adjustments, as near as possible to their equilibrium level I believe that the problem could be easily dealt with by the co-operative action of national stabilisation funds supplemented, on rare occasions, by exchange control.

The principal difficulties, as I see them, are three:

(1) How to devise a system of international control which allows movements of exchange rates *towards* the equilibrium rate but prevents movements *away from* that rate, without introducing a degree of short-term rigidity into exchange rates which would be favourable to speculators. This might perhaps be achieved by various modifications of the I.M.F. plan including a provision that each country, instead of being obliged to adhere to a given *rate* of exchange, would be at liberty to alter its rate within a given *range*, the range itself being altered only with the agreement of the Fund.

(2) How to determine the equilibrium rate (or range of rates) of exchange. The main question here is whether to take account of cyclical changes in the levels of employment in particular countries. There are arguments on both sides here. But on the whole I think that it is salutary that countries should not be allowed to export unemployment. This would mean that if a large scale depression sets in the U.S.A. which has the effect of reducing its imports and expanding its exports, other countries would be allowed to offset this by depreciation.

(3) How to maintain an adequate flow of international lending. While

abnormal capital movements are, as I have indicated, capable of being dealt with, a more difficult problem is that of preventing the abnormal cessation, owing to exchange instability as well as other factors, of 'normal' capital movements. The International Investment Bank may do something to help here, but its assistance will be limited if it refrains from assuming exchange risks. This problem will probably remain with us until the major industrial countries have demonstrated their ability to maintain a steady level of internal demand, employment and prices over a period of years. If they can do this exchange rate adaptations need only be small and need constitute no serious barrier to a revival of international investment.

To bring this over-long letter to an end, I would add that I sympathise a good deal with Dennis Robertson's view that there is really no fully adequate substitute for a measure of flexibility in internal money costs. In the Brave New World I should hope that international adaptations will still be made, to a considerable extent, by changes in national wage and price levels in terms of domestic currency. But it is no use in this day and age hoping for much if any *downward* flexibility in national wage levels. The best we can hope for is that countries whose international position is on the upgrade can be induced to allow their price levels, and *a fortiori* their wage levels, to rise, and that those whose international position is deteriorating can manage to call a halt to the increase in their national wage level, even though they are, at the same time striving to maintain employment. I don't pretend to know exactly how this is to be done!

I am sending copies of this letter to Robertson, Henderson, Robbins and Meade.

Yours sincerely,
MARCUS FLEMING

To J. M. FLEMING, *22 April 1944*

Dear Fleming,

Thank you for your letter of April 6th. The worst of it is that it is too large a subject for correspondence. It would be a matter perhaps for a book, certainly for an article, to deal with the issues you raise. I just add one or two random reflections which I noted down as I read your letter.

I did not say that you should not be attached to the price system. (I share your attachment.) I said you should not be deceived by it. I still feel that the consequences you attribute to exchange depreciation may be based on being deceived as to how the price system works out in practice as compared with the way in which it would work out on certain theoretical assumptions. And perhaps you will not complain of my being a little bit confirmed in this suspicion by your frank confession that, like D.H.R., you are influenced here by an unscientific bias of preference! Of course, I am in favour of exchange alterations on occasion—I have spent much of my life fighting for this liberty, and I am the last person to want the old standards of rigidity to be set up again. But now, not for the first time, I find that these I have converted want to go too far and to reject even that which was partly sound, though instinctively arrived at, in the old orthodoxy.

I should agree that the case where the terms of trade move so strongly as actually to worsen the balance of payments is an extreme one. But long before you have actually reached that conclusion, you will have very probably brought about a quite unnecessary reduction in the standard of life. That is if you prevent wages following the cost of living, which in fact you cannot, that being one of the reasons why, in contemporary conditions, your policy is self-defeating. In this context, I am rather alarmed when I see you arguing that import restriction is as liable as exchange depreciation to be offset by a rise in money wages. Surely that is not so. At the same time, I agree with you strongly in deprecating sliding-scale wage agreements. I know that the present Chancellor of the Exchequer also agrees very much about that.

Surely the right plan is to have both import restriction and exchange depreciation at hand, and use each of them in appropriate degrees and on appropriate occasions.

Finally, I wish you would give me an arithmetical example of the sort of elasticities which you think likely to prevail, so far as this country is concerned, in post-war conditions. I should have supposed, for example, that a 10 per cent depreciation of the exchange would raise the sterling price of imports by nearly that amount.* On the other hand, it would not reduce export costs nearly so much; and then there is the question how much such reduction in export cost as was effected would increase the volume of exports. It seems to me that, taking everything into account, it would not be unplausible to guess that a 10 per cent depreciation of the exchanges might increase the cost of imports in terms of sterling by at least 8 per cent, whilst not reducing their volume by more than (say) 2 per cent; whilst, in the case of exports, it would decrease the cost (say) 5 per cent and, to be generous, let us say, increase their volume by 5 per cent. The net result would be that imports would cost 6 per cent more, whilst exports would bring in the same money as previously. The net result would be that we should have lost 2 per cent of our imports, have parted without reward with 5 per cent of our exports, and would have found ourselves, as the result of these foolish sacrifices, 6 per cent worse off than before on the balance of trade.

I have on purpose, in order to bring the argument home, used figures which are biased so as to produce that result. But you will see how very much you have to alter them if the transaction is going to be proved worth while. So tell me what figures you would like to substitute for those which I have used above merely for illustrative purposes.

Yours sincerely,
[copy initialled] K

From J. M. FLEMING, *29 April 1944*

Dear Keynes,

In many respects I should certainly not repudiate the role of headstrong disciple which you attribute to me in your last letter. But in the present context, arguing as I do for the existence of a relatively high elasticity of reciprocal demand between a country and the outside world, I feel I am acting

* Do you, by the way, assume that when father turns we all turn?—i.e. that all the sterling area countries move with us. Grave disadvantages flow from whichever answer you give—and this, alone, is a reason for not altering rates except for very grave cause.

as a staunch defender of the old orthodoxy against new-fangled heresies—a veritable Old Believer.

You agree with me that the case where the terms of trade move so strongly that exchange depreciation will actually worsen the balance of payments is an extreme one. But I still doubt whether you realise quite how extreme it is. Even the numerical example which you give, and which, as you say, was biased so as to produce the result that depreciation should worsen the balance of trade is not sufficiently biased to achieve that aim. According to your figures a 10 per cent depreciation of sterling would raise the sterling price of imports by 8 per cent and reduce their volume by 2 per cent, so that the sterling value of imports would rise by 6 per cent. As for exports, you say the *cost* would fall by 5 per cent. But you must surely mean that the price of exports *in terms of foreign exchange* will fall by 5 per cent. The *sterling* price of exports will therefore *rise* by 5 per cent, and the volume will rise by 5 per cent. Therefore the sterling value of exports will rise by 10 per cent, and—assuming that exports are initially 80 per cent of imports—the balance of trade will *improve* by some 2 per cent of the value of imports.

The loss of real income involved in the depreciation on your assumptions is not large. We should lose 2 per cent of our imports and an additional 5 per cent of our exports—together equivalent to, say, 6 per cent of the value of imports. But we would gain 2 per cent in securities as a result of the improvement in the balance of trade and 1 per cent for the reduction in the real value of the remaining adverse balance due to the rise in price of export goods. The net loss, which, of course, corresponds to the deterioration in the terms of trade, is 3 per cent of the average of imports and exports, or, say, half of 1 per cent of the national income.

I admit that, on your assumed elasticities, the same effect on the balance of trade could be brought about, with less sacrifice of real income—indeed, with a positive gain in real income—by imposing a 5 per cent tariff or equivalent restriction of imports, *provided that there was no corresponding increase in import restriction overseas*. A 5 per cent tariff, in these circumstances, would enable us to reduce imports by 1 per cent in volume, and 1 per cent in price, thus giving us our improvement of 2 per cent in the balance of trade without having to supply any additional exports.

But if the foreign elasticity of demand for our exports were really as low as you assume, enormous opportunities of gain would be to hand. All that would be required would be to call off the export drive and, indeed, impose a tax on exports, the higher the better. Given an elasticity of demand for our exports of unity, as you assume, the foreigner would continue to supply us with an unchanging volume of foreign exchange, wherewith to pay for our imports. We could then divert resources *ad lib.* from our export trades into producing for home consumption. I am looking forward with keen anticipation to the adoption of this policy by the Treasury!

However, your figures were admittedly only illustrative. I am a little embarrassed by your challenge that I too should quantify my ideas about the elasticities. Such empirical evidence as is available relates to things like the movement of relative international cost levels, which are the upshot of the interaction of the individual elasticities, rather than to the elasticities themselves. But if I *must* proceed *a priori*, I might as well repeat the figures I used for purposes of illustration in a note I wrote last December, of which I enclose a copy. Translating the algebra given in paragraph 13 of the note into arithmetic, and assuming a depreciation of 10 per cent., the results will be as follows:

(*a*) The sterling price of exports will rise by $6\frac{2}{3}$ per cent. The foreign exchange price of our exports will fall by $3\frac{1}{3}$ per cent. The volume of exports will rise by 20 per cent. The sterling value of exports will rise by 28 per cent.

(*b*) The sterling price of imports will rise by 8 per cent. The foreign exchange price of our imports will fall by 2 per cent. The volume of imports will fall by 4 per cent. The sterling value of imports will rise by 6 per cent.

(*c*) If the value of exports (including invisibles) is initially 75 per cent of imports, the improvement in the balance of trade will amount to 15 per cent of the value of imports.

These figures are to be interpreted in the sense of fairly long-term elasticities—taking, say, 3 years to work out—operative in a world in which the various Article VII Agreements, particularly those relating to commerce and money, have been put into effect. It is legitimate to make this last assumption, as this whole controversy arose over the question whether these agreements were not excessively biased in favour of quotas as compared with depreciation.

In order to obtain an equal improvement in the balance of trade by import restriction, it would be necessary, on the assumed elasticities, to impose restrictions equivalent to an additional tariff of over 25 per cent. If this could be done without provoking reprisals, it might be worth while from the purely national point of view. I have worked out the formula for the optimum unilateral tariff, and I find that with the assumed elasticities, the optimum tariff is about 50 per cent. If, therefore, the initial tariff is below 25 per cent, it would pay, *assuming no reprisals*, to impose an extra 25 per cent tariff rather than to depreciate by 10 per cent.

But we cannot assume no reprisals. It has been my whole contention that if we were to try to use the balance-of-payments escape clause in the Commercial Convention as a method of maintaining an over-valued currency, countries which could not or would not follow our example would denounce the Convention and impose restrictions without the pretext of balance of payments difficulties.

In conclusion, let me say that I have learnt a great deal (though it may not be apparent) from this controversy. I would not now deny that there may be a good case for permitting the use of import restriction, under some form of international control, as a means of coping with certain types of short-term disequilibria in the balance of trade. I have in mind, in particular, temporary restrictions designed to maintain the balance during the period following an agreed adjustment in the exchange rate before the latter has had time to exercise its full equilibrating effect. There is even an argument for permitting their use in preference to exchange rate adjustments as a means of offsetting *cyclical* changes in the balance of trade. I am in two minds about this, for quotas or tariffs would cause greater structural difficulties, both at home and abroad, than depreciation, while depreciation would encourage disturbing capital movements. But all these concessions I would make only on condition that there exists an international control over the imposition of import restrictions adequate to prevent their being retained in perpetuity in defence of an over-valued currency. Such an international control might take one of two forms:

(*a*) The Monetary Fund might have authority to *compel* countries to alter their exchange rates in case of fundamental disequilibrium. In exercising this authority, the Fund would be obliged to take account of representations on the part of the Commercial Policy Organisation. Import restriction might then be allowed to be imposed on the strength of more or less automatic criteria affecting the balance of trade.

(*b*) Failing such authority, the power to impose restrictions should depend not on automatic criteria, but on the decision of the Monetary Fund and the Commercial Policy Organisation acting together. The Monetary Fund would, however, have the general responsibility for providing *some* way out of a balance of payments *impasse*, whether by quotas, depreciation, or lending out of its own funds.

Failing some such safeguards as these, the Commercial Policy Organisation, assuming it ever sees the light of day, will, I am convinced, very soon come to an inglorious end.

I am afraid that it would make this letter too long to try to answer all your other points. Some of them may be answered in a letter which I am sending to Henderson, of which I will send you a copy. As regards the sterling area countries, I was assuming that they would maintain parity with sterling, if sterling moved. This is surely much the best thing for our balance of payments as a whole, since if they broke the link with sterling, they would not want to bank their monetary reserves with us. It is arguable that our trade balance might be better if they did not depreciate along with us, but I should have thought that, their economies being complementary with rather than competitive to ours, there was little or nothing in that point.

Yours sincerely,
J. M. FLEMING

To J. M. FLEMING, *2 May 1944*

Dear Fleming,

Your letter of April 29th on exchange elasticities. Yes, you are quite right in your paragraph 2. I made the blunder you attribute to me and apologise. I thought that the result had come out too strongly my way and considered it too hastily to see the obvious reason why.

That, however, only affects the illustration and even the illustration still remains rather formidable. If we take the value of our imports for convenience at £1,000 million, your proposal is that it would be very good business on our part to forgo £60 million worth of goods in order to earn £20 million.

The real source of difference between the judgements we pronounce is discoverable however on page 2 of your letter. Assuredly I agree that if by reducing the price of our exports by 3 per cent we can increase their volume by 20 per cent it will be very well worth doing. But I am afraid it never crossed my head that the right figures could be anything resembling that. Are you not assuming that our competitors would not respond to our change in price by a change in theirs? If one takes a staple article like grey cloth where we are able, let us assume, to sell a certain amount at the world price level, we then reduce our prices by 3 per cent, if no other exporter reduces his price clearly we collar the whole market. But is that likely to happen? I do not think so.

In fact one is up against the usual problems of market leadership and oligopoly. My judgement for what it is worth is that the figures you take in your illustration are widely off the mark. Do you really believe that if we reduce the price of our motor cars by 3 per cent the number of cars we shall export would increase by 20 per cent?

Yours sincerely,

[copy initialled] K

While the discussions on post-war monetary arrangements resulting in Bretton Woods went forward after some delay, the Government was so deeply split on commercial policy that no further steps were possible beyond discussions with the Dominions. The Americans, however, continued to press for a resumption of the commercial policy discussions. In an attempt to help matters forward, Keynes re-entered the fray just before his departure for Bretton Woods.

To SIR RICHARD HOPKINS, *12 June 1944*

Following on my conversation with you I have produced the attached document as a possible means of breaking the deadlock on this subject.

Whilst putting our point of view frankly and perhaps meeting the critics to a considerable extent, I am hopeful that the actual substance of what is said does not depart so radically from the existing draft as to make a renewal of the conversations impracticable. I am getting from Mr. Meade, a statement showing exactly how far this departs from the existing text.

As you know Sir Edward Bridges was interested in this and I have shown the paper to him. He declared himself much encouraged by it and thought it quite possible that this paper might pave the way for the next step.

12 June 1944   KEYNES

ARTICLE VII CONVERSATIONS ON COMMERCIAL POLICY

Mr Hull's invitation to continue these conversations on the expert level should be accepted. But the officials taking part should be instructed to be frank with the Americans on the following aspects of British Commercial Policy, and should regard it as part of their directive to bring the draft Statement of Principles into conformity therewith.

Principles of British Commercial Policy

1. Great Britain both by tradition and self-interest is concerned with the removal of obstacles to international trade and, in particular, the moderation of tariffs. She has never adopted discriminatory trade practices and has no intention of doing so. Her trade policy before the war probably conformed more closely to the objects aimed at in the Mutual Aid Agreement than that of any other country. She is, therefore, in full sympathy with the purposes of the State Department. In particular, she greatly welcomes the proposition of a Multilateral Trade Convention which would govern and over-ride any bilateral arrangements. Moreover in matters of detail she is probably prepared to go further in the desired directions than any other country.

2. Nevertheless her prospective trade position after the war means that safeguards for the balance of trade are indispensable to her. In other respects also it is felt that there is some risk of misunderstanding unless certain fundamental principles of British trade policy after the war are frankly and fully stated. The following categorical statement of our indispensable requirements is not meant to imply that some, or even most of these have not been already met in part or in substance in the existing draft Statement of Principles. For the British officials at the first series of talks were conscious of these requirements and were concerned to see them satisfied. But a careful study of the draft leaves the impression that there may be some dangerous ambiguities in the statement and that the real importance in practice of certain, sometimes obscure, safeguards in the draft may not be sufficiently apparent to all of those whose duty it will be to approve the final result. It also appears that

certain technical methods such as tariffs and subsidies to which the United States is well accustomed, and full-blown state trading, such as is enjoyed by Russia, are dealt with more tenderly than alternative methods better suited to British conditions, although the latter may be more moderate in their effect on the outside world than those which are to be allowed and not, for any obvious reason, more inherently objectionable. This difference of approach becomes even less defensible when it allows countries which already have a relatively high tariff to maintain a permanently higher level than those which in the past have been more moderate in their impositions. It is, therefore, necessary that the British standpoint should be re-stated quite frankly as soon as the conversations are resumed.

3. *Import and Export Programmes*

Experience before the war indicated that methods of unregulated *laissez-faire* were not successful in securing equilibrium between imports and exports, at any rate in the short term. For a country which has normally an export surplus or possesses large liquid reserves to meet an import surplus, this need not be a matter of serious concern. But for many countries these conditions were not fulfilled; and, in the case of Great Britain, they will not be fulfilled after the war. Some latitude, therefore, for official planning of import and export programmes is indispensable to economic health, and, indeed, to the maintenance of solvency and credit. In Great Britain we expect to have to curtail the natural home demand in certain directions so as to release a surplus for export and also to adapt our domestic policy to allow a sufficient expansion of exports; and, on the other side of the account, to limit certain classes of imports to what is essential. This line of policy is not only consistent with, but even required by a healthy international system. The United States may find that equilibrium with the rest of the world requires precisely the opposite policy on their part. The one type of measure should be regarded as not less healthy and desirable than the other. Countries should not merely be allowed as an exceptional indulgence to take measures to secure an equilibrium between imports and exports, but should be positively encouraged to do so; and there should be no suggestion of the contrary. It can be argued that the draft Statement of Principles makes full allowance for all this, especially in the passages which allow for the restriction of imports by countries in balance of trade difficulties. But the underlying principle is not sufficiently clear. Import and export programming should be *expressly* permitted, subject always to provisions intended to secure that the expansion of imports to balance exports is regarded as not less necessary for a healthy equilibrium than the limitation of imports to balance exports. At the same time, such methods, however capable of good use, are also liable to abuse; and it is to the avoidance of these abuses that the Multilateral Convention should address itself. In particular, the general object should be—as Great Britain's most assuredly will be—the expansion and not the restriction of international trade so that equilibrium is reached on the basis of as large a volume of trade both ways as is possible.

Secondly, the divergence produced by import regulation between the world price and the domestic price should not be greater than the maximum divergence permitted by means of tariffs. Above all, the methods adopted should be free from any discriminatory intent.

4. *State Trading and Bulk Purchases*

It is not clear that the draft sufficiently recognises an economic dispensation intermediate between the complete state trading of Russia and the *laissez-faire* policies of the 19th Century when Governments stood aside altogether from acts of commerce. The draft allows a fully state trading country to do almost anything. For example, there is not the slightest interference with a complete policy of import and export programming by such a country. It does not seem reasonable to prescribe, or even to suggest, that only the two extremes are permissible, when, in fact, the great majority of the peoples of the world are likely to pursue an intermediate policy, and may, indeed, in the judgement of some responsible people, be well-advised in doing so. As one of the countries increasingly committed to some version of the intermediate policy, Great Britain can scarcely be expected to commit herself to a draft which even appears to a careless reader to bless the extremes and to suggest that it is only in between that vice is to be found.

This issue comes to the surface particularly in connection with bulk purchasing. The draft Statement can be read to include useful qualifications in this context. But it is important that there should be no ambiguity about the freedom of adherents to the Convention to enter into either short-term or long-term bulk contracts. Nor should barter agreements of a mutual character be entirely excluded where they allow an extension of international trading which would, otherwise, be impracticable; though they should be made subject to special safeguards. Here again the criterion should be whether such arrangements tended to increase the volume and stability of international trade, and whether they were being administered without a discriminatory intent. Too crude a code will break down when it is faced with the variety and multiplicity of natural conditions.

5. *The Equated Price System*

Important cases will certainly occur where a country is importing an article at one price, is producing the same article at another price, and wishes to charge the consumer neither the importing nor the domestic producers' price, but the weighted or equated price of the supply taken as a whole. For certain agricultural products there is great administrative convenience in this system, and there seems no sufficient reason why it should not be permitted. Substantially the same result can be obtained, it is true, from tariffs or subsidies or a combination of the two. But there is no ground for alleging that there is something peculiarly vicious in the technique of the equated price system from which the alternative techniques are, for no apparent reason, supposed to be free. At the same time it would be proper to limit the divergence between the world price and the price to domestic consumers to the maximum difference permitted by any tariffs.

6. *Imperial and other Preferences*

Great Britain has committed herself in the Mutual Aid Agreement to consider the reduction, and even elimination, of Imperial Preferences in return for a sufficient reduction of the world's tariff systems. But she has not agreed that the preference system possesses some special inherent vice from which tariffs and subsidies are free. It must be made clear that Great Britain regards the system of Imperial Preference as a domestic matter which cannot be regarded as involving a discriminatory treatment of foreigners. To treat the preference system as having some extra measure of original sin is, once more, to treat the extremes as legitimate and anything in between as illegitimate. Federal systems, Zollvereins, a Union of Soviet Socialist Republics, Colonial systems, such as that of France, are to be permitted. But arrangements between members of a Commonwealth which are less exclusive are to be eliminated. Great Britain cannot accept this conclusion. At the same time the abatement or elimination of preferences along with the abatement of tariffs and subsidies is another matter. Great Britain is prepared to go a long way in this direction—probably further than others will be ready to go.

7. Whilst high tariff countries can reasonably be allowed at the outset a somewhat greater latitude than low tariff countries, and can be given time in which to accommodate themselves to the general code, in the long run the code, both for old tariffs

and for new tariffs, should be the same for all alike; and in the meanwhile, the measure of divergence between world prices and domestic prices, which is permissible as a result of subsidies, equated prices or import control, should be the highest level currently permitted for any tariff.

8. To make these matters clear is, to an important extent, a matter of presentation. They may be already covered in the Draft Statement to a greater extent than is appreciated at first sight. There is no reason why a plan should not be worked out, directed to the freedom and expansion of international trade, and to the elimination of discriminatory practices, which is fully compatible with the programming of overseas trade, with bulk purchasing, with the principle of equated prices and with the treatment of preferences in relation to tariffs. But the British experts should make it clear that there is no misunderstanding about the above four principles. They believe, moreover, that a modification of the draft along these lines may render it much easier of acceptance by a number of countries which have not yet been consulted. Since the attainment of a Multilateral Convention is the essence of the matter, an improvement in the general acceptability of the Plan may be vital.

On receiving Keynes's note, Sir Richard Hopkins commented.

From SIR RICHARD HOPKINS *to* SIR JOHN ANDERSON, *14 June 1944*

This is urgent only in the sense that Lord Keynes is about to sail. I am sorry I did not manage to send it forward last night.

What happened was this. A short time ago Sir Edward Bridges asked me if I could contribute any idea towards breaking the deadlock on commercial policy. I said to him that I knew Lord Keynes was keenly interested and I judged that he occupied a middle position. Sir Edward then talked to Lord Keynes and Lord Keynes talked to Mr Liesching, Professor Robbins and Mr Meade.

The result was Lord Keynes' memorandum attached which is now with these three who have it quite privately in a personal capacity. He believes they will all bless it in substance. Sir David Waley and Sir Hubert Henderson, whose notes are attached, do much the same. If need be, some more progress could be made between Lord Keynes and his friends by telephone.

To me this is like a breath of fresh air upon a subject which has become obscured by much confusion of thought.

A conceivable course is that the Chancellor, if he were attracted, might come forward with a suggested solution of these lines. I expect Sir Edward Bridges would like to talk to him on the subject before long.

14 June 1944   R.V.N.H.

However, the attempt came to nothing, as Keynes reported to Hopkins.

To SIR RICHARD HOPKINS, *14 June 1944*

COMMERCIAL POLICY

Being a little afraid that the reference to Sir P. Liesching's views in your note on this to the Chancellor might go a little too far (since I had not heard from him since he saw the revised version), I have now rung him up on the telephone. The upshot is as follows:

1. He is of the opinion that it might be extremely useful to reopen the matter on these lines, and indeed that this may be the only way of breaking the deadlock.

2. At the same time he would, of course, wish to reserve his entire freedom of criticism if and when this paper comes to him officially, and he has to advise his President and is not merely in a position of having been given a glance at it in his personal capacity.

3. The line he is likely to take in commenting on it departmentally, is one with which I myself have a great deal of sympathy. He would, I believe, agree with you that this is a 'fresh air' approach; but he believes that in the working out of it a more radical departure would have to be made from the detailed draft they were considering in Washington, than Mr Meade fully appreciates. He does not deprecate this since he thinks it quite likely that the attempt made in Washington to go into so much detail was premature. His point is that the

general principles which I suggest could not easily be translated into the exact arithmetical perfectionist form which Mr Meade had been trying to give them. He thinks that Mr Meade believes that with sufficient ingenuity, something like the old line of approach could be preserved. Sir P. Liesching greatly doubts this. His advice would probably be, therefore, that if these are the lines which Ministers wish to see adopted, it would be a consequence that we should be aiming, with the Americans, at something much more like an agreement on certain broad principles on the right lines, rather than at a frightfully detailed constitutional set-up. I repeat that he does not think that this is necessarily a criticism; but he thinks we should be deceiving ourselves if we were to suppose that by the mere act of re-drafting, the existing document, remaining in other respects in the same general format as at present, could be brought into conformity with the new directive.

As I have said I expect that Sir P. Liesching is very probably right on this. On the other hand, even if we were prepared to come down to detailed arithmetical provisions with the Americans, it is extremely unlikely that the rest of the world could ever be brought to agree with the same arithmetical provisions, which we and the United States would have each worked out on lines not too unsuitable to our own particular cases, but not, for that reason, capable of being fully generalised.

You will see therefore that Sir P. Liesching's state of mind and general attitude, whilst fully sympathetic to the new approach, is a good deal more complicated than anything which I had indicated to you previously.

KEYNES

14 June 1944

On his return from Bretton Woods, Keynes made another contribution to the discussions which had then reached the Ministerial Committee stage. Keynes's paper, with the alterations indicated in footnotes, went forward to the Committee under the Chancellor's signature.

To T. PADMORE, *15 September 1944*

I attach the draft which I promised the Chancellor on barter trade in relation to commercial policy.

As regards what we ourselves did before the war, I have ascertained the following from the Board of Trade.

We ourselves were strictly prevented from entering into discriminatory agreements with other countries by our Commercial Agreement of 1938 with the United States, which is still in force. Article 2 of this Agreement included the principle of the most favoured nation treatment, which in itself is held by the Americans to preclude such arrangements, although it is not perfectly clear that it does. Article 4, however, requires that any import restrictions should be on a non-discriminatory basis, and Article 8 makes a similar stipulation in respect of bulk purchases.

I understand that the reason why we were able to enter into certain Agreements with the Scandinavian countries and also to make the ROCA Agreement with the Argentine, was that in none of these agreements did we ourselves undertake to make minimum purchases. It was only the other parties to the agreements which so engaged themselves. Thus, as mentioned in the draft, it is the commercial agreements which the United States will seek to arrange with other countries, which would be the main obstacle. We can only enter into barter agreements if we can prevent other countries entering into Commercial Agreements with the United States similar to that to which we subscribed in 1938.

I should add that even so, our entering into the ROCA Agreements was subjected to loud clamour and complaint by the Americans. It may be taken as quite certain that they will not voluntarily enter into any future commercial agreements, apart from the special latitude which they will aloow us for the transitional period, allowing any future arrangements of a discriminatory character.

KEYNES

15 September 1944

COMMITTEE ON COMMERCIAL POLICY:
NOTE BY THE CHANCELLOR OF THE EXCHEQUER

In the Report of a Group of Officials on Post-War Commercial Policy which I circulated to my colleagues as C.C.P.(44)1, a suggestion was made that, at the next round of discussions with the American representatives, we might aim at a greater clarity and a wider discretion in the matter of the rights of signatories to the proposed multilateral convention to use the methods of bulk purchases and the quantitative regulation of imports within certain limits on a non-discriminatory basis. The Officials pointed out at the same time that, whilst the meaning of 'discriminatory' is not so clear that the doctrine of non-discrimination can be pushed to its logical conclusion, nevertheless 'express arrangements for directing our purchases to those countries which buy from us would be discriminatory in the sense of Article VII, and are therefore ruled out by the Mutual Aid Agreement'.

In this connection, it seems to me to be important to distinguish two separate issues[7] and, if possible, to clear one of them out of the way at once.

I believe that a school of thought is developing in important organs of the Press and amongst Members of Parliament to the effect that the line of safety for us after the war is to reserve our full rights to enter into discriminatory commercial and also, perhaps, discriminatory currency agreements, not only in the transitional period but permanently. The idea is that we should use our position as an important market, as a bargaining counter, to secure the entry of our exports into the countries from which we buy, by matched bulk purchasing or by the discriminatory use of import licensing or by clearing agreements, or in some other way.

No doubt there is a superficial plausibility in these proposals.

---

[7] Here the words 'namely the policies respectively of *discriminatory* and of *non-discriminatory* bulk purchasing and import regulation' were added.

Nevertheless it is, I think, out of the question for the following reasons that we should seriously intend a policy along these lines:

(1) In Article VII of the Mutual Aid Agreement, as the Officials point out, we have already agreed (subject to a clear qualification that we do not regard this undertaking as applying to preferences) to 'the elimination of all forms of discriminatory treatment in international commerce'. Thus the proposed policy would involve the repudiation of an Agreement which, after prolonged discussion covering several months, we agreed to sign.

(2) If we repudiate this Agreement, we shall be in the position of having received lend lease aid up to date on false pretences, and we shall be deprived of the benefit of the present understanding that the 'consideration' required from us in return for lend lease shall not be such as to burden commerce.

(3) Quite apart from the Mutual Aid Agreement, discriminatory practices on our part are not consistent with our existing Commercial Agreement with the U.S. of 1938, of which Article 4 requires that import restrictions and Article 8 that bulk purchases shall be non-discriminatory. We should, therefore, have to denounce this Treaty.[8] Moreover, it is certain that the U.S. will not sign any Post-War Commercial Agreement which would allow us or anyone else any greater latitude, except as a temporary concession during the transitional period. It follows that the possibility of any commercial treaty with the U.S. would fall to the ground and we should be exposed to the maximum rigour of their tariffs and retaliation.

(4) Moreover, *the other party* with whom we were seeking to enter into a discriminatory agreement, would be placed in just the same position. They, too, would be forced into a commercial

---

[8] The words 'The Bretton Woods proposals, which allow us a latitude to have a discriminatory currency policy during the transitional period, are compatible with our existing Treaty only because our Delegation was successful in persuading Mr Hull to agree to an exchange of letters by which, if the Bretton Woods proposals are accepted, the State Department agree that this overrides the provisions of the Anglo-American Commercial Treaty of 1938.' were added at this point.

rupture with the U.S. and might have to denounce any commercial agreements with the U.S. before they on their side would be free to enter into the proposed agreement with us. Since the barter policy would involve us in such arrangements with a number of countries, we should be inviting a considerable part of the world to enter into a ring with us to undermine the principles of Article VII and break with the U.S. in a field where Mr Hull and the State Department are especially sensitive and where we can expect no popular support in the United States from any quarter. The prospect of our persuading the rest of the world to join with us in this enterprise is very poor.[9]

(5) We (and also any other country joining us) would, if we were to embark on all this, have to give up any hope of getting the post-war financial assistance from the U.S. which is indispensable to the carrying on of our post-war plans for social improvements and an early restoration of the standard of life.

(6) Canada is vehemently of the same opinion as the U.S. in this matter. We should probably be involved in a break with them not less serious than that with the United States.

(7) If all the above considerations were put on one side, nevertheless it would still be exceedingly doubtful whether it is in our interest to encourage a general system of barter trade, which can be used against us just as much as by us. Under such a system other countries could refuse to take our exports unless we took their imports on a scale or of a kind which did not strictly suit us. Before the war we held very strongly that these practices were against the interest of a great trading nation such as ourselves. Personally, I still adhere to this view. Moreover, discriminatory arrangements do, in fact, lend themselves, as the U.S. say they do, to abuses and malpractices such as we shall not attempt ourselves but which may be used against us by other less scrupulous parties. These would be dangerous and uncertain waters in which to launch ourselves, even if the considerations (1) to (5) outlined above had no influence with us.

[9] Paragraph (5) was omitted.

If my colleagues agree with me that it would be little less than crazy to break with the United States on this matter, the sooner we register this conclusion and find some convenient opportunity for making it generally known, the better.

To avoid any possible misunderstanding, let me make it clear:

(*a*) That the above does not apply to the transitional period;— the Americans have already agreed at Bretton Woods to allow us temporarily to continue discriminatory currency practices until we have escaped from our immediate post-war balance of trade difficulties, and we are not likely to need any other instrument than that, since it enables us to require those from whom we buy to spend with us.

(*b*) That the above does not apply to non-discriminatory bulk purchases or import restriction which remain matters for discussion.

(*c*) That, if the arrangements for a saner world which we are hoping to organise in collaboration with the United States and the British Commonwealth and others also, do ultimately break down, then, unquestionably, we have got to think again on this and many other matters.

KEYNES

15 September 1944

During Keynes's visit to Washington for the Stage II negotiations, he continued to take an interest in commercial policy and keep London informed of developments in opinion.

To SIR WILFRID EADY, *13 November 1944*

My dear Wilfrid,

Your letter of October 21st took a full three weeks to get here. There seem no means of knowing whether that will be the time lag, or whether one will get them in about five days. This letter, I may remind you, was largely about your commercial policy talks, and I will stick to that in this reply.

I have had two very long discussions with Pasvolsky on two

successive Sundays, which I can best summarise for your purpose as follows:

1. No definite plans seem to exist, such as we had imagined, for a somewhat larger deputation to arrive in London from Washington before the end of the year. No doubt you will have got into contact with Hawkins by now and have learned from him more than this letter contains. But I feel sure that Pasvolsky has no clear plan in view. His own wishes are that there should be a very small deputation to come to London some time next January. But this is quite another matter from there being any sort of even preliminary decision to that effect. Thus, apart from anything Hawkins may be telling you, there is no desperate urgency.

2. The conversations left me with the decided feeling that, as usual, one is inclined in London to under-estimate the degree of fluidity of ideas on this side, and to regard their proposals as very much more cut and dried than they actually are. Pasvolsky's view is that the paper which emerged from the talks a year ago is very unsatisfactory and needs re-thinking from top to bottom. In particular, he doubts the practicability of a multilateral approach in the sense of universal multilateralism, and would rely more on a small group of major countries to start with. He thinks the plan was faulty in putting no check on subsidies, which in his opinion, with which I concur, is the real menace of the future. As you will have seen from the current plans for subsidising wheat and cotton, there is a party here in favour of subsidising any American export which is on a non-competitive basis down to the point at which it becomes competitive;—on those lines obviously there can be no possibility of reaching equilibrium.

3. In particular, Pasvolsky thinks it was a mistake to get down to detailed drafting before we had thoroughly explored both the difference in our opinion and the extent of our agreement. The paper represents, he thinks, a premature crystallisation of ideas, and thus raises resistances which might be overcome if the

approach were through much more general discussion. Thus you need not think it necessary to counter the existing detailed document by something on similar lines. If the small deputation comes, I fancy that they will be much more disposed to talk at large and to try to get to the bottom of the difficulties.

4. At one point in the conversation, Pasvolsky mentioned that London seemed to be under the impression that the United States wished to force something on us against our will, either by threats or by the offer of inducements. He denied the truth of this. What we want, he pointed out, is to find the right solution; and the first step to this is to discover the greatest common measure of agreement, and to reach a common mind. He thinks this will emerge out of a thorough discussion of the possible alternatives. If we face up to these alternatives in clear and unvarnished form, he is sure we shall shrink from them.

I tried on him rather vaguely the idea of all expedients being equally lawful provided they are applied moderately. I did not think it advisable to carry this suggestion very far, but he reacted to it quite favourably.

5. He thinks it is necessary to make progress on account of two critical dates which are getting nearer. The Lend Lease Act expires on June 30th, and the Trade Agreements Act on June 14th. Legislation to replace or continue these measures will have to be introduced in the early Spring. For that reason, he thinks that we must get together on the whole post-war issue very early next year. He believes that the Lend Lease Act cannot be continued into the second half of next year unless some explanation is given to Congress as to what is to succeed it. They will not readily agree to anything unless they see what it is leading to. And this may well raise post-war policy generally.

Please do not attach either too much or too little importance to these brief notes of lengthy talks. The main point to emphasise is that which I have already mentioned, namely, that ideas over here are fluid, and that we in London, on this and every other matter, always attach to them a fixity and rigidity which they never possess.

Yours ever,
MAYNARD KEYNES

P.S. Opie, who has read this letter, asks me to tell you that he wrote to Ronald on November 1st on the same matter, and somewhat to the same effect, and that if Ronald has not already done so, he might show you his letter.

Finally, in November 1944, the War Cabinet agreed to continue the commercial policy discussions. As a result Harry Hawkins of the State Department and officials from the American Embassy began conversations with Sir Percivale Liesching, Sir Wilfrid Eady, Professor Robbins and Mr Shackle. Keynes watched them from the sidelines with some amusement.

To SIR WILFRID EADY, *1 January 1945*

THE COMMERCIAL POLICY TALKS

Is it a 'commercial consideration' if one supplier offers more convenient financial terms than another, e.g., if he offers the supplies on credit?

If the answer is in the affirmative, as surely it should be on a natural interpretation of the words, then would it be a commercial consideration in deciding on purchase from New Zealand, if New Zealand was prepared to accept payment in sterling which could only be used to purchase British exports?

I am finding the Minutes of the Meetings instructive and entertaining. They must be very wholesome for Mr Hawkins and perhaps for others. Is he, do you think, gradually appreciating what a labyrinth he is trying to work his way into and what nonsense it is to try to settle all these matters by *a priori* rulings, qualified by finding let-outs for all those particular contingencies which one has been clever enough to think of beforehand?

KEYNES

To SIR WILFRID EADY, *4 January 1945*

COMMERCIAL POLICY TALKS

That the term 'commercial considerations' covers such matters as are mentioned in your note was clearly brought out in the discussions. There can be no misunderstanding about that so far as Hawkins is concerned. But the question whether 'commercial considerations' covers the financial terms, though perhaps more important than any of the points that we mentioned, seems to have escaped discussion. I was wanting to know, first of all, how the British members of the Committee would answer this question and, secondly, how much confidence you would feel that Hawkins would answer it in the same way.

It is rather a good example of the perils of the labyrinth along which you are leading him hand in hand. For, whilst 'commercial considerations' seems to be just what the American want at first blush, it is, nevertheless, quite clear that financial terms *are* a commercial consideration. Yet this opens the door to every single one of the practices to which the Americans are most averse. So what?

KEYNES

From SIR WILFIRD EADY, *10 Januay 1945*

On the British side we have no doubt at all that the case you put will be covered by 'commercial considerations'. If a private firm were buying from a supplier who offered credit, and it suited the purchaser to buy on those terms, clearly that would be a 'commercial consideration'.

We get nearer to trouble I think if, for example, in connection with a purchase of commodity 'A', the purchaser, being in turn a supplier of other goods, makes it a condition of the purchase that his own exports shall be taken. We go still nearer to trouble if, for example, a country agrees to purchase a large part of the crop of, say, opium on condition that the Government of the country concerned gives a concession for the exploitation of tramways.

Some of those difficulties came up in discussion about the application of 'commercial considerations' in state trading, and I think the American view is that we must go forward slowly, leaving the International Commercial Organisation, when it is set up, to build up case law about what is proper and improper.

You may have noticed in the minutes of the meeting at which the second part of the American Convention was explained to us that they have two Articles dealing with exchange control and Blocked Balances. I think both Articles will have to come out of the draft Commercial Convention because it won't be easy to reconcile the philosophy of the Convention with the rather more liberal philosophy of Bretton Woods. But it may interest you to know that Hawkins was obviously quite taken aback when I explained that in the transitional period it might well be that we would buy things for sterling and that the sterling would be subject to such agreed restrictions as to its use as applied to the other holdings of sterling by the supplier of the goods. I put it deliberately rather extremely and we are going to run over the whole position at tomorrow's meeting.

10 January 1945   W.E.

To SIR WILFRID EADY, *11 January 1945*

I should doubt if it would be practicable to leave the question raised in your second paragraph below ambiguous. The Chancellor will certainly be asked to explain whether we are or are not free to take such things into consideration. It will not be thought a satisfactory reply to say this would depend upon the view taken of the matter by an as yet non-existent International Commercial Organisation.

I pursue all this, not as a debating point, but as a good illustration of the insoluble riddles which are set up as soon as one tries to have too precise a document. I am sure that the final convention will have to be on much broader lines, if it is to sail past Scylla and Charybdis and all the other snags.

12 January 1945   KEYNES

In the spring of 1945, post-war commercial policy became even more involved with London's current concern over the shape of the post-war economic settlement and the financial assistance available during the transition to more normal conditions, particularly as the Canadian and American governments sought assurances on the shape of Britain's post-war trade policy. At one point Keynes became involved at the highest level when the Prime Minister asked him to attend a meeting to discuss the North Americans' concerns. The other participants at the meeting were Sir Edward Bridges, the Governor of the Bank of England, the Chancellor, the Lord President, the Foreign Secretary, the Dominions Secretary, the Lord Privy Seal and the Paymaster General.

The Anglo-American discussions on commercial policy continued during the spring and early summer of 1945. May also saw a series of Anglo-Canadian talks as noted elsewhere (*JMK*, vol. XXIV, pp. 345–53). As the American discussions continued, Keynes minuted.

To SIR EDWARD BRIDGES, *11 July 1945*

My misgivings about the prudence of having handed the Americans a written statement, which enters into so much detail, are on two grounds,—partly diplomatic, partly on the merits of the statement from our own point of view.

(1) *Diplomatic*

(*a*) Whilst it is made quite clear that the paper has no ministerial authority behind it, it will in practice be difficult to go back on it.

(*b*) It will also be difficult to contest it, if something on these lines emanating from our stable is offered us as a condition of

Stage III assistance, though there will, of course, be no force in this objection, if we are in fact satisfied with the statement on merits.

(c) So much detail apparently settled beforehand is likely to frighten many of those invited to the Conference. The paper has been worked out primarily with a view to composing Anglo-American differences and with almost no regard to other people's problems. I should be surprised if the Dominions and India or European countries or others invited would regard this as an acceptable starting point.

(d) I understand that this is a specimen draft of a statement of principles which will be sent out to the world by the United States on their unilateral responsibility. Thus they will be entitled to work on it and adapt it to their own ideas. If so, there is nothing to prevent them from accepting all our concessions but modifying those passages where we have not met their views fully.

Thus, I think, in American phrase, we are sticking our neck out diplomatically.

(2) *On Merits*

The substance of the statement falls into three parts. A considerable proportion of it is on lines which have been thoroughly discussed and agreed amongst ourselves, and there can be no possible objection. On two matters where Ministers have been particularly interested, namely, agricultural protection and preferences, the paper falls a long way short of accepting the American point of view. I cannot myself see why the Americans should quarrel too much with our agricultural formula, though I think other countries might. So, in spite of Hawkins' having said that they do not at present like our formula, they might conceivably take it in the end. As regards preferences, they will want some more forthright statement.

There remain, thirdly certain paragraphs where I personally feel that the proposals go too far and are not sufficiently qualified. Since I am generally speaking sympathetic to the general approach adopted by our officials, others are likely to feel more strongly about these passages than I do. None of the differences of opinion in question are new ones, and I and others have frequently expressed in past discussions our hesitations about them. The points are the following:

(i) There are no references to shipping subsidies, which are far and away the most dangerous form of subsidy from our point of view. We are offering the Americans a completely free hand. Furthermore, in general we are agreeing that any country can give as much protection as it likes by subsidy, provided it subsidises the whole production of an article and not merely its exports. This allows a rich country like the United States to produce precisely the same effect as protection or as export subsidies by a method no more virtuous than those excluded, but only practicable for a country with a good margin on its budget.

(ii) The discretion we retain for quantitative regulation is insufficient. (This is far and away the most objectionable feature to my thinking.) After the transition period we are not allowed any quantitative regulation, even of a non-discriminatory character, unless the Bretton Woods Fund agrees. The difficulties are thoroughly shirked. The phrase suggests that there was already a clause in the Fund Agreement dealing with this, which there is not. The Economic Section have made several attempts to produce a satisfactory formula, which would demonstrate that a country had difficulties in its balance of payments, but have not yet succeeded to the general satisfaction. I feel the gravest doubts whether we can accept convertibility if we are entirely cut off from using at our own discretion non-discriminatory quantitative regulation. Yet it is precisely convertibility which we hope we can offer the world. You must have some way of shutting off imports which you cannot afford. Of the various alternatives quantitative regulation is at the same time much the most effective and much the most in tune with the modern world. To try and create an international system which excludes quantitative regulation is out of date and, I should have thought, impracticable.

(iii) The passage about state trading is so obscure that possibly no harm is done. Everything depends on what precisely is meant by a state trading body being influenced by nothing whatever except commercial considerations. In practice they never are, or can be, so limited. Bulk purchasing by the state is obviously both desirable and inevitable in the modern world. It is very difficult to reach a satisfactory solution. But I feel a danger in handing over in black and white ideas which are so incompletely thought out.

Finally, I would call attention to an issue where our officials are certainly doing their best to protect the situation. As explained on page 3 of the Minutes of the Seventh Meeting, our proposals are on the basis of a multilateral approach, that is to say, we only come in if a substantial body of other countries come in on the same basis. Hawkins has explained that this is not the American view. They prefer what he describes as the 'multilateral-bilateral' method. This, it seems to me, would be absolutely fatal from our point of view, and our officials were not backward in expressing this same point of view. I have little doubt, in view of what Hawkins has said, that it is the 'multilateral-bilateral' method which the Americans will put forward. Thus we have put them in a position here, as in other respects, to propound principles, which have received some sort of *imprimatur* from our officials, in a form entirely unacceptable to us, but nevertheless differing in a way so subtle and technical that legislatures would not easily be made to appreciate what the difference was.

[copy initialled] K

Keynes's final involvement in the commercial policy negotiations came in the autumn of 1945 during the Loan discussions. Initially Keynes and

London had hoped that the commercial policy issue would not get tied up with the financial negotiations except in the most general and subsidiary way. As a result, the Keynes mission did not initially include experts for such negotiations. However, once it became clear that the Americans expected serious negotiations on what was to become the *Proposals for an Expansion of World Trade and Employment*, an expert team under Sir Percivale Leisching came out from London to handle the trade discussions. As a result, Keynes played a minor part in the discussions, making few interventions in the meetings that followed.

Chapter 3

REPARATIONS, SEPTEMBER 1941–
DECEMBER 1945

Although he had raised the matter in the first draft of his 'Proposals to Counter the German "New Order"',[1] Keynes did not take up the question of the post-war treatment of Germany for almost another year. Then a conversation with Dr Beyen[2] of the Netherlands restimulated his interest and he minuted Lord Catto and others in the Treasury.

To LORD CATTO AND OTHERS, *19 September 1941*

EUROPEAN REPARATIONS

I had a visit a few days ago from Dr Beyen, who told me that his Government were giving increasing thought to the question of reparations from Germany in relation to post-war reconstruction. The Dutch Government are evidently a little anxious lest this issue should be prejudiced by some bold statement by the President and the Prime Minister, after some such occasion as the Atlantic Conference, declaring that there shall be no reparations of any sort or kind. They do not in the least contemplate anything like what happened after the last war. Quite the contrary. But the line to be drawn between reparations and restitution is not a very clear one. They suggest that the whole matter needs careful consideration at not too late a date. They would like to be assured that we are giving some thought to it and that no premature decision will be reached without their having an opportunity to express their views.

Dr Beyen told me that he was endeavouring to influence his Government to accept two general principles:

[1] For this see *JMK*, vol. XXV, pp. 7–16.
[2] Dr Johan Willem Beyen (b. 1897); Alternate President of the Bank for International Settlements, Basle, 1935–7, President, 1937–40; Director, Lever Bros. and Unilever Ltd., 1940–6.

(1) that there should be no question of reparations in cash, but only in kind through deliveries of material, etc.; and

(2) that no deliveries in kind should extend over a period of more than five years after the war at the outside.

He said that their problems fell into the following main groups:

(i) Stolen property of the character of American securities where restitution in kind should be required as a general principle. Shares in Dutch concerns transferred into German or Swiss nominee names must be re-transferred.

(ii) Requisitions of property for current use, of which railway rolling stock, a large part of which has been removed from the country, is an outstanding example. Here the Dutch thought the Germans should be required to restore the rolling stock by replacing what was taken with newly made material. There would be other analogous cases.

(iii) The physical destruction of Amsterdam [Rotterdam?] and some other cities. This is concentrated within comparatively small areas and is probably not a very big figure.

I asked him to try and frame for me some sort of estimate of the order of magnitude of the sums involved. He was not prepared even to guess at this at the moment.

There is also another problem of considerable difficulty. The Germans have taken away a great part of the Netherlands Bank's reserves and replaced them with reichsmark deposits at the Reichsbank, which now comprise a large part of the cover of the Dutch note issue. Is Germany to be required to repay the proper value of these reichsmarks? Clearly for all the countries involved this might amount to a very big figure indeed.

Dr Beyen agreed that the circumstances of different countries would vary very greatly—Belgium and Holland probably very much alike; France different in some respects, but not wholly dissimilar; Czechoslovakia and Greece widely different; Poland another story altogether.

Dr Beyen took the opportunity to say that his Government

hoped not to ask any contribution towards relief after the war. They were quite rich enough to get all the supplies they needed out of their own resources. But they thought that the fact that they were relatively well off in this way, as a result of the frozen American assets and the high earning power of their colonies, should not prejudice their claims against Germany on the above headings.

*　　*　　*　　*

Now, so far as I know, no-one has as yet given a minute's thought to all this. Ought we not to begin thinking about it as one section of our studies of post-war problems? The difficulties both of principle and practice raised are of the greatest possible perplexity.

In the Treaty of Versailles a distinction was made between what we called restitution and reparations, restitution being the return in kind of the same or similar articles which had been stolen or requisitioned. Reparations were stated in terms of cash, which was to be discharged under two heads—partly deliveries in kind spread over a term of years, and partly payments of cash.

Probably it would be easy to agree this time that there should be no cash reparations. But the problems of restitution and of deliveries in kind for reconstruction purposes are not so easily disposed of.

If, as I suggest, a Committee is set up to give some thought to this, I suggest that a representative of the Foreign Office, such as Mr Nigel Ronald, should be a member of it. May I send him a copy of this note?

19 September 1941   [copy initialled] J.M.K.

The upshot from Keynes's minute was a series of discussions in a group made up of Mr N. Ronald, Sir William Malkin,[3] Mr Waley, Mr Henderson and Keynes. For this group, Keynes drafted a series of questions on the principles underlying the post-war treatment of Germany, sending a copy to Ronald on 13 October 1941. He later suggested two additions.

[3]　Sir William Malkin (1883–1945); Legal Adviser to Foreign Office, 1914–45.

REPARATIONS

I

1. Is there to be a difference in the economic treatment of victors and vanquished?

2. Is there to be a distinction between non-enemy countries which are Allies and those which are not?

3. Is France to be treated in this connexion as a fully allied country? For example, should France, having had the bulk of her foreign assets frozen at an early stage, be allowed to receive back the whole of them and sustain the rest of any claims she may have equally with everyone else?

II

1. If there is to be a difference in the economic treatment of victors and vanquished, what limitations are to be set to the demands against the enemy countries?

2. On the assumption that the enemy countries will not be required to pay reparations in the sense of that term after the last war, and that no claims are made for destruction of buildings, etc. by bombardment or in the course of operations, what limitations should be set to the demands made on them?

3. Should different treatment from the above be required for any particular classes of destruction, such as ships?

4. Should they be required to restore property which is capable of being identically returned in specie, such as securities, works of art, etc.?

5. Should they be required to replace property which has been requisitioned or carried off, such as rolling stock, cattle, agricultural implements, the contents of factories, etc., by deliveries similar in kind?

6. Should this same principle extend to raw materials currently produced which have been requisitioned or carried off?

7. Should they be required to repay contributions in cash or services exacted from the occupied countries?

8. Should they be required to repay credits at the Reichsbank in favour of the central banks of the occupied countries which will constitute the main cover for the note issues of those countries?

9. How is enemy property in the hands of custodians or frozen in U.S.A. to be treated? Should it be returned? Or retained without compensation? Or set off against the above claims?

III

1. Should the aggregate of the contributions exacted in any of the above forms be limited to what could be transferred in kind within a period of say five years, contributions in cash, or contributions in kind over a longer period, being excluded?

2. If, as is probable, the most reasonable interpretation of the above claim leads to a much larger sum than Germany could contribute in kind over a period of say five years, what order of priority should be established?

3. Should the order of priority depend on the nature of the claim or on the need of the claimant?

4. In particular, should those countries, such as Holland or France, which will after the end of the war presumably recover large frozen assets in the shape of gold and dollar securities, be required for this reason to take a lower place in their claims against Germany than for example Poland, whose assets in that form are insignificant?

5. Should any regard be had to the fact that certain countries, again France, Holland and perhaps Belgium in particular, will hold very much larger liquid assets in gold and dollar securities than we shall ourselves?

6. Should the claims of individual countries be considered at all (apart from identical restitution of securities and works of art)? Or should we exact from the enemy countries such contributions as seem reasonable, pool the proceeds, and use

them as a fund for European relief and reconstruction according to need?

7. If the enemy countries receive relief immediately after the war which they do not pay for immediately, should they pay by instalments? And if so, should claims for such payments rank before or after the items in II above?

IV

1. If a declaration were to be made that there would be no difference in the economic treatment of victors and vanquished, would this mean that all the above claims are wiped off, or that the enemy countries would be entitled to prefer (or set off) similar claims against ourselves and our allies?

2. If the phrase 'no reparations or indemnities' were to be used, which of the above claims would it exclude? Clearly it should not exclude identical restitution of securities and works of art? Where would the line be drawn?

3. Is there any reply, however guarded, which can be made safely to enquiries from Allied Governments in London?

To SIR HORACE WILSON, *20 October 1941*

REPARATIONS

(1) I have had a meeting about this with Mr Nigel Ronald of the F.O. and Sir W. Malkin. We thought the most useful thing we could do would be to draw up a catechism of questions requiring a decision, mainly with a view to indicating the complexity of the problem and giving a warning note against the use of loose phrases.

I attach a copy of this catechism. I have nothing at present to add to it except that perhaps the following additional clause might be added:

If the purchase by German interests of holdings in banks and companies of occupied countries are cancelled, what is to happen if the Germans have paid in local currency U.S. $ for the shares which they have acquired?

I should also like to add one overriding rider somewhat as follows:

The chief thing that matters is that Ministers should not suppose that the chief thing that matters is to avoid the mistakes made last time.

(2) Since our discussion and in response to the attached version of the catechism, I have the enclosed letter from Mr Ronald asking what is the next step.[4] You will see that he and Sir W. Malkin have had a word with Mr Eden on the subject.

[copy initialled] J.M.K.

As far as one can gather, the discussions resulted in little beyond a Treasury memorandum, dated 5 December 1941, entitled 'Compensation to be Required from the Enemy'. This memorandum raised the possible issues involved and warned Ministers against statements which might prove impossible to fulfil and against using language which might lead to charges of bad faith from ex-enemy countries after the war. However, it never received wide circulation, probably because of the opposition of other Departments.

These matters rested until the summer of 1942, for, beyond some informal discussions amongst interested officials, nothing happened until Hugh Dalton, President of the Board of Trade, circulated a memorandum on 28 August entitled simply 'Reparations'. In it he suggested that officials should work out a plausible German plan for dealing with a defeated Britain, turn it around to fit the case of a defeated Germany, suggest changes to meet the interests of other members of the United Nations and then suggest why this should not be the course adopted. He then went on to suggest that the Europeans had made a muddle of reparations policy (and much else) in the inter-war period, but that the time had come for a re-examination of the issues of reparations and post-war economic security. On this Cabinet paper, Keynes wrote

4 Not printed. [Ed.]

REPARATIONS: NOTES ON MR DALTON'S MEMORANDUM

Mr Dalton is now in favour of the examination of this subject by an official committee. This is what we have been suggesting for some little time past. The proposed membership of the Committee seems suitable. Presumably we shall agree to his proposal. The first task of this Committee will be to examine the Treasury Memorandum and Mr Dalton's Memorandum, and it is, therefore, unnecessary perhaps to discuss the latter in detail at this stage. But I add a few preliminary remarks.

(1) The President's own Memorandum is interesting and deserves careful thought, since, whether it is right or wrong, it represents a point of view which is likely to be widely held. It is for the Committee to clear its mind as to whether his general approach is really advisable. The attached annex, however, ('A Technical Note') does not add much to knowledge, and as regards policy it is difficult to discover any echo in it of the President's ideas. This is not, I think, the D.O.T. paper to which Mr Dalton refers in paragraph 6 of his own document. Since A.P. (42) 10 does not seem to fill the bill, I do not think I can have seen the paper in question.

(2) Mr Dalton much under-estimates, in my opinion, the difficulty of the dilemma between ruining Germany and milking her.

(3) It is quite true that in 1919 the problem of reparations was attacked on old *laissez-faire* principles and pre-1914 international commerce and finance, and that, if organised enslavement is substituted for this, much more substantial results might be obtainable over a period of years. It would certainly be useful for Ministers to decide whether they favour something tending in the direction of organised enslavement, since a broad decision about this would affect much else.

(4) Mr Dalton misapprehends, I think, the purpose of the Treasury paper, a copy of which is attached. This was in course of preparation a year ago. One of its purposes was to prevent

premature declarations being made by a responsible Minister which would not only preclude what Mr Dalton wants but also much more moderate measures. It indicated very briefly some of the claims for restitution, which will be likely to take precedence of reparations, and also the question of the order of priority between these. It certainly was not the intention of the Treasury to exclude from this the cost of armies of occupation. The suggestion was that the reparations in kind which were envisaged would absorb the probable capacity for five years. The principal difference of opinion with the President of the Board of Trade would appear to be whether it would be advisable to continue the reparation period over a much more extensive length of time than five years.

(5) It does not seem likely that this country would benefit financially either under the proposals of the Treasury Memorandum or under those of Mr Dalton. But perhaps this is not his intention.

(6) He says that it would be interesting to see worked out more vindictive proposals with a view to passing judgment on them when it is seen what they are really like. An interesting first essay in this direction is Dr Einzig's article published in the *Economic Journal* last week.[5] I attach a copy. Dr Einzig has explained the same ideas in more detail in a book.[6]

(7) The official committee may not be able to get very far without some instruction from Ministers on very broad questions, in particular whether it is a case of a policy 'until the pips squeak', and also, whatever the immediate policy is, whether it should be designed to be for some short period, such as five years, or of a more enduring character.

[copy initialled] K

3 September 1942

[5] P. Einzig, 'A Plan for Germany's Economic Disarmament', *Economic Journal*, June–September 1942.
[6] P. Einzig, *Can we win the Peace?* (London, 1942).

The result of the Dalton memorandum and the subsequent discussions was an Inter-Departmental Committee on Reparation and Economic Security with Sir William Malkin as Chairman. The other members included Keynes, Professor Robbins, J. E. Meade, E. W. Playfair, N. B. Ronald, P. Liesching, H. M. G. Jebb[7] and Rear-Admiral R. M. Bellairs.[8] The Committee met thirty-three times between 18 November 1942 and 31 August 1943 when it submitted a report.

Keynes took an active part in the work of the Committee, including its report. The two papers he circulated were both influential and appear below; the second is in revised form.

GERMANY'S CONTRIBUTION TO THE COST OF KEEPING THE PEACE OF THE WORLD

The provisional conclusion of the Committee on Reparation and Economic Security which met with least criticism and is most likely to be adopted was the recommendation for the complete demilitarisation of Germany pressed to an extreme degree. If Germany is thus demilitarised, the question of guaranteeing her frontiers will necessarily arise. Presumably it is intended either that there should exist an international police force or that certain Powers should between them undertake to maintain armaments, possessing sufficient force to deal with any likely contingency threatening world peace.

Now, the direct financial consequence of this is to relieve the German budget, more or less permanently, of a very large sum; whilst the budgets of those Powers responsible for keeping the peace of the world are burdened with a heavy charge, also for a more or less indefinite period.

[7] Hubert Miles Gladwyn Jebb (b. 1900), 1st Baron Gladwyn 1960; Private Secretary to Permanent Under-Secretary of State for Foreign Affairs, 1937–40; Ministry of Economic Warfare with temporary rank of Assistant Under-Secretary, 1940; Acting Counsellor in Foreign Office, 1941; Head of Reconstruction Department, 1942; Counsellor, 1943; Assistant Under-Secretary of State, 1946–7; Deputy Under-Secretary of State, 1949; Permanent Representative of U.K. to United Nations, 1950–4; British Ambassador to France, 1954–60.

[8] Roger Mowbray Bellairs (1884–1959); Representative on League of Nations Permanent Advisory Commission, 1932–9; Admiralty, 1939–46.

One can assume that, so long as there is an army of occupation in Germany, she will be responsible for meeting all local expenses incurred in German currency. But occupation might not continue so long as the quasi-permanent arrangements for the maintenance of peace; and, in any case, the sum involved would fall far short of meeting the full costs even of the armies of occupation, since their armament and equipment would be supplied from abroad and a considerable part of the pay and allowances of the troops would be expended outside Germany.

To indicate the order of the sums involved, it may be mentioned that British defence forces of 1 million in post-war conditions would probably cost not less than £500 million a year, including the cost of the Navy and the Air Force. This is, of course, a very rough figure, since the way in which the forces are divided between the three Services makes a big difference. In any case, however, this force of 1 million would be far short of the total forces required by all those concerned to maintain world peace.

The sum of which the German budget would be relieved by complete disarmament with their much larger numbers would not be less than this. Moreover one element in the relief thus afforded to Germany is insufficiently measured by the financial cost:—the prohibition of conscription, by giving Germany the additional industrial use of young men in the prime of their activity, would have an economic value much in excess of their army pay.

Now the contrast between our budgetary situation, with a burden of (say) £500 million, and the German budgetary situation, relieved of a similar or a larger sum, would make all the difference to her capacity and to ours to finance costly schemes of social improvement and amelioration. The amount of which Germany is relieved is at least six times as great as the increased cost of social insurance, children's allowances and the health services under the beveridge scheme in its early years. It is not far short of our total budgetary expenditure on the social services, education, housing, agriculture and trade.

It is natural to wish that the benefits of defeat and the burdens of victory should not be more financially disproportionate than is inevitable. I see no means of redressing the anomaly completely, for the old, familiar, insoluble problems of 'Reparations' would arise from an attempt to make Germany find in cash available outside her frontiers a fixed sum of anything like the internal expenditure of which complete disarmament will relieve her. Yet, unless some fairly far-reaching measures are taken to deal with this anomaly, it is hard to believe that public opinion will permanently acquiesce in the situation when its real character and consequences are understood.

For this reason I suggested at a recent meeting of the Committee that we should consider some technique by which Germany can be required to pay over annually a large sum to those financially responsible for maintaining the peace of the world, whether this is an international body or a combination of Allies. The method suggested was one by which the whole of the gross receipts obtained by Germany for her exports would be canalised through an international institution, e.g. a special account in the books of the Clearing Union, into which all countries purchasing German exports would obligate themselves to pay the gross amounts due. A certain proportion, (say) one-quarter or one-third, of these gross sums would then be transferred direct to the account of the international body concerned with maintaining the peace, the balance being transferred to Germany to pay for her imports and other general purposes. German exporters would, of course, be paid in full by the German Government, the difference being charged on the German budget.

It is not possible to predict how much money this would yield. In a good year such as 1928 German exports were valued at about £m1,000. In a bad year such as 1935 they fell below £m300. In 1938 they were about £m350. At post-war prices one would expect them not to fall below £m500, and with a revival of world trade they might well recover to £m1,000. These figures indicate how difficult it would be to put on Germany a fixed external charge equivalent to the internal charge which she escapes through demilitarisation, but also that the annual charge, whilst falling short of this, might in favourable circumstances reach £m200 or even more. This particular formula overcomes some of the main difficulties of collecting reparations, and I believe that its advantages will appear even greater on close study. It would be going beyond the scope of this paper to develop these points in detail at the present stage. The general conception might be:

(1) That Germany would be required for a limited period of years to provide restitution and physical reparation in kind and in labour services;

(2) that she would be required to meet all local costs of occupation;

(3) that the gross proceeds of her exports would be canalised as above, say 20 per cent being transferred to international defence account during the early period, rising to 33 per cent when her liability for physical reparation and occupation costs becomes less or ceases;*

(4) that, to prevent this from acting as a further encouragement to the practice of autarky, she should be required to keep her impediments, direct or indirect, to imports within prescribed limits.

Certain secondary advantages of this treatment of her export-proceeds deserve mention:

(a) The machinery thus set up would be ready and available to impose a complete financial blockade in the event of a breach on her part of any of her undertakings. Any such breach could be penalised so long as it lasted by increasing the proportion of her export-proceeds to be withheld up to any figure, even 100

---

* Some allowance might have to be made for the value of imported materials embodied in exports.

per cent if necessary, according to the gravity of the offence. It would be of very great advantage to have at hand over the long period, and not merely during occupation, a heavy (and graded) sanction which did not involve warlike action.

(*b*) It is only through a German contribution to the costs of maintaining peace that the United Kingdom can expect any mitigation of the financial burdens of victory.

(*c*) The actual method suggested is particularly convenient to our interests for the following reason. If Germany is thereby discouraged from developing a large volume of exports, we are relieved of a serious competitor. If she is not discouraged, we receive a useful contribution towards meeting our adverse balance of trade.

(*d*) A similar system could be applied to Japan, and perhaps to Italy and other Axis allies in appropriate measure. The advantage to us pointed out under (*c*) above would apply not less in the case of Japan.

There is nothing harsh or unjust in requiring from Germany and Japan even over the long period a contribution to the cost of preserving world peace at least equal to the burden which we should be assuming ourselves. On the contrary, it would be an intolerable conclusion that they alone should escape from any share in this long-drawn-out future sacrifice which their own conduct had made an inescapable element in world policy.

21 December 1942   KEYNES

RESTITUTION AND REPARATION
THE DECLARATION TO BE MADE BY GERMANY

The Declaration to be made by Germany

The German Government acknowledges that she has by her unprovoked aggression and reckless acts of pillage and destruction caused damage and incurred costs and liabilities to the Governments and nationals of the United Nations beyond her capacity to make good. She, therefore, submits to an act of general bankruptcy towards all the external creditors of herself and her nationals; and undertakes the future tasks, surrenders and obligations set forth below, by way of a partial composition of all such costs and liabilities.

The Acts to be performed by Germany

1. The title to all assets and property in German ownership but physically situated in the territory of any of the United Nations and to all claims on the nationals and residents of any of the United Nations shall pass to the ownership of the Government of the territory in question.

2. Where pre-war German territory is transferred to one of the United Nations, the same principle shall apply to all German assets, property and claims (and also to liabilities) within the transferred territory.

3. All gold, securities, works of art, rolling stock, ships, live-stock, the equipment of factories and any other moveable assets taken by Germany out of the territory or from the ownership of the nationals of any of the United Nations, whether or not Germany shall have purported to make payment for them, shall be returned in specie to the Government of the United Nations affected, where they still exist and can be identified.

4. The same principle shall apply to the return of all assets except that immoveable assets shall also be included, which have been taken involuntarily from German nationals or ex-nationals (whether or not payment has been made for them) on grounds of racial discrimination.

5. Claims due from one Axis government or central bank to another shall be cancelled.

6. Neutral governments shall be allowed to set off German assets in their jurisdiction in respect of the claims of themselves and their nationals against the German Government and its

nationals, and Germany shall default on any excess of its liabilities above such set-off.

7. Any excess of German claims over liabilities on neutral countries, all assets in German ownership physically situated in neutral territory, and any gold remaining to Germany shall be transferred to the United Nations Relief Administration towards the cost of Germany's post-war relief.

8. Germany shall make such deliveries in kind or services of the following description required by the claimant Governments towards making good loss and damage as it shall lie within her power to perform within the period of occupation:–

    (i) the services of labourers;

    (ii) machine tools and the equipment of factories existing at the date of the armistice;

    (iii) ships and railway rolling stock;

    (iv) timber, bricks, cement, steel billets, structural steel and other semi-manufactured and finished products required for the erection of buildings and the restoration of the means of transport;

    (v) coal and potash;

    (vi) the performance of 'tasks' to restore buildings and the means of transport.

They shall not include live-stock, food-stuffs, or raw materials and manufactured products other than those specified above.

9. The provision that the deliveries demanded shall lie within the power of Germany to perform shall be interpreted by a Reparation Commission which shall observe the following principles:–

    (i) The total value of such deliveries by Germany shall not exceed 15 billion reichsmarks at the prices and wages ruling in Germany in 1938;

    (ii) no deliveries shall be required which cannot be supplied at a cost reasonably commensurate with the resulting value;

    (iii) no deliveries shall be required which would have the

effect of reducing the standard of life in Germany below a stipulated level;

(iv) no deliveries shall be required which impair, disproportionately to their value, Germany's productive capacity;

(v) a failure to make deliveries which are consistent with these conditions may be punished by an extension of the period of delivery.

10. All supplies and services available within Germany and required for the use of the armies of occupation and for the Missions of the United Nations shall be transferred without charge.

11. The whole of the gross receipts due to Germany for her exports shall be canalised through an international institution, e.g. a special account in the books of the Clearing Union, into which all countries purchasing German goods and services shall obligate themselves to pay the gross amounts due.

12. The cost of relief and rehabilitation supplies, in excess of the sources of payment available under 7 above, shall be a first charge against these receipts, but may be collected by instalments if the United Nations Relief Administration so decide.

13. 20 per cent of such receipts up to £m500 and 25 per cent of such receipts in excess of £m500 shall be transferred to an international fund for the maintenance of peace, towards the cost of naval and military armaments, whether national or international, required to ensure world peace.

14. The payments required under 13 above shall only be payable during the initial period of occupation to the extent that they exceed the value of the transfers under 8 and 10 above.

15. The above composition shall be comprehensive and shall comprise Germany's total liability in respect of the external claims upon her existing at the date of the termination of hostilities; that is to say, she shall have no further liabilities to make external payments beyond the above in respect of the external debts of her nationals, of the liabilities of the Reichsbank

in respect of balances or clearing accounts and of notes circulating outside Germany territory, or of the loss and damage she has caused.

16. The Governments of the United Nations shall be responsible for making such compensation out of the above, or otherwise, as each of them shall see fit to satisfy the claims of their own nationals against Germany and German nationals.

Allocation of Deliveries in kind between the United Nations

17. Each of the Governments of the United Nations shall declare whether or not they desire to claim an allocation of the deliveries to be made under 8 above.

18. Those Governments which renounce their claims shall form an assessment committee which shall determine the respective proportionate shares of those Governments claiming an allocation.

19. Those Governments which make a claim shall furnish the assessment committee with a general statement directed to showing the net reduction in the value of their national property at the end of the war compared with the beginning. This statement shall set forth:

(*a*) the replacement cost of the immoveable property within their territories destroyed or injured in the course of hostilities or occupation, not replaced or made good by the end of the war;

(*b*) the loss of moveable property existing at the beginning of the war not replaced or made good by the end of it or by restitution under 3 above, in the shape of ships, rolling stock and other means of transport, and of live-stock;

(*c*) any other special losses of property by pillage or destruction, not offset by corresponding gains in other directions, not including normal obsolescence and wear and tear;

(*d*) the value of the net disposal of gold and external property and the net increase of external indebtedness, which has occurred during the war.

20. The assessment committee shall also take account of any gains accruing to a claimant Government out of the other clauses of this settlement or out of arrangements made between the United Nations relating to debts and assets or through the United Nations Relief Administration, and to any net increment of national wealth accrued during the period of the war in the shape of increased gold holdings, decreased external obligations, increased external assets and the like.

21. The assessment committee shall not enter into details or attempt any exact valuation of the claims in terms of money, but, by the exercise of broad judgement on the above facts as laid before them, shall assign to each claimant Government a percentage share of the reparation deliveries to be made by Germany or by other Axis Governments.

Soon after the completion of the Malkin Report, Keynes, then in Washington for discussions surrounding Article VII of the Lend Lease Agreement, suggested he discuss the Report with officials in the State Department interested in the same problems. When the Minister in charge of the Article VII mission, Mr Law, asked London for permission on 16 September for Keynes's discussion, there ensued a considerable delay before on 29 September a meeting of Ministers concerned refused permission, partly, one suspects, because of Keynes's previously published views on reparations and also because the no-dismemberment assumption concerning post-war Germany in the Report had not been the subject of Ministerial discussion. However, during the delay, Mr Law presumed that no reply from London implied consent and Keynes spoke on 28 September from the notes below.

To SIR WILLIAM MALKIN, *29 September 1943*

My dear Malkin,

I enclose a copy of a summary of our reparation paper from which I spoke at the State Department yesterday. I hope you will feel that I have got the perspective right and not missed out anything essential. You will see that to a very great extent I have retained the actual language of the original.

During the meeting on September 28 my exposition occupied most of the time, though a good many questions were asked. I heard subsequently, however, that they were considerably interested, and even excited, in what was put before them and are very much disposed to explore matters further. I anticipate, therefore, that there will be further meetings. I expect you will also be hearing all about this from Ronald.

Yours ever,

KEYNES

The attached paper gives the notes from which I spoke at a meeting in the State Department on Tuesday, September 28, 1943, at which the following were present:

Mr Law	Mr Myron Taylor
Mr Ronald	Mr Acheson
Lord Keynes	Mr Berle
	Mr Harriman
	Mr Finletter
	Mr Pasvolsky
	Mr Dunn
	Mr Matthews

Mr Law began by explaining that these proposals had no Ministerial authority as they had not yet been considered by Ministers. It was thought, however, that it might be useful if we shared with our American friends some of the suggestions of our own Interdepartmental Committee.

As it was not possible to cover the whole of the ground in the course of discussion, I left in their hands a few copies of these notes which cover a slightly wider ground than my oral discourse. It will be observed that so far as possible the actual language of the original has been used.

KEYNES

28 September 1943

347

RECOMMENDATIONS OF THE BRITISH
INTERDEPARTMENTAL COMMITTEE
ON REPARATION AND ECONOMIC SECURITY

I. *Introduction*

The Committee found it necessary to proceed on the basis of certain hypotheses in order that the position under review might be sufficiently definite, without of course expressing any opinion as to how far these hypotheses would prove valid. Of these the principal are the three following:

1. They did not consider that they were charged with the task of deciding the advisability of exacting reparations from Germany since this cannot be determined in isolation and in ignorance of the other provisions of the peace settlement. They regarded it as their task to recommend the most suitable methods in the event of such a policy being adopted.

2. Their recommendations are based on the assumption that, whilst there may be important territorial changes at the frontiers, Germany will not be broken up into several constituent parts but will remain a substantial unitary State.

3. In recommending what seemed suitable in the case of Germany they have not considered whether the same sort of provisions would be equally applicable to other enemy States.

In addition to these hypotheses the Committee worked in conformity with what seemed to them to be certain overriding general conditions, of which the most important were these:

1. The conditions of the Atlantic Charter, taken in conjunction with certain authoritative interpretations, did not appear to them to exclude such interference with Germany's normal economy as may be necessary to ensure that she is kept disarmed and incapable of commencing another war of aggression. But they clearly ruled out such measures as the total de-industrialisation of Germany or any interference with her

economic life not reasonably required either to obtain such reparation as she could provide or to ensure that she is not again in a position to disturb the peace of Europe. Moreover, while it would be manifestly unfair to ensure that the German standard of living is maintained at a higher level than that of countries she has overrun, measures which would have the effect of unduly depressing that standard or impairing the opportunities for peaceful employment would be inconsistent with the Atlantic Charter.

2. It is advisable that as much as possible of what has to be done should be of a once-and-for-all character within a limited period after the termination of hostilities. The feelings and interest which we shall have in common at that time may be much stronger than subsequently, so that it should be easier to secure common and agreed action.

3. In so far as any provisions may have to continue in operation over a longer period, it is important that they shall not only appear just to the United Nations now but shall continue to appear ten or twenty years after the war to be sufficiently just to command their full co-operation in carrying them out. Reparation and disarmament are both words which are charged with emotional content and suffer from association with a past failure. They could only too easily be made into a cause of division among us and a rallying point of German resentment and propaganda.

4. As regards economic security, it seemed to the Committee that there was no object in piling up additional safeguards if those already provided would be sufficient if there were a firm and continuing resolution of the United Nations to apply them. Measures of economic security are no substitute for the will to use force to suppress a potential aggressor. It is important not to recommend secondary measures which will not be necessary if the primary measures are functioning. For if by excessive precaution the measures adopted seem arbitrary and unjust a generation hence they may by reaction infect the will of the

peoples and governments of the United Nations to maintain peace at any cost.

II. *Division of the Subject Matter*

We were charged with the consideration of two subjects to a large extent distinct, namely, reparation and economic security. They are, however, connected inasmuch as the measures for economic security may easily reduce the capacity of Germany to pay reparation; whilst on the other hand, as an offset to this, the disarmament provisions may increase German's long-term economic strength and should therefore, be balanced by a contribution from her to peace-keeping, to which I will return later.

I will take reparation first. We interpreted our terms of reference under this head to cover all the financial and economic claims against Germany of whatever character which could be made by the United Nations at the end of the war.

We found that these claims fall very conveniently into four headings, namely: 1, restitution; 2, reparation; 3, the contribution to peace-keeping; 4, pre-war private claims.

III. *Restitution*

We interpreted 'restitution' to cover all forms of identifiable property taken by Germany from the nationals of the United Nations, including property which though no longer identifiable is capable of being restored in virtually identical or closely similar form.

We recommended that no distinction should be made between property taken without payment, property requisitioned and paid for and property acquired by voluntary, or what purports to be voluntary, sale at the market price. These distinctions might be relevant as between a United Nations Government and its own nationals, but should not, we thought, affect Germany's liability to restore the property.

Our recommendation is that all such property should be restored in so far as it can be identified.

The principal categories of claims under this heading would be as follows:

(*a*) *Gold*. The best information we could obtain indicated that Germany has taken something in the order of $500 million, chiefly from Holland, Belgium and Poland. In addition to this there were seizures at an earlier date from Austria and Czechoslovakia valued at $50 million. There may also be claims in respect of diamonds and other precious stones.

(*b*) *Works of Art*. This head should be understood in a broad sense, including in addition to works of art proper, historical and cultural treasures, the contents of libraries, the equipment of learned or technical institutions, and so forth. Under this heading it might be reasonable to propose that where it has been shown that a particular article has been removed and cannot be recovered, Germany should be required to deliver an article of corresponding interest and value.

(*c*) *Securities*, in industrial and other concerns in the occupied countries.

(*d*) *Rolling stock, inland water transport and ships.*

(*c*) *Factory equipment*.

(*f*) *Miscellaneous*, such as pedigree stock, agricultural equipment and miscellaneous loot.

We recommended that all claims to restitution be limited to property existing before the outbreak of hostilities and should not cover the requisition of current output.

IV. *The Basis of Reparation Claims*

The various types of claim for damage which could conceivably be made range from compensation for particular types of damage up to a claim for the total costs of the war. Since it is evident that such claims even if confined to certain limited categories are likely greatly to exceed Germany's capacity to pay, no Allied country can on any basis of division hope to receive more than a small proportion of its claim. It follows that classification of claims according to whether they should or should not rank is only important as affecting the different shares of the different claimant Governments, and would not affect the aggregate amount which Germany is required to pay, which will in any case be the largest sum which it seems advisable to demand. The makers of the Treaty of Versailles were suffering or pretending to suffer, or acquiescing in the imputation of suffering, from the illusion that their total claims against the enemy could be met. It became necessary therefore that they should establish and justify a detailed inventory of claims. With their disillusion and the world's experience behind us the Committee felt themselves excused from a similar task. Our problem today, in their view, is simpler and more limited. The purpose and the only object of considering which claims should rank is in order to reach a method of arriving at a broad answer to such questions as what should be the Russian percentage share of the whole available receipts from Germany, what should be the British share, and so on. In the view of the Committee it is simply not worth while to devote an immense amount of time and labour to assessing the claims of each Allied country and to discussing the merits of the different classes of claims with a view to the distribution between the Allies of the compensation recovered. What is required is some equitable and comparatively simple criterion which could be applied on broad lines without going into unnecessary detail.

Our recommendation is therefore that round figures for the proportionate share of the different members of the United Nations should be settled by the governments concerned as part of a broad-bottomed bargain. This does not mean that they should not be based on certain general principles, which indeed the Committee proposed and which I will describe in a moment. In this way broad decisions might be reached which would not violate the requirements of justice or reasonable expectation, and are at the same time capable of sustaining instructed criticism and of satisfying or at least not outraging a range of uninstructed public opinion widely varying within and between each of the United Nations.

In arriving at the broad principles on which the round figures for proportionate percentages might be based, we proceeded mainly by *excluding* a number of potential claims which one government or another might be expected to put forward.

Taking the broadest possible claim first, we felt that there would be grave difficulty in arriving at a fair division of the available proceeds based on an estimate of the general costs of the war incurred by each Ally. Costs have taken a great variety of forms and are not easily reduced to a common measure. On a somewhat similar principle we excluded a number of claims which might be proffered by the countries which have been the subject of occupation on the ground that these costs seemed to correspond in character to the costs of the war incurred by those nations which continued active hostilities. For this reason, we recommended the exclusion from the computation of all occupation costs and the like levied by the German authorities on occupied areas, claims in respect of German bank notes circulating in occupied areas, and similar exactions and sacrifices, including the whole of the claims against Germany in respect of clearing balances with the Reichsbank.

We emphasise the justice and reasonableness of this conclusion because it may be hotly contested by some of the Allies which have suffered occupation. For example, book credits at the Reichsbank arising out of the clearings constitute a large part of the assets of the central banks of the occupied countries and of the cover for their note issue. Nevertheless, for the Allies concerned to substitute their own obligations will only put the occupied areas in the same position as they would have been in if they had not been occupied. The Allied countries which succumbed to occupation should not for that reason be excused the burden of ending the war with a heavy increase of domestic debt. It was therefore one of the recommendations at which the Committee arrived with least hesitation, that we should stand absolutely firm on allowing no priority to any of the classes of claim arising out of occupation. Under the heading of restitution we have already proposed to allow the occupied areas the full measure of satisfaction which is physically practical. This already puts them in a somewhat favoured position in certain respects compared with the claims of those countries which have not been occupied.

Another class of claim which may be pressed from some quarters but which we nevertheless decided to exclude, was in respect of personal injury and loss of life. From some points of view it is logical that this should be included in the basis of apportionment; there may well be political feeling in various countries in favour of it; and those countries which have suffered heavy casualties in the war or whose civilians have been murdered in large numbers may be expected to hold strong feelings in this regard. Nevertheless, the inclusion of this item would raise the most serious difficulties, both statistical and in respect of valuation. Above all, how are we to assess the value of human life in relation to the value of property? Moreover, we found no reason to suppose that the inclusion of this difficult basis of claim would be likely to bring out a significantly different basis of apportionment than that which we had in fact proposed to adopt.

As a result of these various exclusions, we found ourselves left with only one category of claim, namely, in respect of losses of property directly caused by the enemy. It is quite true that if we were to follow a purely logical line of argument it might be difficult to distinguish between the loss of property directly caused by the enemy and the loss of property consumed in the form of our own war expenditure for the purpose of defeating the enemy. This, however, would result inevitably in including the general costs of the war and even more. For we should be led on from one category of claim to another and might even find it difficult to give a logical reason why, for example, losses should not be included arising out of the disorganisation of internal economy, the need for resettlement of the evicted people, the loss of productive power by malnutrition, and so forth. Moreover, as has already been emphasised, there is no reason to suppose that to try to bring all these claims into hotch-potch would improve the essential justice of the proportional division of the proceeds which we could arrive at on a simpler basis.

We were thus led to the conclusion that it would be wiser to confine the basis of claims for reparation to the loss of non-military property, moveable and immoveable, directly caused by the enemy in the course of military operations. Moreover, in default of agreement about a better formula, we felt that there were strong grounds for thus devoting the available proceeds of reparation to the physical damage to United Nations' property caused during hostilities, if only because the form of reparation which on other grounds we decided to recommend was specifically designed to repair such damage. At the same time, whilst the proportionate division should be primarily based on this criterion, it seemed to us that the heads of Governments in making the final assessment should, if necessary, feel free to take into general account such other considerations (e.g. loss of life, loss of external assets, and the like) as they might deem relevant to the final settlement.

Our recommendation with a view to the carrying out the above basis of apportionment runs as follows:

(a) The compensation to be obtained from Germany should be assessed on the basis of the amount of the loss of moveable and immoveable non-military property destroyed or injured in the course of operations (not including losses arising out of occupation) if they occurred—

355

(i) on land in any area occupied by German forces or in or over which German forces had been engaged in operations;

(ii) at sea, before Japan's entry into the war in any area; after Japan's entry into the war in the area east of the American Continent but west of the Cape of Good Hope in the south, and of longitude 62° east in the north, including the Mediterranean but not the Red Sea;

subject to deduction in respect of property acquired by transfer of territory or by subsequent restitution in the shape of ships, rolling stock and other means of transport, or live-stock, and also, in order to avoid duplication, of the value of any claims made by the Allied Governments concerned against any of Germany's allies.

(*b*) The assessment should take the form not of absolute sums but of percentages of the compensation obtained from Germany. Thus each claimant Government would secure a proportionate share of the compensation obtained from Germany in roughly the same ratio as that of its losses under the above head to the total losses.

(*c*) The percentages of compensation on the above basis would be agreed by heads of Governments without entering into details or attempting any exact valuation of the claims, but by the exercise of broad judgement on the facts produced by each claimant Government. As mentioned above, the heads of Governments should be free, if they deem proper, also to take into account such other considerations as they may deem relevant. If the governments are unable to reach a decision on the percentages to be allotted, it will be necessary for them to agree upon some impartial authority to settle the matter.

(*d*) It should be left to each of the Allied Governments concerned to decide what to do with the compensation which it received, e.g. whether and how the amounts received should be divided between its different classes of claimants, the extent to which those amounts should be used for the relief of the general taxpayer, and so on. It would be open to any Government which saw fit to do so to employ some of the compensation received in relief of claims (e.g. those for personal injury) which might not have been taken into account for purposes of assessment and apportionment.

V. *The Allied Claim on Germany for Peace-keeping*

The eighth point of the Atlantic Charter provides for the disarmament of the aggressor nations. The direct financial consequences of this measure will be to relieve Germany of a major continuing charge on her budget and her national resources generally. The prohibition of military service, moreover, will release to industry the services of a large number of young men in the prime of their activity. Since on this occasion it is not proposed that the victorious powers should disarm, there will be no offsetting economies to those who will be charged with the task of preserving the peace of Europe and of the world at large. Until provision is made otherwise, this will come about equally whether the task of peace-keeping is entrusted wholly to a combination of national forces or partly to some international body.

In the case of the United Kingdom it is estimated that, if we were spared the budgetary cost of the minimum national armaments which we are likely to require after the war, the relief would be at least six times as geat as the increased cost of social insurance, children's allowances and the health service under the Beveridge scheme in its early years, and would be not far short of our total budgetary expenditure on the social services, education, housing, agriculture and trade. It will seem intolerable to public opinion that the result of the war should be to fix such a burden on our shoulders and wholly to relieve Germany of any corresponding charge. If the disarmament of Germany is accompanied by any form of guarantee of her new frontiers from aggression or from changes unauthorised by an international body, the comparison, particularly as the years go by, will be still more glaring. The fruits of defeat, economic and financial at least, will seem, at any rate to the victors, unduly sweet. A structure, so based, may soon become precarious, as memories relax and fade.

It seemed to the Committee therefore that there should be a substantial contribution from Germany to the financial cost of keeping the peace, continuing so long as the disarmament provisions themselves remain in force. This is perhaps the most novel feature of the recommendations taken as a whole. As will appear in the sequel, the Committee recommended that Germany's contribution in respect of reparation proper should be limited to a short period of years and that such continuing contribution as it was practicable and right to place upon her should be exclusively devoted to the above purpose as a contribution for peace-keeping.

Since the percentage dividend on the total reparation claims estimated according to the formula we recommend, which Germany will be capable of fulfilling within a limited period, is likely to be comparatively small (perhaps not more than 10 percent and almost certainly less than 25 percent) it may seem at first sight difficult to justify the diversion to this other purpose of such later continuing cash payments as Germany may be in a position to make after the initial period is over. The justification of this proposal is mainly political and psychological.

When the period of occupation is at an end, the method we propose for collecting cash payments from Germany will require a general international collaboration on the part of substantially all those countries with which Germany conducts trade. The continued effective operation of such a method will be much facilitated if the proceeds are applied to what is really an international purpose. Moreover, as the injuries of the war recede into the distance, the current daily task of upholding the peace of the world will be a purpose much more easily justified to the public opinion of all countries than a dead sequel to the past. Such a contribution will involve no financial discrimination

358

against Germany. Indeed, she would be contributing to the costs of maintaining peace a relatively smaller sum in proportion to her production than the rest of us. Moreover, if plans mature even in part for an international police force, it will be a very great convenience that there should be available an international source of finance to defray what might be a substantial proportion of the cost.

The Committee felt entitled, therefore, to recommend this proposal as a constructive contribution to the peaceful evolution of the future, which did not excuse Germany from her proper financial responsibility. They explained that it had been much in their minds to discover equitable terms for future application which ran a chance of commencing themselves to public sentiment in the changing conditions of the future. It is one thing to impose certain conditions which can be executed once and for all, here and now. It is another thing to impose duties of execution on the future. Where the latter are involved counsels of moderation are called for and policies which do not depend too much on what *has* happened but find their justification in contemporary needs.

VI. *The Limits of Germany's Capacity to Pay.*

The critics of the reparation provisions of the Treaty of Versailles did not argue that Germany had *no* capacity to pay. The complete failure of these provisions to effect their purpose and the evil consequences of the attempt to apply them have led to the false conclusion widely entertained today that any attempt to exact payments from Germany after the war will be fruitless.

In the judgement of the Committee there is no sound basis of fact or argument for such a conclusion. On the other hand, the difficulties in the way of fixing the scale or the aggregate amount of what is likely to prove practicable and reasonable in the changing conditions of the future are easily seen to be insoluble. Events will almost certainly upset a particular figure in one direction or the other and this would serve to discredit not only the details but the principles of the settlement.

On the one hand, Germany's position will have deteriorated through the loss of all her external assets and of her shipping; by such loss of territory as results from the treaty of peace; by extensive damage from the air; by the failure to maintain plant and transportation in good repair; by the exhaustion of stocks of raw materials and consumable goods, by a vast number of casualties amongst men in the prime of life; and possibly from the destruction caused by invasion—in short, 'by all the unmeasured ruin in strength and hope of many years of all-swallowing war and final defeat'.

On the other hand, as the war itself has demonstrated beyond any doubt, Germany is an immensely efficient industrial organisation capable of a vast and sustained output. If the skill and industry and determination which she has devoted to evil purposes can be diverted to the works of peace, her capacity over a period of years should be very great. But we cannot say how great until we have much knowledge, now unattainable, of the economic conditions of the post-war world.

The Committee concluded therefore that it would be useless and unwise to name specific figures as a measure of the liabilities which it is proper that the treaty of peace should place on the shoulders of Germany. It is better that we should aim at an elastic formula which will be automatically adjusted to the facts of the future as they disclose themselves.

VII. *The Forms of Germany's Capacity to Pay*

The Committee turned in the light of the general considerations already mentioned to consider the forms in which Germany can meet the various claims on her apart from the restitution of identifiable property already dealt with. They concluded that the main categories are the following:

(i) Once-for-all deliveries of financial or capital assets, including gold.

(ii) Once-for-all deliveries of materials, raw or manufactured, out of stock.

(iii) Annual deliveries in kind from current output.

(iv) The performance of tasks in Allied territory by organised German labour.

(v) The services of labourers not organised for special tasks to be made available outside Germany.

(vi) The provision of the requirements within Germany of the armies of occupation.

(vii) Annual payments in cash to be provided out of the excess of Germany's exports over her imports.

For reasons already given, it seemed advisable that the claims for reparation proper should be limited to what lies within Germany's capacity to meet under the first five items, that is to say, reparation will be met exclusively out of existing assets and out of deliveries in kind and services; whilst Germany's contribution to peace-keeping will be met out of annual cash payments over the exchanges.

Deliveries in kind, especially of certain types of material to repair buildings and the means of transport, seemed to be very suitable during the early period after the war whilst these works of restoration are being intensively carried out in the war devastated areas. Moreover, during this period it should be within the power of the Allied Governments to exercise the supervision and, if necessary, the compulsion which might be required to ensure that the stipulated deliveries are on the required scale.

On the other hand, an indefinite prolongation of such a system might prove seriously wasteful. It would delay and impair the restoration of normal trade in Germany, to the disadvantage not only of herself but also of her neighbours and competitors. It would introduce an artificial and unreal element into the economic life of Europe, which would certainly not be worth while if it were on a small scale and would be still more undesirable if it were on a large scale. The Committee therefore recommended that deliveries in kind should be limited to what can be performed within a short period after the war, say five years.

These considerations apply even more forcibly to the employment of German labour abroad for more than a brief period. This expedient may have a proper place in the punitive measures of the early days, when punishment to fit the crime will have its palpable justification even in German eyes. But it involves political dangers and may, on grounds of humanity, fail to command support for any long period. It is therefore required for a period of not more than three years. If it is our policy that all Europe should settle down as soon as possible into the normal habits and sentiments of peace, assuredly a short period should be set to exactions in kind and services.

After the expiry of five years the contribution to peace-keeping, the details of which will be mentioned later, should come into effective operation and not until then.

VIII. *The Reconstruction Commission*

It will not be possible, either now or on the termination of hostilities, to form the final estimate of what Germany can reasonably be expected to provide, or to insert any figures of deliveries in any instrument to which it may be possible to obtain a German signature at or shortly after the time of the Armistice. It appeared therefore to the Committee that the only practical solution would be to entrust the task of deciding what deliveries Germany shall be required to make and of controlling the modalities of such deliveries to an inter-Allied organisation which might be called the Reconstruction Commission. It will be the duty of the Commission to prepare from time to time schedules of the deliveries to be made by Germany and to be satisfied that the deliveries demanded lie within the power of

Germany to perform. For this purpose the Commission should have complete discretion in authorising deliveries, but should take into account all relevant considerations, including whether required deliveries—

(*a*) Are at a cost reasonably commensurate to the resulting value.

(*b*) Will not have the effect of unduly reducing the standard of life in Germany.

(*c*) Will not impair disproportionately to their value Germany's productive capacity.

(*d*) Are not needed as exports to pay for Germany's immediate essential imports.

(*e*) Will not seriously impair disproportionately to their benefits to other countries Germany's capacity to provide employment for her industrial population.

The Committee considered various alternatives for the composition of the Reconstruction Commission. One solution suggested would be a Commission composed of, say, a United States Chairman, a Russian Vice-Chairman, a United Kingdom representative, a representative selected by the Western European powers, and a representative selected by the Eastern European powers. It would be possible to devise other solutions, but this is mainly a political question which will have to be settled according to the political situation at the time.

Since undue interference with Germany's normal export trade is undesirable and would probably result in its being necessary to assist her financially, the Committee came to the conclusion that it would be equitable to require deliveries in kind only for such articles as could be employed in the work of reconstruction, leaving other articles to be obtained from Germany by purchase in the ordinary way.

IX. *Assets and Deliveries and Services to be Made Available by Germany for Reparation*

To take over German property rights and interests in the territory of each of the United Nations is a particularly simple form of reparation, since it involves no transfer of foreign exchange. The peace treaties concluded after the last war provide a precedent. It is recommended therefore that the title to all such property rights and interests and to all claims by German nationals against the nationals of any of the United Nations should pass to the ownership of the government of the territory in question. The sum so received should be credited towards the proportionate share of the receiving Government in reparations.

The deliveries in kind to be required can be divided into those to be met from stocks immediately available after the conclusion of hostilities and those to be met from future current production.

The following is a summary of deliveries which might be required from stock—

(i) Machine tools, the equipment of factories, mines, etc., and agricultural implements.

(ii) Ships, inland water transport, railway rolling stock and motor transport.

(iii) Any stocks of raw materials in excess of normal peace-time working stocks.

(iv) Livestock.

Deliveries in kind from future current production can be classified as follows:

(i) The supply of timber, bricks, cement, steel billets, structural steel and other semi-manufactured and finished products required for the erection and equipment of buildings and the restoration of the means of transport.

(ii) Ships, inland water transport and railway rolling stock.

(iii) Agricultural machinery and implements, nitrogenous fertilisers and potash for the restoration of agriculture.

Reparation in the shape of services might take the form of—

(i) The performance of tasks by organised bodies of German labour to restore buildings and the means of transport.

(ii) Services of labour not organised for special tasks.

Objection may be seen to a proposal which condemns large numbers of Germans to what may be regarded as amounting in effect to a form of forced labour for a term of years. Nevertheless so valuable a form of reparation cannot be neglected, particularly as it is known that some Allied countries are likely to demand it. Such objections as are inherent in the proposals can be reduced by fixing the maximum number of men and a definite period of years for this form of employment. It is recommended that the maximum number to be employed shall be three million in the first year, two million in the second year and one million in the third year. The Reconstruction Commission should be entitled to give broad instructions covering the selection of labourers, having regard to their age and the nature of their war record. For example, the labourers might be drawn from the Gestapo, the S.S., the Nazi Party and the demobilised German armed forces, including the S.A., in that order.

In order to avoid a burden on the German exchange, the Allied Government concerned should be expected to supply housing and subsistence for the labourers and any pocket-money paid to them; while the German Government would be responsible for clothing them and providing any necessary subsistence to their dependents in Germany.

It is impracticable at the present time to make any close estimate of the probable value of Germany's total contribution towards reparations within the terms of years indicated. But the Committee was of the opinion that it might be of the order of, say, $4 billion at 1938 prices, or possibly $6 billion at the level of prices prevailing after the war.

X. *The Contribution to Peace-Keeping*

This contribution, beginning after the reparation deliveries have been completed, would take the form of a cash payment remitted over the exchanges through an excess of Germany's exports over her imports.

The machinery suggested for the collection of this payment is that the whole of the gross receipts due to Germany for her exports should be canalised through an international institution and that of the sum so received a certain proportion would be transferred to a special account to be used in such way as the United Nations might direct as a contribution to peace-keeping, only the balance being made available to Germany. That is to say, the proceeds of a certain proportion of Germany's gross exports would be thus retained. It is suggested that the proportion might be worked out as a basic 10 percent, increased to 20 percent on any excess of Germany's exports in any year over the equivalent of $1 billion, and 25 percent on any excess over $2 billion. German exporters would, of course, be paid in full by the German Government, the difference being charged on the German budget. This proposal raises a number of technical questions which would need study. But the Committee was of the opinion that none of these problems would be insuperable. The formula and machinery indicated seemed to them preferable to any alternative that they had before them.

XI. *Other Claims on Germany Arising out of the War*

It is important that within the limits of her capacity Germany should pay for such relief as she obtains. It seems inevitable that she will require at first an amount of imports, foodstuffs and other materials in excess of her available exports. Taxpayers in Allied countries providing relief may well be ready to make sacrifices for the benefit of Allies whose territory has been devastated, but would naturally object to doing so for the benefit of the state responsible for the devastation. There are, moreover, other countries which though they may not make contributions to international relief, would be called upon to pay for relief goods supplied to them.

The Committee therefore recommended that provision for the payment by Germany for such relief as she obtains should be made in the following ways:–

(*a*) Any gold remaining in Germany after the return of gold removed from occupied territory should be used towards the cost of Germany's post-war relief.

(*b*) Any excess over liabilities to any neutral country of German claims and assets in German ownership physically situated in neutral territory should be similarly transferred to the relief authorities.

(*c*) The cost of relief for Germany in excess of the above sources of payment should be a gross charge on the receipts due to Germany for her exports in subsequent years collected by such instalments as the relief authorities may decide. The machinery for the collection of these sums will be the same as that proposed in regard to the contribution for peace-keeping.

As regards the cost of occupation, Germany shall be required to provide without charge all the supplies, accommodation and services available within Germany and required for the use of the forces of occupation, and so much of the pay of the members of these forces as they receive in German currency, leaving each of the Allies concerned to meet direct and incidental costs arising outside Germany, towards which, however, the contribution for peace-keeping will be available after the first five years.

XII. *The Treatment of Pre-war Claims on Germany*

The Committee was in some perplexity how best to handle this matter, and limited themselves to expounding three alternative solutions:–

Since any payments made by Germany after the war in respect of pre-war claims must directly or indirectly serve to reduce her capacity to make payments on account of reparations or peace-keeping, one alternative seemed to be to wipe out private pre-war claims against Germany so as to leave the whole of Germany's capacity intact to meet claims arising out of the war and subsequent developments. If this clean-cut solution were to be adopted it would amount to an act of general insolvency on the part of Germany and there might be psychological and political advantage in adopting a solution which involved an explicit acknowledgment by Germany of the abject situation to which she had brought herself. In this case Germany might be called on to make a formal declaration recognising her state of insolvency. It might run somewhat as follows:

Germany acknowledges that she has by acts of pillage and destruction caused damage and costs and incurred liabilities to the Governments and nationals of the United Nations far beyond her capacity to make good. She therefore acknowledges that she is in a state of general insolvency towards all the external creditors of herself and her nationals ... (and so forth).

This would not preclude individual Allied Governments from making such compensation to their nationals as they might see fit. But it would have the advantage that neither in fact nor in appearance any preference would be given to owners of property in Germany over others who had suffered as a result of German action. It would also facilitate the adoption of the proposal that all war-time clearing balances due from Germany should be wiped out in order to make way for a clear and logical solution of the problem of reparation; for if pre-war money claims are kept alive the door might be opened to special pleading for keeping alive money claims which have arisen since the outbreak of war, in spite of the fact that this date provides a fairly clear dividing line. A similar treatment of neutral claims against Germany would also be very considerably facilitated.

On the other hand, there are a number of serious disadvantages in this solution. It involves the surrender to the German Government of the property of the United Nations in Germany. This surrender would, to say the least, be a paradoxical outcome of victory. Political refugees from Germany who did not desire to return to reside in Germany would lose their property. Market organisation, factories, patents, etc., in Germany belonging to companies and individual nationals of the United Nations would be transferred to German competitors. These are channels and stimuli of external trade, sources of technical knowledge and centres of economic intelligence, and their loss would involve some sacrifice to our foreign trade. The cancellation of the Dawes and Young Loans would be involved, in spite of the fact that the circumstances of their issue involve a certain responsibility for some of the Allied Governments.

An alternative solution would be to establish a moratorium, say of five years, in respect of the pre-war claims but in other respects leave them undisturbed so that claimants would in due course have the right to take such legal steps as might lie in their power to resume possession. In this case, there would have to be a declaration to the effect that nothing in the reparation settlement affects money claims against the German Government or its nationals by the United Nations or their nationals arising out of arrangements made before the war, or property rights and interests belonging to them before the war and situated in Germany; and that the German Government shall therefore preserve in, and where necessary, restore to, their original ownership the above claims and property. This is by far the simplest solution to work out and does not raise any difficult legal questions between the Governments of the United Nations and their nationals. It is also free from most of the objections to the more drastic solution mentioned above.

The third alternative is to make a compromise between the other two by which the external money claims over the German exchange at the end of the war are cancelled with the exception, however, of claims in respect of the Dawes and Young Loans, whilst the property rights and interests of the United Nations or their nationals situated in Germany are reserved and treated in the same way as in the second alternative.

XIII. *The Economic Aspects of Security*

The Committee was also asked to consider what economic measures might usefully be taken to prevent future German aggression.

Before making their positive recommendations, the Committee emphasised certain over-riding considerations:

(*a*) There is no economic difficulty in keeping Germany impotent to wage major war so long as her aggressors retain the will to do so. The mere denial to her of weapons of war leaves her at the mercy of her armed neighbours. On the other hand, it is impossible to devise any measures, economic or otherwise, which will of themselves permanently keep Germany impotent if her conquerors lose their will to enforce them.

(*b*) Nevertheless, economic measures could greatly contribute to the task of maintaining security by so weakening Germany as to render the task of recreating her war economy difficult, protracted and unpromising; by detecting quickly any steps which she might take to this end; and by increasing the power of the United Nations to use economic pressure as a sanction.

(*c*) At the same time drastic and complete measures of an economic character would involve a high degree of control. Moreover, long-term measures are the most important since it is only after a period of time that the danger of renewed aggression by Germany could develop. Yet there are obvious objections to long continuing control of the normal activities of German citizens. We therefore concluded that any measures which it would be desirable to maintain for a long period should either depend on control from outside Germany, or be of a kind to appeal to public opinion as being so thoroughly justifiable and as interfering so little with the normal economic life of Germany that there would be no difficulty in setting on foot measures of sanction if infringements took place.

With these general principles in view, the following recommendations were framed:

(1) Since the Atlantic Charter contemplates the total disarmament of Germany, there will be no justification for her to possess an armament making industry. Germany should therefore be forbidden to manufacture military, naval and air armaments, civil aircraft and aero engines, including any separately manufactured components; and the existing plant employed in their manufacture should be destroyed or removed.

(2) The suggestion has been put forward in several quarters that Germany's machine tool industry should be destroyed after the war, or at least greatly reduced. The arguments in favour of such a course are that an expansion of the machine tool industry would provide the first warning that aggression was contemplated and that if Germany had to start from scratch we could have some time to prepare our own rearmament, or alternatively to take steps to check German rearmament. Nevertheless, the arguments against such a total prohibition were, in the opinion of the Committee, convincing. The machine tool industry is an integral part of the engineering industry and it would be virtually impossible for a country to possess a large and progressive engineering industry without a machine tool production. The prohibition of such production would involve an interference with Germany's economic life inconsistent with the over-riding considerations mentioned above.

(3) There are a number of raw materials which taken together are essential to Germany's war effort which she must import from outside her own territories. The Committee considered therefore whether it is possible to institute any system of control or limitation of these supplies. After a careful examination of the details, the Committee reached the following relatively limited recommendations:

(i) The following commodities should be regarded as of

significant importance for the prevention of German rearmament; manganese, chrome, tungsten, molybdenum, nickel and oil.

(ii) Germany should supply statistics of her imports, production, consumption and stocks of these commodities.

(iii) Germany should not hold more than six months' stocks of any of these commodities without the permission of the competent Inter-Allied Commission.

(iv) The Commission should, if they are dissatisfied with the effective operation of provisions (ii) and (iii), be entitled at any time to insist that none of these commodities should be imported into Germany except under their licence.

(4) Germany's ability to carry on war for any length of time has been directly due to her pre-war development of processes for the production of synthetic materials, notably oil and buna rubber. The committee considered very carefully the particular cases of synthetic oil, synthetic rubber and nitrogen fixation. On a balance of considerations they were of the opinion that Germany's normal economy would be unduly interferred with if their positive recommendations were to extend beyond the case of synthetic oil. The Committee limited themselves, therefore, to a recommendation that all synthetic oil plants in Germany should be destroyed on the entry into force of the peace treaty and their reorganisation forbidden so long as Germany remains disarmed.

(5) On the other hand, that Germany should conform to general principles discouraging undue autarchy should in no way conflict with her ultimate prosperity. The Committee recommended therefore that Germany should be required to abandon and abstain from practices which impede the intention of the United Nations to promote mutually advantageous economic conditions between nations and to conform to any arrangements made by the United Nations for this purpose.

(6) The Committee included in their examination the question of financial controls, in particular, the control of the

Reichsbank and international shareholding in German industry. As regards the former, the Committee concluded that it would be generally contrary to our interests to impose stringent measures of financial control upon Germany once the initial period after her defeat has passed. They were also unable to make a recommendation in favour of international shareholding in German industry whilst not, however, wishing to rule out this possibility altogether if some useful special application could be found for it.

(7) Finally, the Committee considered the effect on economic security of possible transfers of German territory. The question whether particular portions of German territory should be detached or transferred to neighbouring states is one to be decided on review of a number of considerations of which the economic aspect of security is only one, and by no means the most important. The Committee limited themselves therefore to pointing out certain considerations relating to particular territories which have a bearing on the economic aspect of security since they may affect her ability to prepare for and conduct another war. They prepared a summary of certain information relevant in this context relating to the Saar Basin, Upper Silesia, East Prussia, and Austria. These details show that Germany's economic capacity to wage war could be considerably influenced in the aggregate by certain transfers of outlying German territory.

28 September 1943

The October 1943 Conference of Foreign Ministers in Moscow discussed, to some extent, the post-war treatment of Germany, but left the dismemberment issue to one side, if only because both Mr Hull and Mr Eden admitted that their Governments had not made up their minds on the issue. The Conference resulted in the setting up of a European Advisory Commission in London to study and make recommendations on questions surrounding the termination of hostilities in Europe to the Governments concerned.

At the Teheran Conference at the end of November 1943 Churchill, Roosevelt and Stalin discussed, again with little advanced preparation, the dismemberment of Germany. They agreed that some sort of partition scheme for post-war Germany was desirable, but left the details to the European Advisory Commission.

In the course of 1944 Keynes was occasionally involved in discussions of the post-war treatment of Germany with Mr Playfair, the Treasury representative on the Economic and Industrial Planning Staff set up in February 1944 to consider the post-war treatment of Germany. As the result of instructions received in May, the E.I.P.S. spent the summer of 1944 working on the economic aspects of proposals to dismember Germany into three sovereign states. By the end of August, E.I.P.S. had completed their work on the question and sent a report on the 'Economic Aspects of Dismemberment' to the inter-departmental Committee concerned with general armistice and post-war problems. On reading the report Keynes wrote to Mr Playfair.

To E. PLAYFAIR, *13 September 1944*

I have read the attached with much interest. I should like, if you could spare the time, to have another meeting with the same party as before, when you are back. At the previous party I spent most of my time expounding my doubts and scepticisms. But perhaps there are also some more constructive things to be said.

The paper below has not dissuaded me from favouring dismemberment. I still think that is the right starting point. On the other hand, you do succeed in showing that it involves many problems not yet considered. But why not consider them? It seems to me that you are in danger of wasting too much grey matter on the less probable alternative and not enough on the more probable.

For example, there are other alternatives than surrounding each of the three parts with an independent tariff barrier. For example, the tariffs might be what *we* decided they should be and might thus in practice be a mixture. Also, we might require deliveries of food from the West to the East, and deliveries of currencies by the East to the pool, thus spreading the required burden over the whole. Another idea would be to incorporate the North-West in a tariff union with Belgium and Holland; to incorporate the South in a tariff union with Austria; and to incorporate the East in a tariff union with Poland and Czechoslovakia.

I fancy there is room for much more ingenuity if one starts with dismemberment. I do not feel that any of you have as yet allowed your minds to play as freely as you might about its possibilities.

[copy initialled] K

13 September 1944

Keynes's arrival in America for the negotiations on Stage II of lend lease brought him up against the Morgenthau Plan for the pastoralisation of Germany.[9] Mr Morgenthau had raised the proposals at the Quebec Conference in September 1944 when Churchill agreed to accept much of the spirit of the proposals, despite Mr Eden's strenuous objections that the Government had made no such decision. In the end, however, neither Churchill nor Roosevelt took the Plan any further. Keynes had first heard of the Plan through newspaper reports, and informal discussions with Lord Cherwell, who had been at Quebec, and Harry White, the author of the Plan.[10] However, on 5 October, Keynes received the following note from Mr Morgenthau.

From H. MORGENTHAU, *5 October 1944*

My dear Lord Keynes,

I am enclosing herewith a highly confidential document, which is the Treasury Plan on how to deal with Germany. According to our understanding, you are not to show this to anybody except the Chancellor of the Exchequer.

[9] Program to Prevent Germany from Starting a World War III.
[10] For other Keynes comments on the Plan, see *JMK*, Vol. XXIV, pp. 130–1, 133–5.

After you have read it, I will be glad to have you discuss it with Harry White and myself.

Sincerely yours,

H. MORGENTHAU

PROGRAM TO PREVENT GERMANY FROM STARTING
A WORLD WAR III

1. *Demilitarisation of Germany*

It should be the aim of the Allied Forces to accomplish the complete demilitarisation of Germany in the shortest possible period of time after surrender. This means completely disarming the German Army and people (including the removal or destruction of all war material), the total destruction of the whole German armament industry, and the removal or destruction of other key industries which are basic to military strength.

2. *New Boundaries of Germany*

(*a*) Poland should get that part of East Prussia which doesn't go to the U.S.S.R. and the southern portion of Silesia. (See map in 12 Appendix.)

(*b*) France should get the Saar and the adjacent territories bounded by the Rhine and the Moselle Rivers.

(*c*) As indicated in 4 below an International Zone should be created containing the Ruhr and the surrounding industrial areas.

3. *Partitioning of New Germany*

The remaining portion of Germany should be divided into two autonomous, independent states, (1) a South German state comprising Bavaria, Wuerttenberg, Baden and some smaller areas and (2) a North German state comprising a large part of the old state of Prussia, Saxony, Thuringia and several smaller states.

There shall be a customs union between the new South German state and Austria, which will be restored to her pre-1938 political borders.

4. *The Ruhr Area* (The Ruhr, surrounding industrial areas, as shown on the map, including the Rhineland, the Keil Canal, and all German territory north of the Keil Canal.)

Here lies the heart of German industrial power. This area should not only be stripped of all presently existing industries but so weakened and controlled that it can not in the foreseeable future become an industrial area. The following steps will accomplish this:

(*a*) Within a short period, if possible not longer than 6 months after the cessation of hostilities, all industrial plants and equipment not destroyed by military action shall be completely dismantled and transported to Allied Sections as restitution, all equipment shall be removed from the mines and the mines closed.

(*b*) The area should be made an international zone to be governed by an international security organisation to be established by the United Nations. In governing the area the international organisation should be guided by policies designed to further the above stated objective.

5. *Restitution and Reparation*

Reparations, in the form of future payments and deliveries, should not be demanded. Restitution and reparation shall be effected by the transfer of existing German resources and territories, e.g.,

(*a*) by restitution of property looted by the Germans in territories occupied by them;

(*b*) by transfer of German territory and German private rights in industrial property situated in such territory to invaded countries and the international organisation under the program of partition;

(*c*) by the removal and distribution among devastated countries of industrial plants and equipment situated within the International Zone and the North and South German states delimited in the section on partition;

(*d*) by forced German labor outside Germany; and

(*e*) by confiscation of all Germany assets of any character whatsoever outside of Germany.

6. *Education and Propaganda*

(*a*) All schools and universities will be closed until an Allied Commission of Education has formulated an effective reorganisation program. It is contemplated that it may require a considerable period of time before any institutions of higher education are reopened. Meanwhile the education of

German students in foreign universities will not be prohibited. Elementary schools will be reopened as quickly as appropriate teachers and textbooks are available.

(*b*) All German radio stations and newspapers, magazines, weeklies, etc. shall be discontinued until adequate controls are established and an appropriate program formulated.

7. *Political Decentralisation*

The military administration in Germany in the initial period should be carried out with a view toward the eventual partitioning of Germany. To facilitate partitioning and to assure its permanence the military authorities should be guided by the following principles:

(*a*) Dismiss all policy-making officials of the Reich Government and deal primarily with local governments.

(*b*) Encourage the reestablishment of state governments in each of the states (lander) corresponding to 18 states into which Germany is presently divided and in addition make the Prussian provinces separate states.

(*c*) Upon the partition of Germany, the various state governments should be encouraged to organise a federal government for each of the newly partitioned areas. Such new governments should be in the form of a confederation of states, with emphasis on states' rights and a large degree of local autonomy.

8. *Responsibility of Military for Local German Economy*

The sole purpose of the military in control of the German economy shall be to facilitate military operations and military occupation. The Allied Military Government shall not assume responsibility for such economic problems as price controls, rationing, unemployment, production, reconstruction, distribution, consumption, housing, or transportation, or take any measures designed to maintain or strengthen the German economy, except those which are essential to military operations. The responsibility for sustaining the German economy and people rests with the German people with such facilities as may be available under the circumstances.

9. *Controls over Development of German Economy*

During a period of at least twenty years after surrender adequate controls, including controls over foreign trade and tight restrictions on capital imports, shall be maintained by the United Nations designed to prevent in the

378

newly-established states the establishment or expansion of key industries basic to the German military potential and to control other key industries.

10. *Agrarian program*

All large estates should be broken up and divided among the peasants and the system of primogeniture and entail should be abolished.

11. *Punishment of War Crimes and Treatment of Special Groups*

A program for the punishment of certain war crimes and for the treatment of Nazi organisations and other special groups is contained in section 11.

12. *Uniforms and Parades*

(*a*) No German shall be permitted to wear, after an appropriate period of time following the cessation of hostilities, any military uniform or any uniform of any quasi-military organisations.

(*b*) No military parades shall be permitted anywhere in Germany and all military bands shall be disbanded.

13. *Aircraft*

All aircraft (including gliders), whether military or commercial, will be confiscated for later disposition. No German shall be permitted to operate or to help operate any aircraft, including those owned by foreign interests.

14. *United States Responsibility*

Although the United States would have full military and civilian representation on whatever international commission or commissions may be established for the execution of the whole German program, the primary responsibility for the policing of Germany and for civil administration in Germany should be assumed by the military forces of Germany's continental neighbors. Specifically, these should include Russian, French, Polish, Czech, Greek, Yugoslav, Norwegian, Dutch and Belgian soldiers.

Under this program United States troops could be withdrawn within a relatively short time.

On receiving the plan, Keynes wrote to the Chancellor.

To SIR JOHN ANDERSON, *6 October 1944*

My dear Chancellor,

Alas! Mr Morgenthau has been as good as his word and has sent me a copy of the Treasury plan, on the understanding that I show it to no one except yourself. You will also see from the attached letter that he is inviting me to discuss it with himself and Harry White—presumably after October 16th when he returns to Washington. It may be somewhat embarrassing, but I suppose I shall have to do my best.

I have some reason to think that Cherwell also has a copy on the condition that he shows it to no one. Presumably the Prime Minister and, one would imagine, the Foreign Secretary must have read the full text when they were at Quebec. But I feel doubtful whether they took an actual copy home for the use of the Foreign Office. If they did, no doubt it is already generally available to the Ministers concerned. On the other hand, the position may be as I surmise above.

You will see that the document is by no means as crude as the information first to hand might have suggested. Indeed, there are some parts of it with which I at any rate find myself in considerable sympathy. Unfortunately it is the most vulnerable paragraph, namely paragraph 4, which has received all the attention, and here it seems to me that they quite clearly shirk the essential difficulty.

The paragraphs with which I strongly sympathise are paragraph 8* and paragraph 14 (provided, as is evidently intended, paragraph 14 applies to us equally with the U.S.A). In my judgement, as you will be already aware from the memorandum I wrote on the boat lately sent you, a policy on our part different from what is recommended in paragraphs 8 and 14 in this memorandum must inevitably let us in for financial responsibility of a crippling character beyond what we can support for

---

* Except that §8 goes much too far for the early initial period.

any protracted period. They also seem to me to represent the mere commonsense of the situation.

Nor do I dissent from paragraph 5, which only differs from our own proposals in excusing Germany from deliveries of current produce in kind, this proposed relief being quite a proper offset to the severity of the other conditions. Paragraphs 7 and 10 obviously deserve serious consideration. No objection to paragraphs 1, 11, 12 and 13.

Paragraph 9 is important, but requires further development. In my own opinion it is not technically impossible to organise something of this kind. There may be a good deal to be said for it as being at any rate much easier to maintain, and in other respects vastly preferable to an attempt at excessive internal control.

Paragraph 6 has a germ of an idea in it, but is plainly carried too far and expressed in an objectionable form.

Paragraphs 2 and 3 are simply part of the dismemberment problem already under discussion.

That leaves us with paragraph 4, which is the only part of the plan which has received any prominent attention, and this is, as I have said above, the most vulnerable part. You will observe that the area in question is far wider than what one generally understands by the Ruhr. There is not the faintest indication how the large population of this extensive area is to be kept alive. In its present form this part of the proposal looks quite hopelessly impractical, creating intolerable conditions of a kind which world opinion could not conceivably allow, without any hint as to how they can be ameliorated.

Nevertheless, the plan as a whole has not received quite fair treatment as the result of the isolation of this particular paragraph from the rest.

My latest impression of the atmosphere is that we have not heard the last of this plan.* The State Department are furious

* This is confirmed by the extract from *Time* below (which is generally better informed than the rest of us). *Time* is here correcting an earlier report which it gave last week. [Not printed. Ed.]

that Mr Morgenthau should have gone behind their back. But they have not, so far as I know, put up any alternative which is nearly so concrete or definitive. It is also clear that apart from details the President is sympathetic to this general line of approach. It is therefore up to those who hold a different view to produce something equally definite; and for those who think that this draft contains some useful features to try to make sense of it, and in particular eliminate or drastically modify the absurd paragraph 4.

None of my business, as I am only too well aware. All the same, it is a subject in which at one time, in other contexts, I was supposed to take an interest.

Yours ever,

[copy initialled] K

Although it does not seem that Keynes discussed the Plan in detail with Morgenthau or White, he did have a conversation with Roosevelt on the post-war treatment of Germany before returning to London. The results of this conversation were reflected in a note he wrote soon after his return.

From a letter to E. J. PASSANT,[11] *30 December 1944*

At one time I was myself playing with the idea of dismemberment. But I was never in favour of making that permanently compulsory. My notion was to gain twenty years' time and then let them do what they liked.

I find the whole question full of perplexity. But, at the moment, I am against dismemberment, partly, at any rate, for the reasons which you set forth so convincingly.

The present trend of opinion amongst those whose opinions matter seems to me to be towards annexation, including in this the project of Rhenania, though Rhenania, as I have heard it discussed, includes not only what lies to the West of the Rhine,

---

[11] Ernest James Passant (1890–1959); Fellow and Lecturer in History, Sidney Sussex College, Cambridge, 1919–46; served in Foreign Office, 1939–41; Naval Intelligence Division, Admiralty, 1941–5; Research Department, Foreign Office, 1945–6; Librarian and Keeper of the Papers, Foreign Office, 1946–59.

but also a considerable population in the Ruhr. My belief is that, if a decision had to be reached in the near future, the separation of Rhenania would be part of it. The great difficulty there is that the population involved is much too great to be capable of being dealt with by transfer.

At any rate, I think it is the policy of annexation, together with the associated problem of transfers of population, which now requires more particular and detailed attention than the project of dismemberment, either in drastic or in a less drastic form.

What frightens me most in the whole problem is that these issues are extremely likely to be settled by those (as I know by first-hand conversations), who have not given continuous or concentrated thought to it. The best consolation is that, whatever you may hear talked about and however confidently, you may be quite sure that up to date no real decision whatever has been taken on the matters of main importance. This is a state of affairs which is necessarily a frightful nuisance to all those concerned with working out details and policies. Nevertheless, it may be the course of wisdom. That, in truth, is my own position at the moment. I am against reaching any important decisions whatever about the more distant future until events have provided us with more data.

You are admittedly in no way constructive in your paper. I make no complaint of that. For, in fact, there is *no* good solution. *All* the solutions which are being talked about are, not only bad, but very bad. This, however, is an added reason for suspending judgement in the hope that history and the course of events will provide something better for us than we are capable of inventing for ourselves.

January 1945 saw Keynes reporting his American impressions to E.I.P.S., as Whitehall prepared for the Yalta meetings of February 1945. At these meetings, the Big Three agreed on the partition of Germany, that Germany must pay in kind for losses caused by her in the war, that reparations would go to the countries which had borne the main burden and suffered the heaviest casualties in the war, that reparations in kind would take the form of removals of property, annual deliveries and direct labour services, and that the Allied Reparations Commission would meet in Moscow later in the year. The Americans and the Russians proposed a global total of $20 billion for reparations, half to go to the Soviet Union, as a guide to the Reparations Commission. The British refused to accept any figure.

After Yalta, Keynes again returned to the German issue with two notes to the Chancellor on dismemberment.

To SIR JOHN ANDERSON, *26 February 1945*

THE DISMEMBERMENT OF GERMANY

Sir W. Eady has shown me the draft on this matter which he has submitted to you. I admire his paper and am in general agreement. The purpose of this note is, partly to supplement very briefly what he has said so well, and partly to put greater emphasis on certain aspects or connected problems.

I. *Political considerations*

(i) A dismembered Germany, one part of which is under Russian, and others under Western European, influence means that there is a direct frontier between these two spheres. Is this not very dangerous compared with the alternative of a buffer state in the shape of a unitary Germany, which is not strong enough to be a danger but not, in the long run, so weak that it can be ignored?

(ii) The dismembered parts will be at the outset so weak economically that a bourgeois economy on the Western model can scarcely be expected to survive. These weak states will be seed-beds of social revolution in Europe.

(iii) The centripetal forces in Germany, the strength of which Sir W. Eady rightly emphasises, may, therefore, take the form of politico-social suction to assimilate the Western sections to

384

the Russian section, as a first step towards forming a unitary German U.S.S.R. Surely this is how we ought to expect it all to end. And is that just what we want? If this happens, it disposes in a sense of objection (i) above, but only to bring it back again with the frontier further West.

(iv) Public opinion here, in the U.S., in the British Commonwealth and in Western Europe has not been in any way prepared for such a solution. I should expect that a large and responsible section of opinion will vehemently oppose it. So far as U.S. is concerned, the likelihood of their pulling out as much and as soon as possible will be greatly increased.

(v) There is a manifest incompatibility between the proposed policy of dismemberment and the proposed policy of reparations. It is not practicable to have both. Even Mr Morgenthau's plan recognises this and was based on the assumption of 'No reparations'.

II. *Our own immediate economic interests*

This plan has to be thought of in the context of our Occupation Policy and our Reparation Policy. The difficulties here are not created by the Dismemberment Policy and still await a solution even if dismemberment is not adopted; but dismemberment would seriously aggravate them.

I seek an answer to the following questions:

(*a*) Do we intend to occupy Germany for more than the minimum period, two years at the most, in the face of the President's decision that he will withdraw after two years?

(*b*) Do we take any responsibility to maintain a minimum standard of life in the areas for which we are responsible?

(*c*) If so, who is going to pay for it?

(*d*) If we administer beyond the minimum military period, do we administer so as to make a good job of the place or to make a bad job of it?

(*e*) Since to make any sort of a good job of it will require the provision of a large amount of working capital, who, in that event, is going to pay for it?

I am not aware that any serious attempt has been made to face the difficulties behind these questions or even to discuss them on the ministerial level.

No doubt we shall refrain from making the *same mistakes* as last time. But that is not much comfort.

KEYNES

26 February 1945

To SIR JOHN ANDERSON, *27 February 1945*

THE DISMEMBERMENT PROPOSALS

Reflecting on our conversation yesterday, my own feeling based, I confess, on very little, about the psychology underlying the Russian proposals, is as follows.

I believe that they are mainly moved by motives of revenge and the aim of the destruction of Germany. They also have a naive belief in the possibilities of reparation. I do not believe that a far-sighted conception of the political balance of power in Western Europe (as distinct from Eastern) plays an equally prominent part in their present thoughts. Very likely something of the kind is at the back of the heads of some of them. But this, I should say, is not where the steam comes from for driving the policy forward.

Nevertheless, if we allow ourselves to agree to a policy which lends itself in the long run to certain secondary ends, then in the long run, say 10 years hence, we shall duly reap the consequences, even though these consequences are not the main object at the present time.

The conclusion I draw from the above is that there is much room for diplomatic skill. Within limits there is no radical divergence between the short-term Russian policy and ours. Our perplexity is that whilst an extreme version of their policy might work, it cannot, in fact, come to pass. The reason why we may appear sometimes to go towards the other extreme is not for any affection for the other extreme, but because of our inability to see how any intermediate policy, or at any rate an intermediate policy leaning to the Russian extreme, can possibly work. Nevertheless, there is not here necessarily such a radical difference of objective that we could not work together to secure a result; whilst at the same time diverting the Russians from a particular version of their policy which would have undesirable long-term consequences.

Therefore it is our job to start thinking all over again right from the beginning in the light of what happened at Yalta. I believe that a whole set of new ideas are required to bridge the gap safely.

KEYNES

27 February 1945

On 28 February, Keynes submitted a draft covering note to a draft Treasury memorandum for the War Cabinet. The covering note in a slightly revised form went to the Cabinet on 9 March.

REPARATIONS AND DISMEMBERMENT

1. The following conditions are essential in our interests. I hope that those who negotiate in detail on our behalf will be instructed to regard their satisfaction as indispensable:–

(1) We must not ourselves incur any expense arising out of the supply of permitted imports into Germany, whilst Germany is simultaneously expected to make reparation deliveries, whether these are of a once-for-all or of a current and continuing character. For this would mean, in fact, that *we* were paying the German reparations to the recipients. We must, therefore, put it in the forefront of our conditions that relief and other supplies, which are agreed to be necessary to put Germany in a position to pay any reparations at all, shall be a first charge on any deliveries taken from here, and must be paid for in the first

instance (in the appropriate proportions) by those receiving the deliveries, so long as the supplies required are exceeding the value of the deliveries obtainable.

(2) The permitted imports into Germany shall be on a scale consistent with the Prime Minister's statement that 'It is not the purpose of the Allies to leave the people of Germany without the necessary means of subsistence.' Nor shall there be any deliveries of any description inconsistent with this statement.

(3) No once-for-all deliveries shall be taken from any zone unless the German Control Commission have decided, in agreement with the occupying power, that they can be taken without risk of creating conditions which are contrary to the administrative interests of the occupying power.

(4) An occupying power shall not be expected to take responsibility for securing any reparation deliveries beyond what it judges to be within the capacity of its zone.

(5) We should give no undertaking at the present stage to occupy Germany for a longer period than that for which the four occupying powers are each and all prepared to make themselves responsible. Any further commitment for a longer period must be a matter for consideration when the time comes.

2. It is most unlikely that Germany will be in a position, after meeting her necessary imports, to make current reparation deliveries on a substantial scale in the first 5 years after the war. In the next 5 years much more should be possible; but there is no basis at the present time for a realistic estimate of the probable amount. Whatever may be obtained later, the net reparations in the first 5 years will consist mainly, or entirely, of the once-for-all deliveries (though the equivalent value of even these may be needed in large part to cover necessary imports) and the services of German labourers. It is most important, therefore, that the latter (i.e. services) should be included in the reparation account.

3. No equipment or stocks shall be taken from parts of Germany which are to be detached from German sovereignty,

whether for inclusion in Poland or (as may be the case in the West) to form a zone under international control.

4. Dismemberment will greatly impair Germany's capacity to make reparations. Indeed, reparations and dismemberment should be considered as being mainly alternative penalties. A sound scheme of reparations implies and requires a unitary German Government which can be made responsible for that delivery. To dismember Germany under the occupation of 4 several Powers, who cannot themselves take the responsibility of procuring reparation deliveries from their zone, does not lend itself to the working out of any sound scheme of reparations (or, I should add, any sound scheme at all) on any lines hitherto discussed.

5. Subject to the above, let the reparations be as large as possible. But let there be no misapprehensions in the minds of any of us about the realistic prospects.

6. Some of the arguments and the facts as I see them, lying behind and justifying these conclusions, are set out more fully in the following note. In particular, I develop in this note the special difficulties in which we ourselves shall be involved in the zone for which we are to take initial responsibility, if a Russian policy were to be accepted which fails to observe the conditions which I have set forth above as being, in my judgement, indispensable to our own interests.

[copy initialled] K

28 February 1945

The War Cabinet considered the memorandum on 22 March and merely decided to discuss the issue at a later date. When it actually did so, it agreed to set up a Committee on Reparations backed by the usual parallel official committee. Keynes became a member of this official committee, chaired by Sir Wilfrid Eady and Sir David Waley, which was to prepare instructions for the British representatives involved in the post-Yalta discussions. For this committee he attempted to draft a covering note highlighting the issues involved. This draft, with its Annex providing a possible global breakdown of reparations payments to each recipient, based heavily on an earlier paper by Austin Robinson, saw several revisions and extensions before going to the Ministerial Committee on Reparations on 30 April under Sir John Anderson's signature.

To SIR WILFRID EADY, *23 April 1945*

The attached draft is not intended to cut across Mr Playfair's 'Draft Instructions to the British Delegation' or Sir D. Waley's 'Machinery for Executing Reparation'. I am well satisfied with both of these documents and have no material criticisms on either of them. This paper is rather intended as a covering paper to the Draft Instructions in order to high-light those matters which are particularly controversial, even amongst ourselves, or on which no clear guidance has yet been given.

The Annex, in which I attempt an alternative to a global figure for reparations, is intended as a trial balloon to see what you think of it. If we decide in favour of this kind of approach, there would of course have to be a few appropriate modifications in the Draft Instructions. As I have said in the course of that paper, it appears very complicated, but the complications seem to me to arise (and to have not yet been dealt with) in almost exactly the same form whether the approach here suggested is adopted or any other approach.

KEYNES

23 April 1945

THE DRAFT INSTRUCTIONS ON REPARATIONS

The attention of the Ministerial Committee is drawn particularly to the following matters arising out of the attached Draft Instructions, likely to prove controversial, where clear-cut Ministerial decisions might prove very helpful to the British Delegation:

1. *Should an aggregate global figure be put on reparations?*

Argument for: The Russians are believed to attach importance to a very high figure as necessary to satisfy their public opinion.

Arguments against:

(i) Any figure which is fixed Ministers will have to defend as reasonable before British and American public opinion. We face the dilemma of an obviously unrealistic figure which will evoke memories of last time and will in fact break down, and a realistic figure which is much too low in relation to the damage done and the measure of Germany's guilt and also for Russian political and propaganda purposes.

(ii) There is no process of calculation by which a figure can be reached prior to an accurate knowledge of the extent to which German productive capacity has been destroyed and to decisions

(*a*) on dismemberment;

(*b*) on the measures necessary for security;

(*c*) on the scale of the once-for-all deliveries;

(*d*) on the kind of economic life and general set-up for Germany at which we shall aim during the period of occupation.

(iii) There are many serious difficulties in valuation, including especially—

(*a*) the basis of valuation of labour-services, whilst on the other hand, to omit this item from the total, as the Russians propose, would be to exclude what may prove to be the largest source of contribution, and thus make any substantial total still more difficult to justify;

(*b*) the basis of valuation of once-for-all deliveries of plant and installations in Germany;

If the decision is to resist a global figure, a possible alternative approach might be worked out.

2. *The basis of sharing reparations*

(i) Should we regard it as our business to secure a fair share to the Allies not represented at Moscow?

(ii) Should we agree finally to a given share for Russia in advance of a general agreement about the basis of sharing?

3. *Should any conditions be placed on the employment of German labour outside Germany?*

For example—

(i) Should the labourers be chosen only from members of the Nazi party, whether at present prisoners of war or not, or from Germans now between certain age limits?

(ii) Should the whole system of force labour be limited to a relatively short period such as five years?

(iii) Should any attempt be made to differentiate the conditions of employment from what might reasonably be described as servitude? In other words, should the labourers, or the German Government on their behalf, have any *rights*?

(iv) Should the period of service of a particular individual be limited to a period such as one or two years? Or do we contemplate that men, some of whom may already have been prisoners of war for some time, should be parted from their wives and families for a considerable period after the war? If the latter, should we stipulate that there should be no fresh recruitment after two years?

(v) Should every European Ally be offered the opportunity to indent on German labour?

(vi) Do we ourselves wish to do so?

4. *The principle of restitution*

(i) The European Allies will argue vehemently for a wide interpretation of restitution of stolen goods as distinct from reparation of damaged property, i.e. they will consider as restitution everything required to make good the loss and damage to their economy during the occupation. The Malkin Committee recommended against a wide extension but admitted a compromise to the extent of allowing restitution of similar goods in the cases of gold, live-stock and means of transport. Ministers have rejected this compromise. Is it clear that our Delegation should support the Russians and oppose the French on this issue without entertaining any compromise? The most difficult case is gold. For example the Belgians entrusted some of their gold to the French for safe keeping; this gold fell into the hands of the Germans; the French have honourably accepted responsibility and have returned an equivalent quantity of their own gold to Belgium. Are we to maintain that the French have no claim in respect of the above against any gold found still remaining in German hands? Live-stock has been driven off, rolling stock has been seized, from the Western European Allies. Are we clear that we will refuse them any support if they demand that these claims fall, at least in part, under the heading of restitution? Should we admit such claims, but debit them to the recipient as part of their agreed overall share of reparations?

(ii) Should Italy, Austria and the satellites generally receive the benefits of restitution at least in the narrowest sense?

5. *Austria*

Should we accept the Russian demand to subject Austria to reparation, with every expectation that anything taken from Austria on this ticket will have to be restored to her on some other ticket at the expense of ourselves or America?

6. *The Reparations Commission*

(i) Should such a body be established with wide powers?

(ii) Should it include representatives of all accepted claimants to reparation?

(iii) What should be its relations (*a*) to the German Control Commission, (*b*) to the Commanders of the several zones?

Important questions will arise on these points on which a separate memorandum is submitted.

7. *What is the status of the Moscow discussions?*

(i) Are these discussions of a preliminary character for the exploration of the ground and with a view to each delegation reporting its own conclusions to its own Government? Or is it considered essential, or at least highly desirable, that an agreed definitive conclusion should be reached?

(ii) Is it intended that the conclusions, if any, should be referred to a wider body which would include all claimants to reparations?

(iii) Is it possible at this stage to go further than an exchange of views on a matter so closely intertwined with decisions on other matters which will not fall within the Moscow agenda and have not been settled as yet outside them?

AN ALTERNATIVE TO A GLOBAL FIGURE FOR REPARATIONS

It is suggested that no attempt should be made to reach a common denominator of value for (*a*) once-for-all deliveries of plant and installations, (*b*) labour services and (*c*) current deliveries of materials; and, therefore, no global figure in terms of money should be fixed in advance or even calculated after the event.

In place of this, each claimant would be entitled to indent for a proportionate share of each category taken separately.

It would be a condition of this approach that the proportionate shares for each should be fixed with some reference to the scale of the claimants' demands for the others, as well as to other broad considerations.

The following is an illustration how such a plan might be worked out:

(i) A body representing the Control Commission, the Commanders of the zones, the Reparation Commission and the several claimants would make an inspection and a census of German plant and installations to establish the following matters—

(*a*) the quantity which could be taken compatibly with the general long-term policy of the Allies towards the German economy of which must be taken (or destroyed) in the interests of security;

(*b*) the particular articles falling within (*a*) for which one or more of the claimants have a fancy;

(*c*) the relative value of the different articles in a common, conventional unit (not money) as determined by an independent corps of American experts appointed for the purpose.

The relative demands of the various claimants (including overlapping claims) would then be added up in terms of the conventional unit. If the total demand of any claimant relatively to the demands of the others was in excess of his basic proportion, he would be asked to abate it appropriately by cutting out some of those of his demands which overlapped with the demands of other claimants. Any remaining overlapping claims would be adjusted by an agreed give-and-take which would aim at the final result being in accordance with the basic proportions for sharing.

(ii) Each claimant would state the number of German labourers on which it wished to indent and the period. If the total fell within Germany's maximum capacity as agreed by the Reparations Commission, all claims would be met in full. Otherwise they would be abated, first by abating the claims of any country asking for more than its basic proportion relatively to the others, and after this proportionately. No money value would be placed on this source of reparations, any more than on the once-for-all deliveries. In both these cases there would be no limit except Germany's maximum capacity in the event.

(iii) There remains the third category of current deliveries. These should exclude food and manufactured products and should be restricted to a specified list of raw materials and semi-manufactured products such as coal, potash, timber, steel, cement, bricks. These should be handled in a somewhat different fashion. As before, the different claimants would indent on what they wanted in accordance with annual programmes, and their overlapping demands would be tidied up on the same principle as that just described. But in these cases values would be determined by the Reparations Commission in accordance with the world prices ruling at the date in question. Moreover Germany's liability to pay for approved imports, in so far as it had not been discharged by any of the other means discussed in (iv) below, would be a first charge on these current deliveries (and only on these, *not*, that is to say, on reparation categories (i) and (ii) above). That is to say, if in any year such liabilities were x per cent of the current reparation deliveries, the recipients of the deliveries would have to pay in cash x per cent, the excess of the liabilities would have to be carried forward to the next year.)

(iv) The following assets to be set aside to cover the cost of permitted German imports and to be used in the following order:

(*a*) proceeds of German exports other than reparations;

(*b*) German assets in neutral countries;

(*c*) any gold not required for restitution;

(*d*) part payments under (iii) above for current reparations deliveries.

(v) The basic proportions might be as follows, on the assumption that U.K. does not indent for labour services:

Russia, 50 per cent; U.K., 17½ per cent; Poland, 7½ per cent; France, Holland, Czechoslovakia, Belgium, 5 per cent each; Jugoslavia, Greece, 2½ per cent each.

These proposals may seem, and indeed are, exceedingly complicated. But the complication arises out of the problems to be solved, not out of the proposed solution. They are all of them latent in any settlement and can only escape notice so long as we confine our attention to paper proposals without considering the practical difficulties in the way of carrying them out.

To E. PLAYFAIR, *25 April 1945*

THE PREAMBLE TO THE DRAFT INSTRUCTIONS ON REPARATIONS

Now that I see the revised text, I realise that it is in some respects deficient as a result of detaching the Annex which I drafted at the same time. For certain matters which ought to have come in the preamble were omitted for the reason that they were appearing in the Annex. I suggest, therefore, the following additions—

A new paragraph 2 as follows:

2. *The character of current deliveries*

(i) Should current deliveries exclude food unless (which is most unlikely) a surplus of foodstuffs is developed in excess of Germany's total demands?

(ii) Should manufactured articles be excluded, whether capital goods or consumption goods?

(iii) In short, should current deliveries be restricted to a specified list of raw materials and semi-manufactured products such as coal, potash, timber, steel, cement, bricks?

Add to the present paragraph on *The basis of sharing reparations*—

(iii) Would a sharing basis on some such lines as the following be acceptable, on the assumption that the U.K. proportion relates to deliveries other than labour services? Russia, 50 per cent; U.K., $17\frac{1}{2}$ per cent; Poland, $7\frac{1}{2}$ per cent; France, Holland, Czechoslovakia, 5 per cent each; Belgium, Jugoslavia, Greece, $2\frac{1}{2}$ per cent each.

I note two minor misprints:

1(i), 5th line, for 'and a realistic figure' read 'or a realistic figure'.

3(ii) for 'force labour' read 'forced labour'.

The official Committee continued to meet throughout May. As Keynes told R. H. Brand on 13 May

> We have been spending recently an inordinate amount of time talking nonsense about reparations. Not that we should be blamed for it. We talk nonsense because there is no sense available. Ministers still have to exercise their prerogative of adding or subtracting nonsense. So we are still some way from finality.

In the end the British attitude towards reparations settled down to the following. There would be no global sum for reparations until Germany's capacity to pay became clear, for as yet there had been no final decisions on the territorial extent of Germany, her dismemberment, or her economic organisation. The first charge on German assets should be the German standard of life, occupation expenses and imports. The cost of imports should be the first charge on German reparations deliveries. Subject to the above, there should initially be limited once-for-all deliveries of capital goods followed by limited deliveries in kind of non-food raw materials and semi-manufactures over a ten-year period with a reconsideration of the issue after five years. Labour services could also find use, subject to stringent safeguards.

The Reparations Committee set up at Yalta met for the first time at the end of June 1945. Before the meeting of the Big Three at Potsdam in July, all the Commission needed to do was fix a series of percentages for distribution of the proceeds and related points, but the Commission had reached no agreements as to details before the Potsdam conference.

The meetings at Potsdam were themselves characterised by disagreements. Nevertheless, in addition to setting the post-war boundaries of Germany and agreeing that for purposes of reparations Germany should be treated as a single economy, those involved set a number of parameters within which the reparations problem would be solved:

(*a*) reparations should come principally, but not exclusively from industries producing munitions and implements of war;

(*b*) sufficient resources should remain in Germany to enable the Germans to subsist without external assistance and provide them with a standard of living not exceeding the average of European countries excluding the U.K. and the U.S.S.R. as well as cover occupation costs;

(*c*) the German economy should be decentralised;

(*d*) the first charge on exports of current production and stocks should be imports; and

(*e*) the occupying powers would draw reparations from their own zones of occupation except that the U.S.S.R. would receive 25 per cent of the industrial equipment so removed from the Western zones.

Keynes's final involvement in the reparations issue came when Professor C. B. Hoover[12] working under the terms of the Potsdam Agreement estimated that to maintain the German standard of living at the level of the 1930–8 European average implied an attempt to maintain production and consumption at the 1932 level. If this were done, he argued, given the post-war position of Germany it would prove impossible to balance the necessary imports with exports, much less cover occupations costs or allow for reparations. When the Hoover Report became public, it was the subject of considerable controversy and Hoover wrote to Keynes. Both Hoover's letter and Keynes's reply appear below.

From PROFESSOR C. B. HOOVER, *30 November 1945*

My dear Keynes,

As you may have heard, I spent some four months on a temporary assignment in Germany as economic advisor to our occupational authorities. In connection with the necessity for trying to carry out the Potsdam Agreement, I prepared a report which showed the extreme difficulty, if not impossibility, of carrying out a reparations policy aimed at the de-industrialisation of Germany while at the same time leaving sufficient capital resources in the truncated Reich to maintain a minimum standard of living.

When this report was made public it was heavily attacked in our press and radio by those who wished to follow a policy founded upon revenge and destruction of all industrial military potential, whatever the cost. The report

[12] Calvin Bryce Hoover (b. 1897); Professor of Economics, Duke University, from 1927; Economic Adviser, U.S. Department of Agriculture, 1934; Consultant, National Resources Planning Board, 1937; Advisory Commissioner, Council of National Defence, 1940, Price Administration and Civilian Supply, 1941; Economic Adviser, U.S. Group Control Commission in Germany 1945.

has gradually, however, obtained support from American economists and is currently receiving corroboration from the reports from Germany of Byron Price and General Eisenhower.

Realising the effect which your *Economic Consequences of the Peace* had upon international opinion in the period between the two wars, I venture the hope that at an appropriate and convenient moment you might express your opinion on a reparations policy for this war.

I fully realise the almost certain inadvisability of doing anything of the sort now in view of the current negotiations in connection with the loan. I realise further that your official position might render my suggestion inadvisable for action even at some future time. My deep concern that we should as far as possible forestall action in Germany which would make a truly desperate situation even worse and which might delay European reconstruction indefinitely is the excuse for my suggestion.

Sincerely yours,
CALVIN B. HOOVER

To PROFESSOR C. B. HOOVER, *6 December 1945*

My dear Hoover,

I heard about the substance of your report on the German position in relation to reparations policy and find myself very much in sympathy with it. At an earlier stage I was considerably concerned in discussions on this matter. But eventually I got to feel so hopeless about any sensible or even possible result, that I disengaged myself from so distasteful a subject. Our original ideas on this matter a year or more ago were in my opinion not too bad. But, for reasons which are only too obvious, they have fallen by the way. There cannot, in my opinion, be the smallest doubt that your criticisms are well founded and that only a change in policy can prevent great misfortunes.

All the same, I am afraid that this expression of opinion must remain private and personal to yourself, I can only regain complete freedom of public expression by ceasing to be officially connected with other matters. Perhaps that day may not be far off, but, at the moment, I have to behave like, at any rate, a demi-semi-official. This time I have not too bad a conscience about that because, as I have mentioned, I am not, as I was last time, personally mixed up in responsibility for this subject. And also because I believe that this time, both here in the U.S.A. and also in England, the majority share my views; whereas, last time, I was a voice crying in the wilderness and had, therefore, to cry loudly.

Sincerely yours,
[copy initialled] K

Appendix

SELECTIONS FROM THE ARTICLES
OF AGREEMENT OF THE
INTERNATIONAL MONETARY FUND

ARTICLE IV. PAR VALUES OF CURRENCIES

. . . . . .

SEC. 3. *Foreign exchange dealings based on parity.* The maximum and the minimum rates for exchange transactions between the currencies of members taking place within their territories shall not differ from parity

(i) in the case of spot exchange transactions, by more than one percent; and

(ii) in the case of other exchange transactions, by a margin which exceeds the margin for spot exchange transactions by more than the Fund considers reasonable.

SEC. 4. *Obligations regarding exchange stability.* (*a*) Each member undertakes to collaborate with the Fund to promote exchange stability, to maintain orderly exchange arrangements with other members, and to avoid competitive exchange alterations.

(*b*) Each member undertakes, through appropriate measures consistent with this Agreement, to permit within its territories exchange transactions between its currency and the currencies of other members only within the limits prescribed under Section 3 of this Article. A member whose monetary authorities, for the settlement of international transactions, in fact freely buy and sell gold within the limits prescribed by the Fund under Section 2 of this Article shall be deemed to be fulfilling this undertaking.

SEC. 5. *Changes in par values.* (*a*) A member shall not propose a change in the par value of its currency except to correct a fundamental disequilibrium.

(*b*) A change in the par value of a member's currency may be made only on the proposal of the member and only after consultation with the Fund.

(*c*) When a change is proposed, the Fund shall first take into account the changes, if any, which have already taken place in the initial par value of the member's currency as determined under Article XX, Section 4. If the proposed change, together with all previous changes, whether increases or decreases,

(i) does not exceed ten percent of the initial par value, the Fund shall raise no objection;

(ii) does not exceed a further ten percent of the initial par value, the Fund may either concur or object, but shall declare its attitude within seventy-two hours if the member so requests;

(iii) is not within (i) or (ii) above, the Fund may either concur or object, but shall be entitled to a longer period in which to declare its attitude.

(*d*) Uniform changes in par values made under Section 7 of this Article shall not be taken into account in determining whether a proposed change falls within (i), (ii), or (iii) of (*c*) above.

(*e*) A member may change the par value of its currency without the concurrence of the Fund if the change does not affect the international transactions of members of the Fund.

(*f*) The Fund shall concur in a proposed change which is within the terms of (*c*) (ii) or (*c*) (iii) above if it is satisfied that the change is necessary to correct a fundamental disequilibrium. In particular, provided it is so satisfied, it shall not object to a proposed change because of the domestic social or political policies of the member proposing the change.

. . . . . .

ARTICLE V. TRANSACTIONS WITH THE FUND

. . . . . .

SEC. 3. *Conditions governing use of the Fund's resources.* (*a*) A member shall be entitled to buy the currency of another member from the Fund in exchange for its own currency subject to the following conditions:

(i) The member desiring to purchase the currency represents that it is presently needed for making in that currency payments which are consistent with the provisions of this Agreement;

(ii) The Fund has not given notice under Article VII, Section 3, that its holdings of the currency desired have become scarce;

(iii) The proposed purchase would not cause the Fund's holdings of the purchasing member's currency to increase by more than twenty-five percent of its quota during the period of twelve months ending on the date of the purchase nor to exceed two hundred percent of its quota, but the twenty-five percent limitation shall apply only to the extent that the Fund's holdings of the member's currency have been brought above seventy-five percent of its quota if they had been below that amount;

(iv) The Fund has not previously declared under Section 5 of this Article, Article IV, Section 6, Article VI, Section 1, or Article XV, Section 2 (*a*), that the member desiring to purchase is ineligible to use the resources of the Fund.

(*b*) A member shall not be entitled without the permission of the Fund to use the Fund's resources to acquire currency to hold against forward exchange transactions.

SEC. 4. *Waiver of conditions.* The Fund may in its discretion, and on terms which safeguard its interests, waive any of the conditions prescribed in Section 3 (*a*) of this Article, especially in the case of members with a record of avoiding large or continuous use of the Fund's resources. In making a waiver it shall take into consideration periodic or exceptional requirements of the member requesting the waiver. The Fund shall also take into consideration a member's willingness to pledge as collateral security gold, silver, securities, or other acceptable assets having a value sufficient in the opinion of the Fund to protect its interests and may require as a condition of waiver the pledge of such collateral security.

. . . . . .

SEC. 7. *Repurchase by a member of its currency held by the Fund.* (*a*) A member may repurchase from the Fund and the Fund shall sell for gold any part of the Fund's holdings of its currency in excess of its quota.

(*b*) At the end of each financial year of the Fund, a member shall repurchase from the Fund with gold or convertible currencies, as determined in accordance with Schedule B, part of the Fund's holdings of its currency under the following conditions:

(i) Each member shall use in repurchases of its own currency from the Fund an amount of its monetary reserves equal in value to one-half of any increase that has occurred during the year in the Fund's holdings of its currency plus one-half of any increase, or minus one-half of any decrease, that has occurred during the year in the member's monetary reserves. This rule shall not apply when a member's monetary reserves have decreased during the year by more than the Fund's holdings of its currency have increased.

(ii) If after the repurchase described in (i) above (if required) has been made, a member's holdings of another member's currency (or of gold acquired from that member) are found to have increased by reason of transactions in terms of that currency with other members or persons in their territories, the member whose holdings of such currency (or gold) have thus increased shall use the increase to repurchase its own currency from the Fund.

(*c*) None of the adjustments described in (*b*) above shall be carried to a point at which

(i) the member's monetary reserves are below its quota, or

(ii) the Fund's holdings of its currency are below seventy-five percent of its quota, or

(iii) the Fund's holdings of any currency required to be used are above seventy-five percent of the quota of the member concerned.

SEC. 8. *Charges.* (*a*) Any member buying the currency of another member from the Fund in exchange for its own currency shall pay a service charge uniform for all members of three-fourths percent in addition to the parity price. The Fund in its discretion may increase this service charge to not more than one percent or reduce it to not less than one-half percent.

(*b*) The Fund may levy a reasonable handling charge on any member buying gold from the Fund or selling gold to the Fund.

(*c*) The Fund shall levy charges uniform for all members which shall be payable by any member on the average daily balances of its currency held by the Fund in excess of its quota. These charges shall be at the following rates:

(i) *On amounts not more than twenty-five percent in excess of the quota:* no charge for the first three months; one-half percent per annum for the next nine months; and thereafter an increase in the charge of one-half percent for each subsequent year.

(ii) *On amounts more than twenty-five percent and not more than fifty percent in excess of the quota:* an additional one-half percent for the first year; and an additional one-half percent for each subsequent year.

(iii) *On each additional bracket of twenty-five percent in excess of the quota:* an additional one-half percent for the first year; and an additional one-half percent for each subsequent year.

(*d*) Whenever the Fund's holdings of a member's currency are such that the charge applicable to any bracket for any period has reached the rate of four percent per annum, the Fund and the member shall consider means by which the Fund's holdings of the currency can be reduced. Thereafter, the charges shall rise in accordance with the provisions of (*c*) above until they reach five percent and failing agreement, the Fund may then impose such charges as it deems appropriate.

(*e*) The rates referred to in (*c*) and (*d*) above may be changed by a three-fourths majority of the total voting power.

(*f*) All charges shall be paid in gold. If, however, the member's monetary reserves are less than one-half of its quota, it shall pay in gold only that proportion of the charges due which such reserves bear to one-half of its quota, and shall pay the balance in its own currency.

ARTICLE VI. CAPITAL TRANSFERS

SECTION 1. *Use of the Fund's resources for capital transfers.* (*a*) A member may not make net use of the Fund's resources to meet a large or sustained outflow of capital, and the Fund may request a member to exercise controls to prevent such use of the resources of the Fund. If, after receiving such a request, a member fails to exercise appropriate controls, the Fund may declare the member ineligible to use the resources of the Fund.

(*b*) Nothing in this Section shall be deemed

(i) to prevent the use of the resources of the Fund for capital transactions of reasonable amount required for the expansion of exports or in the ordinary course of trade, banking or other business, or

(ii) to affect capital movements which are met out of a member's own resources of gold and foreign exchange, but members undertake that such capital movements will be in accordance with the purposes of the Fund.

. . . . . .

SEC. 3. *Controls of capital transfers.* Members may exercise such controls as are necessary to regulate international capital movements, but no member may exercise these controls in a manner which will restrict payments for current transactions or which will unduly delay transfers of funds in settlement of commitments, except as provided in Article VII, Section 3 (*b*), and in Article XIV, Section 2.

ARTICLE VII. SCARCE CURRENCIES

SECTION 1. *General scarcity of currency.* If the Fund finds that a general scarcity of a particular currency is developing, the Fund may so inform members and may issue a report setting forth the causes of the scarcity and containing recommendations designed to bring it to an end. A representative of the member whose currency is involved shall participate in the preparation of the report.

SEC. 2. *Measures to replenish the Fund's holdings of scarce currencies.* The Fund may, if it deems such action appropriate to replenish its holdings of any member's currency, take either or both of the following steps:

. (i) Propose to the member that, on terms and conditions agreed between the Fund and the member, the latter lend its currency to the Fund or that, with the approval of the member, the Fund borrow such currency from some other source either within or outside the territories of the member, but no member shall be under any obligation to make such loans to the Fund or to approve the borrowing of its currency by the Fund from any other source.

(ii) Require the member to sell its currency to the Fund for gold.

SEC. 3. *Scarcity of the Fund's holdings.* (*a*) If it becomes evident to the Fund that the demand for a member's currency seriously threatens the Fund's ability to supply that currency, the Fund, whether or not it has issued a report under Section 1 of this Article, shall formally declare such currency scarce and shall thenceforth apportion its existing and accruing supply of the scarce currency with due regard to the relative needs of members, the general international economic situation, and any other pertinent considerations. The Fund shall also issue a report concerning its action.

(*b*) A formal declaration under (*a*) above shall operate as an authorization to any member, after consultation with the Fund, temporarily to impose limitations on the freedom of exchange operations in the scarce currency. Subject to the provisions of Article IV, Sections 3 and 4, the member shall have complete jurisdiction in determining the nature of such limitations, but they shall be no more restrictive than is necessary to limit the demand for the scarce currency to the supply held by, or accruing to, the member in question; and they shall be relaxed and removed as rapidly as conditions permit.

(*c*) The authorization under (*b*) above shall expire whenever the Fund formally declares the currency in question to be no longer scarce.

. . . . . .

ARTICLE VIII. GENERAL OBLIGATIONS OF MEMBERS

SECTION 1. *Introduction.* In addition to the obligations assumed under other articles of the Agreement, each member undertakes the obligations set out in this Article.

SEC. 2. *Avoidance of restrictions on current payments.* (*a*) Subject to the provisions of Article VII, Section 3 (*b*), and Article XIV, Section 2, no member shall, without the approval of the Fund, impose restrictions on the making of payments and transfers for current international transactions.

(*b*) Exchange contracts which involve the currency of any member and which are contrary to the exchange control regulations of that member maintained or imposed consistently with this Agreement shall be unenforceable in the territories of any member. In addition, members may, by mutual accord, co-operate in measures for the purpose of making the exchange control regulations of either member more effective, provided that such measures and regulations are consistent with this Agreement.

SEC. 3. *Avoidance of discriminatory currency practices.* No member shall engage in, or permit any of its fiscal agencies referred to in Article V, Section 1, to engage in, any discriminatory currency arrangements or multiple currency practices except as authorized under this Agreement or approved by the Fund. If such arrangements and practices are engaged in at the date when this Agreement enters into force the member concerned shall consult with the Fund as to their progressive removal unless they are maintained or imposed under Article XIV, Section 2, in which case the provisions of Section 4 of that Article shall apply.

SEC. 4. *Convertibility of foreign held balances.* (*a*) Each member shall buy balances of its currency held by another member if the latter, in requesting the purchase, represents

(i) that the balances to be bought have been recently acquired as a result of current transactions; or

(ii) that their conversion is needed for making payments for current transactions. The buying member shall have the option to pay either in the currency of the member making the request or in gold.

(*b*) The obligation in (*a*) above shall not apply

(i) when the convertibility of the balances has been restricted consistently with Section 2 of this Article, or Article VI, Section 3; or

(ii) when the balances have accumulated as a result of transactions effected before the removal by a member of restrictions maintained or imposed under Article XIV, Section 2; or

(iii) when the balances have been acquired contrary to the exchange regulations of the member which is asked to buy them; or

(iv) when the currency of the member requesting the purchase has been declared scarce under Article VII, Section 3 (*a*); or

(v) when the member requested to make the purchase is for any reason not entitled to buy currencies of other members from the Fund for its own currency.

. . . . . .

ARTICLE XIV. TRANSITIONAL PERIOD

SECTION 1. *Introduction.* The Fund is not intended to provide facilities for relief or reconstruction or to deal with international indebtedness arising out of the war.

SEC. 2. *Exchange restrictions.* In the post-war transitional period members may, notwithstanding the provisions of any other articles of this Agreement, maintain and adapt to changing circumstances (and, in the case of members whose territories have been occupied by the enemy, introduce where necessary) restrictions on payments and transfers for current international transactions. Members shall, however, have continuous regard in their foreign exchange policies to the purposes of the Fund; and, as soon as conditions permit, they shall take all possible measures to develop such commercial and financial arrangements with other members as will facilitate international payments and the maintenance of exchange stability. In particular, members shall withdraw restrictions maintained or imposed under this Section as soon as they are satisfied that they will be able, in the absence of such restrictions, to settle their balance of payments in a manner which will not unduly encumber their access to the resources of the Fund.

. . . . . .

ARTICLE XV. WITHDRAWAL FROM MEMBERSHIP

SECTION 1. *Right of members to withdraw.* Any member may withdraw from the Fund at any time by transmitting a notice in writing to the Fund at its principal office. Withdrawal shall become effective on the date such notice is received.

. . . . . .

ARTICLE XIX. EXPLANATION OF TERMS

In interpreting the provisions of this Agreement the fund and its members shall be guided by the following:

(*a*) A member's monetary reserves means its net official holdings of gold, of convertible currencies of other members, and of the currencies of such non-members as the Fund may specify.

. . . . . .

(*i*) Payments for current transactions means payments which are not for the purpose of transferring capital, and includes, without limitation:

(1) All payments due in connection with foreign trade, other current business, including services, and normal short-term banking and credit facilities;

(2) Payments due as interest on loans and as net income from other investments;

(3) Payments of moderate amount for amortization of loans or for depreciation of direct investments;

(4) Moderate remittances for family living expenses.

The Fund may, after consultation with the members concerned, determine whether certain specific transactions are to be considered current transactions or capital transactions.

ACKNOWLEDGEMENTS

We wish to thank Professor L. S. Pressnell, Professor Lord Robbins and Mr J. K. Horsefield for assistance in the preparation of this volume.

Crown copyright material appears with the permission of the controller of Her Majesty's Stationery Office, while the material from the *Morgenthau Diaries*, available in the Franklin D. Roosevelt Library at Hyde Park, New York, appears with the permission of the National Archives and Record Service.

DOCUMENTS REPRODUCED IN THIS VOLUME

Where documents come from the Public Record Office their call numbers appear before the date.

ARTICLES

Note by Lord Keynes (on F. D. Graham's 'Keynes vs Hayek on a Commodity Reserve Currency'), *Economic Journal*, December 1944   *page* 39–40

Objective of International Price Stability, The, *Economic Journal*, June–September 1943   30–3

MEMORANDA, NOTES AND COMMENTS

Alternative to a Global Figure for Reparations, An (T236/255), 23 April 1945   394–7

Bank for Reconstruction and Development, The, to T. Padmore (T231/354), 9 June 1944   48–54

Bretton Woods (T236/157), 14 June 1945   196–206

Commercial Policy, to Sir R. Hopkins (T236/378), 14 June 1944   311–12

Commercial Policy Talks, The, to Sir Wilfrid Eady (T236/378), 1 January 1945   320–1

Commercial Policy Talks, to Sir Wilfrid Eady (T236/378), 4 January 1945   321

Committee on Commercial Policy (T247/2), 15 September 1944   314–17

Conference on International Monetary Fund, to Sir R. Hopkins (T231/365), 7 June 1944   43–7

Dismemberment of Germany, The, to Sir J. Anderson (T247/87), 26 February 1945   384–6

Dismemberment Proposals, The, to Sir J. Anderson (T247/87), 27 February 1945   386–7

Draft Instructions on Reparations, The (T236/255) 23 April 1945   390–4

Germany's Contribution to the Cost of Keeping the Peace of the World, 21 December 1942   337–41

I.M.F.—Drafting Queries, The (T231/ECA21/019A), 17 September 1944*   134–40

* This file has unfortunately been mislaid at the Public Record Office since the editor took copies of this document. The old Treasury reference was ECA 21/019A; the new Treasury class is T231.

International Montetary Fund, The, 29 December 1944   146–54

International Monetary Fund, Textual Doubts, to T. Padmore (T247/38), 20 September 1944   140–1

Monetary and Commercial Bilateralism, from D. H. Robertson (T247/28), 27 May 1944   24–5

Monetary and Commercial Bilateralism, to D. H. Robertson and Sir W. Eady (T247/27), 31 May 1944   25–6

Monetary Conference, The, to Sir D. Waley (T247/28), 30 May 1944   40–3

Monetary Proposals, The, to T. Padmore (T247/35), 28 April 1944   1–3

My Notes on Mr Pasvolsky's Memo (T247/94), 5 January 1942   239–42

Note on the International Monetary Fund, A: An Essay in Rabbinics, from D. H. Robertson (T247/38), 31 July 1944   114–17

Note on a Note on the I.M.F., A: An Essay in Metarabbinics (T247/38), 9 August 1944   118–22

Note on a Note on a Note on the I.M.F., A: An Essay in Common Sense, from D. H. Robertson (T247/38), 29 August 1944   126–7

Notes for the Chancellor on Bretton Woods (T247/39), 15 February 1945   188–92

Overton Committee Draft Report, to S. D. Waley (T247/2), 31 December 1942   251–3

Post-war Commercial Policy (T247/2), 15 January 1943   256–60

Preamble to the Draft Instructions on Reparations, The, to E. Playfair (T236/255), 25 April 1945   397–8

Project of a Commercial Union, to Sir Wilfrid Eady (T247/2), 20 November 1942   248–50

Quantitative Regulation of Imports (T236/302), 9 February 1944   284–7

Questions on Treatment of Post-War Germany (T247/86), 13 October 1941   331–3

Recommendations of the British Inter-departmental Committee on Reparation and Economic Security, 28 September 1943   348–73

Reparations (T247/86), 3 September 1942   335–6

Reparations, to Sir H. Wilson (T247/86), 20 October 1941   333–4

Reparations and Dismemberment (T247/87), 28 February 1945   387–9

Report of the Overton Committee on Commercial Policy, The, to Sir D. Waley (T247/2), 1 February 1943   262–5

Restitution and Reparation (T247/86), 1 March 1943   341–6

Savannah, to Sir E. Bridges (T236/169), 12 February 1946   209–10

Savannah Conference on the Bretton Woods Final Act, The (T247/83), 27 March 1946   220–38

Sir H. Henderson's Criticism of the Overton Draft Report on Post-War Commercial Policy (To Sir Wilfrid Eady and others), 4 January 1943   253–6

MINUTES

To Anderson, Sir John, from Sir R. Hopkins (T247/2), 14 June 1944   310–11
To Catto, Lord, and others (European Reparations) (T247/86), 19 September 1941   328–30
From Compton, E. G., 17 February 1943   296–70
To Compton, E. G., 17 February 1943   270
To Compton, E. G., 19 February 1943   271
From Compton, E. G., 24 February 1943   272
To Bridges, Sir E. (T247/2), 11 July 1945   323–6
To Dalton, H. (T247/83), 29 March 1946   220
From Eady, Sir Wilfrid (T236/378), 10 January 1945   321–3
To Eady, Sir Wilfrid (T236/378), 11 January 1945   322–3
From Eady, Sir Wilfrid (T247/39), 24 January 1945   168–70
To Eady, Sir Wilfrid (T36/255), 23 April 1945   390
To Eady, Sir Wilfrid (T247/40), 21 June 1945   184–5
To Hopkins, Sir Richard (T247/2), 12 June 1944   304–10
To Hopkins, Sir Richard, from R. H. Brand, 23 July 1944—excerpt   113
To Padmore, T. (T247/2), 15 September 1944   313
To Playfair, E. (T247/61), 13 September 1944   374–5
From Robertson, D. H., to Sir H. Henderson and Sir D. Waley (T236/302), 16 March 1944   289–91
From Robertson, D. H. (T247/28), 22 May 1944   23–4
To Waley, Sir D., Sir Richard Hopkins and T. Padmore (T247/35), 14 July 1944   93
From Wilson, Sir H. (T247/94), 23 January 1942   244
To Wilson, Sir H. (T247/94), 27 January 1942   244

PUBLISHED LETTERS

To *The Economist*, 29 July 1944   84–5
To *The Times*, 18 May 1944   8–9
To *The Times*, 23 August 1944   128
To *The Times*, 29 August 1944   128–9

DOCUMENTS REPRODUCED IN THIS VOLUME

UNPUBLISHED LETTERS

To Addison, Lord (T247/35), 17 May 1944   6–8

To Anderson, Sir John (T160/1375/F17942/010/03), 21 July
    1944—excerpt   105–8

To Anderson, Sir John (T247/87), 6 October 1944   380–2

To Bernstein, E. M., 19 November 1944   154–5

From Bernstein, E. M. (T247/40), 15 May 1945—excerpt   193

To Bernstein, E. M. (T247/40), 29 May 1945   193–5

To Brand, R. H., 8 February 1945—excerpt   185–7

To Brand, R. H., 13 May 1945—excerpt   398

From Brand, R. H., 23 January 1946—excerpt   206–7

To Brand, R. H., 8 February 1946—excerpt   208–9

To Catto, Lord, 4 July 1944   77–83

To Catto, Lord, 22 July 1944—excerpt   98

To Eady, Sir Wilfrid, 9 November 1944—excerpt   148

To Eady, Sir Wilfrid (T236/378), 13 November 1944   317–20

From Eady, Sir Wilfrid (T247/39), 25 January 1945   170–1

To Eccles, D., 17 February 1943   271

From Eccles, D., 18 February 1943   271

To Fleming, J. M. (T236/302), 13 March 1944   287–9

From Fleming, J. M. (T236/302), 6 April 1944   291–7

To Fleming, J. M. (T236/302), 22 April 1944   297–9

From Fleming, J. M. (T236/302), 29 April 1944   299–303

To Fleming, J. M. (T236/302), 2 May 1944   303–4

To Graham, Benjamin, 31 December 1943   36–8

To Graham, Professor F. D., 31 December 1943   34–6

To Henderson, Sir Hubert, 4 January 1943   253

From Hoover, Professor C. B., 30 November 1943   399–400

To Hoover, Professor C. B., 6 December 1945   400–1

To Hopkins, Sir Richard (T231/365), 25 June 1944   59–64

To Hopkins, Sir Richard (T231/365), 30 June 1944   66–71

To Hopkins, Sir Richard (T231/365), 22 July 1944   108–112

To Hopkins, Sir Richard, from R. H. Brand, 23 July
    1944—excerpt   113

To Kahn, R. F. (T236/302), 13 January 1944   283–4

To Kahn, R. F., 13 March 1946   217

To Malkin, Sir W. (FO371/35309), 29 September 1943   346–7

To Meade, J. E. (T247/2), 15 December 1942   272–5

From Meade, J. E. (T247/2), 17 December 1942   275–8

To Meade, J. E. (T247/2), 18 December 1942   279–80

From Meade, J. E. (T247/2), 22 December 1942   280–2
To Morgenthau, H.(OF 277/64A), 13 July 1944*   88–90
To Morgenthau, H. (T247/38), 17 July 1944   94–6
To Morgenthau, H. (*Morgenthau Diaries*, vol. 756, p. 70), 19 July
  1944   97
From Morgenthau, H. (T247/87), 5 October 1944   375–9
To Morgenthau, H. (draft) (T247/39), January 1945   156–9
To Morgenthau, H., from Sir John Anderson (T247/39), 1
  February 1945   175–7
From Morgenthau, H., to Sir John Anderson (T247/39), 8 June
  1945   183–4
To Opie, R., draft (T247/94), 5 January 1942   242
To Opie, R., 13 February 1942   245–6
To Overton, Sir A. (T247/2), 3 February 1943   261–2
From Overton, Sir A., 9 February 1943   265–6
To Overton, Sir A., 12 February 1943   266–9
To Passant, E. J. (T247/87), 30 December 1944—excerpt   382–4
From Pasvolsky, L. (T247/69), 27 April 1942   246
To Pasvolsky, L. (T247/69), 22 May 1942   247
To Pasvolsky, L. (T247/35), 24 May 1944   28–30
To Pethick-Lawrence, F. W. (T247/35), 16 May 1944   3–4
From Robbins, L. C. (T247/39), 17 January 1945   171–3
To Robbins, L. C. (T247/39), 19 January 1945   174–5
To Robertson, D. H. (T247/38), 9 August 1944   117–18
To Robertson, D. H. (T247/64), 14 August 1944   122–4
From Robertson, D. H. (T247/38), 29 August 1944   124–6
From Robertson, D. H. (draft) (T247/39), January 1945   159–62
From Robertson, D. H. (T247/39), 21 January 1945   162–3
To Robertson, D. H., 23 January 1945   163
To Robertson, D. H. (T247/39), 8 February 1945   163–4
From Robertson, D. H. (T247/37), 12 February 1945   164–5
To Robertson, D. H. (T247/40), 14 February 1945   166–7
From Robertson, D. H. (T247/39), 17 February 1945   167
To Robinson, J. V., 9 September 1944   129–32
From Robinson, J. V., 14 September 1944   132
To Robinson, J. V., 16 September 1944   133
To White, H. D. (T247/35), 24 May 1944   26–8

* Since the editor examined these documents the Treasury has reported that the relevant file of OF 277/64A has been inadvertently destroyed. A Public Record Office search for the papers in other departmental files has so far been unsuccessful.

To White, H. D. (T247/35), 14 July 1944   93–4
To White, H. D. (T247/65), 6 October 1944   142–6
To White, H. D. (T247/39), 6 February 1945   177–82

SPEECHES, MINUTES OF MEETINGS ETC

House of Lords Debates, 16 May 1944—excerpt   4–6
House of Lords Debates, 23 May 1944—excerpts   9–21, 22–3
International Monetary Conference, Minutes of Second Informal
    Meeting with Dominion and Indian Representatives
    (T231/364), 25 June 1944   56–8
Note of an Informal Meeting between the U.K. and U.S.
    Delegations at Atlantic City (T231/361), 26 June 1944   65–6
Opening Remarks at the First Meeting of the Second Commission
    on the Bank for Reconstruction and Development (T247/32),
    3 July 1944   72–7
Remarks on Savannah (T247/83), 8 March 1946   214
Speech at Inaugural Meeting of Governors of Fund and Bank
    (T247/83), 9 March 1946   215–17
Speech in Moving to Accept the Final Act at the Closing Plenary
    Session (T247/65), 22 July 1944   101–3
Statement to Commission II (T247/64), 21 July 1944   100–1
Statement to Meeting of Commission I, 10 July 1944*   81–7
Statement at Executive Plenary Session at Bretton Woods
    (T247/64), 20 July 1944   99–100
Statement to Governors of Fund and Bank (T236/170), 16 March
    1946   218–19

BROADCAST

Statement for B.B.C. on International Bank for Reconstruction
    and Development (T231/353), 22 July 1944   103–5

TELEGRAMS

To Anderson, Sir John (no. 68 REMAC), 14 July 1944*   90–2
To Bridges, Sir Edward (T236/170), 13 March 1946—excerpt   217–18

* Since the editor examined these documents the Treasury has reported that the relevant file of ECA 21/07 has been inadvertently destroyed. A Public Record Office search for the papers in other departmental files has so far been unsuccessful.

DOCUMENTS REPRODUCED IN THIS VOLUME

To Catto, Lord, 28 July 1944   113
To Hopkins, Sir Richard (T231/365), 8 July 1944   83–4
To Treasury (no. 2 REMAC) (T236/169), 7 March 1946   211–13

PUBLISHED DOCUMENTS

International Monetary Fund, Selections from Articles of
   Agreement   402–10

INDEX

Abnormal war balances, 8, 22

Acheson, Dean, Assistant Under-Secretary of State, U.S.A., 64, 212; at Bretton Woods, 59, 87–8, 102; at reparation talks, 347

Addison, Lord (Christopher Addison): opens monetary debate in House of Lords, 12, 13, 15, 20, 22, briefed by JMK, 6–8

Ad valorem duties, 252

Africa
  East and West African colonies, 254
  North African iron ore, 270
  South Africa, 42, 218, 231

Agrarian programme for Germany, 379

Agricultural machinery, 254; tractors, 262, 263–4
  and reparations, 331, 351, 364, 365

Agricultural products, 308–9

Agriculture, 268, 339, 357
  finance for post-war development, 104
  and the Overton Report, 257, 261, 263–4
  Ministry of, 263–4
  protection for, 285, 324

Aircraft, 379; production, 371
  Ministry of Aircraft Production, 265

Air Force, 338; damage from the air, 360

Albery, Sir Irving, M.P., 1

Alcohol, 110–11

Allied Reparations Commission, *see* Reparations Commission

Allies, 10
  'Allied Claim on Germany for Peace-keeping', 357–9
  Allied Forces, 376
  Allied Governments in London, 333
  at Atlantic City, 59
  and costs of occupying Germany, 367
  occupied Allied countries, 354
  reparations claims, 331, 333, 352, 353, 356, 361, 365, 368, 392–3; position of France, 331
  relief from, for devastated territories, 366–7
  role in post-war Germany, 395, in Morgenthau's plan, 377

U.K. war debts to, 86
war effort, 86

Allies, European
  discussions with British on Joint Statement (IMF), 3, 20, on the 'Boat' revision, 61
  views on principle of restitution, 392–3

American
  aid, 24, 59, 212, 229–30, 316; *see also under* Loans
  bluff, 251, 255
  climate, 70, 82, 83, 84, 107, 123–4, 214, 217
  economists, 240–1
  idea of management, 217, 225, 'leak' technique, 244
  lawyers, 68, 70, 78
  steel production, 270
  see also United States of America

American Delegations
  to Bretton Woods, 61, 84, 85, 87, 93, 125, 130, 145, 168, 170–1; appointed 'without commitment', 43, 63, 98; preliminary meetings with British Delegation at Atlantic City, 65–6; good relations with British, 105–6, 109; differences between White and other members, 79; as hosts of Conference, 110–11. *See also* Bretton Woods
  Deputation for commercial talks in London (1944–5), 318–19
  to Savannah, 209, 221–2, 227

American Embassy in London, 320
  Ambassador, *see* Winant, John Gilbert

Amsterdam, 329

Anderson, Sir John, Chancellor of the Exchequer until August 1945
  commercial policy negotiations, 63, 244, 246, 298, 310–11, 312–13, 322, 323; 'Committee on Commercial Policy: Note by the Chancellor of the Exchequer', 314–17
  and Monetary Proposals (International Monetary Fund): speech on, 2, 3, 27; instructions for Delegation, 47, 71, 92, 96, 109; dissatisfied with Exchange

Anderson, Sir John (*cont.*)

Clause, 65, 66, 92, 93–4; on location of Fund Office, 87, 88, 90, 94; drafting queries, 134, 140, 141–2, 149, 151, 161, 162, 163; letter to Morgenthau on discrepancy, 154, 163, 168, 173, 175, 177, 178, 182–3, 186, 203, 204–5, and his reply, 183–4

plans for Parliamentary debate on Bretton Woods, 93–4, 155, 163, 164, 169, 173, 174, 177–9, 187, 204; 'Notes for the Chancellor on Bretton Woods', 188–92

proposed visit to U.S.A., 80–1

relations with Bank of England, 61, 67

reparation negotiations, 375, 379–82, 390; memo to, 'The Dismemberment of Germany', 384–7

list of letters, 415

Reports and memoranda to, 2, 90–2, 105–8

Anglo-American

discussions on commercial policy (1945), 323–7. *See also under* Commercial policy

discussions on post-war economic policy, 283, 346

Anglo-American Loan Agreement (December 1945), 167, 206, 233, 316, 400; negotiations, 189, 326–7

Anglo-American Trade (Commercial) Agreement (1938), 58, 191, 248, 313, 314, 315; JMK's conversations on, in Washington (1941), 239, 242; date of expiry, 319

Anti-Americanism, 3, 6, 29–30

Aquitania, 209

Arbitrage, 124

Argentina

meat exports, 240; ROCA Agreement, 313

Payments Agreements, 25

sterling balances, 122–3, 125

Armaments, 337, 338, 344, 357, 370; German armaments industry, 371, 376

Armies

British defence forces, 338

German, 376; prohibition of military service, 357

of liberation, 72

of occupation, 336, 344, 361; in Germany, 338

Arnold, American lawyer at Bretton Woods, 102

Article VII (Mutual Aid Agreement), *see* Mutual Aid

Articles of Agreement of the International Monetary Fund, 96 n 24, 98, 113, 192; correspondence on, with Joan Robinson, 129–33; Britain's accession to, 206; problem of amendment procedure, 149

Article I: purpose of the Fund, 200–1

Article IV, Par Value of Currencies, 93, 402–3; (3), 133, 139–40, 142–3, 402, 407; (4) (a), 171, 402; (b), exchange transactions, 127, 133, 170–1, 402, 407, and Article VIII, 135, 137, 138–9, 142–3, 148, 168; (5) (c), 169, 402–3; (e), 403, a Russian clause, 131; (6), 402, 403. *See also* Exchange Adjustment Clause

Article V, Transactions with the Fund, 114, 403–5; (1), 403, 406, 408; (3), use of the Fund's resources, 115, 199, 402–3; (4), waiver of conditions, 130, 403; (5), 402, 405; (7), repurchase, 125, 131, 403–4; (8), provision for charges, 130, 131, 171, 404–5

Article VI, Capital Transfers, 114–15, 406; (1), 115, 403; (3), 115, 117, 131, 155, 408

Article VII, Scarce Currencies Clause, 155, 406–7; (2), 130, 406–7; (3) (b), 134, 153, 155, 183, 403, 406, 407, 408

Article VIII, General Obligations of Members, 79, 114, 407–8; ambiguities, 126, 164–5, 166–7, 171–2, 173; (2) (a), Avoidance of Restrictions on Current Payments, 8, 114, 116, 118–20, 134, 407, Robertson's interpretation, 124–5, 135–6, 137–8, 148, 172, inconsistency with VIII (4)(b), 138–9, 141–4, 148–54, 156–8, 160–2, 165, 168–9, 170, 202–3, queries on, 158–9, 182–5, proposed redrafts, 142–3, 145, 146, 155, 171, draft letters to Morgenthau on, 156–9, 175–6, reply, 183–4; (4), Convertibility of foreign-held balances, 47, 114–16, 134, 136–7, 143, 144, 150, 408; relation to other Articles, 115, 127, 135, 153, 407, *and see above*, (2); and Indian sterling balances, 116–17; let-out clause, 144

Article XI, Relations with Non-Member Countries, 139–40

Article XIV, Transitional Period, 158, 176, 408–9; (1), 195, 199, 408; (2), Exchange restrictions, 134, 153, 155, 406, 407, 408

Article XV, Withdrawal from Membership, 139, 403, 409

Article XIX, Explanation of Terms, 167, 409–10

Article XX, 402

Articles of Agreement (*cont.*)
  Article XXII, on permitted restrictions,
    172, 175
Asia, 72, 101
Assets
  of Bank for Reconstruction and Develop-
    ment, 74, 75
  of central banks in occupied countries, 353
  frozen during World War II: Dutch, 330,
    332; French, 331, 332; enemy, 332
  German: under terms of restitution, 342–
    3; included in German capacity to pay,
    361, 364–5, 377; in neutral countries,
    367, 396; external losses, 360; post-war
    charges on, internally, 396, 398
  overseas, U.K., 86
  in reparation claims, 355
  as security for International Monetary
    Fund, 404
Associated Nations, 72
Atlantic City
  preliminary drafting Conference for Bret-
    ton Woods (June 1944), 40, 41, 55;
    Committee arrangements, 41–3, 60–1;
    minutes of meeting, 56–8; U.K. and
    U.S. delegations, 65–71
  climate, 70, 82, 97 n 25
Atlantic Conference, 328
Atlantic Charter, 348–9, 357, 371
Attlee, Clement, Lord President of the Council, 323
Auctions, of import licences, Meade's idea,
  273 n 5, 274, 277–8, 281–2
Australia
  Delegation at Atlantic City, 56; at Bretton
    Woods, 98, 112; quota problem, 69, 79,
    98; joins I.M.F. in 1947, 98 n 27
  observers at Savannah Conference, 231
Austria, 229, 373, 375
  gold seized by Germany, 351
  in Morgenthau's plan for Germany, 376
  Russian demand for reparations from, 393
Axis countries, 341, 342, 346; allies of Ger-
  many, 356

Balance of payments
  international: under International Mone-
    tary Fund, 199, 200–4, 302; role of
    creditor countries, 14; in transitional
    period (Article XIV), 45, 285–6, 409;
    under Article V, 125, Article XXII, 172,
    175
  under Bank for Reconstruction and De-

velopment, 51, 73, 105; equilibrium
    through credit for exports from third
    countries, 109
  under proposed Commercial Conven-
    tion, 172, 173, escape clause, 294, 301–2;
    under proposed Commercial Union, 248,
    273 n 5, 282, 290
  of sterling area, 302
  U.K., post-war problem of, 239, 242;
    Meade's memorandum on, 283; under
    Overton Report, 256–7, 260; and quan-
    titative regulation of imports, 260, 285,
    325, *vs* depreciation of rate of exchange
    to produce equilibrium, 287–9, 292, 296,
    298–304
  U.S., favourable balance, 121, 306–7
Balance of power, 386
Balance of trade
  Britain's post-war problem, 129, 132, 260,
    285, 305, 317; import regulations pre-
    ferred to tariffs as aid for, 261, 264, 266–
    7, 269, or to exchange depreciation, 299;
    Fleming's view, 292–3, 294, 295, 300–3;
    transitional arrangements under Joint
    Statement of Principles, 307; and post-
    war German exports, 341
  U.S., and scarce currency clause, 189,
    192
Balances
  abnormal war, 8, 22
  bank, 161
  foreign-held, *see under* Article VIII
  international, U.K. as custodian of, 165
  'old', 117
  see also Sterling balances
Balfour of Burleigh, Lord, 187; exchange with
  JMK in Lords' debate on International
  Monetary Fund, 21–3, 24, 25–6
Balkan Unions, 251
Balogh, Thomas, economist
  letter to *The Times* on the monetary pro-
    posals (18 May 1944), 8, 24; reply, 8–9, 23
  'World Monetary Policies' (*The Times*,
    August 21, 22, 23, 1944), 127; letters
    on (JMK, August 24, 29), 128–9
  'Baloghian' views, 26
Bancor, 10, 32
Bank of the Argentine, 122–3
Bank of Canada, 113
Bank of England
  agents in New York, 170; representatives at
    Savannah, 210
  capital investment, 269–70

Bank of England (*cont.*)
 comments on JMK's paper on Bank for
  Reconstruction and Development, 54
 foundation, 250th anniversary, 83, 113
 and International Monetary Fund, 123,
  165, 168, 232, 236
 in Low cartoon, 95
Bank of England, Governor of, *see* Catto, Lord
Bank for International Settlements (B.I.S.),
 221; proposal to liquidate, 96, 97, 98
Bank rate, 16
Bank for Reconstruction and Development
 early plans for discussions on, 40, 41, 63;
  memorandum on American and U.K.
  draft papers (9 June 1944), 48–54; instructions to British Delegation, 54–5;
  'Boat Draft' revision of American proposals, 55, 59, 61–2, 64, 67; discussions
  at Atlantic City, 56, 66, 77; Governor of
  Bank of England consulted, 67
 at Bretton Woods (July–September 1944):
  JMK as Chairman of Commission II,
  70–1, 87–8, 102, his opening address,
  72–7; meetings and discussions on, 83,
  84, on articles of agreement, 87; JMK
  seconds report at Executive plenary
  session, 100–1; statement on, for BBC
  evening news, 103–5
 support for in U.S., 91; plans to rail-road
  through Congress, 147–8, 180, 186; alternative plan of American bankers, 164,
  167, 179, 180–1, 186–7, 188, 189–90;
  amendments to Bretton Woods Bill affecting Bank, 196–8; 'sea-change' after
  Bretton Woods, 232–3
 capital subscriptions, 49, 50, 53, 54; target
  for capital funds, 104
 location: difference with Americans, 84, 87,
  88–90, 206; Washington chosen in preference to New York, 211, 212, 218, a
  defeat for U.K., 220, 221
 management, 53
  Alternates, 218–19, 223, 226, 227, 228
  Board of Executive Directors, 194, 212,
  218–19, 221, 223, 226, 227, 228, 237;
  American Director, 194, 197, 212, 229
  Board of Governors, 197, 221, 226, 237;
  American Governor, 196–7; British
  Governor (JMK), 210, 234–5
  Executive Board, 198
  President, 212, 213, 237, 238; staff, 237
 relations with National Advisory Council
  (U.S.), 194, 197–8, 211–12, 228, 229

 salaries, 218–19, 223–4, 237, 238
 voting power, 53
 quotas, 54–5
 scope of operations, 49–51, 109, 188, 198;
  not the answer for U.K. post-war problems, 205–6
 for further details see under Assets; Balance
  of Payments; Bretton Woods
Bankers, 16, 161
 American, 79, 81, 147, 194, 222; counter-
  proposals to I.M.F., 164, 167, 186–7,
  188, 189–90, Report, 179, 180–1; accept
  modified Bretton Woods Bill, 196–7,
  201–2, 206; New York bankers, 211
 international, 38
Barter
 agreements, 12, 240, 248, 308
 trade, in relation to Commercial Policy,
  313, 314–17
BBC, statement by JMK and White on Bank
 and Fund, 103–5
Beaverbrook, Lord, Lord Privy Seal, 323;
 visit to U.S.A., 80–1
Beckett, William Eric, Foreign Office Legal
 adviser: with British Delegation to
 Bretton Woods, 54 n 12, 56, 57, 58, 102,
 177, his 'magnificent job of work',
 110; supports JMK's interpretation of
 Articles, 140, 141
Beit, Sir Alfred, M.P., 1
Belgium
 on Drafting Committee (IMF), 42, 43;
  delegates at Bretton Woods, 55, 100, at
  Savannah, 218, 238
 JMK's journey through devastated areas in
  1918, 100
 reparation claims, 329, 351, 393, 397,
  398
 also mentioned, 375, 379
Bellairs, Admiral Roger Mowbray, 337
Bennet, Viscount, open debate in House of
 Lords on post-war economic policy, 4, 19
Berle, Adolf, Assistant Secretary of State,
 U.S.A., 347
Bernstein, Edward Morris, U.S. Treasury:
 negotiations on I.M.F., 68, 142, 182,
 with Robertson, 83, 109, 124; present at
 interview between JMK and White, 146;
 interpretation of Article VIII, 152,
 154–5, 160, 164, 165, 168, 184, of Article
 XXII, 175, 177, of Article I, 201; 'only
 a Levite among the Priests', 193
 list of letters, 415

Beveridge, Sir William, Welfare Scheme, 338, 357

Bevin, Ernest, M.P., 36, 205

Beyen, Johan Willem, Dutch banker: on Dutch reparation plans, 328–30

Bible, 10

Big Three, at Potsdam, 398. *See also* Churchill, Winston; Roosevelt, Franklin; Stalin, Josef

Bilateralism
argument against, 190–1; misunderstood by Pasvolsky, 239–40; JMK mistaken for advocate of, 241–2, 243, 245, 246
bilateral agreements, and Meade's commercial union project, 248, 273, 276–7, 279–81
commercial bilateralism, and monetary multilateralism, difference with Robertson on, 23–6
vs. monetary proposals of Bretton Woods, 165n; correspondence on, in *The Times*, 8–9; support for, in Parliament, 27, 178, 180
not the right policy for Britain, 12, 305

Birmingham group of M.P.s, 187

Black market, in foreign exchange, 133, 137–8, 142, 143, 170–1

Blocked
balances, 240, 322
blocking, under Article VIII (IMF), 118, 120–1, 134–5, 143, 156, 184
currencies, 23, 25–6, 156, 190
financial blockade, 340
IMF subscriptions, 44

Board of Trade, 236, 239, 270, 313; proposals on post-war commercial policy, 248, 256–10, *see also* Overton Committee
President of the Board of Trade, *see* Dalton, Hugh; Overton, Sir Arnold

Bolton, G. L. F.: adviser to British Delegation at Bretton Woods, 54 n 12, 56, 82, 98, 117, supports JMK on interpretation of Articles, 140; Bank of England representative at Savannah, 210, 230

Bonds, *see* Securities

Booms, 201

Boothby, R[obert] J. G., M.P., 1–2, 24, 129, 132

Bourgeois economy, 384

Brand, R. H., British Treasury official in Washington, 59–60, 158, 180, 213, 219 n 41; member of British Delegation to Bretton Woods, 54 n 12, 92, 108, 147; negotiations, 79–80, 182, with White, 146, 163, 184; differs from U.K. view of Directors' role, 209; might deputise for JMK at Savannah, 210
list of letters, 415

Brassert, Messrs, iron and steel works designers, 272

Brazil
cotton, 252, 254–5
representative on I.M.F. Drafting Committee, 42

'Brazil', as genetic term, 164–6

Brenner, Mr, lawyer at Bretton Woods, 102

Bretton Woods Bank, 233, 234. *See* Bank for Reconstruction and Development

Bretton Woods Bill (U.S.A.): passes House of Representatives in amended form, 196; memorandum on, 'Bretton Woods' (14 June 1945), 196–206

Bretton Woods Act, 212, 233

Bretton Woods Monetary Conference (July 1944)
preparations: the 44 nations invited to attend, 40, 72, 83, 103, the 'monkey-house', 41, 42, 63; delegations 'ad referendum', 41, 96, 98, 'without commitment', 63; conference procedure arrangements, 58; 'Drafting Conference', *see* Atlantic City; no 'fait accompli' for Bretton Woods, 67, plans 'rather incoherent', 70–1
at Bretton Woods: the three Commissions JMK chairman of II (the Bank), 71, 87–8, for details of Commission I *see* International Monetary Fund, for II *see* Bank for Reconstruction and Development; Commission III ('other measures' for international financial cooperation), 71, 96–7
committees, 77, 83, 87, 93, 96, 97, 107, 127, 151, 156, 160; drafting committee of Articles, 171–2; Ad Hoc Committee, 170
President of Conference, Morgenthau, 88
report on first week, 83–4, on Conference as a whole, 105–10; pressure of work, 106–7, 172; a heated meeting, 124–5; a successful experiment in international cooperation, 109
Conference extended from 19 July to 22 July, 96; end of Plenary Conference, 106, 123; closing 'love feast', 112; JMK's role, 112–13, 215

Conference (*cont.*)
Final Act, 98, 100; moved by JMK, 101–3, 112; consideration by Congress, *see under* U.S.A.: Congress; Parliamentary discussions, 147–8, 155, 176–81 *passim*, 192, 'Notes for the Chancellor on Bretton Woods', 188–92; Savannah Conference on Final Act, *see* Savannah Conference
problems of interpretation, *see* Articles of Agreement
Bretton Woods Fund, 233, 234, 325. *See* International Monetary Fund
Bretton Woods Plan
concerned with currency and exchange, not commercial policy, 128–9; relation to commercial agreements, 173, 174–5, 315 n 8, 317, 322; advantages to Britain, 192
date for adherence to Plan (31 December 1945), 205–6
Bridge, Roy Arthur Odell, Bank of England representative at Savannah, 210
Bridgen, J. B., member, Australian Delegation at Atlantic City, 56
Bridges, Sir Edward, Permanent Secretary to the Treasury: concern with commercial policy, 304, 310, 311, 323
memoranda addressed to, 209–10, 323–6
telegram to, 217–18
British
farmer, 287
national character, 30
sentiment on gold standard, 85
steel production, 270
British Ambassador in Washington, 111, 236
see also Halifax, Lord
'British Commercial Policy, Principles of', 305–10
see also Commercial policy
British Control, *see* Exchange control
British Delegation to Bretton Woods
members, led by JMK, 54 n 12, 'a magnificent team', 107, 109; appreciation from Americans, 106, 110; their powers 'ad referendum', 47, 63, 96, 99; instructions, 47; recommendations on Bank for Reconstruction and Development, 49–55
discussions on board the *Queen Mary*, 55, 82; 'Boat drafts' on Fund and Bank, 55, 59, 64, 67
at Bretton Woods, 71, 96, 102, 160, 315 n 8, on July 11th, 170–1; report to Lord Catto (4 July 1944), 77–83; statement by JMK on behalf of the Delegation, 86–7;

report to Sir John Anderson (21 July 1944), 105–8, to Sir Richard Hopkins, 108–12; instructions from London, 115–16, 121; the 'final scene', 112–13
see also under International Monetary Fund
British Delegations
at Atlantic City (June–July 1944), 55–6; informal meeting with Dominion and Indian representatives, 56–8; reports to Sir Richard Hopkins, 59–64, 66–71; meeting with American Delegation, 65–6; daily meetings, 66–7
at Savannah (March 1946), 209–10, 214, 218; report to Hugh Dalton, 220–38; defeated on location issue, 220–2; compromise on role of Executive Directors, 222–4; successful on role of Governors, 226; views on outcome of Conference, 227–32
at post-Yalta discussions (1945), 389; draft instructions for, 390–7
British Empire, 12, 191
British Loan, *see* Anglo-American Loan Agreement
Broches, Mr, lawyer at Bretton Woods, 102
Brooks, H. E., Principal, Treasury: Secretary to U.K. Delegation at Atlantic City, 56, 59, 140, 170, his 'sterling and beautiful qualities', 110; note on text of I.M.F., 141; suggested for Savannah, 210
Brown, Ed (Ned), of Chicago, 161, 213
Bruce, Stanley Melbourne, Australian High Commissioner in London, 3
Budgets, 252
German, 337, 339, 366; of victors and vanquished, 337–9, 357
I.M.F. and Bank, 225
U.K., 210
Buffer state, 384
Buffer stocks: advocated by JMK, 35, 37, 38, 40, 249, by J. M. Fleming, 291
Bulk purchase
in Bretton Woods plan, 22, 25, 128
in Meade's commercial union project, 249, 274
in post-war commercial policy, 310, 326; State Trading and Bulk Purchase, 307–8; on a non-discriminatory basis, 313, 314–5, 317
Burgess, W. Randolph, 167
Burma, 230
Butter, 22, 26

Cabinet (War Cabinet), 67, 80, 92; disagreements over Article VII, 155; dissatisfaction with Article VIII, 157, 176; delay debate on Bretton Woods until after Congress pronouncement, 187; commercial policy discussions, 283, 320; note to, on Reparations and Dismemberment, 387–9; set up Ministerial and Official Committees on Reparations, 389–90

Economic Section, 163, 325

Cambridge, 159

Canada

aid for Britain, 60, 80; discussions on Mutual Aid, in Ottowa, 113, at Bretton Woods, 71

Anglo-Canadian talks on commercial policy (1945), 323; insistence on multilateral approach, 191

Delegation to Atlantic City, 56

Delegation to Bretton Woods, 93, 124, 160, 162, 172; and Article VIII, 165, 170, 171; represented on Drafting Committee for I.M.F., 42

Delegation to Savannah (1946), 209, 218, 222, 224, 226; appointments as Executive Directors, 228; close relations with U.K. Delegation, 230–1

exports, and I.M.F., 114

Treasury, 113

Canada, Minister of Finance, see Ilsley, James Lorimer

Capital

capital repayments of Bank for Reconstruction and Development loans, 52

export of, under IMF, 159, 161, 182; import, to redress balance of trade, 295

invested in oil refineries, 267, in iron and steel plant, 268, 269–70

working capital for post-war Germany, 386

Capital goods, 50, 200; as reparations, 397, 398

Capital imports, in post-war Germany, 378

Capital movements (transactions)

abnormal, Fleming on, 293, 296–7, 302

under Article VI, 406, Article XIX, 409–10

under Clearing Union proposals, 172

international, and domestic rate of interest, 16

under International Monetary Fund, 9, 195, 205, 406; rights of member states to control, 17, 131, 406, of central banks and individuals distinguished, 119–21

'Current international transactions', 206, 407–8, 409–10; difference with Robertson, 114–22, 126–7, 164–7; ambiguities in draft Articles, 134–6, 142–6, 151–2, 154, 184–5, 203, denied by Morgenthau, 183–4, proposed redraft, 155

Capitalist countries, 33

Cartels, 249

Casaday, L. W., American Treasury attaché in London, 27; goes as observer to Bretton Woods, 55

Catto, Lord, Governor of the Bank of England, 67, 323; Catto exchange clause, 44–5, 62, 68, 78; proposed principle for the Fund, 46–7

Minutes addressed to, 328–30

telegram to, 113

Central banks

in Axis countries, 342

under Clearing Union plan, 31

role in International Monetary Fund, 114, 123, 208–9, 220–1, 'instrument and agent of their Government', 15; obligation to redeem balances, dispute with Robertson, 116–17, 118–21; rights of individuals and of central banks distinguished, 119–21, 135, 141, 143, 144, 158–9, 167, 182; ambiguities in draft Articles, 134, 138, 183–4; in proposed redraft, 155

in occupied countries, 332, 353

Chancellor of the Exchequer, see Anderson, Sir John; Dalton, Hugh

Chang, lawyer at Bretton Woods, 102

Chatham House, JMK speaks at, 164, 179, 187

Cherwell, Lord, Paymaster General, 323; at Quebec Conference, 375, 380

Chetty, Sir Shanmukkam, Indian delegate at Bretton Woods, 80

Children's allowances, 338, 357

Chile, 42, 125, 162

China

and I.M.F.: on Drafting Committee, 42; at Bretton Woods, 55; quota, 69; voting power, 130

post-war commercial policy, 255, 257; asks for stabilisation loan, 229

Delegates at Savannah, 215; Vinson's stooge, 217, 222

also mentioned, 50

Churchill, Winston, Prime Minister, 60, 185, 328

Churchill, Winston (*cont.*)
asks JMK to attend meeting on North America, 323
at Potsdam, 398
Quebec Conference, 375, 380
at Teheran Conference, 374
at Yalta, 383; statement on reparations, 388
Civil Service
American, 224
British, at Bretton Woods, 110
International, 220–1, 223; question of pay, 223, 236–7
Clark, J. M., American economist, 240
Clark, William Clifford, Canadian Deputy Minister of Finance, 60; at Bretton Woods, 80
Clarke, Richard William, Assistant Secretary, Treasury: at Ottawa, 113
Clayton, William Lockhart, Under-Secretary of State for Economic Affairs, U.S.A., 212; refuses Presidency of Bank for Reconstruction and Development, 237
Clearing agreements, 314
Clearing balances, due from Germany, 368
Clearing Union, International, 31, 35, 249, 261
debate on, in House of Lords (1943), 9–10, 13
escape clause, 254, 256, 257, 282, 290
and German reparations, 339, 344
relation to I.M.F. proposals, 10, 13, 172, 202; to other plans, 265, 273, 276, 277
Coal, as reparations, 343, 396, 397
Cobbold, Cameron Fromanteel, Deputy Governor of the Bank of England: redrafts Article VIII(2), 146, 155, 161; leads talks on Bank and Fund in Washington (1946), 208, 210
Cobbold clause, on exchange, 78
Collado, Emillo, Export–Import Bank: adviser at Bretton Woods, 102; appointed American Executive Director of the Bank for Reconstruction and Development, 228
Colombia, 42
Colonies
British Crown, 13
colonia systems, 309
Dutch, 330
Commerce
commercial agreements (treaties), 128–9, 191, 313
commercial bilateralism, *see* Bilateralism

no commitments on, in I.M.F. monetary proposals, 8–9, 19, 128–9, 190
U.K. as a commercial nation, 11–12
Commercial Convention, Hawkins's proposal (1943), 172–3, 175, 301–2, 308, 318–19, 322
Commercial policy
Article VII (Mutual Aid), agreement not to cause burden on trade, 190, 309, 314, 315; conversations on (1943), 292, 294, (1944, after Bretton Woods), 63, 304–10
under Article XIV (I.M.F.), 409
Board of Trade proposals, based on Meade's Commercial Union project (November 1942), 248–50; considered by Overton Committee, 250; majority report, 250, 251–3, 262–5; minority report (Henderson), 250, 253–6; notes on both reports, 'Post-War Commercial Policy', 256–60; further correspondence on, 261–9; proposals go through Cabinet, 283, 289; note on quantitative regulation of imports, 286–7
Bretton Woods not concerned with, 128; consistent with 'very foolish' policies, 129; Monetary Agreement independent of commerce, 131–2, should not be considered in relation to, 174, 175
British principles of, 305; in relation to Statement of Principles, 305–7, 310, 318; memorandum, 'Commercial Policy' (June 1944), 311–12
post-war, proposed talks on, 28, 283; opposition to American proposals in Lords and Commons, 27, 28–9; deadlock on, 63, 304, 310–11; Americans urge resumption (1944), 304, 317–18; Ministerial Committee on, 312; memorandum on barter trade in relation to commercial policy (September 1944), 313, 314–17; discussions with Pasvolsky on, in U.S., 317–20
talks resumed in London (November 1944), 320, 323; correspondence with Eady on 'commercial consideration', 320–3; minute on statement handed to Americans (July 1945), 323–6
U.S. loan negotiations become tied to commercial policy issue (autumn 1945), Lieshing heads team of experts, 327
Commercial Policy Organisation, 302
Commercial Union, Meade's project, adopted by Board of Trade, 248; comments on,

Commercial Union (*cont.*)
  'Project of a Commercial Union' (JMK, 20 November 1942), 248–50; correspondence on, with Meade, 273–82
Committee of Economic Development, 206
Commodities, 37, 38
  Article VII talks on, 63
  commodity reserve money, 36
  'commodity standard', 31, 33, 35
  commodity trade, 287
  composite commodity, 35, 37, 38
Common sense, 102, 129, 380; Robertson's 'Essay' on, 126–7
Commonwealth, 12, 21, 40, 235, 254, 317, 385
  gold production, 85
  and Imperial Preference, 309
  representatives at Atlantic City, 56, 66, at Bretton Woods, 71, at Savannah, 230, 231; quotas and voting power under I.M.F., 69, 70, 130
  see also Australia; Canada; India; New Zealand
Communist countries, 33
Competition, 257, 291, 341, 361, 369; and subsidies, 318
'Composite commodity', 35, 37, 38
Compton, Edmund Gerald, Assistant Secretary, Treasury: consulted on steel production, 269–70, 271–2
  Minutes to and from, 414
Conference of Foreign Ministers, Moscow (October 1943), 373–4
'Conference on International Monetary Fund' (memorandum, 7 June 1944), 43–7
Conferences, *see* Atlantic City; Bretton Woods; Moscow; Potsdam; Quebec; Savannah; Teheran
  projected post-Bretton Woods conference, 180, 181, 196
Confidence, 200, 216, 220, 230
Conscription, 338
Conservatism, 123
Conservative M.P.s, 1–2
'Consideration' (lend lease), 315
  commercial consideration, 320–3
Consumers, 252, 255, 291, 308
  consumer goods, 266; as reparations, 397
  consumption, 265, 301, 378; in post-war Germany, 378, 399
Control Commission, 395

Convertibility
  convertible currencies, 409; gold convertible currencies, 55, 143
  'convertibility': need for definition, 55 n 13; in the Bretton Woods Pickwickian sense, 121; undertaken by members of I.M.F., 8–9, 11, not required during transitional period, 45–6; should not include past accumulations of balances, 47; multilateral, 58
  'obligation' of convertibility of foreign-held balances under Article VIII of I.M.F., 58, 185, 186, 325, 408; limiting circumstances, 150–1; ambiguity of draft terms: correspondence with Robertson on, 114–21, 124, 126, 160, 161, 164–7; queries on, 134–5, 182; letter of Morgenthau on, 156–9, 175–7, reply, 184; proposed amendment, 145; Eady's view, 168; correspondence on, with Robbins, 171, 174; under terms of American amendment, 201, 202–3
  of sterling: pre-war standard practice, 9, 11–12; problem of wartime sterling balances, 83, 116–17, 121–2, 126–7; zero-day for full convertibility, 126
Cost-levels, relative international, 292–3, 294, 301
Cost of living, 4
  index, 294
  see also under Wages
Costa Rica, 42
Cotton, 252, 254–5, 318
Cox, Oscar, American lawyer at Bretton Woods, 102
Credit
  through Bank for Reconstruction and Development, 51, 104–5, 109, 203; a 'mutual pool of credit insurance', 76, 104
  under Clearing Union plan, 31
  contraction of, abjured as instrument of domestic policy, 16
  for current exports in transitional period, 58
  from International Monetary Fund, 190, 204
  wages and credit policy under an international currency scheme, 32–3
  see also Loans
Creditor countries
  drain of gold to, 32
  Germany's external creditors, 368
  under I.M.F., 122–3, 125, 127, 159, 182; and import restrictions, 254

Creditor countries (*cont.*)
  responsibility for equilibrium in international balance of payments, 14, 105
  role in Bank for Reconstruction and Development, 50, 52, 54
  U.S.A. as, 121
Crown Colonies, 13
Crowther, Geoffrey, writer and journalist, 187
'cruzeiros', 165
Cuba, 42, 43; Cuban sugar, 162
Currencies
  black market in, 138
  blocked, 23, 25–6, 156, 190
  Bretton Woods monetary proposals' main concern with, 8, 128, 190
  convertible, 167, 409; gold convertible currencies, 55
  currency agreements, 5
  currency stabilisation loans from Bank for Reconstruction and Development, 55
  hard currencies, 273 n 5
  under International Monetary Fund, 132, Article V, 125, 403–5; interconvertibility, 8, 11, 13, under Article VIII, 114, 134–5, 137–8, 159, 161, 162, 164–5, 168, 182, 407–8, in redrafted Article, 155; let-out for currency reserves, 120, other limitations, 150, 317; alterations to par value, 45, under Article IV, 402–3, and under Clearing Union plan, 290
  national currencies: under gold standard, 17–18, 'linked to gold' under I.M.F., 85; under Bank for Reconstruction and Development, 73; need for link with international currency, 39, 195
  paper currency, 53
  valued in terms of composite commodity, 35, 37, 38
  see also Bilateralism; Convertibility; Depreciation; Gold; International currency; money; scarce currencies
Current payments, *see under* Article VIII of Article of Agreement (I.M.F.)
Currie, Lauchlin, Foreign Economic Administration, 240
Curtin, John, Prime Minister of Australia, 3
Customs Unions, 249–50, 251, 376
Cyclical
  changes in balance of trade, 302
  changes in employment levels, 296
  Trade cycle, 13
  see also under Fluctuations
Czechoslovakia
  and International Monetary Fund: on

Drafting Committee, 42, 43; at Bretton Woods, 55; at Savannah, 215
  reparations, 397, 398; in Morgenthau's plan, 379; claim for war damage, 329, 351
  tariff union with East Germany and Poland, proposed for, 375

Daily Express, 178
Dalton, Hugh
  President of Board of Trade in Coalition Government (before July 1945), 311; reparations plan, 334, 337, 'Notes' on, 335–6
  Chancellor of Exchequer in Labour Government (from August 1945), 219, 237; Report on Savannah Conference addressed to, 220–38
Dawes Loan, 369–70
Debtor countries
  under Bank for Reconstruction and Development, 105
  in Clearing Union scheme, 249
  under International Monetary Fund, 55, 125, 130, 159, 182
Default, on Bank for Reconstruction and Development loans, 52, 53, 75, 76
Deflation, 16
de Kock, M. H., Deputy Governor of South African Bank, 231
Democratic Party, U.S.A., 63, 82
Denmark, 23–4
  bacon factories, 274
Depreciation
  of currencies, 5; under I.M.F., 65, 127, 138, 143, 151, protected from competitive depreciation, 85, 189
  of exchanges, to correct balance of trade, 150, 283–4, 289–304; *vs* quotas, 287–9, 292
Depressions, 169, 192. *See also* Slumps
Deshmukh, Sir Chintaman, Governor of Bank of India: member of Indian Delegation at Atlantic City, 56, 80, at Savannah, 231
Deutsch, J. J., member of Canadian Delegation to Atlantic City, 56, 58, at Bretton Woods, 125
Development loans: under Bank for Reconstruction and Development, 53, 73, 104–5; uncertain position under International Monetary Fund, 195
Diamonds, 351
Disarmament, of Germany, 348, 349, 371, 376;

Disarmament, of Germany (*cont.*)
  total demilitarisation, 337–41; effect on
    her Budget, 338, 339, 357–8
Discrimination
  Article VII (Mutual Aid) non-discrimina-
    tory trade agreement, 132, 133, 292,
    314, 315, 316
  Bretton Woods 'non-discriminatory trade
    and currency policy', 190, under Article
    VIII, 408; commitment accepted by
    U.K., except for preferences, 256,
    259–60, 309, 315, and other planning
    practices, 310
  and bulk-purchasing, 308, 310
  Commercial Agreement with U.S.A. (1938)
    forbids, 313, 315, 316
  I.M.F. members committed to refrain
    from, 12, 23, 132, except during transi-
    tional period, 24, 136, 317, or in case of
    scarce currency, 192
  non-discriminating import regulation, 307,
    313, 314, 317; in Meade's Commercial
    Union plan, 273 n 5, 274, 275–8, 280–2
  support for discriminatory commercial and
    currency agreements in Press and Parlia-
    ment, 314–17
  U.K. policy always opposed to, 305
Disequilibrium, *see* Equilibrium
Dismemberment
  'Dismemberment of Germany, The' (26
    February 1945), 384–6
  'Dismemberment Proposals, The' (27
    February 1945), 386–7
  'Dismemberment, Reparations and' (9
    March 1945), 387–9
Dollars
  'compensated dollar', 31
  convertibility into, under Article VIII
    (I.M.F.), 116–17, 121–2, 125, 126–7,
    136, 138, 162, 165, under Article V, 125
  dollar influence and I.M.F., 207
  frozen dollar securities, 332
  and gold convertibility, 143
Domestic policy
  and domestic demand, 267, 306
  under I.M.F., 7, 18, 403; power to control
    domestic rate of interest, 16–17
  'new model' (1944), 19
Dominica, 42
Dominions
  discussions on Article VII, commercial
    policy (1944), 3, 283, 304, 324; reaction
    to Overton Report (1942), 252, 257, 264;
    under Meade's Commercial Union pro-

ject, 276; interests ignored in Anglo-
    American talks (1945), 324
  as sterling area countries, 12
  talks on I.M.F. proposals (1944), 20, on
    Bank for Reconstruction and Develop-
    ment, 48; representatives at Atlantic City,
    56, 58, 62
  see also Australia; Canada; India; New
    Zealand
Dominions Secretary, *see* Stanley, Oliver
Drafting Committee, *see under* International
  Monetary Fund
draftsmen, 96
Drozniak, Governor of the Bank of Poland: at
  Savannah, 231
Dunn, Mr, of the State Department, U.S.A.,
  347
Dutch
  delegation at Bretton Woods, 96
  Government (Netherlands), 328
  shares taken over by Germany, 329
  soldiers, to police postwar Germany, 379

Eady, Sir Wilfrid, Second Secretary,
  Treasury, 24, 43, 126, 173
  at Atlantic City, 54 n 12, 56, 63, 82; talks
    with Indian representatives, 79–80
  at Bretton Woods, 92, 108, 123; takes
    charge of sections on management,
    109–10; role in deadlock over interpre-
    tation of Article VIII, 124, 141, 146, 160,
    168–71, 174, 184–5; conducts prelimi-
    nary discussions in Washington for
    I.M.F. inaugural meeting, 208, 209, 210
  in Canada, 210
  chairs War Cabinet Committee on Repara-
    tions, 389–90; paper on dismember-
    ment of Germany, 384
  conversations with Americans in London
    on commercial policy, 320; exchange of
    'notes' on, 320–3
  memoranda and minutes addressed to,
    25–6, 184–5, 248–50, 253–6, 320–1,
    322–3, 390; minute from, 321–2
  list of letters, 415
Eastern Europe, 386
Eccles, David McAdam, Ministry of Production: on steel production, 270–1
  list of letters, 415
'Economic Aspects of Security' (September
  1943), 370–3
Economic Consequences of the Peace, 400–1
Economic and Industrial Planning Staff
  (EIPS), 374, 383

Economic Journal
JMK as editor, 30, 34, 36, 38; succeeded by
Harrod (February 1945), 164
'The Objective of International Price
Stability' (JMK, note on Hayek's 'A
Commodity Reserve Currency'),
June–September 1943, 30–3, 38
'Keynes *vs* Hayek on a Commodity Reserve
Currency' (Frank Graham), December
1944, 36, 39; 'Note by Lord Keynes' on,
39–40
'A Plan for Germany's Economic Disarm-
ament' (Paul Einzig), June–September
1942, 336
Economic nationalism, 292
Economic security, post-war, 191–2, 334, 349.
See also Commercial policy
Economic and Social Council, *see* United
Nations Organisation
Economic theory, 240
Economic warfare, 85
Economist, 178; letter from JMK (29 July
1944), 84–5
Economists
American, 240–1, 400
and I.M.F., 101, 147; their lips sealed in the
service of Government, 178; as perma-
nent staff for Fund and Bank, 237, 238
'new doctrines' accepted by, 16
spring fever among, 291
views on cure for disequilibrium, 287
Ecuador, 42
Eden, Anthony, Foreign Secretary (before 25
July 1945), 90, 96, 323, 334
at Conference of Foreign Ministers,
Moscow (October 1943), 373; at Quebec
(September 1944), 375, 380
Education, 339, 357; in post-war Germany,
377–8
Efficiency: relation to money costs, 31, 32;
efficiency wages, 32, 37, 38
Egypt
and I.M.F., 42; representatives at Bretton
Woods, 83; at Savannah, 217, 231
sterling balances, 83, 117, 122
Einzig, Paul, American economist
'A Plan for Germany's Economic Dis-
armament' (*Economic Journal*, June–
September 1942), 336
article on I.M.F. in *The Financial Times* (23
August 1944), 124, 127; doubts on
drafting of Article IV raised by, 132, 133,
137–8, 142

Eisenhower, General, 400
Elasticity
of exchanges (or of reciprocal demand for
imports and exports), 288, 298–9,
299–303; under I.M.F., 57, *see also* 85
in loan policy of Bank for Reconstruction
and Development, 50
in relation of national to international currency, 39
and reparation figures, 360
Elliott, Walter, M.P., 2
Employment
and exchange rates, 293, 296, 297
in Germany, 363
import regulation to stabilise, 268
policy, 291
prospects under I.M.F., 105
see also Full employment; Unemployment
Enemy countries, 331, 332, 333, 348
Engineering industry, 262–3, 265–6;
German, 371
England
climate, 110, 214
ready for a new world, 214, 401
see also United Kingdom
Equated price system, 308–9, 310
Equilibrium
in balance of international payments, under
I.M.F., 14, 51, 130, 296; aided by Bank
for Reconstruction and Development,
73, 105, 109; impossible with American
subsidies, 318
in balance of trade, 285; short- and long-
term disequilibrium, 295
between exports and imports, post-war,
306–7
internal and external, under Monetary Proposals, 7; exchange adjustment to correct
disequilibrium, 33, 45, 79, 169, 287–8,
402–3
see also Balance of Payments
Escape (saving) clause
for abnormal war balances, 8, 22
on import restrictions, based on Clearing
Union plan, 254, 256, 257, 269, 282, 294,
301
waiver clause in Articles of Agreement,
I.M.F., *see* Article V
see also 'Let-out'
Ethiopia, 42; Vinson's stooge at Savannah,
217, 222
Europe
advantages to, of Bank for Reconstruction

Europe (*cont.*)
and Development, 48, 188; European Executive Directors, 228
at commercial policy talks (1945), 324
Delegations at Savannah, 230
as location of Fund headquarters, 94
occupied countries, 72
standard of life, 399
also mentioned, 101, 169, 276, 293, 362
see also Eastern Europe; Western Europe
European Advisory Commission (1943), 373–4
European Allies, *see* Allies, European
'European Reparations' (19 September 1941), 328–30
Exchange Adjustment Clause (I.M.F.), 43 n 9, 44, 46; U.K.'s provisional acceptance, 47; Catto's proposed revised clause, 44–5, 55, 57; discussed at Atlantic City, 64–6, 78–9; version presented to Commission I, 83; agreement reached with Americans, 92, 93; Australian view, 98
see also Article IV
Exchange control
under Article VII (Mutual Aid), 294
under Article VIII (I.M.F.): British, 119–20, 126, 135–7, 141, 143–4, 152, 161; general, 126–7, 136, 144, 154–5, 159, 182, 183, 407–8
and control of capital movements (Article VI), 131, 144, 406
in draft Commercial Convention, 322
also mentioned, 235, 296
Exchange equalisation, 291
Exchange rates
under Articles of Agreement (I.M.F.), 139–40, 150, 169
under Clearing Union plan, 32–3, 34
flexible, 296; *see also under* Depreciation
optimum level, 283–4
Exchanges
adjustment, to keep internal and external equilibrium, 7, 33
in American Bankers' plan, 187
Bretton Woods' concern with, 128
British procedure for supporting, 178
free exchange for members of Bank for Reconstruction and Development, 75
'Live and Let Live' on, 136
under I.M.F.:
Article IV, 127, 133, 162, 402–3; intention disputed, 135, 137, 138–40, 142–3, 170–1

Article VIII, agreement to refrain from discriminating practices, 12, 23, 137, 165, 166, 203, 407; restrictions permissible during transitional period (Articles VII, XXII), 58, 172, 175, 407, 408–9; difference with Robertson on, 118–19, 122–3, 137–8, appeal to White for clarification, 143–5
Article XI, 139
procedure for altering, 5, 14–15, 85; safeguards against rigidity, 189
spot transactions, 402
stability, 33, 125, 162, 200, 296, 402; *vs* elasticity, difference with U.S. on, 57, 65–6
also mentioned, 235, 290
see also Black Market; Parity of exchange
Expansionist policy, 2
under Article I (I.M.F.), 200–1, Article VI, 406
under Article VII (commercial policy), 306–7, 310
of Bank for Reconstruction and Development, 73, 104, 194
for British business overseas, 285–6, for export industries, 4
urged by Committee of Economic Development, 206
Experts
at conversations on Commercial Policy (June 1944), 304, 310, 326, for Anglo-American Loan, 327
responsible for drawing up Joint Statement on the Establishment of an International Monetary Fund, 4, 6, 19, 20–1; Indian, 116–17
for reparations control, 395
as staff members of Bank for Reconstruction and Development, and I.M.F., 15, 75, 207, 225
'technical' group at Bretton Woods, 193
Export-Import Bank, 206, 233; tied loans, 229
Chairman, 197, 212, 233
Export industries, 4; export drive, 300
Export trade
and Article VIII, 183–4
costs, and exchange depreciation, 299
a necessity to U.K., 29–30
Exporting countries, exporters
and Bank for Reconstruction and Development, 75
under International Monetary Fund, 161, 164–5, 190

Exporting countries, exporters (*cont.*)
   and proposed import licences, 274–5, 277–8
Exports
   British, 229; post-war expansion, 7, 254,
      306; export productive capacity, 239
   credit for, 58
   and I.M.F., 8, 12–13, 22–3; under Article
      VIII, 114, 116; and recourse to I.M.F.
      funds, 201
   German, *see under* Germany
   relation of foreign price to total receipts for,
      289, to total value, 303–4
   subsidies for, 248; in Overton Report, 252,
      254–6, 262, opposed in minority report,
      256, 260; American, 318
   see also Balance of trade; Trade
Exports and imports
   demand and supply for, and market mech-
      anism, 292–5
   effect on, of exchange depreciation, 298–9
   post-war programmes for, 306–7, 308, 310
   and rate of exchange, 288
   reciprocal arrangements for: under Bretton
      Woods Plan, 128–9; not permissible
      under Article VII, 314–15; and 'com-
      mercial considerations', 320, 322
   U.K., relative make-up, 265–6
   see also Balance of payments
Ezekiel, Mordecai, American economist, 240

Factories
   contents of, and reparations, 331, 342, 343,
      351, 364
   foreign-owned, in Germany, 369
Federal Reserve Bank, New York, 211, 222;
      talks with British Delegation at, 221
Federal Reserve Board, 21, 61, 161, 169;
      rivalry with New York Federal Reserve
      Bank, 211, 222
   Chairman of the Board, 197, 212, 233
Finance
   financial controls of post-war Germany,
      372–3
   'financial terms' and commercial policy,
      321–2; finance negotiations become in-
      volved in commercial issue, 327
   financiers, 66, 101
   and National Advisory Council, 212,
      233
Financial News, 27
Financial Times, The, 124
Finletter, Mr, 347
Fisher, Irving, compensated dollar, 31

Fleming, John Marcus, Economic Section,
      Cabinet office: 'Quotas *vs* Depreciation'
      (February 1944), comments on, 287–9,
      290; correspondence on market mechan-
      ism *vs* interventionism, 291–304
   list of letters, 415
Fluctuations
   long- and short-term, 37
   seasonal, cyclical and emergency, and
      I.M.F. loans, 199–204
Food
   bulk purchase of, 22, 25–6, 274
   imports (U.K.), 265, 293; war-time, 290
   in post-war Germany, 290, 366; excluded
      from reparation payments, 343, 396, 397
   see also Butter; Wheat
Foreign Economic Aid (F.E.A.), 45
Foreign Ministers' Conference (October
      1943), Moscow, 373–4
Foreign Office, 90, 236, 330, 380
Foreign Secretary, *see* Eden, Anthony
France
   campaign in (1944), 62 n
   Colonia system, 309
   Delegates at Savannah, 215, 218, 226, 231,
      views on pay of international civil ser-
      vants, 224, 225
   President of the Republic, 224
   reparation claims, 329, 332, 393, 397, 398;
      status as an Allied country, 331; in
      Morgenthau's plan for Germany, 376,
      379
   wages agreements (Matignon, 1936), 294
   see also French Committee
Free market, and exchanges, 122, 126–7, 136,
      161
Free trade, 132, 250; Overton Report biased
      in favour of, 251, 253, 255, 258; U.K.
      qualified support for, 259–60
Free will, 14, 23; voluntary action, 24,
      26
Freedom, 143
French Committee: represented on Drafting
      Committee for I.M.F., 42; at Bretton
      Woods, 85, 231
Fuel, Ministry of, 264
Full employment
   and money-wages, 33, 37–8
   U.K. committed to, 4–5, 7, 132; I.M.F. an
      aid to, 19
   in U.S.A., 189, 191
'Fund', term preferred to 'Bank' for Recon-
      struction and Development Bank, 55

INDEX

Gambling, Mr, and his girls at Bretton Woods, 107–8, 110

Gardner, W. R., U.S.A. Delegation at Atlantic City, 65, 124

German Control Commission, 388, 394

Germany

capacity to pay, 332, 352, 359–62, 366, 368, 389, 398

deindustrialisation, 142; ruled out by Interdepartmental Committee on Reparations and Economic Security, 348–9; Morgenthau's 'pastoralisation' plan, 375, 376–9, comments on, 380–2; Hoover's view, 399–400

demilitarisation, plan for, 337–40; disarmament, 357–8, under Atlantic Charter, 348–9, 371; in Morgenthau's plan, 376

dismemberment, question of: not included in Malkin Report (1943), 346, 348; not discussed at Foreign Ministers' Conference, 373; considered at Teheran, 374; Report on, by Economic and Planning Staff (1944), 374; JMK's early view, 374–5, later view, 382–3; memoranda on, 384–9; in Morgenthau's plan, 381; reparations and, 391, 398; Yalta agreement on partition, 383

Einzig's 'Plan for Germany's Economic Disarmament', 336

exports, to pay for peace costs, 339–41, 344, 358, 361, 363, 366–7, 396, to pay for necessary imports, 396, 399; imports, 340, 372, 387–8, 398

German aggression, 341, 357, 368, 370–1

Government, 339, 365, 366; proposed Declaration to be made by, 341–6

industrial efficiency, 360; iron works, 267; engineering industry, 371; synthetic materials, 372

pre-war claims on, 367–70

reparations, see Reparations

retreat in 1918, 100

standard of living, 344, 349, 363, 385, 398; Churchill's statement on, 388; Potsdam agreement on, 399

transfer of territory from, 342, 348, 356, 360, 373, 388–9; in Morgenthau's plan, 377; Potsdam agreement on, 398

'Germany's Contribution to the cost of Keeping the Peace of the World' (21 December 1942), 337–41

Gilbert, Sir Bernard William, Second Secretary, Treasury, 82

Gold

'a barbarous relic', 16, 85, see also 132

buying and selling countries, 170–1, 290; under Article IV, 137, 139, 402, Article V, 405

as collateral security (I.M.F.), 404

drain of, to creditor countries, 14, 32, 189

exchange rates fixed in terms of, 34, 38, 39; under Clearing Union plan, 35; currencies linked to, under IMF, 85

export of, to correct balance of trade, 295

gold convertibility, 143; 'gold convertible' currencies, 55

gold quotas, under Article V, 131, 404–5, 408; holders of, 40, 85, 332

as monetary reserves, 85; under Article XIX, 167, 409

option to redeem foreign-held balances in, under Article VIII, 116 n, 127, 134

production of, 35, 40, 85

restitution of, by Germany, 342, 343, 345, 346, 351, 361, 393, 396; of frozen gold securities, 332; retained for German relief, 367, 396

and scarce currencies, 407

subscriptions in, for Bank for Reconstruction and Development, 49, 50, 54, 75; as guarantees for Bank bonds, 75

transactions in, under Article VII, 407

Gold reserves, 35, 49; under Article VIII (I.M.F.), 150–1, 157, 165, 176, 408

Gold and Silver Commission (1887), 195

Gold standard

effect on prices, 30–1, and on wages, 31–2, 33

International Monetary Fund not a return to, 2, 17–18, 27, 28; U.S. view, 57; Bevin's view, 205

JMK bitterly opposed to, 17, misquoted on, 84–5

in Low cartoon, 95

Goldenweiser, Emanuel Alexander, economist, Federal Reserve System, 65–6

Gordon, Donald, Canadian Treasury, 113

Governments

44 represented at Bretton Woods, 40; location of I.M.F. to be decided by, 88–90, 91; European Governments and Washington as h.q., 212; proposals for payment of national executives of Bank and Fund, 218–19, 224

economists in the service of, 178

international loans guaranteed by, 188

433

Governments (*cont.*)
monopoly of exchange dealings, 126, 136
powers under proposed Commercial
Union, 249, 252, 275
see also National sovereignty; *and under*
separate countries
Graham, Benjamin, American economist, 34,
35; views on buffer stocks, 38, 40
letter to (31 December 1943), 36–8
Graham, Professor Frank, American
economist
comments on article by JMK in *Economic
Journal* (June–September 1943), 34–6
'Keynes *vs* Hayek on a Commodity Reserve
Currency' (*Economic Journal*, December 1944), 39; 'Note by Lord Keynes'
on, 39–40
Greece
and I.M.F., 42, 43, 195
in Morgenthau's plan for Germany, 379
war damage, 329; reparations, 397, 398
Gregory, Sir T. E., member of Indian Delegation at Atlantic City, 56, 57, 58, at
Bretton Woods, 80
Gridley, Sir Arnold, M.P., 1
Groups, political and geographical, for commercial policy arrangements, 249–50,
251, 259–60
Guarantees: for Bank for Reconstruction and
Development loans, 50–1, 54, 55, 73–7;
guarantee commission, 51–2; guarantee
fund, 55
Guatemala, 42; delegates at Savannah, 217;
Mr Vinson's stooge, 222
Guest, Keen and Baldwins, Port Talbot steel
works, 270
Gutt, Camille, former Belgian Finance Minister: proposed as Managing Director for
I.M.F., 238

Haiti, 42
Halifax, Lord, U.K. Ambassador in Washington, 59, 241, 242
Hammersley, S. S., Conservative M.P., 1, 187
Hannon, Sir P. J. H., leader of Birmingham
group of M.P.s, 187
Hansard, 26, 28
Hansen, Alvin, American economist, 240;
delegate, Atlantic City, 66
Harriman, William Averell, 347
Harrod, Roy, succeeds JMK as editor of
Economic Journal (February 1945), 164
Hawkins, Harry, U.S. State Department, 64

Hawkins Conversations on post-war commercial policy in Washington, 172, 173,
175, 242, 243, 245; in London (January
1945), 320–1, 322, 326
Hayek, F. A.
'A Commodity Reserve Currency' (*Economic Journal*, June–September 1943),
30, 36; note on ('The Objective of International Price Stability', JMK), 30–3
'commodity standard', 31, 35, 39, 40
Health service, 338, 357
Henderson, Sir Hubert
comments on Drafting Queries paper
(JMK), built on a mare's nest, 140–1
minority report on Overton Committee
commercial proposals, 250, discussed by
JMK, 253–6; JMK's 'half way' position
on, 256, agrees on keeping quantitative
control of imports, 257–8, 273, 284;
Committee's rejoinder, 261
letter to Meade on import licences, 279;
letter from D. H. Robertson, 289
takes part in discussions on reparations, 330
also mentioned, 297, 302, 310
list of letters, 415
Hermann Goering Iron Works, 267, 269, 272
Hinchinbrook, Lord, M.P., 2
History, 383
Hoarding, 31
Holland
frozen and liquid assets, 332
and I.M.F., 42, 43
possible tariff union with Belgium, 375
war damage and reparation claims, 329,
351, 397, 398
see also Dutch; Netherlands
Honduras, 42; representatives at Savannah,
217
Hoover, Calvin Bryce, Economic Adviser,
U.S. Group Control Commission in
Germany: Report on Potsdam reparations policy, 399–401
list of letters, 415
Hopkins, Sir Richard, Permanent Secretary,
Treasury, 59, 105, 113, 162, 241
memoranda addressed to, 43–7, 304–10,
311–12
minutes: from Brand, 113; to Sir John
Anderson, 310–11; telegram to, 93
list of letters, 415
House of Commons
and International Monetary Fund: debate
on Joint Statement (May 1944), 3–4, 6,

House of Commons (*cont.*)
   7, 27, 28; opposition to commercial
      proposals, 28–9; unlikely to accept
      Articles without redrafting, 134, 149,
      151, 173, 174; question of further debate,
      155, 158; views on management, 207
   taught by JMK to hate gold, 132
   see also M.P.s; Parliament
House of Lords
   speech by JMK on post-war policies (16
      May 1944), 4–6
   debate on International Monetary Fund,
      monetary proposals (23 May 1944), 6–8,
      26–7, 40; speech by JMK, 9–21; alter-
      cation with Lord Balfour of Burleigh,
      21–3, 24, 25–6
   opposition to I.M.F. commercial proposals,
      27, 28–9
   talks with Members on I.M.F., 179, 187
   see also Parliament
Housing, 339, 357, 378
   bricks and building labour as reparations,
      343, 361, 364, 365, 396, 397
Hull, Cordell, U.S. Secretary of State: state-
      ment on U.S. foreign trade policy, 20;
      negotiations on I.M.F. commercial
      policy, 304, 315 n 8, 316; at Foreign
      Ministers Conference in Moscow, 373

Iceland, 42
Ilsley, James Lorimer, Canadian Minister of
      National Revenue: at Bretton Woods,
      71, 80; at Savannah, 230
Imperial
   preference, 260, 276, 309–10
   sentiment, 27, 28
   trade, 23
Import restrictions
   under Commercial Agreement with U.S.
      (1938), 313, 315
   correspondence with Meade on (1942),
      272–82; memorandum, 284–7
   in Draft Statement of Principles, 307, 310
   vs exchange depreciation, 288–91
   import licences, 128; discriminatory,
      during transitional period, 136, 314;
      under Article VIII, 184; in Meade's
      Commercial Union scheme, 274–5,
      277–9, 281–2, 'ad valorem', 282
   quantitative: in Overton Report, 253,
      257–8, 262, 264, 265; preferable to
      tariffs, 258, or other system of import
      control, 325–6; non-discriminatory, 259,

260, 314, 317, 325–6; under escape
      clause based on Clearing Union plan,
      254, 256, 257, 269, 282; to support
      balance of trade, 261; to foster new
      industries, 266–9
   by quota, 248, 263; 'The Protective Inci-
      dence of Import Quotas' (Fleming),
      281–2
Importers, 162, 167, 274; importing countries,
      266
Imports
   of capital, 295
   demand for, in a trade cycle, 13
   German, *see under* Germany
   loans for, from Bank for Reconstruction
      and Development, 50
   for relief, I.M.F. funds not available for,
      200
   U.K., need for post-war reductions, 254,
      264
   see also Exports and imports
India, 42, 162
   delegates at Atlantic City, 55, 56, 58; at
      Bretton Woods, 71, 79–80, 117; at Savan-
      nah, 218, good relations with British,
      231; quota problem, 58, 69, 79; sterling
      balances problem, 71, 83, 85, 116–17,
      121–2
   views on commercial policy, 252, 257; in-
      vited to talks on (1945), 324
   war effort, 86
Indian Civil Service, 208–9
Industry
   Bank for Reconstruction and Development
      loans for, 104–5
   German, 371–3, 376, 377–9 *passim*, 398;
      manpower for, through demilitarisation,
      338, 357
   industrial countries, 36, 264, 297
   new (infant) industries, 249, 252, 257, 268
   in Report of Overton Committee, 257, 262,
      265, 267–8
   see also Engineering; Manufactures; Trade
Inflation, 16, 66, 201, 293; distinguished from
      expansion, 73; inflationary spiral, 294
Insurance, 76; Social Insurance, 338, 357
Inter-Allied Commission, 372
Inter-Departmental Committee on Repara-
      tion and Economic Security, 337, 339,
      347, 374; recommendations, 348–73
Interest
   on Bank for Reconstruction and Develop-
      ment bonds, 109

Interest (*cont.*)

and commission on Bank for Reconstruction and Development loans, 51–2, 55, 76

on I.M.F. long-term loans, 203

see also Loans; Rate of interest

International co-operation, in the economic field, 4, 7, 13, 21; Bretton Woods' success as, 6, 14, 109, continued at Savannah, 214, 221; no idea of, among Americans, 217; proposed U.K. office for, 235

Marshall's optimism on, 195

'internationalism', 29

International currency, 10, 31, 32–3, 38−9

International finance, 211, 221, 229; shareholding in German industry, 373

International financial co-operation, Commission III at Bretton Woods for, 71

International investment, 52–3, 54, 55

International Investment Institution, 19; International Investment Bank, 297

International Monetary Fund (I.M.F.)

'Joint Statement by Experts on the Establishment of an International Monetary Fund', published as White Paper (April 1944), 1, 4–6; 'The Monetary Proposals', 1–3; debate on, in House of Commons, 3–4, in House of Lords, 9–23

preparations for Monetary Conference (May 1944), 40; 'The Monetary Conference', 41–3; Treasury discussions, 43; 'Conference on International Monetary Fund' (June), 43–7; instructions to British Delegation, 47

Atlantic City, Drafting Conference, 40, 41–3, 55–62, 64–70; Boat Drafts, 55, 64, 65, 68; drafting queries (September 1944), 134–40; 'Textual Doubts', 140–1; 'The Bretton Woods Draft of I.M.F.' (October), 142–6; memorandum on (December), 146–54; proposed re-draft of Article VIII, 155; 'Bretton Woods (Interpretation of Article VIII)' (January 1945), 156–9; 'history of the drafting problem', 160, 162, 170–2, 174–5, 182–3

at Bretton Woods (July 1944), 70–1, 77–83, 85, 87–96; JMK's opening address, 72–7; JMK misrepresented on purpose of Monetary Fund, 84–5; Conference extended, 96

Commission I (for I.M.F.), 71, 83, 97; statement by JMK, 86–7; Report, 98, 99, seconded by JMK, 100–1

Executive Plenary Session, statement by JMK, 99–100; Final Act, moved by JMK (22 July), 101–3; statement on Conference for BBC (JMK and White), 103–5; JMK signs Final Act for U.K., 154

post-Bretton Woods changes, 232–3

and Congress, *see under* United States of America: Congress

information furnished to Fund, 198

location: difference with U.S. on, 87, 88–92, 94, 96, 206; U.K. prefers New York to Washington, 211–12; Washington decided on, 218, 220

management, 15, 55, 69–70, 109, 168–9, 220–1, 225

Alternates, 215, 218–19, 223, 226, 227, 228, 234–5

Assembly, 15

Executive Directors, 70, 206–9, 218–19, 220, 224, 226–8, 234; role, 222–3, representatives, not delegates, 207; American, 194, 197, 212, 228, 229; British, 210, 234–7; Executive Board, 204

Governors, 215, 220, 237, 'ornamental personages' only, 197, 221; American, 196–7; British, 234–5, (JMK), 206, 210; Board of Governors, 70, 88, 89, 91, 185, 197, 202, annual meeting, 226, Chairman, 226; Executive, or Steering Committee, 226; JMK Vice-chairman, 226

Managing Director, 206–7, 208, 212–13, 221, 237–8

President, 212–13, 237

remuneration, 213, 218–19, 223–6, 236–7

Secretariat, 141, 145–6, American, 170; staff of international civil servants, 220–1, 223, 237, British, 234, 238

member nations: 44 represented at Bretton Woods, 40, 41, 63, 72, 83, 89, 103, 206–7; relations with Americans, 106; language and other problems, 107; applause for JMK, 112–13; rights and obligations: sovereign rights on exchange regulation, 34, 93, on international capital movements, 115; obligation to prevent black market in foreign currency, 133, 170. *See also* under Articles of Agreement, 402–10

Non–Members, 139

'Note on the International Monetary Fund (An Essay in Rabbinics)' (Robertson), 114–17; 'A Note on a Note...' (JMK),

I.M.F. (*cont.*)

118–21, 122; rejoinder, 'I.M.F.', 124–7

philosophy of Fund, 123, 135, 141, 166; American 'idea' of, 65

quotas, 47, 58, 130, 131, 205; British share of aggregate, 13, 69, 286; differences on, 69, 79, 98; and location of Fund, 87, 88; Quota Agreement (Low cartoon), 95; under Article V, 403, 404–5

recourse to funds, 199–204; purpose of Fund under Article I, 200, 204; for aid in cyclical fluctuations, 13, under proposed American amendment, 199–204; conditions governing use of funds (Article V), 403–5; not intended for large capital transactions, 9, 144, 406, nor for relief or war debts, 13, 87, 199–200, 205, 408–9; 'the place of last resort', 130, 131 exhaustion of drawing rights, 115, 116, 157, 172, 176, 184; suspension, 47, 66, 135, 150; ineligibility, 79, 406

in relation to commercial policy, 286, 302, 325, 409

repurchase of currency, 404–5

service charges, 130, 405, 409

subscriptions, 55, 73, 122–3

withdrawal from Fund, 65, 68, 78–9, 139, 409

see also Articles of Agreement; Atlantic City; Bretton Woods; Exchange Adjustment Clause; Savannah Conference; Scarce currencies; Voting power

International police force, proposal for, 337, 339, 358; for policing of Germany, 379, 380

International Purchasing and Selling Combinations, 249

International Zone, 389; in Morgenthau's plan, 376, 377

Intuition, 15

Investment

domestic, and I.M.F., 201

foreign: under terms of Articles of Agreement, 9, 286, 409; through Bank for Reconstruction and Development, 52–3, 54, 55, 74, 104–5; through International Investment Bank, 297

investment market, 74; American, 213

see also Loans

Invisible exports, 301; income, 172

Iran, 42

Iraq, 42

Iron

iron ore, low- and high-grade, 267–8, 269–71

iron and steel works, 268, 271; German, 267, 269

pig, and scrap iron, 270

see also Steel

Iron ration, 13, 157, 176

Isolationism

in U.K., 3, 6; economic, 192

in U.S.A., 81, 82, 91, 251, 257

Italy

applies for membership of I.M.F. and Bank for Reconstruction and Development, 229

as an ex-enemy country, 341, 393

Japan: entry into war, 356; attack on Pearl Harbour, 59; as an Axis country, 341

Jebb, Hubert Miles Gladwyn, Head of Reconstruction Department, U.S.A., 337

Joint Statement by Experts on the Establishment of an International Monetary Fund, White Paper (April 1944), 1, 45–6, 47, 55, 125, 127; discussed with European Allies, 3; debate on, in House of Lords, 4, 6, in Commons, 65; agreement on, with U.S. Treasury, 44

see also International Monetary Fund

Journalists, 101, 187

see also Press

Jugoslavia, 42, 397, 398

Kahn, Richard F., Ministry of Supply, 217, 272; comments on Meade's memorandum, 283–4

list of letters, 415

Kelchner, Mr, convener at Savannah Conference, 216

'Key-currency', 160, 162, 168

Keynes, John Maynard (Lord Keynes, JMK)

activities: 1941: in Washington, Lend Lease discussions, 239, 242, 243, 245, 246, 247; later discussions in London, 245–6

(September) discussions on Reparations, 330–4

1942–3: contributions to commercial policy discussions, 248–50, 251–3, 253–60, 262–5, 268–9

(November–August 1943) member, Inter-Departmental Committee on Reparation and Economic Security, 337–46

Keynes, John Maynard (*cont.*)

1943: (September) Article VII talks, Washington, 346; speech to State Department on reparations, 346–73

1944: (April), meetings with M.P.s on I.M.F. proposals, 1–3, 25; discussions with European Allies, 3; (May), speeches on Joint Statement in Lords, 4–6, 9–21, exchange with Lord Balfour, 22–3; (June), paper on Article VII conversation, 304–10, memorandum to Hopkins, 311–12

leads Delegation to Bretton Woods (June–July), 47, 54 n 12, 310; on the *Queen Mary*, 55, 61, 64; in New York, 55, 59–60; at Atlantic City Drafting Conference, 56–8, 60–2, 64–70; at Bretton Woods, 71, 77–84, 88–92, 170–2, 182–3; chairman of Commission II (Bank), 70, 71, 83, 87–8, opening remarks (3 July), 72–7; misrepresented on I.M.F. and gold standard, 84–5; statement on sterling balances, 86–7; gets Conference extended, 96; crisis over Bank for International Settlement, 96–8; Statement at Executive Plenary Session (20 July), 98, 99–100; seconds Report on Bank (21 July), 100–1; moves Final Act (22 July), 101–3, 112, signs for U.K., 154; Statement on Bank and Fund for B.B.C., 103–5; report to Chancellor of Exchequer on Bretton Woods, 105–8, to Hopkins, 108–9

concluding 'love feast', 112; tribute to JMK, 112–13; 'in at the official birth', 209

(July–August), in Ottawa, 113, 117, 123–4

(September), raises drafting queries with Treasury, 134–40, with Chancellor of Exchequer, 140–1, with Americans, 142–6, 148–55, 177; letter to Morgenthau, 156–9, 161–3, 171, 175–7, 182, 183–5 contributions to commercial policy discussions, 312–17, 320, 323–6

(October–December), Stage II negotiations, Washington, 142, 146, 153, 178, 186, 317–19, 375, 382; talk with Roosevelt, 382

1945: (February), talks at Chatham House on I.M.F., 164, 179, 187, with members of House of Lords, 179, 185, 187, 192, briefs Chancellor of Exchequer for talks with M.P.s, 188–92

(March), member, official committee on reparations, 389–90, 398–9, drafts instructions, 390–8; later disengages himself from reparations policy, 400–1

(Spring and summer), takes part in commercial talks, 323–6

(June), Stage III negotiations, Washington, 206; (Autumn), Anglo-American Loan discussions, Keynes Mission, 326–7

1946: (March), leads Delegation to Savannah Conference, 209–10, 214, 217–18; on the *Queen Mary*, 209n, 210; stops off at Washington, 210–13, 221; attends Inaugural Meeting of Bank and Fund, as British Governor of both, 206, 210, speech (9 March), 215–17; Vice-Chairman, Executive Committee, 226; statement on remuneration of Directors and Alternates, 218–19; concluding speech in opposition, 222; cheered unanimously at the end, 232 n 50; report to Chancellor of Exchequer on Conference, 220–38

broadcast, 103–5

health, 59, 70, 82–3; signs of strain, 83, 84, worried press reports, 97 n 25, 98; a heart attack, 107; advised to get into a warm climate, 209

opinions; cocktail parties, 110–11; gold standard, 17, 85, 132; lawyers, 68, 102; unemployment as an economic weapon, 16–17; 'the voice of Authoritarians and Totalitarians', 290; World War I reparations policy, 400–1

personal: celebrates Concordat between King's College, Cambridge, and New College, Oxford, 71, and 250th Anniversary of foundation of Bank of England, 113

in Low cartoon, 95

tour of Belgium in 1918, 100

works: *Economic Consequences of the Peace*, 400

Keynes, Lydia, wife of JMK: with JMK in U.S.A., 59, 71, 82, concern for his health, 70, 98, 209

King's College, Cambridge, 71

Labour

conditions of, in the post-war world, 73, 104

labourers' services as reparations, 343, 361, 362, 365, 384, 388, 392, 396, 398, forced labour, 365, 377, 392, 398; problem of valuation, 391, 394, 395–6

Labour M.P.s, 187
labour circles, 38
Laissez-faire
a dead world, not likely to be resurrected, 264
equilibrium between imports and exports not secured by, 306
intermediate policy between Russian state trading and, recommended, 307–8
and Meade's import licences scheme, 275
Overton draft report based on, 253
Pasvolsky's belief in, 239, 240; Fleming's vestigial belief, 288–9, 291; Robertson's pockets of, 289
in World War I reparations policy, 335
Latin-American countries, and I.M.F.: vote-pooling for management, 226; experts appointed as Executive Directors, 228; representatives at Savannah, 232, 238
Law Mission on Article VII, in Washington (Autumn 1943), 283, 346
Law, Richard Kidston, head of Law Mission, 346, 347
Lawyers, 101, 102, 161
American, 68, 70, 78, 169
company law, 273
legal advisers at Bretton Woods, 102, 138; problem of legal interpretation of Articles of Agreement, 140, 151–2, 158, 177, 182, 200–1
League of Nations, Economic Committee, 234
Lee, Frank G., Treasury Representative in Washington, 59, 60
Lend-lease, 29
settlement terms under Article VII of Mutual Aid Agreement, 190, 239, 315, 346
Lend Lease Act, expiry date (30 June 1945), 319
Stage II negotiations on, 375
Lerner, Alec, 296
'Let-out' sentence in Article VIII, section 4(b), 150, 408; confusion over draft at Bretton Woods, 124–5, 154, 156, 160; difference with Robertson on, 115–16, 134, 135–7, 160–2, 165–6; American views, 144, 152; Chancellor of Exchequer's dilemma, approach to Morgenthau on, 151, 157–9, 168–9, 173, 175–7, 182, his reply, 183–4; suggested amendment, 153; in American Bretton Woods Bill, 202

Liberalism, 109
Liberated countries, 72, 104–5
Liberia, 42
Liesching, Percivale, Second Secretary, Board of Trade, 63
consulted on commercial policy talks, 310, 311–12; takes part in Anglo-American talks, London (January 1945), 320; leads team of Experts for trade discussions in Washington, 327
member, Inter-Departmental Committee on Reparations and Economic Security, 337
Little Englandism, 12
Livestock, and reparations, 331, 342, 343, 345, 356, 364, 393; pedigree, 351
Loans
American tied loans, 188
through Bank for Reconstruction and Development, 49–51, 73–5; guaranteed loans, 48, 49, 50–1, 75–7, 104; interest and charges under Guarantee Commission, 51–2, 53, 55, 76
untied loans, 54, 55, 109, 229, American, 188; stabilisation loans, 55, 194–5, 198, 229; for relief and reconstruction, 72, 104–5, 188, 198, 199; for world economic expansion, 73, 104; tied to overseas expenditure, 104–5; under proposals of American bankers, 189–90
for commercial purposes, 235
Export-Import Bank, tied loans, 229
International Investment Bank loans, 296–7
international loans guaranteed by governments, 188
I.M.F. funds not for permanent loans, 203–4
U.K. loan programme (1946), 210. *See also* Anglo-American Loan Agreement
see also Credit; Investment
Loftus, P. C., M.P., 2
London
Allied Governments in, 333
European Advisory Commission set up in, 373–4
as international financial centre, 9, 11, 12, 161, 191; money market, 126, 136; sterling balances in, 122–3, 125
as seat of Government, 318, 319–20; opposition to Fund, 90, 94, 108; criticism of Article VIII, 115–16, 119, 121; queries over interpretation, 142, 153; reports to, from Bretton Woods, 105, from Wash-

London (*cont.*)
  ington, 211, 317, from Savannah, 232; instructions from, 185
  talks in: Dominions discussions on Article VII, 3, further talks projected, 64; Anglo-American conversations, 318
  also mentioned, 55, 84, 146, 238
Long run, 386–7
Lord President of the Council, *see* Attlee, Clement
Lord Privy Seal, *see* Beaverbrook, Lord
Low, David: 'It can't be ours!', cartoon, 95
Luxemburg, 42
Luxford, Mr, U.S. legal adviser at Bretton Woods, 102, 146; advice on interpretation of Article VIII, 148–9, 154, 177, 182
Luxury, 29
Lyttelton, Oliver, 60; his gaffe, 59, 60

Macey, Miss, JMK's secretary in Atlantic City, 71, 82; in Washington, 102
Machine tools: as reparations, 343, 364; German machine tool industry, 371
Malaya, 230
Malkin, Sir William, Legal Adviser to Foreign Office: discussions on reparations policy (1941), 330, 333, 334
  chairman, Inter-Departmental Committee on Reparation and Economic Security, 337; Malkin Report, 346, 393, JMK's speech on, in Washington, 346–7, 348–73
  letter to, 346–7
Manufactures, 22
  advantages to, of Bank and Fund, 105
  British imports, 264; and exports, 265–6
  in Meade's Commercial Union scheme, 249
  semi-manufactured, 265, 266–8; as reparations, 343, 364, 396, 397, 398, finished products excluded, 343, 396, 397
  textiles, and export subsidies, 254–5; rayon, and tariffs, 264
Market mechanism, 291–2, 303–4
Marshall, Alfred
  Evidence before Gold and Silver Commission (1887), 195
  Tabular standard, 31
Matignon agreements on wages and cost of living, 294
Matthews, Mr, State Department, 347

Mayflower, 102
Meade, James E., Economic Assistant in Cabinet Office, 140, 293–4
  correspondence on Article VIII, 168, 173, 174; on import restrictions, 272–82
  member, Inter-Departmental Committee on Reparations and Economic Security, 337
  memoranda: 'The Post-War International Settlement and the U.K. Balance of Payments', 283–4; with JMK, 'Quantitative Regulation of Imports', 284–5
  'pockets' of *laissez-faire*, 289
  Project for a Commercial Union, adopted by Board of Trade (1942), 248, 250; assists in commercial policy discussions (1944), 304, 310, 311–12
  list of letters, 415–16
Melville, L. G., Australian delegate at Atlantic City, 56, 57, 69, at Bretton Woods, 112; observer at Savannah, 231
M.P.s, 314; meetings with JMK (April 1944), 1–2, 25, (February 1945), 164; meetings with the Chancellor of the Exchequer, 164, 177, 178–9, 187, 188
Mendés-France, Pierre, Minister of National Economy, leader of French Delegation at Bretton Woods and Savannah, 231
Mexico: represented on White's Drafting Committee, 42–3; Vinson's stooge at Savannah, 217, 222
Microphones, 101, 107
Monetary Agreement, *see* International Monetary Fund
Monetary authorities
  under Article IV (I.M.F.), 137, 402; Article VIII, 143, 185
  and Bank for Reconstruction and Development loans, 51
'Monetary and Commercial Bilateralism', exchange of views on, with Robertson, 24–6
'Monetary Conference, The', Memorandum (30 May 1944), 41–3. *See also* Bretton Woods; International Monetary Fund
Monetary Proposals (Plan), *see* International Monetary Fund
Money
  cheap, 17
  earmarked, 195
  flight of hot, 16, 296
  and international price stability, 5, 31–2
  money-stream, 290

Money (*cont.*)
see also Currencies; International currency; Quantity theory

Monick, Emmanuel Georges Michel, Governor of the Bank of France, 224

Monopoly
Government, of exchange dealings, 126, 136, 144–5
monopolistic bodies, 275
see also State trading

Morgenthau, Henry, Secretary, U.S. Treasury, 27, 102
I.M.F.: invites representatives of 44 Governments to Bretton Woods, 40, to be without commitment, 47, 63; calls Drafting Conference at Atlantic City, 40; President of Conference, 88; at Bretton Woods, 59, 87–8; negotiations with British Delegation, 90–2, 96–7, 173; problem of drafting queries, 154, 169, draft letter to, on interpretation of Article VIII, 156–9, 161, 162, 163, 168, letter as sent, 175–7, 178, 182; reply 183–4
personal relations with JMK, 81, 96, 98, 106, 187; correspondence on location of Fund, 88–90, 94–6, on Bank for International Settlement, 97
brings Fund and Bank before Congress, 147, 171, 181; accepts amendments to Bretton Woods Bill, 196
post-war Germany: concern with de-industrialising, 142; plan for 'pastoralisation', 375–9, 385, JMK on, 380–2
in Low cartoon, 95
list of letters, 416

Moscow, 108, 112
Allied Reparation Commission meet in (1945), 384, 392, 394
Foreign Ministers Conference (1943), 373–4

Most favoured nation (M.F.N.), 240, 276, 279, 280, 313

Motor-cars, 240, 254, 304; motor transport and reparations, 364; motoring expeditions in Canada, 113, 124

Multilateralism
commercial: and currency, 25–6, under Bretton Woods Agreement, 129, 190; advocated by JMK for post-war policy, 241–3, 245, 257, 259; tariff concessions contingent on, 255, 256; difference with Meade on, 273, 276–7, 279, 280–1; John Williams on, 290–1; Multilateral Trade
Convention in line with British policy, 305, 307, 310, 326; Chancellor of Exchequer's note on, 314; Pasvolsky's doubts, 318; American 'multilateral-bilateral' view, 326
under Article VII (Mutual Aid), 131, 294
multilateral convertibility, 58, 114, 116, 200, for sterling balances, 85; monetary, and commercial bilateralism, 23–4
see also Bilateralism; Convertibility

Mutual Aid, talks with Canadians on, 7, 113

Mutual Aid Agreement, 190, 305, 309, 314
Article VII, 301; for greater freedom of trade, 258, 294, 314, anti-discrimination, 314, 315, 316; discussions on (1942), 239, (1944), 3, 292; conversations on Commercial policy under, 63, 346, memorandum on (June 1944), 304–10

Nathan, Lord, 22, 187

National Advisory Council on International Monetary and Financial Problems, set up under Bretton Woods Act, 197–8, 211–12, 233–4; chairman, Vinson, 229

National Foreign Trade Week (U.S.A.), 20

National income, 37, 300

National sovereignty, under International Monetary Fund, 46, over parity of exchange, 47, 68; difference between U.K. and U.S.A., 57, 65, 78

Navy, 338

Nazis, 365, 379, 392

Netherlands
post-war reconstruction and reparations policy, 328–30
representatives at Bretton Woods, 55
see also Dutch; Holland

Netherlands Bank, 329

Neutral countries, 342–3, 367, 368, 396

New College, Oxford, 71

New Deal, 228

Newfoundland, iron ore, 269, 270

New Hampshire, home of the Bretton Woods Agreement, 40, 42, 105

New York
Bank of England Agents in, 170
British Delegation for Atlantic City arrive in, 55, 59, pass through en route to Bretton Woods, 66, return to U.K. via, 123; JMK returns to (1946), 210, 221
money market, 127, 143; the Black Market of the world, 171
Robertson in, 122

New York (*cont.*)

turned down as headquarters for Bank and Fund, 211, 221

New York Times

campaign against the Monetary Plan, 62–3

report of JMK's speech on I.M.F. and the gold standard, 85

New Zealand, 42; export arrangements and I.M.F. regulations, 22, 25–6, 320

Nicaragua, 42

Non-conformists, Senator Tobey, 81–2

Non-member countries of I.M.F., 139–40

Norman, Montagu, former Governor of the Bank of England: elevated to peerage (1944), 113

North America, 191

Northamptonshire: iron ores, 269; Corby iron and steel works, 272

Norway, 42; representatives at Bretton Woods, 55; demand for liquidisation of Bank for International Settlements, 96

'Objective of International Price Stability, The' (JMK, *Economic Journal*, June–September 1943), 30–3

Occupied countries, 72; reparations for, 331–2, 353–4, 355–6, under Morgenthau's plan, 377; return of gold taken from, 367; purchases by Germans of holdings in banks and companies, 334

occupation of Germany, 340–1, 343, 344, 358, 367, 388, 389, 391, 398, 399; occupying powers, 388, 399; military occupation of Germany, under Morgenthau's plan (paragraphs 8, 14), 378, 379, 380; armies of occupation, 344, 367

Oil

imports, 263, 264, 267

refining, 262, 263, 266–7, 269

synthetic, German plants for, 372

Oligopoly, 303

O'Neal, Mr, evidence before Congress Committee on International Monetary Fund, 194

Opie, Redvers, Treasury representative in Washington, 41, 182, 184, 320; member, British Delegation at Bretton Woods, 54 n 12; and Pasvolsky's memorandum on possible Anglo-American conflicts over post-war economic policy, 239, 242–3, 244, 245–6

Orthodoxy, and the I.M.F. monetary proposals, 17, 19

Ottawa, 113, 117; climate, 123–4

Overdrafts, 31

Overseas Finance (O.F.), for international co-operation and reconstruction, 235–6

Overton, Sir Arnold, President of the Board of Trade (1942), 248, 256; as chairman of interdepartmental committee adopts Meade's project of a commercial union, 248; majority and minority reports, 250, comments on, 251–3, 253–6; rejoinder to minority report, 256, comments on, 256–60; correspondence on, 261–9

list of letters, 416

Padmore, T., Private Secretary to Chancellor of the Exchequer: memoranda and minutes addressed to, 1–3, 48–54, 93, 140–1, 313

Panama, 42

Paper currency, 53

Paraguay, 42

Parity of exchange

under British Exchange control, 119

under I.M.F. Articles of Agreement, 79, 93–4, 118, 125, 139, 154, 162, 170, 402–3; sovereign rights over, 47, 93

Parliament

and International Monetary Fund, 92, 108, 185, 193; fears for national sovereignty under, 45, 65; delegates' decisions on, to be *ad referendum* to Parliament, 47; Chancellor of Exchequer prepares for criticism from, 66, 93, 142, 154, 157, 163, 169, 186; sensitive on location of Fund, 94, on convertibility, 145; discussions on Bretton Woods, 155, 176–7, 177–8, 192

new (Labour) Parliament, June 1945, 205

see also House of Commons; House of Lords; M.P.s

Passant, Ernest James, Naval Intelligence Division, Admiralty: letter to, 382–3

Pasvolsky, Leo, economist, of U.S. State Department, 26

informed of Lords' debate on I.M.F. monetary proposals and commercial policy (1944), 28–30; relations with British Delegation on I.M.F., 61, 63, 64, 71; talks with JMK on commercial policy, 317–20

memorandum 'Possibilities of Conflict of British and American official views on Post-war Economic Policy' (1941), notes on (JMK), 239–47

list of letters, 415

Patronage, and I.M.F., 225, 237

Paymaster General, *see* Cherwell, Lord

Payments Agreements, 24, 25

Peace, 77, 100–1; Germany's contribution to keeping world peace after World War II, 337–41, 344, 357–9, 366

Pearl Harbour, 59

Peru, 42, 125, 162

Pethick-Lawrence, F. W., M.P.: speech on I.M.F., 3, 7, 27; Chancellor of Exchequer speaks with, 187
list of letters, 416

Philippines, 42

Pigou, A. C., late Professor of Political Economy in Cambridge, 159, 195

Pips, 'until the pips squeak', 336

Planning, 253, 258, 291–2
of international investment, by Bank for Reconstruction and Development, 52–3, 54
of post-war trade, 5, 129, 132

Plastic industries, 263, 266

Playfair, E. W., Treasury Representative on Economic and Industrial Planning Staff, 374; member, Inter-Departmental Committee on Reparation and Economic Security, 337
'Draft Instructions to the British Delegation' (1945), 390, revised text, 397
memorandum addressed to, 397–8; minute, 374–5

Plumptre, A. F. W., Canadian delegate to Atlantic City, 56

Poland
coal, 23
and I.M.F., 42, 195; delegates at Bretton Woods, 55, at Savannah, 222, 231
post-war plans for, 375, 389; in Morgenthau's proposals for Germany, 376, 379
reparation claims, 329, 351, 397, 398

Politics
American, 164, 167, 186, 189, 194, 221, 228
and economics, 38, 57, 255
and I.M.F., 62, 180, 189, 234
political refugees, 369
politicians, 21, 101, 216
reconstruction, a political problem, 363
Russian, and reparation, 391

Pooling, 76, 226, 332–3

Population, transfers of, 383

Potash, as reparations, 343, 365, 396, 397

Potsdam, Big Three at (July 1945), 398–9; Potsdam Agreement, 399

Practical politics, 39, 180

Preferences
and Article 7, 258, 315
'Imperial and other Preferences', 309–10
as means to foster special groupings, 249–50, 251, 259–60
vs tariffs, 240, 276, 309–10
U.K. sticks out for, 324

Press
British: favourable reaction at first to I.M.F. monetary proposals, 26–7, 28, later hostility, 178–9, 180–1; hostile to commercial policy proposals, 29, push for full discriminatory rights, 314; pessimistic on Bretton Woods, 83; and bankers' counter-proposals, 188, 196
JMK talks to Press men, 179, 187; press reports on his health, 97–8; statement at press conference misreported, 84–5; articles by JMK, 16, at Savannah, 213–14
U.S.: opposition to Monetary Plan, 62–3, 81; reports on I.M.F. affairs, 82, 201, 226, 375; White's press conferences, 70–1, 84–5, 'his own' press, 78; discussions on post-war policy (1942) kept from, 245; attack on Hoover report (1945), 399
see also individual newspapers and journals

Price, General Byron, 400

Prices
buffer stocks to assist stability, 37, 291
cost-price structure, 290
dumping price, 269
equated prices, 310
and import regulations, 269, 285, 307; for import licences, 279–80; under State trading, 286–7
price competition, pre-war, 268; Fleming's belief in, 291, 293, 295, 297–8
price controls, in Germany, 378
of primary commodities, 4–5
an unsatisfactory index to real social costs, 288
world prices and reparations, 396
'The Objective of International Price Stability', 30–3

Primary commodities, 4, 249

Private enterprise, 206; international cartels between private interests, 249, 250

Production
German, 269, 378, 399
of gold, 35, 40, 85
producers' ramps, 40

Production (*cont.*)
productivity, and Bank for Reconstruction and Security, 105; German productive capacity, 363, 391
of steel, 269–72
subsidies for, 325; quantitative restriction of imports to aid home producers, 285, 286–7
Production, Ministry of, study of steel production, 270–2
'Project of a Commercial Union' (20 November 1942), 248–50
Property, and reparations: requisitioned or stolen by Germans, 329, 331, 350–1, 377, 393; losses caused by enemy action, 345, 354–6, 384; German property in transferred territory, 342; German property rights in U.N. territories, 364; ownership of property in Germany, 368–70; enemy property in U.S.A., 332; German losses, 360; in Yalta Agreement, 384
'Proposals to Counter the German "New Order"' (1940), 239, 328
Proposals for an Expansion of World Trade and Employment, 327
Protection, 266
maldistribution of resources under (Fleming), 294–5
protective tariffs, 265
and quantitative import restrictions, in Meade's Commercial Union scheme, 273, 275–6, 280; 'The Protective Incidence of Import Quotas' (JMK), 281–2
by subsidy, 325
see also Preferences; Subsidies; Tariffs
Prudence, 86, 89, 108, 289, 323
Prussia, 376, 378; East Prussia, 373
Psychology, 39–40, 243, 358, 368, 386
Public opinion
British: converted to new model of domestic policy, 16, 19; opposed to Exchange Adjustment clause, 65; sensitive on location of Fund, 94; suspicious of Article VIII, 176; on the burdens of victory, 339, 357–8
German, 370
international, and *Economic Consequences of the Peace*, 400
on reparations, 391
of U.N. members, 353; on a possible German U.S.S.R., 385
U.S.: commercial proposals shaped for, 29; British concern for, 71; bored by Bretton Woods, 82; opposed to location of Fund in New York, 211
Purchasing power, 73, 105; minimum purchases, 313; purchasing power parity, 293
see also Bulk purchase

Quantity theory of money, 31–2
'Quantitative Regulation of Imports', 284–7; *see also* under Imports
Quebec Conference (September 1944), 375, 380
Queen Mary, Cunard liner, 55, 209n, 210
Quotas
and import restrictions, 254, 263, 273 n 5, 278, 279; 'The Protective Incidence of Import Quotas' (Meade), 281–2
for primary products, 249
'Quotas versus Depreciation' (Fleming), correspondence on, 287–9, 292–7, 301–2
see also under Bank for Reconstruction and Development; International Monetary Fund

Rabbinics, Robertson's 'Essay' in, 114–17; 'An Essay on Metarabbinics', reply from JMK, 118–22, 123
Racial discrimination, and reparations, 342
Radio, 378, 399; broadcast statement on Fund and Bank, 103–5
Railways, 131–2
rolling-stock, requisitioned by Germany, 329, 331, 342, 343, 345, 351, 356, 364, 393
Raisman, Sir J., member of the Indian Delegation at Atlantic City, 56, 80, 127
Rasminsky, L., Foreign Exchange Board, Canada
member of the Canadian Delegation at Atlantic City, 56, 57, 58, 62; at Bretton Woods: on Article VIII, 124, 160, 172; Reporting Delegate of Commission I (I.M.F.), 98, 99, 100, 125; at Savannah, 228
Rate of interest, 16, 17. *See also* Interest
Raw materials
in Germany, 360; imports, 371–2; as reparation, 331, 343, 361, 364, 396, 397, 398
producing countries, 37
and subsidies, 252
U.K. imports, 264, 265, 293; cover for, by loans from Bank for Reconstruction and Development, 50

Reconstruction
    funds for: from proposed International Investment Institution, 19; from Bank for Reconstruction and Development, 51, 72, 73, 104, 188, 198, through National Advisory Council (U.S.A.), 234, and Overseas Funds (U.K.), 235; not from UNRRA, 72, 103, nor from I.M.F., 195, 199–200
    for Italy, 229
    reconstruction period, 13, 14
    reparations for, 328–30, 363; Reconstruction Commission, 362–3, 365; Hoover on, 400
    after World War I, 100
Red tape, 111
Reichsbank, 329, 332, 344–5, 353, 373; Reichsmark deposits, 329
Reich government, 378
Relief and rehabilitation
    distinguished from reconstruction, 72
    for enemy countries, 333, Germany, 343, 366–7, 387–8
    funds for, provided by UNRRA, 103, 188; aid from Overseas Funds, 235; not directly financed by I.M.F., 195, 199–200; possible use of reparations for, 333, 344
    Netherlands not likely to ask funds for, 330
    see also UNRRA
Reparation Commission, 343, 384, 394–6, 398
Reparations
    basis of claims, 351–7
    in cash, 329, 330, 331
    deliveries in kind, 329, 330, 336, 340, 343, 361–2, 363, 364–5, 383–4, 387–8, 391, 394; current deliveries, 396, 397–8; allocation, 345–6, 394–5
    priority, 332, 336, 354
    in services, 331, 340, 343, 361–2, 365, 388, 391; allocation, 392, 394–8
    total value, 343, 384, 391, 394–7; duration of period for paying, 332, 336, 362, 365, 388; allocation, 384
    'European Reparations', minute to Treasury (September 1941), 328–30; queries on treatment of victors and vanquished (October 1941), 331–4; Treasury memorandum (December 1941), 334
    'Reparations: Notes on Mr Dalton's Memorandum' (September 1942), 335–6; Interdepartmental Committee on Reparation and Economic Security set up, JMK a member, (November 1942), 337; meetings, 272; papers by JMK, 337–41, 341–6; Malkin Report (September 1943), 346–7, 348–73
    in Morgenthau's plan for post-war Germany, (1944) 377, 381
    Yalta agreement on (February 1945), 383–4, 385; reparations and dismemberment, notes on (February 1945), 385, 386, 387–9; Committee on Reparations set up, JMK a member (March 1945), 389, 398; 'Draft Instructions on Reparations' (JMK, April 1945), 390–4, 'An Alternative to a Global Figure for Reparations', 394–7, 397–8
    Potsdam agreement on (July 1945), 398–9; Hoover Report (November 1945), 399–401
Republicans, U.S.A.
    opposition to I.M.F. monetary plan, 62–3, 81, 82; 'brought round' to support Fund and Bank, 91; Bretton Woods Bill accepted by, with amendments, 196
    Republican Isolationists, 196
Re-purchase clause (I.M.F.), 193, 404–5
Reserves
    free reserves, Bank for Reconstruction and Development, 76
    Indian, 116
    I.M.F.: central reserve fund, 55, 73; of members, under terms of Articles, 169, 285–6
    monetary, 13; under Article XIX, 167, 409, Article V, 404, 405
    and quantity theory, 31
    of sterling area, 302
    U.K. shortage of liquid reserves, 306
Restitution, 340, 350–1, 354, 356, 360, 392–3; distinguished from reparations, 328, in Treaty of Versailles, 330; takes precedence of reparations, 336
    in kind, 329, 330; of securities and works of art, 331, 332, 333, 342, 351; in Morgenthau's post-war plan for Germany, 377, 381
    'Restitution and Reparation,...' (December 1941), 341–6
Restrictions; on current international payments, *see under* Article VIII of Articles of Agreement; on exchanges, *see* Exchanges; on imports, *see* Import Restrictions
Rhine, 376, 382
'Rhenania', 382–3

Rights and obligations
of individuals and central banks under I.M.F., 119–20; over convertibility, 135–6, 141, 143–4, 159, 168
of German labour used for reparation services, 392

Risk
in Bank for Reconstruction and Development loans, 51, 52, 54, 74–5; mutual credit insurance pool against, 104
exchange risks, 51, 297

Robbins,, Lionel C., Cabinet Office
member, British Delegation to Bretton Woods Conference, 54 n 12; at Atlantic City, 56, 66; at Bretton Woods, 83, 172 n 38; on JMK, 56, 84, 97 n 25, 112
correspondence on interpretation of Article VIII, 171–5
at London Commercial Policy talks (1945), 320
member, Inter-Departmental Committee on Reparations and Economic Security, 337
list of letters, 416
also mentioned, 140, 141, 168, 289, 297, 310

Robertson, Dennis H., Treasury
Bretton Woods: member of British Delegation, 43 n 9, 47, 54 n 12; at Atlantic City, 56; at Bretton Woods, 83, his outstanding ability, 109–10; British representative on Committee for Article VIII, 83, 116–17, 124–5, 137, 160, 162, 170; difference with JMK on interpretation, 114–17, 118–22, 126–7, 134–8, 140, 141, 161, 164–5, 166, 167; difference on Article V (currency subscription), 122–4; Robbins on the propriety of his conduct, 171–2
correspondence on monetary and commercial bilateralism, 23–6
faith in *laissez-faire*, 289, in exchange mobility, 269–91, 297, 298
succeeds Pigou as Professor of Political Economy at Cambridge, 159; 'dead' in respect of Bretton Woods, 163
list of letters, 416
Notes: 'Monetary and Commercial Bilateralism', 24–5; 'Note on the International Monetary Fund: An Essay in Rabbinics', 114–17; 'An Essay in Common sense', 126–7; Minute to Sir H. Henderson and Sir D. Waley, 289–91

Robertson, Jack, 162

Robinson, Austin (E.A.G.), 390

Robinson, Joan, correspondence with JMK on Articles of Agreement, 129–33

Robinson, W. S., Australian financier, at London talks on Article VII, 3

Rocky Mountains, 28

Ronald, Nigel
member, British Delegation to Bretton Woods, 54 n 12, 92, 98, 108
at the Foreign Office, 320, 330; group discussions on reparations, 330, 333, 334; member, Inter-Departmental Committee on Reparations and Economic Security, 337

Roosevelt, Franklin D., President of U.S.A.
and Bretton Woods, 60; appoints Delegation without commitment, 63; tied up with re-election prospects, 62–3, 82, 147; instructs delegates on Washington as location for Fund and Bank, 222
and reparations, 328, 382; at Yalta, 383–4; policy on occupation of Germany, 385
at Teheran Conference (1943), 374; at Quebec (1944), 375; at Potsdam (1945), 398

Rotterdam, war damage, 329

Rowe-Dutton, E., Principal Assistant Secretary, Treasury, 126; attempts redraft of Article VIII 2(a), 146, 155, 161, 168; Secretary of Delegation at Savannah, 210, 230, on the closing scene there, 232 n 50

Rubber: buna rubber, 372

Ruhr
annexation proposals, 382–3
in Morgenthau's plan for the partition of Germany, 376, 377; JMK's view, 380, 381–2
steel industry, 269

Russia (U.S.S.R.)
gold production, 85
and I.M.F.: on Drafting Committee, 42; voting power, 70, 130; Delegation at Bretton Woods, 107, 108, 109, the black sheep received into the fold, 112; Article IV 5(e) a 'Russian' clause, 131; Article IV a problem for, 145; Delegation at Savannah, 215
post-war commercial policy, 255, 257; State Trading, 250, 306, 307
reparations, 352, 392, 393; press for high global figure, 384, 391; proposed half-share of total, 383, 397, 398

Russia (U.S.S.R.) (*cont.*)
role in proposed partition of Germany, 384–5, 386–7, 389, 399; in Morgenthau's plan, 376; Russian soldiers to police Germany, 379; revenge motive, 386
war effort, 86
also mentioned, 40, 363

Saar, 373, 376
Salvador: invited to Bretton Woods, 42; representatives at Savannah, 222
Savannah, climate and appearance, 214, 217
Savannah Conference (March 1946)
American 'line' at, 211–13
British Delegation, led by JMK, 209–10; his speech at Inaugural Meeting of Governors of Bank and Fund, 215–17; report on Conference, 220–38; moral leadership of British group, 230–1
meetings on location of Fund and Bank, and role and remuneration of management, 220–7; mellow note to end on, 232
Scandinavia, 313
see also Denmark; Norway; Sweden
Scarce currencies, 58, 119–20, 193; under Article VII (I.M.F.), 130–1, 134–5, 173, 183, 189, 192, 406–7, Article V, 403
Scarce resources, 40, 291
Schacht, Dr Hjalman Horace Greeley, 9
Schachtian minds, 9, 23, 24
Scientific habit of mind, 21
Securities
of Bank for Reconstruction and Development, 50; bonds, 75, 109
Consols, 120
and reparations, 329, 331, 332, 342, 351
also mentioned, 300
Self-interest (of a nation), 254, 259, 305; enlightened, 14, 247
Service charges, 405, 409. See also under Loans
Shackle, R. J., Board of Trade: at London talks on commercial policy, 320
Shakespeare, William: *Hamlet*, 149
Shinwell, Emanuel, M.P., 2
Shipping
German losses, 360
subsidies for, 256, 258, 260, 262, 325
Transatlantic liners, see *Aquitania*; *Queen Mary*
war damage to, 331; restitution, 342, 343, 345, 351, 356, 364

Shroff, Mr, Indian delegate at Bretton Woods, 80, 86
Silesia, 376; Upper Silesia, 373
Sierra Leone, 270
Silver, as collateral security, 404
Sinclair, Sir Robert, Ministry of Production, 60
Slumps, 22, 33, 132, 201
see also Depressions; Fluctuations
Smuts, General Christian, 3
Snelling, A. W., Secretary to the U.K. Delegation, Atlantic City, 56, at Bretton Woods, 110
Social costs, 288
Social revolution, 384–5
Social welfare, 290–1, Beveridge scheme, 338–9, 357; improvements, 316
South Africa, 42; Delegation at Savannah, 218, 231
South America, 225, 257; Delegations at Savannah, 222
see also under separate countries
South Wales, steel works, 270
Southby, Sir Archibald, M.P., 1
Soviet Union, 384; Union of Soviet Socialist Republics, 309
see also Russia
Spain
iron ores, 270
Spanish moss, in Savannah, 214, 215
Spearman, A. C. M., M.P., 1, 3
Speculation, 291, 296
Stabilisation
of commodities, by buffer stocks, 35
of cost of living, 4
currency, loans for, 55, 194–5, 198, 199
of exchanges, see under Exchanges
of industry and employment, import regulations for, 268, 273 n 5, 282
of international trade, 308
Stage Two, 59, 105; discussions in Washington (Autumn 1944), JMK at, 142, 375
Stage III, 205–6, 324
Stalin, Josef, one of the 'Big Three', at Teheran, 372, Yalta, 383–4, Potsdam, 398–9
Standard of life
Bank for Reconstruction and Development's role in improving, 73, 104
and exchange depreciation, 288, 298
German post-war, 344, 349, 363, 385, 398;

Standard of life (*cont.*)
    Churchill's statement on, 388; Yalta decision, 399
  in post-war Britain, 190, 191, 290, 316
Stanley, Oliver, Dominions Secretary, 323
State trading, 249, 261, 263–4, 267, 278, 286–7; role in flow of expenditure, 291; and 'commercial considerations', 322
  'State Trading and Bulk Purchases', 307–8, 326
Statisticians, 237, 238
Steel production, 266, 268, 269–72; steel products as reparations, 343, 364, 396, 397
Stepanov, M. S., Chairman, Russian Delegation to Bretton Woods, 112
Sterling
  convertibility: traditional, 9; London as financial centre depends on, 11–12; zero-hour for full convertibility, 126, 136; under Article VIII, 118, 119–22, 126–7, 134–6, 152, 164–5
  external and internal value, 16
  foreign held, and commercial bilateralism, 23–4, 25
  and gold standard, under I.M.F., 205
  sterling exchange, 283–4, 293, 302
  during transitional period, 322
  and value of exports and imports, 300–1
Sterling area
  under I.M.F. monetary proposals, 2; advantages to, 9, 11, better than empire or sterling area bilateralism, 191, 241; quotas for, 13; under Article VIII, 161; and Executive Directors, 207
  a matter to handle slowly in 1946, 231
  representatives at Savannah, 231
  and sterling exchange movements, 299n, 302
Sterling balances
  Indian and Egyptian, wartime, 71, 83, 85; statement on (JMK), 86–7; under Article VIII, 116–17, 160, 166
  in London, 122–3, 125
Stettinius, Edward, Assistant Secretary of State, U.S.A., 59
Stewart, Walter, American economist, 240
Stirling, J. A. G., Board of Trade: in Washington, 242, 243, 245
Stormtroopers (S.S., S.A.), 365
Strabolgi, Lord, 4
Subsidies
  as an adjunct to market mechanism, 291
  to British farmers, 287

  for cost of living, 294
  effect on consumption, 265
  to foster new or needy industries, 249, 265
  in Overton Report, 251–2
  in proposals on Commercial Policy, 306, 318; British proposals, 325
  state trading preferable to, 261, or import regulation, 268; equated price no more objectionable than, 308–9, nor preferences, 309–10
  see also under Shipping
Supply Departments, 265
  Ministry of Supply, 272
Sweden, iron ore, 269
Swiss nominee names used for shares taken by Germany, 329
Synthetic materials, 372

Tabular standard, 31, 39, 40
Taft, Robert, Republican Senator, 91
Talmud, 118
Tange, A. N., Australian Delegate to Atlantic City, 56
Tariffs
  ad valorem, vs import licences, correspondence on, with Meade, 273 n 5, 274–6, 278, 279–80, 281–2
  as alternative to currency depreciation, 5; Robertson on, 290, 294–5, 300, 302
  American, 240, 255, 276, 306
  under Anglo-American Commercial Treaty of 1938, 315
  under Article VII of Mutual Aid Agreement, 292, 294, 309–10
  Great Britain's policy on, 305–6, 307
  'optimum unilateral tariff' (Fleming), 301
  in Overton draft Report, 251–2, 264; JMK's proposed alternative, 254–6, 257–8, 259–60; correspondence on, 265, 268–9
  vs preferences, 240, 276, 309–10
  state trading preferable to, 261, 286
  tariff unions, and dismemberment of Germany, 374–5
Taxation
  and the price system, 288, 291
  and salaries for international civil servants, 223, 224, 225, 237
  subsidies met out of, 265
Taylor, Myron, State Department, U.S.A., 347
Teheran Conference (November 1943), 374
Telegraph, The, 27

Terms of trade, 283; effect on, of movements in the rate of exchange, 288, 294, 295–6; possible effect of, on balance of payments, 298, 300

The Times
Ambassador in Washington denied a copy, 111
letter to Balogh (JMK, 20 May 1944), 8–9, 21, 23; other letters from JMK, 16
lukewarm or hostile to I.M.F., 178
report of debate in Lords on Monetary Proposals (23 May 1944), 26–7
'World Monetary Policies' (T. Balogh, 21, 22, 23 August 1944), 127; correspondence on, 128–9

Theunis, Georges, Belgian Delegate at Bretton Woods
journey through war-devastated Belgium in 1918 with JMK, 100
Reporting Delegate for Commission II (Bank for Reconstruction and Development), 100

'Third countries', 109, 125

Timber, as reparations, 343, 364, 396, 397

Time, 381n

Time-lags, 72, 195, 317

Tobacco, 121, 290

Tobey, Charles William, Republican Senator: member of American Delegation at Bretton Woods, 81–2

Totalitarianism, 38; Lord Keynes speaks in the voice of, 290

Towers, Graham Ford, Canadian Delegation at Bretton Woods, 80; nominated as candidate for Presidency of Bank, 213; refuses Managing Directorship of Fund, 237

Trade
German, post-war, 378
planning *vs* market-mechanism for, 292
U.K., 8–9, 316; advantages to, of I.M.F. monetary proposals, 11, 12–13, of Bretton Woods proposals, 129, 190–1; Imperial Trade, 23; not sufficiently considered in Overton Report, 256, alternatives proposed, 256, 258–60; and Meade's import licence scheme, 278; Budgetary expenditure on, 338–9, 357
Washington trade discussions (1945), 327
see also Balance of trade; Exports; Free trade; State trading

Trade agreements, 24, 25

see also Anglo-American Trade Agreement, *and under* Discrimination

Trade cycle, 13

Trade, international
advantages to, of Bank for Reconstruction and Development, 52, 54
barter agreements for, 308
and exchange rates, 296
Great Britain's policy on, 305
and I.M.F.: facilitation of growth under, 200, 307, 310; and Article VIII, 168–9; not affected by Article VI, 406

Pasvolsky's belief in *laissez-faire* for, 239–40
restrictions on, 4, 58, 124

Trade policy, discussions on (1941), 239
see also Commercial policy

Trade Unions, 36, 38

Transitional period
under Article VII (I.M.F.), 134, 199–200; under Article VIII, 114, 116, 117, 126, 136, 184; Article XIV, 408–9
duration: five years, 24, 43 n 9, 47; difference with Americans on, 57–8, 62, 68–9
Exchange Adjustment Clause problem, 44, 47, 55
in Joint Statement of Principles, 45–6; negotiations on, at Atlantic City, 66, Bretton Woods, 79
post-transition terms for dollar–sterling exchange, 161, for quantitative regulation of imports, 325
rationing during, 290
safeguards for U.K. during, 8, 11, 189, 190, 250, 285–6, 313, 314; saving clause for abnormal war balances, 22; concession on discrimination, 315, 317
tied loans of Export-Import Bank during, 229
and U.K. reserves, 13, 286

Transport
costs, 269, 270
German, 360, 378
as reparations, 343, 345, 351, 356, 361, 364, 365, 393
see also Aircraft; Railways; Shipping

Treasuries: role in I.M.F., 208, 220, 221; under Article VIII, 158, 182

Treasury (U.K.)
Economic Section, 236
experts in monetary discussions (1944), 20; discussions on Fund and Bank, 43
instructions from, 123; telegram, 78

Treasury (U.K.) (*cont.*)
JMK: minutes and papers submitted to, 133, 168, 328–30; reports, 211–13, 220–38
memoranda: 'Compensation to be Required from the Enemy' (1941), 334, 335–6; on Reparations and Dismemberment (1945), 387, 389, covering note (JMK), 387–9
relation to I.M.F., 232, 235–6
representatives: in Ottowa, 113; Washington, 236; on Overton Committee, 248, 250
Treasury files, 125
views on commercial multilateralism, 24, 26; on currency depreciation, 292, 294
Truman, President, 224
Turkey, Karabuk steel works, 272

Undeveloped countries, 104
Unemployment
'export' of, 5, 296
German, 378
I.M.F. as a means to prevent, 13, 192
JMK's long fight against, 16–17
to keep wages down, 31–2, 33, and Trade Unions in order, 36, 38
Unitas, 10, 32
United Kingdom
advantages to, of Bank for Reconstruction and Development, 48; British share of capital subscription, 49
'British Commercial Policy', 305–7; *see also under* Commercial Policy
financial aid from U.S., 316. *See also* Anglo-American Loan Agreement
and I.M.F., 90, 94, 99, 162, 169, 176; advantages of, to U.K., 11–15, 188–9; share in monetary reserves, 13, prospect of exchange stability, 66; member of Drafting Committee, 42; reservations on joining, 46, difference with U.S. on proposals, 57–8; voting power, 70; U.K. interests, and Management, 89, 207, problem of staffing, 234–8, and salaries, 218–19, 224; Final Act signed for U.K. by JMK, 154; Accession to Articles of Agreement (1945), 206. *See also under* International Monetary Fund.
Ministers, 312, 334, 347, 386, 391; and reparations, 393, 398, Ministerial Committee on, 389–90; salary of Prime Minister, 224

poor communications with Washington, 67–8, 84, 111, 123
post-war problems, 4–5, 29, 247, 259; 'infant' industries, 262–3; trade policy, 323
reparations, 352, 384, 396, 397–8; British attitude towards, 398; policy on occupation of Germany, 385–6, 387–9, 399; representative on proposed Reconstruction Commission, 363
war effort, 29–30, 86; deferred indebtedness, 11, 86–7; the burden of victory, 10–11, 341, 357, 393
see also Anglo-American; British; England; London; Parliament; Treasury
United Nations
and Bank for Reconstruction and Development, 72, 197
Britain's war burden unique among, 11, 29, 86
Missions, 344
and reparations, 349, 352–3, 355, 368–70; allocation of deliveries in kind between, 345–6; restitution of assets and property, 342, 364
role in peace-keeping arrangements for Germany, 366, 370, 372, in Morgenthau's plan, 377, 378–9
United Nations Monetary and Financial Conference, 97, 98. *See also* Bretton Woods
United Nations Organisation (U.N.O.), 207, 211, 221; Economic and Social Council, 221, 234, 235
United Nations Relief and Rehabilitation Administration (UNRRA)
funds provided for rehabilitation, not reconstruction, 72, 103–4, 188
German post-war relief, 343, 344
management, 227; voting system, 58
role in allocation of reparations, 346
also mentioned, 235
United States of America
Administration (Government), 20, 40, 46, 161, 323; and Senator Tobey, 81; relations with Congress, 91, 255, eased by National Advisory Council, 233–4; Morgenthau's influence with, 92; concern with full employment, 191–2; and Bretton Woods, 205, insist on Washington as location of Fund and Bank, 211–12, 222; Cabinet Committees, 212, 233
and Bank for Reconstruction and Development, 77, 91; capital subscription, 49;

United States of America (*cont.*)

U.S. the main source for bank loans, 74, 75, 234, for untied loans, 109, 229–30; American location for, 84, 87–8, 90, 211–12, 218; American Directors and management, 194, 197, 198, 213, 228, 229

cartels, 250

commerce: commercial talks with U.K. (1944), 304, 311–12, 314, 317–27; insistence on non-discrimination, 315–17; commercial agreements, 313, 315–16, *see also* Anglo-American Trade Agreement; Secretary of Commerce, 197, 212, 233

cotton, 252, 254–5, 318

a creditor country, 121; surplus exports, 104, surplus for overseas investment, 306–7; rich, 325, a land of steaks and ice-cream, 112

Congress: and Bretton Woods, 71, 161, 207; sovereignty over Delegation maintained, 63, 65, 125, 171; insist on U.S. location of Fund, 90–1; trouble with Article VIII, 138; debate in House of Commons waits on Congress action, 147–8, 155, 158, 176–7, 178, 187, 192; amendments to Articles, 169, 171, 181, accepted by Treasury, 194–5, 196–206; 'railroading' the Final Act through, 147, 149, 179–80, 186, 211–12; debate on, 192–5, Bill passes House of Representatives, 196; in Bankers' counterproposals, 167, 189–90, 197

commercial policy talks, 245, 255

Congressional committees, 179, 158, 193

Congressmen: and bankers, on I.M.F., 79, 81, on Bank for Reconstruction and Development, 164, 179; isolationists, 257

Lend-Lease Act renewal, 319

relations with Administration, 91; altered by National Advisory Council, 229, 233

Constitution, 143; an obstacle to multilateral commercial agreements, 273, 276

financial power, 188

and International Monetary Fund: voting power, 15, 69, 70, 130; on Drafting Committee, 42; formula for quotas, 58, 69, 130; under Article IV (par value of currencies), 138, 143, under Article VII (scarce currencies), 173, 189, 192; American Directors and Executives, 194, 197, 212, 226, 237, staff members, 224–5, 229.

See also under International Monetary Fund

President, 197, 198, *see also* Roosevelt, Franklin; presidential elections (1944), 30, 62–3, 82, (1948), 228

Senate: Committees, 81, Banking Committee, 213; Republican Senators, 81–2, 91; Bretton Woods Bill goes through, 196

and Stage Two, 59–60; discussions in Washington, 142, 375

State Department

commercial policy: and Pasvolsky's memorandum (1941–2), 239, 241, 243, 244; free trade element, 251, 258; committed to Article 7 (Mutual Aid Agreement) on multilateral trade, 305, 316, allowances for U.K. transitional difficulties, 45, 315 n 8; conversations on commercial policy (1944–5), 63, 173, in London, 64, 320

discussions with Foreign Office (U.K.) on World Organisation, 90

I.M.F.: relations with Bank and Fund, 228–9; on location of Fund, 92

reparations: addressed on, by JMK, 346–73; reaction to Morgenthau's plan, 381–2

a tribute to (JMK, May 1944), 21

Statue of Liberty, 143

Treasury:

Bretton Woods Conference, 43; Joint Statement of Principles, 44; concern for U.K. transitional difficulties, 45; plans for Bank for Reconstruction and Development, 48–9, 77; co-operation with British Delegation, 105–6; drafting problems, 139, 152, 184; talks on Bank and Fund with technical experts, 193; gets the Bill through Congress, 194, in a re-drafted form, 196, with amendments, 201, 204; will pass on 'headaches' to new institutions, 228–9

negotiations with France, 231

plan for de-industrialisation of Germany (Morgenthau's plan), 375, 376–9; comments on (JMK), 380–2

Secretary of the Treasury, 197, 212, 233. *See also* Vinson, Judge Frederick Moore

Treasury lawyers, 102

in World War II: restitution of stolen American securities, 329; assets frozen in America during, 330, 332; role in proposed Reconstruction Commission, 363,

United States of America (*cont.*)
  in Morgenthau's plan for post-war Germany, 379, 380; represented at Teheran Conference, 374, at Yalta, 383–4, at Potsdam, 398; JMK talks with Roosevelt on Germany, 382, reports on his American impressions, 383; likely to pull out of Germany soon, 385; and reparations, 395, American public opinion on, 395, 401; Hoover Report, 399–400
U.S.S.R., *see* Russia; Soviet Union
Urban land planning, 291
Uruguay, 42

Varvaressos, proposed Greek delegate for Bretton Woods, 43
Velocity of circulation, 31
Venezuela, 42
Versailles, Treaty of, 330, 352, 359
Victors and vanquished, 331, 333, 339, 358
Viner, Professor Jacob, 240
Vinson, Judge Frederick Moore, Secretary of U.S. Treasury, 228–9
  at Bretton Woods, 88
  discussions with JMK on Savannah, 210, 211–13; opening speech, 215; his stooges, 217–18, 222; Chairman of Executive Committee, and of both Boards of Governors, 226; on remuneration of Managing Director and President, 213, holds his hands close on appointments, 237–8; insists on location of Bank and Fund at Washington, 211, 221–2
  Chairman, National Advisory Council, 229, 233, Export and Import Bank, 233
  political ambitions, 228
Voting power
  Bank for Reconstruction and Development, 53
  for Bretton Woods procedure, 58
  International Monetary Fund, 69–70, 89, 130, 405; for changing constitution, 204; of Executive Directors, 228
Wages
  in conditions of full employment, 33, 37–8
  effect on, of import restrictions, 295, 298
  external pressure on, 32, 35, 39–40
  must follow cost of living, 288, 298; Fleming's view, 294
  national tendency to rise, 31, 35
  and prices, 31, 33, 37, 289, 297
  sliding-scale arrangements, 294, 298
  stable efficiency wages a political, not economic problem, 35, 38

wage policy under an international currency scheme, 32–3
Waley, Sir Sigismund David (Sigi), Under Secretary, Treasury
  comments on Overton Report, 261, 262; answered, 262–5
  correspondence sent to, 63, 64, 71, 117, 123, 289; memoranda to, 41–3, 251–3; minute, 93
  discussions on reparations, 330; joint chairman, Reparations Committee, 389; 'Machinery for Executing Reparation', 390
  note on commercial policy, 310
War
  casualties, 354, 360, 384
  chest, 169, *and see* 176
  costs, 352, 353, 354–5
  crimes, 379; guilt, 391
  debts, 58, 345; U.K., 86–7; not to be settled through I.M.F., 87, 199–200, 205–6
  devastation, 72; in World War I, 100; in World War II, 100–1, 329, 331, 341–2, 345, 368; devastated countries and cities, 104–5, 329, 361, 366–7, 377; at sea, 356
  economy, 370
  effort, 10–11, 29, 86
  prisoners, 392
  restrictions, 8, 11, 183, 290
Wardlaw-Milne, Sir John, M.P., 2
Washington
  Article VII conversations (July 1944), JMK at, 63–4, 346
  climate, 27, 123
  communications system with London, 68, 111, 317; exchange of documents, 175
  conference of experts on monetary proposals (February 1944), 21
  JMK visits to, in 1941, 102, 239; before Savannah (1946), 210, 221
  location of Bank and Fund in, 211, 212, 218, 221–2; cost of living for staff, 225
  as seat of Government, 188, 205, 241, 251, 311, 380; preliminary discussions for inaugural meetings of Bank and Fund, 208; Washington Committees, 233
  Stage II discussions, JMK at (October 1944), 141, 142, 146, 147, 178, 186, 317
  U.K. representatives in: Robertson, 123; managers and directors of Bank and Fund, 235–7
Weekly Economic Summary, 196
Weapon Production
  Director General of (U.K.), 269

Weapon Production (*cont.*)
German, 269; armament industries, 376, 398
Western Europe, 40, 363
delegations at Savannah, 222, 231
gold holdings, 85
and partition of Germany, 384–5, 386–7
'Restitution' for West-European Allies, 393
Wheat
exports, American subsidies for, 252, 318
imports, U.K., 264, 285, 286
Wheeler, F. H., Australian Delegate to Atlantic City, 56
White, Harry Dexter, U.S. Treasury
at Atlantic City: discussions with JMK, 56, 61, reported to Commonwealth delegates, 56–8, 59; chairs meetings, 67
Bretton Woods: his curious conception of the conference, 41; first thoughts on Bank and Fund, 193; his Drafting Committee, 42–3; complicated programme, 60–1, optimism on outcome, 62–3, 81; meetings with JMK behind the scenes, 66–7; points discussed, 68–9, 79; Chairman of Commission I on Fund, 70, 99, 102; policy on press, 70–1, 78, 84; trouble with his Delegation, 79; difference with British over location of Bank and Fund, 87; statement on Bretton Woods to BBC news, 103; 'all in' after late night committees, 107
early discussions with JMK on national sovereignty in exchange matters, 34; exchange of views on Catto exchange clause, 62, 68, 78, on Exchange Adjustment clause, 65, agreement reached on Article IV (parity), 93, 148, 187
consulted on interpretation of Article VIII, 137, 141, 142–6, 148–53, 156, 175; sends no reply, 146; not impressed by problem, 150, 163, 168, 169; issue raised again, 177, 182, 186
evidence before Congress Committee on Bretton Woods Bill, 193–4; railroads both Fund and Bank through Congress, 147, 179, 186
views on role of Executive Directors, 206–7, 208–9; ruled out as Managing Director of Fund, 213; appointed Director of Bank, 228
at Savannah, 227, on the last night, 232;

friendly relations throughout with British delegation, 64, 67, 81, 106, 235
interest in de-industrialisation of Germany, 142; author of Morgenthau Plan, 375, asks for JMK's views, 376, 380, 382
list of letters, 416–17
Whitehall, 106, 241, 245, 383; I.M.F.'s close link with, 232
Williams, Professor John H., of New York, 122, 123, 167
Wilson, Sir Horace, Permanent Secretary, Treasury
memorandum addressed to, 333–4
minute to, 244; minute from, 243–4
Winant, John Gilbert, U.S. Ambassador in London, 63, 245, 246
Wolcott, Congressman: amendment to I.M.F. Articles of Agreement, 195, 196, 198
Works of art, restitution of, 331, 332, 342, 351
World Organisation, projected, 89–90
World War I
Armistice, 100
'dreadful mistakes' of post-war policy, 100, 328, 334, 386, 391; reparations, 331, 335, 359; JMK's personal involvement, 401
international lending racket, 53
peace treaties, 364
World War II
'coming battle' (May 1944), 30; campaign in France, 62n; bombardment, 331, war in the air, 360; loss of life, 354, 360
end of war, and establishment of International Monetary Fund, 46; transitional period to last 5 years from, 47
Japan's part in, 59, 341, 356
see also Reparations; War
World War III, programme to prevent, 376–9

Yalta Conference (February 1945), 383–4, 387; Reparations Committee set up, 398; post-Yalta discussions, 389
Young Loan, 369–70
Yugoslavia, *see* Jugoslavia

zero-hour, 117, 126, 136
Zollverein, 251, 309
Zones: of occupation for Germany, 388, 389, 394, 395, 399; international, 376, 377, 389